The Shakespeare Controversy

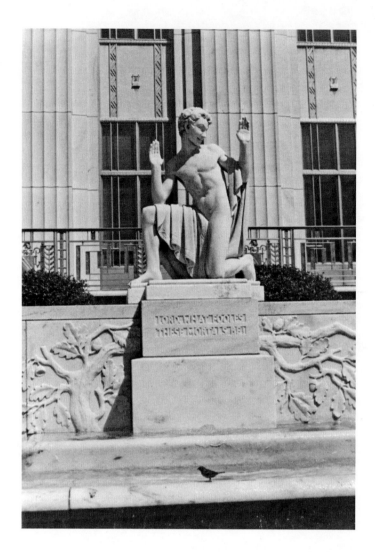

The Shakespeare Controversy

AN ANALYSIS OF THE AUTHORSHIP THEORIES

Second edition

Warren Hope and *Kim Holston*

McFarland & Company, Inc., Publishers

Jefferson, North Carolina, and London

Frontispiece: Statue of Puck, outside the Folger
Shakespeare Library, Washington, D.C.

LIBRARY OF CONGRESS CATALOGUING-IN-PUBLICATION DATA

Hope, Warren, 1944–
The Shakespeare controversy : an analysis of the authorship
theories / Warren Hope and Kim Holston. -- 2nd ed.
p.   cm.
Includes bibliographical references and index.

ISBN 978-0-7864-3917-1

illustrated case binding: 50# alkaline paper ∞

1. Shakespeare, William, 1564–1616 — Authorship.   I. Holston,
Kim R., 1948–   II. Title.
PR2937.H66   2009
822.3'3 — dc22   2009014103

British Library cataloguing data are available

Cover image ©2009 Shutterstock

Manufactured in the United States of America

*McFarland & Company, Inc., Publishers
Box 611, Jefferson, North Carolina 28640
www.mcfarlandpub.com*

Warren Hope offers his share of this book
to Jessie and Jason
as a charm against the dark
incantations they are bound to meet
in prefaces to Shakespeare.

Kim Holston offers the same
to Courtney and Michael.

Acknowledgments

Whether or not they considered the issue important, these people deserve our thanks: Jacqueline Bellows and Elizabeth S. Wrigley of the Francis Bacon Library; Joan Powell of Interlibrary Loan at Haverford College Library; Ben Primer, university archivist, Princeton University's Seeley G. Mudd Manuscript Library; Carol Sue Lipman, president, Shakespeare Authorship Roundtable; the late A. Bronson Feldman; Anne Swigart; Gary Goldstein; the late Steve Morris; Harriet Pattison; Matthew N. Proser, president, Marlowe Society of America; Jane Swan of West Chester University; Keith Smith; Chris Bankes; Sarah A. Polirer, curatorial assistant, Harvard University Archives; Karen L. Green, registrar, the Folger Shakespeare Library; Nancy Spellman; Celeste Ashley; James McKee; and Ruth Loyd Miller. For this 2nd edition we used many online sources as well as West Chester University's Francis Harvey Green Library and the University of Delaware's Morris Library. We appreciate the help of the Interlibrary Loan staff at Chester County Library, Exton, PA, and Bettina Smith, Silver Spring, MD.

Contents

Preface

Heretical ideas tend to be at first ignored, then ridiculed, and finally attacked. The histories of the Shakespeare controversy that appeared prior to the original edition of the present work were part of an attempt to ridicule the Shakespeare authorship question. Since our history appeared in 1992, the ante has been raised, and the authorship question in general and the Oxfordian hypothesis in particular have come under serious, straightforward attack. What prompted this attack is the growing interest in and popularity of the Oxfordian hypothesis. The editors of respected periodicals, Justices of the Supreme Court, and PBS producers all publicly asserted or demonstrated by their actions that the Shakespeare controversy was worthy of serious attention. The adherents of the Stratfordian hypothesis — mostly, but not exclusively, professors of English in colleges and universities — finally felt obliged to respond.

This seismic shift in the Shakespeare controversy led us to prepare a second edition of our history of the subject. Doing so gave us the chance to correct some errors in the first edition as well as to add to both the text and the bibliography — bringing both up to date. The text has been expanded by the inclusion of three new chapters, and the annotated bibliography has grown exponentially through the addition of multitudinous entries.

What interested us most in the original edition was tracking the growing recognition that something was rotten with the authorship of Shakespeare's works and the way this recognition led to what we accept as the correct solution to that problem. In this revised edition we had to confront a range of new scholarship. In broad terms, that scholarship consists of (1) growing support for the Oxfordian hypothesis, (2) various kinds of attacks on that hypothesis by Stratfordians, and (3) a kind of eclectic mass of material that argues for the agnostic position, makes a case for additional candidates, or attempts to strengthen either the Oxfordian or the Stratfordian view. The controversy seems to be moving less to a clearcut resolution than to a general acceptance of the legitimacy of the scholarly pursuit of the question.

One concrete sign of this tendency is the Declaration of Reasonable Doubt About the Identity of William Shakespeare, a declaration that is identified with no specific candidate for the Shakespeare honors but simply insists on the freedom to doubt the traditional attribution of the plays and poems. Mark Rylance and Derek Jacobi, the British actors, drew attention to the Declaration by choosing to sign it publicly. There are now almost 1,400 signers of the Declaration. (See www.DoubtAboutWill.org.) Other signs of this tendency are courses in "authorship studies" that are now offered in colleges and universities both here and in the United Kingdom. It will be fascinating to see how such ventures fare.

In the meantime, we continue to hope that readers will share our conviction that both the early pioneers of the Shakespeare controversy and recent participants in it deserve our time and attention.

Introduction

Doubts that William Shakspere (let us not spell it "Shakespeare") of Stratford-on-Avon wrote the plays and poems attributed to him have been expressed in print for more than two hundred years. The question of Shakespeare's identity has engaged the wit and energy of a wide range of people — from Mark Twain to housewives in suburban London and from Sigmund Freud to school teachers in the American Middle West. Yet the histories of this subject are marked by a dreary sameness.[1] They are all written from the same point of view: there is no Shakespeare authorship question, really, only a gabble of cranks who think there is. It is as if dwellers on the flat earth decided to write up the evolution of the notion that the world is round.

This history of the subject is very different. It is written from the point of view that there is an authorship question, that it is important, and that the correct answer to it has already been found and broadcast among us. More of us would be aware of these truths if a gabble of cranks did not vociferously deny them. In short, this is a history written in opposition to the currently prevailing view — a view that will pass.

Clifford Simak, the very highly regarded science fiction writer, appears to share our faith in humanity's ability to determine the truth of this matter in the long run. In his novel *The Goblin Reservation*, a book set in the distant future, he writes that Time College established, "two or three years ago, that the Earl of Oxford, not Shakespeare, had been the author of the plays." We take encouragement from the fact that Simak offers support for our own reading of the history of the authorship question. We, too, are convinced that Time (not the college) will eventually establish that "William Shakespeare" was Edward de Vere, the Seventeenth Earl of Oxford. What we track in this book are the efforts of a number of people which culminated in that recognition of Shakespeare's identity, and the consequences, thus far, of that recognition.

The result is a kind of inversion of the history of the subject as it has been written to date. People who have been denounced as lunatics are seen as truth-seekers. Great writers who have been said to have spoken ironically on this subject are taken at their word. Cranks become respected authorities and respected authorities become mere cranks. A whole host of people who have been torn from their contexts and misrepresented are put back where they belong and permitted to show at least a glimpse of their true colors.

Our aim is to be critically selective, not exhaustive. We focus on those individuals and writings that move the question toward its solution. Much of what has been written on the authorship question merely restates a case that had been previously made by others — necessary at the time as a way of gaining popular support, no doubt, but not of lasting interest. Then, again, the sheer number of sometimes preposterous candidates proposed as Shakespeare has only served to discredit the question generally. Many of the earliest treatments of the subject were slight, or dubious, or failed to engage the interest of the public, thus leaving the question much as they found it. As a result, we begin in earnest with Delia Bacon — not because she was the earliest writer on the question but because she was the first to treat it as a cultural riddle worthy of serious attention and it has been treated that way by at least some others ever since. On the other hand, we end our history in 2007 — when two works appeared that sum up the current state of the question. References to and descriptions of many works that deal with the controversy from its vague beginnings to its definitive present will be found in Part II of this work, the chronologically arranged annotated bibliography (which includes titles published as recently as 2009).

It must be understood, though, that Delia Bacon did not emerge from a vacuum. She had predecessors. The first published doubts about the authorship of Shakespeare's plays seem to have surfaced in 1769 with the anonymous publication of a book entitled *The Life and Adventures of Common Sense: An Historical Allegory*. In this allegory, a character called Wisdom has a commonplace book filled with rules for dramatic writing and other unusual matter. Wisdom meets a "person belonging to the Playhouse" who is described in terms of the legends that were gathering around the name of Shakespeare. This person obtains Wisdom's commonplace book and becomes a playwright — "his name was Shakespeare!" While not probing the question of authorship directly, this book, which has been attributed to a physician named Herbert Lawrence, at least shows that a need to explain Shakespeare's knowledge was then felt by some.[2]

Then there is the strange story of the Rev. J. Wilmot, D.D., rector of Barton-on-the-Heath near Stratford. Wilmot seems to have single-handedly all but convinced himself that Francis Bacon, rather than William Shakspere of neighboring Stratford, wrote Shakespeare's plays and poems. He gave this opinion and his reasons for it to James Cotton Cowell, a young man who had undertaken to prepare a paper on Shakespeare for the Ipswich Philosophical Society. Cowell found the results of his research unsatisfactory — "Everywhere was I met by a strange and perplexing silence," he records. Rummaging near Stratford, though, he turned up the Reverend Wilmot and that gentleman, Cowell informed his fellow philosophers, "does not venture to say definitely Sir Francis Bacon was the author; but, through his great knowledge of the works of that writer, he is able to prepare a cap which fits him amazingly."

Cowell reported Wilmot's views to the Ipswich Philosophical Society on February 7, 1805, and it is through a record of this talk that we learn of Dr. Wilmot's opinions. Wilmot himself felt compelled to burn the papers that contained his heretical musings. News of his doings reemerged only in the twentieth century. If Cowell looked into the matter further, he kept his findings to himself. Something of the trepidation with which these men broached the subject can be sensed by Cowell's confession that the Reverend Wilmot's tentative thesis had made of Cowell "a Pervert, nay a Renegade to the faith I have proclaimed and avowed" before the philosophers of Ipswich. Before divulging Wilmot's name, Cowell swore the members of the society to secrecy.[3]

This fear may have been rooted in the economic meaning of Shakespeare for Stratford. Pilgrims had already begun to visit the place and locals greeted them with outstretched palms. John Adams visited the town with Thomas Jefferson in April 1786, and recorded his impressions: "Three Doors from the Inn, is the House where he was born, as small and mean, as you can conceive. They shew Us an old Wooden Chair in the Chimney Corner, where He sat. We cutt off a Chip according to the Custom. A Mulberry Tree that he planted has been cutt down, and is carefully preserved for Sale."[4]

The first bold call for an inquiry into the authorship came in 1848, when Joseph Hart, an amateur boating enthusiast, and later the American consul at Santa Cruz, published his *The Romance of Yachting*. Hart remarked that "destitution of authentic incidents marks every stage" of Will Shakspere's life, declared the attribution of the plays and poems to him to be a fraud, and urged a search for the actual authors.[5] Hart did not seem to think that a solitary individual could have accomplished the feat. These statements and others similar to them paved the way for Delia Bacon. The history of the question really begins with her.

We will use Shakspere to refer to the citizen of Stratford and Shakespeare to refer to the author of the plays and poems, except for when we are quoting others. Traditional scholars argue that this is a distinction without a difference, that it is making too much of the inconsistent orthography of the Elizabethan period. But that inconsistent orthography points to consistent pronunciation: the name's first syllable is "shacks" or "shocks," not "shake" or "shakes."

PART I

Chapter 1

A Founding Mother: Delia Bacon

Expose thyself to feel what wretches feel.

For too long, critics have depicted Delia Bacon as a tragi-comic figure, blindly pursuing a fantastic mission in obscurity and isolation, only to end in silence and madness. What this stereotype has accomplished is to permit critics to write off with a sigh or a snicker, depending on the critic's sensibility and perspective, Delia Bacon's work without bothering to try and understand it or considering the context in which her work was produced.

This is not at all to say that the stereotype is without basis. On the contrary, her sad story establishes an archetype for the story of the Shakespeare authorship question at large — or at least one element of it: an unworldly pursuit of truth that produces gifts for a world that is indifferent or hostile to them. But we get ahead of ourselves. For now, Delia Bacon's story.

I

Delia Salter Bacon was born in a log cabin at Tallmadge, Ohio, near what is now Cleveland, on February 2, 1811.[1] She was one of the six children born to David Bacon, a protestant missionary in what was then the West, and his young wife, Alice Parks Bacon. The family sprang from New England roots. Delia's grandfather, Joseph Bacon, who settled as a preacher in Woodstock, Connecticut in 1764, was descended from Michael Bacon, a member of the Massachusetts Bay Colony as early as 1640. These intimate connections with Protestantism and the colonization of America shaped her outlook for life. In a piece on the life of Sir Walter Raleigh she wrote, "the wild old forest echoed with Sabbath hymns and sweet old English nursery songs, and the children of the New World awoke."[2] She saw herself as an awakened child of the New World, and saw American culture as the growth of an Elizabethan transplant.

Tallmadge, Ohio, consisted of 12,000 acres of "wild old forest" that David Bacon planned to establish as a community of the God-fearing. Political and economic conditions, culminating in the War of 1812, temporarily halted the Western migration. The New England Congregationalists who were to people his dream community never materialized. The family, in desperate financial shape, returned to Connecticut. David Bacon tried to eke out a living as a preacher and teacher, but died, defeated and exhausted, at the age of forty-six. His widow dispersed the children, placing them with family and friends. Delia was placed in the Hartford home of friends, Delia Williams, perhaps the woman she had been named for, and her husband, an attorney. They were a childless couple and if Delia's material wants were met, the atmosphere of the home was reportedly grim.

She was fortunate to attend a school for girls founded by Catherine Beecher. Although there must have been difficulties, Delia Bacon's intellect thrived in this environment. Years later, Catherine Beecher stated that if she were "to make a list of the most gifted minds" she had ever met, male or female, the names of Delia Bacon and four of her other young students would have to be on it.

By May 1826, that is, at the age of fifteen, it became necessary for Delia to earn her own living. Always bold and enterprising like the Elizabethans she admired and studied, and perhaps inspired by the example of Catherine Beecher, she set out, with the assistance of her slightly older sister, to establish a school of her own. She made attempts in several locations, but without success. Martin Pares reports that these efforts "came to an end in the summer of 1830 in disappointment, sickness, and insolvency."[3] It may have been with memories of these efforts in mind that she wrote in an aside while discussing Raleigh's unofficial academy, "Where the teacher is, there must the school be gathered together. And a school in the end there will be: a school in the end the true teacher will have, though he begin it, as the barefoot Athenian began his, in the stall of the artisan, or in the chat of the Gymnasium, amid the compliments of the morning levee, the woodland stroll, or in the midnight revel of the banquet."[4] This at least suggests the dedication with which she pursued her aim, no matter how meager the apparent results.

Delia Bacon (Print Collection, Miriam and Ira D. Wallach Division of Art, Prints and Photographs, New York Public Library, Astor, Lenox and Tilden Foundations).

Following the failure of these attempts to establish a school of her own, she taught privately or was an employee in the schools of others that were already established.

It is perhaps no coincidence that a period of "disappointment, sickness, and insolvency" led to her first book, *Tales of the Puritans*, which was published anonymously in 1831. This publication made a few things clear — that she aspired to be an author, that she had read widely, and that her mind naturally turned to history for its materials of contemplation. A collection of romances for women, the book enjoyed a modest success. She later wrote a short story, with the self-revelatory title "Love's Martyr," which was selected to win a $100 prize, even though the first published short story of Edgar Allan Poe was among her competition. And she tried her hand at a play or, rather, what she described as a dialogue, not intended for stage production, that took the American Revolution for its scene. Theodore Bacon, her nephew, records that the failure of this verbose piece made her give up the dream of earning her living as a writer for a time.

Eventually she found another and more congenial alternative to school teaching in lecturing. Although the example of the feminist, Margaret Fuller, may have encouraged her, she was something of a pioneer in this field, too.[5] Mrs. Eliza Farrar, the wife of a Harvard professor, begins the chapter on Delia Bacon in her *Recollections of Seventy Years* in this way: "The first lady whom I ever heard deliver a public lecture was Miss Delia Bacon."[6] Listeners were repeatedly struck by the knowledge, passion, and power of Delia Bacon as a lecturer. In fact, many of her listeners who have left recorded impressions feel obliged to go outside the human category to describe her, making her a sibyl, an oracle, or a muse: "Graceful and intellectual in appearance, eloquent in speech ... and full of inspiration, she looked and spoke the very muse of history."[7] This placement of her beyond the human in people's minds seems to have had two dominant effects. First, she was no doubt often lonely and made to feel alone, if not alien, in the Boston, Hartford, New Haven, and New York of the 1840s. Second, her listeners were left with a lasting impression of her, but they tended to forget what she said. "Of those lectures she wrote out nothing — not even notes. All their wisdom came fresh and living from the depth of her ready intellect. And for that very reason there is now no trace of what would be so valuable."[8] Too few of her admirers had the foresight to record what they had heard.

Fortunately for Delia Bacon — and us — not all of her admirers were of this type. Some gave her practical support and aid — opening their homes to her for lectures and discussions or giving her letters of introduction to potential audiences in other cities. And some of these did also leave a slight record of the things she said. Mrs. Eliza Farrar was that kind of listener:

> She was so much admired and liked in Cambridge, that a lady there invited her to spend the winter with her as her guest, and I gave her the use of my parlor for another course of her history to the time of the birth of Christ, and I can never forget how clear she made it to us that the world was only then made fit for the advent of Jesus. She ended with a fine climax that was quite thrilling.[9]

This report, scant as it is, deserves a little attention. First, Delia Bacon did not conceive of history as a mass of random events or as a sequence of events arising from the economic and political life of humanity alone. Quite the contrary, like her Puritan forebears, she saw history as purposeful, an evolutionary movement prompted, at least in part, by Providence. It was typical of her that she applied her outlook even to the birth of Jesus. As we will see, she also applied it to the timing of the appearance of Shakespeare on the stage of the world.

Second, the effect of Delia Bacon's presentation on Mrs. Farrar is recorded in terms that unconsciously reflect the repressed sexuality of Delia Bacon's society — "She ended with a fine climax that was quite thrilling." This current of repressed sexuality put Delia Bacon at the center of a scandal that had repercussions throughout and beyond the Congregationalist community in New Haven.

Delia Bacon's love affair with the Reverend Alexander McWhorter, a young divinity student at Yale and a member of a wealthy New Jersey family, now reads like a tragedy of errors. McWhorter was twenty-three years old at the time; and Delia was thirty-five. They lived in the same hotel in New Haven and were initially thrown into contact, it seems, when they took meals. Delia, ever the true teacher in search of a school, used her rooms as a kind of salon, a place for intellectual discussions with individuals who attended by invitation. It was considered an honor to be invited.

Alexander McWhorter wished to join the group, but had never been formally introduced to her. Nonetheless, she learned of his wish and wrote him an invitation. He apparently used this written invitation to suggest to friends that Delia had designs on him and was guilty of gross impropriety. He accepted the invitation, though, and in fact made many more visits. He even continued to visit her when her family objected to the situation and took her out of the hotel to live at her brother's home. Eventually, although the situation and its attendant notoriety so affected her nerves that she withdrew to a retreat for a "hydropathic cure," McWhorter followed her there.

A reporter who dealt with the case in *The Philadelphia Times* of December 26, 1886, writes:

> He was completely fascinated by the brilliant talk of a refined and cultivated woman to whom the whole field of belles lettres was a familiar garden. They read and studied together, and, with two such natures, it was only natural that their talk should be more of books than of love. She even confided to him her favorite theory that ... Shakespeare was not the author of Shakespeare's Plays.... He approved these ideas and encouraged the delusion in its incipient stages. Then, when he tired of the flirtation ... he turned viciously upon his uncomplaining victim and contemptuously characterized an affair, that had begun with baseness on his part, as literary intimacy.[10]

This testimony is interesting because while the author misses no opportunity to misrepresent and disparage Delia's work on Shakespeare, he clearly sees her as the victim in the affair with McWhorter.

In a misguided attempt to protect Delia's reputation, her brother, the Reverend Leonard Bacon and other family members, announced her engagement to McWhorter. The divinity student publicly denied their engagement, adding that while Delia had proposed a number of times, he had never agreed. Leonard Bacon brought charges against "the clerical Lothario" in an effort to have McWhorter's license to preach revoked. Yale's Dr. Nathaniel Taylor, a teacher of McWhorter's who perhaps wished to diminish Leonard Bacon's influence in the community, rushed to McWhorter's defense. Twenty-three Congregational ministers heard evidence in the case and voted twelve to eleven to vindicate McWhorter.

Delia was, of course, humiliated. The scandal was bruited far and wide. According to Catherine Beecher, "No talk of private scandal had ever before been known to create so extensive an excitement." Irving Wallace, in his informative and entertaining chapter on Delia Bacon in his *The Square Pegs*, connects this public humiliation to her work on Shakespeare:

> After the trial Delia went to Ohio to recover and to bury herself in the books of another, and happier, age. When she returned to New England and her lectures, she was a new woman and she had a mission. For she had found in history a man she disliked even more than the faithless McWhorter. This man, she would soon announce, was William Shakespeare, pretender and mountebank.[11]

Now it is a shrewd guess that the animus Delia Bacon aimed at Will Shakspere of Stratford helped to siphon off some of the feelings that McWhorter had generated in her. When she describes the actor as "an insult to genius and learning," McWhorter of the Yale Divinity School may well be in her mind's eye as well as the Divine Will of Stratford. But the fact remains that her theory had developed as a result of years of historical researches and reflection that took place before she met Alexander McWhorter. Her sense of public shame no doubt increased her desire to publicly right a wrong. It no doubt also made her realize more fully than ever before the protection offered by anonymity to a public figure. But the McWhorter affair does not diminish at all her work on Shakespeare.

Indeed, she may well have gained by it — not just illumination on the relation between the public and the private life, the impact of various modes of communication on society, and the need for those who have or desire power to control or at least influence those modes of communication, but it is possible, at least, that McWhorter helped to reinforce her method. As a divinity student, he was full of "the higher criticism"—textual criticism of the Bible and researches into the life of the historical Jesus, in Albert Schweitzer's phrase. He seems to have constructed a theory himself. He argued that a peculiar grammatical construction in the Hebrew of the Old Testament was a forecast to the initiated of the birth of Jesus. This practice of closely reading texts in order to wring from them meanings that lie beneath their surfaces could have, through conversation, given new authority to Delia Bacon for her own findings. Finally, the bravery with which she overcame the ridicule and humiliation associated with the scandal may have helped give her the courage she needed to launch a bold, straight-forward attack on the literary idol of the English-speaking world and beyond.

What certainly crystallized in her mind following the MacWhorter affair—and there may have been an element of flight in this—was the need to go to England to further her Elizabethan researches and discover proofs of her theory. She found the sympathetic aid required to make this wish possible through Ralph Waldo Emerson, who had said of Shakespeare that he could not "marry" the life "to the verse."[12] He took time from his own writing and lecturing on Abolition to help her in a number of ways. For one thing, he listened to her with understanding, something many of her best friends refused to do. He read her letters on Shakespeare with real interest and wrote back with sincere admiration. He interested the editors of *Putnam's Monthly* in publishing a series of articles by her on Shakespeare, a scheme that was to help her finance her stay in England. Finally, he introduced her to Charles Butler, a wealthy New York banker with intellectual interests. Butler offered to finance Delia's round-trip passage to England and support her there for six months.

In May, 1853, Delia left New York harbor on board the *Pacific* bound for Liverpool. She arrived there on May 24, armed with letters of introduction from Emerson, the financial backing of Butler, and her own learning and determination. Within a month of reaching London, she used one of Emerson's letters and visited with Jane and Thomas Carlyle at their home in Cheyne Walk. The Carlyles, aware of her mission, also invited a friend who was interested in Francis Bacon and later became one of his biographers.

Ralph Waldo Emerson (courtesy of the National Archives).

In a letter to her sister, Delia describes this visit in terms which demonstrate her sense of humor but also succinctly state the main point of her work on Shakespeare:

> They were perfectly stunned. They turned black in the face at my presumption. "Do you mean to say," so and so, said Mr. Carlyle, with his strong emphasis; and I said that I did; and they both looked at me with staring eyes, speechless for want of words in which to convey their sense of my audacity ... I told him [Carlyle] he did not know what was in the Plays..., and no one could know who believed that that booby wrote them. It was then that he began to shriek. You could have heard him a mile.

Here, in brief, is the main point of all her labors: she wanted to know what was in Shakespeare's plays — what they meant, what they taught about life — and she had become convinced that the traditional attribution of them to Will Shakspere of Stratford was an obstacle to that knowledge.

Despite this audacious and auspicious beginning, her fate in England was not a lucky one. She attracted few friends, admirers, or converts to her cause. The Carlyles remained extremely kind, but totally unconvinced. In fact, Carlyle urged her to comb the documents of the period — contending that only documentary evidence would persuade people. Delia insisted that this would be a part of her work, but she worked mostly on developing her case from a careful reading of the pertinent texts. She soon jettisoned her plan to return to America after a relatively short stay in England. As a result, she soon lived in poverty as well as intellectual isolation.

The plan to support herself by her pen also took longer to put into action than she had originally expected. The first of her articles appeared in *Putnam's Monthly* in January, 1856 — and the first was also the last. The editor attached this note to the piece:

> In commending the publication of these bold, original, and most ingenius and interesting speculations on the real authorship of Shakespeare's Plays, it is proper for the editor of *Putnam's Monthly*, in disclaiming all responsibility for their startling view of the question, to say that they are the result of long and conscientious investigation on the part of the learned and eloquent scholar, their author; and that the editor has reason to hope that they will be continued through some future numbers of the magazine.[13]

Nathaniel Hawthorne (courtesy of the National Archives).

The learned and eloquent scholar, their author, also had reason to hope that the articles would appear in future numbers of the magazine. She counted on the payment for them to keep a roof over her head and put food on her table. No more from her pen ever appeared in the magazine, however. The reasons given for this disappointment vary. Some claim her friends and family, in another misguided attempt to protect her reputation, urged the editor to discontinue the series. Others claim that professional Shakespearean critics such as Richard Grant White used their influence to silence the heretical Delia. But it seems just as likely that later installments advanced the argument too slowly and in such verbose, repetitive, and oracular prose that the editor rejected them.

Another loss resulted from this loss of a livelihood. Part of the manuscript for her book, apparently a complete "Life of Raleigh," that she hoped would first appear in *Putnam's*, was eventually sent by Emerson to his brother, William, in New York, for safekeeping. When the manuscript was rejected and Delia asked that it be returned to her in England, William Emerson sent it on its way to Concord with a house guest of his, Sophy Ripley. The parcel was lost on the way and with it went Delia's faith in Emerson. Her financial difficulties became crushing and she decided to seek relief from someone in England. Whether it was Providence, shrewdness, or luck that turned her thoughts to Nathaniel Hawthorne, the brother-in-law of her friend Elizabeth Peabody, cannot be stated with assurance, but it is certainly the case that she could not have found a more generous, humane, and devoted champion. She must have realized that when he responded to her letter immediately with these words:

> I would not be understood, my dear Miss Bacon, as professing to have faith in the correctness of your views. In fact, I know far too little of them to have any right to form an opinion: and as to the case of the "old Player" (whom you grieve my heart by speaking of so contemptuously) you will have to rend him out of me by the roots, and by main force, if at all. But I feel that you have done a thing that ought to be reverenced, in devoting yourself to this object, whatever it be, and whether right or wrong; and that, by so doing, you have acquired some of the privileges of an inspired person and a prophetess — and that the world is bound to hear you, if for nothing else, yet because you are so sure of your own mission.[14]

Hawthorne was better than his word. He corresponded with her, went to see her when he was in London, announced to her landlord and other creditors that he would be personally responsible for her debts, and financed the publication of her book, in both England and America. He also provided the book with a sympathetic preface. It is not too much to say that, except for Hawthorne and his generosity, the book that raised the Shakespeare authorship question as a cultural riddle of the first importance would never have appeared.

After so many difficulties and disappointments, the mere publication of the book was not enough for Delia Bacon. It may well be that in her isolation she had imagined that the book would cause a mass and immediate conversion to her point of view. If so, she was very much mistaken. As Hawthorne wrote, the

> ponderous octavo volume ... fell with a dead thump at the feet of the public.... A few people turned over one or two of the leaves, as it lay there, and essayed to kick the volume deeper into the mud; for they were the hack critics of the minor periodical press in London, than whom, I suppose, though excellent fellows in their way, there are no gentlemen in the world less sensible of any sanctity in a book, or less likely to recognize an author's heart in it, or more careless about bruising, if they do recognize it.[15]

Delia's heart was bruised. She even turned against Hawthorne, snapping at the one hand that would support her, complaining that in his preface he failed to announce that he accepted her theories in toto. He had not done so because he did not accept them. What he did accept, and remained grateful for, was her "interpretation of the Plays" and the "wide scope," "high purpose," and "richness of inner meaning" she found in them.

Months before the publication of her *The Philosophy of the Plays of Shakspere Unfolded* (1857), ill and worn out, she moved from London to Stratford-on-Avon. With her book written, in some way her work done, she perhaps felt a longing for death that showed itself in a growing conviction that the truth of the origin of the Shakespeare works could be found in a grave. She had earlier sought permission to open Bacon's tomb, but without success. She now haunted the church at Stratford, worrying about whether she should open Will Shakspere's tomb. Eventually, her mind gave way and she was installed in a private mental institution nearby.

Her nephew and first biographer, Theodore Bacon, tells how she came to return to America. Lieutenant George Blagden Bacon, of the U.S. Navy, was returning home through England following a two-year tour of duty on "an American frigate in the China Seas." He determined to seek out his relative, unaware of her condition and whereabouts. He was shocked by what he learned of her. He delayed his departure and arranged to take Delia home with him. The family placed her in an institution in Hartford, where she died on September 2, 1859. She was buried in New Haven.

II

Two political upheavals, the American and French Revolutions, make up part of the backdrop for Delia Bacon's thought and work. These upheavals brought in their wake a new spirit, a new outlook, that elevated humanity's reasoning faculty as an authority. With an almost religious fervor, people thought for themselves, toppled venerated idols, reexamined old dogmas, and set out to discover the truth. In the year of Delia Bacon's birth, 1811, the English poet Samuel Taylor Coleridge reflected this fervor by applying the new spirit of inquiry to Shakespeare. "Does God choose idiots," Coleridge demanded of his listeners during a series of lectures on Milton and Shakespeare in London. "Does God choose idiots by whom to convey divine truths to men?"[16] This is the very question that Delia Bacon considered in her "William Shakespeare and His Plays: An Inquiry Concerning Them" in *Putnam's Monthly*.

She put the question this way:

> Shall this crowning literary product of that great epoch, wherein these new ages have their beginning, vividly arrayed in its choicest refinements, flashing everywhere on the surface with its costliest wit, crowded everywhere with its subtlest scholasticism, betraying, on every page, its broadest, freshest range of experience, its most varied culture, its profoundest insight, its boldest grasp of comprehension — shall this crowning result of so many preceding ages of growth and culture, with its essential, and now palpable connection with the new scientific movement of the time from which it issues, be able to conceal from us, much longer, its history? — Shall we be able to accept in explanation of it, much longer, the story of the Stratford poacher?[17]

Delia Bacon does not simply answer these questions with what Melville called a "thunderous no" and go on to argue in favor of her own explanation of the origins of the Shakespearean works. She might have fared better if she had — at least, *Putnam's Monthly* might have published more of her work if she had. Instead, she attacked and restated the question from a number of angles.

For instance, she chastises her contemporary critics for feeling able to add to our knowledge of Homer, a figure who, as she says, is "antehistorical," who lived and worked before the invention of writing, before memories were recorded and collateral documents kept. This fact of the circumstances in which Homer thrived does not cause modern critics to throw up their hands. Yet they have failed to apply the tools of modern historical and literary criticism to the figure of Will Shakspere of Stratford, despite the fact that he thrived centuries after the spread of writing and years after the press had begun to do its good work. Why? She answers, "the critics themselves still veil their faces, filling the air with mystic utterances which seem to say, that to this shrine at least, for the footstep of the common reason and the common sense, there is yet no admittance."[18]

This position is clearly an intolerable outrage and an insult in Delia Bacon's eyes. She is convinced that there is no shrine from which common reason and common sense should be banned. So she devotes a good deal of space to considering why the critics are attracted to their position, a position that condemns them to ignorance and a loss of integrity. To deal with this question she considers the conditions that obtained when the legend of the authorship began.

"The common disposition is to receive, in good faith, a statement of this kind, however extraordinary — the natural intellectual preference of the affirmative proposition at hand, as the explanation of a given phenomenon ... might serve to account for this result at a time when criticism, as yet was not,"[19] she states, describing the lack of criticism at the time of the publication of the First Folio, 1623. But this reason cannot explain the continued acceptance of an "extraordinary" statement at a time when Homer is being anatomized and even the origins of religion are being probed. Instead, she argues that some critics of Shakespeare's works are relieved by the darkness that surrounds their origin. Part of the attraction of that darkness is the ability to attribute the production of the works to nature unschooled and untouched by art, to the appearance of "superhuman genius" where it should be least expected. These critics delight in the spectacle of nature mocking reason, laughing at history, and placing its prodigal achievement out of the reach of criticism. Some critics, she argues, find this liberating because it frees them from the limits of reason and allows them to make of Shakespeare anything they please.

Even for critics of this type, debased as she clearly thinks they are, the popular legend of the authorship can only be maintained by severely limiting what they find in Shakespeare's works and by grotesquely distorting what those works mean. As a result, she contends, two Shakespeares already exist in the writings of critics. One is the deer-stealing youth who grew up to be an actor and successful theatrical manager. The other is the author of the plays and poems. She identifies these two Shakespeares with Hamlet and the players he addresses:

> Condemned to look for the author of Hamlet himself— the subtle Hamlet of the university, the courtly Hamlet, "the glass of fashion and the mould of form"— in that dirty, doggish group of players, who come into the scene summoned like a pack of hounds to his service, the very tone of his courtesy to them, with its princely condescension, with its arduous familiarity, only serving to make the great, impassable social gulf between them the more evident — compelled to look in that ignominious group, with its faithful portraiture of the players of that time (taken from the life by one who had had dealings with them), for the princely scholar himself in his author, how could we understand him — the enigmatical Hamlet, with the thought of ages in his foregone conclusions?[20]

Having established the existence of two distinct Shakespeares in contemporary criticism, the player and the poet, she considers what should be done about the name Shakespeare. She tackles this subject, too, from a number of points of view. She decides that the poet, the author, chose to merge his identity with that of the player. More importantly, for her, she is convinced that the poet did so in order to hinder criticism, that is, in order to conceal the intellectual treasure of the plays and poems in apparent trifles, of no lasting interest to anyone, not even their supposed author. She draws this conclusion as an historian, as a student of the Elizabethan age. The attribution of the plays to the Stratford citizen, a man with at best a limited education and no aim in life higher than buying New Place and retiring to it, effectively inverts the point of view of the true author. This is the way she shrewdly summarizes the point of view of the poet and the distortion that the popular legend of authorship causes:

> But for this prepossession [the popular theory of authorship] in that daring treatment of court-life which this single play of Hamlet involves, in the entire freedom with which its conventionalities are handled, how could we have failed to recognize the touch of one habitually practiced in its refinements? how could we have failed to recognize, not in this play only, but in all these plays, the poet whose habits and perceptions have been moulded in the atmosphere of these subtle social influences? He cannot shake off this influence when he will. He carries the court perfume with him, unconsciously, wherever he goes, among mobs of artisans that will not "keep their teeth clean," into the ranks of "greasy citizens" and "rude mechanicals;" into country feasts and merry-makings; among "pretty low-born lasses," "the queens of curds and cheese," and into the heart of that forest "where there is no clock." He looks into Arden and into Eastcheap from the court standpoint, not from these into the court, and he is as much a prince with Poins and Bardolph as he is when he enters and throws open to us, without awe, without consciousness, the most delicate mysteries of the royal presence.[21]

It must be pointed out that in Delia Bacon's view there is nothing of snobbery in any of this. Instead, it is the result of common sense reflecting on the circumstances that existed during the reign of Elizabeth. As she writes, perhaps especially addressing those literary critics who have failed to consider the technological differences between Shakespeare's time and their own,

> we must take into account the fact that, at the time when these works were issued, all those characteristic organizations of the modern ages, for the diffusion of intellectual and moral influences, which now everywhere cross and recross, with electric fibre, the hither-to impassable social barriers, were as yet unimagined.... The Englishman who but reads *The Times*, today, puts himself into a connection with his age, and attains thereby a means of enlargement of character and elevation of thought and aims, which, in the age of Elizabeth, was only possible to men occupying the highest official and social positions.[22]

She therefore concludes that the name Shakespeare can be legitimately maintained if it is understood that it refers to the author, not the player, and if it is not permitted to distort our understanding of the work — if we read it aware that it was written from the standpoint of the court, rather than that of either Eastcheap or Arden. For Delia Bacon, reading the plays from this standpoint is a requirement "now too grave and momentous to permit of any further postponement."[23]

Why should the way we read the plays of Shakespeare be a "grave and momentous" matter? Delia Bacon's answer is that the author, or authors, were well aware of the religious and social function of the theater in the ancient world and determined to use the Elizabethan stage for similar purposes. The plays of Shakespeare were not mere entertainments, but attempts to guide and mould the masses of the future, a freer age. Because of the popular attribution of the plays to Will Shakspere, she claims, we have blinded ourselves to the meaning of the poet, a poet who "would have all our life, and not a part of it, learned, artistic, beautiful, religious." The passion behind her plea clearly springs from her sense of the waste of life that will result from continuing to ignore the lessons Shakespeare has to teach.

III

The passages quoted at some length from Delia Bacon's article in the previous section were intended, in part, to convey a sense of her style. That style has been a cause of complaint for years, even among sympathetic figures. Hawthorne, for instance, lamented that her book contained "a great amount of rubbish, which any competent editor would have shovelled out of the way."[24] Nearly one hundred years later, Martin Pares, unlike Hawthorne a convinced Baconian, continued to lament the lack of an editor: "The book is in fact a laborious, profound, but quite remarkable and valuable piece of literary criticism, which in the hands of a skillful editor might almost have become a classic."[25]

These comments approach a just estimation of Delia Bacon's *The Philosophy of the Plays of Shakspere Unfolded*. Her style was perhaps better suited to arousing the interest of listeners in a lecture hall in Boston than to conveying information to a reader. It is a rhetorical, oratorical style. Its lengthy, gasping, convoluted sentences can have a numbing effect. But just when you think she has disappeared beneath the surface forever, she soars up with a brilliant fish flopping in her beak. Except for some tiresome repetitions, it is hard to know precisely what could be safely cut. Just as you are ready to give up on a paragraph as an incomprehensible slab of words, one of her sharpest insights emerges from it. To a much larger extent than is at first apparent, her tedious, long-winded outpourings do repay the efforts of what she calls "the not undiligent reader." Her style serves to promote thought rather than to convey information.

For instance, there is not now, more than one hundred years after the publication of the book, a clear consensus on what her theory of the Shakespeare authorship was. She has been classed as a Baconian, as an advocate of dual authorship who attributes the plays and poems to both Raleigh and Bacon, and as an advocate of a group theory of authorship, attributing the works to Raleigh, Bacon, Spenser, and others. People of good faith can draw these conclusions for the very good reason that Delia Bacon is ambiguous on the subject. Nonetheless, drawing these conclusions do her an injustice because they necessarily misrepresent her position. Her position is clear and she states it early: "The question of the authorship of the great philosophic poems which are the legacy of the Elizabethan Age to us, is an incidental question in this inquiry, and is incidentally treated here."[26]

Who wrote the plays is for her a merely literary question — and she is after bigger game, to use a phrase of Mark Twain's. She wishes to show clearly what the plays contain, what they mean, and what they imply for the life of humanity on this globe. She indicates that Raleigh was involved in the production of the Shakespeare works at least by starting an unofficial academy, a school, a school where Shakespeare studied. She clearly suggests that this school is shown to us in action in *Love's Labours Lost* — but does not say whether the founder of the school or the student wrote the play. She argues that Raleigh hauled his books around in trunks just as Brutus does in *Julius Caesar* — but does not say whether this means to her that he wrote the play or was a model for Shakespeare's portrait of the Roman. She says that Raleigh "became at once the center" of a collection of "elder wits and poets" that included Sir Philip Sidney, Thomas Lord Buckhurst, Henry Lord Paget, Edward Earl of Oxford, and others; and she states that this group laid "the shining foundations" of the monument that is Shakespeare's work. Whether these foundations include plays that Shakespeare was familiar with and learned from, or early works attributed to Shakespeare, or plays that were eventually reworked and issued as Shakespeare's, she does not say. She does not say because such questions are not of primary importance to her and they could divert her readers from what she cares about most. Often she is content to say "the poet, be he who he may" and let it go at that.

What she is concerned to show is that Shakespeare's works contain an application to the human condition of the New Learning; and that Shakespeare's works therefore parallel and complete Bacon's application of the New Learning to the natural, physical world. Her conclusion takes up the problem that Bacon, as he is known to us in the record, does not seem to be the kind of man the poet she writes of is. That she deals with this problem indicates the prominence she gives to Bacon in the production of Shakespeare's plays and poems. One of the many ironies we are faced with when we consider Delia Bacon's fate is that most of her followers have concentrated on who the playwright was almost to the exclusion of dealing with what he said and meant.

What he meant from Delia Bacon's point of view can best be learned from her analysis of *King Lear*. She devotes more than one hundred pages of her book to that analysis and every one of those pages, despite their stylistic defects and difficulties, is well worth reading. Her analysis of the play remains to this day unsurpassed.

It is characteristic of her that she opens her analysis not with *Lear* at all, but with a general consideration of the poet's attitude toward sovereignty and a specific consideration of the contortions the poet was forced to go through in order to voice that attitude in *Richard II* and *Henry V*. She is convinced that Shakespeare was obsessed with the question of the legitimacy of monarchy. She clearly sees the Tudor dynasty as the result of a usurpation of power, the "double crown of military conquest and priestly usurpation,"[27] and indicates that the poet viewed it in the same way. This conclusion was reached by the poet through the application of scientific inquiry to the case. She argues that the usurper Bolingbroke gave voice to a discovery of the poet's:

> Of course, poor Bolingbroke, fevered with the weight of his ill-got crown, and passing a sleepless night in spite of its supposed exemptions ... might surely be allowed to mutter to himself, in the solitude of his own bed-chamber, a few general reflections on the subject ... that nature in her sovereignty, imperial still, refused to recognize this artificial difference in men, but still went on her way in all things ... classing the monarch with his "poorest subject."[28]

Now, this recognition that nature treats all men, regardless of rank, in much the same way was, even in the time of Elizabeth, "proper, and obvious enough." Nonetheless, to treat even this subject frankly, in a pamphlet, say, would have been seen as a threat to the monarch and duly punished. The writing hand of John Stubbes was chopped off because he had the audacity to oppose the French Alliance through marriage to Elizabeth in a pamphlet. It is the dramatic treatment, the fact that the potential criticism of sovereignty is expressed by a sovereign, keeping his own council, that protects the author. One of the reasons Delia Bacon's sentences are so long is because they are so packed with ideas. While presenting this argument, for instance, she pauses mid-sentence to write, "the poet appears, to have had some experience of this mortal ill [insomnia], which inclines him to put it down among those which ought to be excluded from a state of supreme earthly felicity."[29]

She immediately complicates this relatively simple case by considering the treatment of sovereignty in *Henry V*. The "brave and gentle hero of Agincourt," the night before battle, disguises himself as a private soldier and, in plain prose that befits his assumed station, probes the man that resides behind royal ceremonies: "I think the King is but a man as I am, the violet smells to him as it doth to me; all his senses have but human conditions. His ceremonies laid by, in his nakedness, he appears but a man." The use of the disguise here, of course, promotes dramatic irony. But more than that, the fact that a monarch disguised as a private speaks, makes the speech permissible; to have a private talk this way on a public stage could have caused regal eyebrows to raise. Further, it must be remembered that for Delia Bacon this dramatic use of disguise merely mimics another use of disguise in life. The author is a courtier—a courtier whose concern for the common good causes him to worry about the amount of power granted any individual, even a monarch. Indeed, the author's sympathies are with the monarch: "He thinks that wretched victim of that most irrational and monstrous state of things, on whose head the crown of an arbitrary rule is placed, with all its responsibilities, in his infinite unfitness for them, is, in fact, the one whose cause most of all requires relief."[30] Delia Bacon here makes Shakespeare a forerunner of Oscar Wilde, that rebel of the ruling-class who, in his *The Soul of Man Under Socialism*, argued that the rich need to be liberated from the burdens placed on them by their property and the concerns it causes.

Despite this kind of sympathy, the author's views are literally dangerous. He protects himself by concealing his identity in the form of a player and theatrical manager, a rustic with little education, at best, who cares neither about the common good nor the responsibilities of a ruler, but only wishes to stage an entertainment that will produce some cash. The disguises the author uses in life and on the stage establish layers, protective layers: the author speaks through Will Shakspere of Stratford, who speaks through a mock monarch in a play, who assumes the disguise or role of a private soldier. It is for this reason that Delia Bacon describes what she has done in her book as presenting the philosophy of the plays unfolded.

Before going on to analyze a much more radical critique of monarchy than she has thus far considered, Delia Bacon concludes,

> the Poet of Shakspere's stage, be he who he may, ... is a poet who is infected and, indeed, perfectly possessed, with the idea, that the true human leadership ought to consist in the ability to extend the empire of man over nature,—in the ability to unite and control men, and lead them in battalions against those common evils which infest the human conditions,— not fevers only but "worser" evils, and harder to be cured, and to the conquest of those supernal blessings which the human race have always been vainly crying for.[31]

It is from the height of this position that she sees the question of the poet's identity as merely a literary one.

Delia Bacon calls *King Lear* "the grand social tragedy" because it is, to her, an experiment that allows the poet to define "the human social need, in all its circumference ... as the basis of the human social art."[32] She describes the experiment of *Lear* as equivalent to the Tudor experiment. "a king, who, nurtured in the flatteries of the palace ... thought that he could still be a king, and maintain 'his state' and 'his hundred knights,' and their prerogatives ... merely on grounds of respect and affection, or on grounds of duty, when not merely the care of 'the state,' but the revenues and power of it had been devolved on others."[33] This king, she says, was engaged in an "experiment very similar to the one which he [the poet] found in progress in his time, in that old, decayed, riotous form of military government, which had chosen the moment of its utter dependence on the popular will and respect, as the fitting one for its final suppression of the national liberties ... the experiment of the unarmed prerogative."[34]

The poet, a courtier, had little control over the result of this experiment in life. In his play, however, the result could be enlightenment. Lear, homeless and locked out in the storm, becomes not the spokesman for monarchy but for humanity. He states what Delia Bacon takes to be "a general prescription" for rulers of all types:

> Take physic, pomp;
> Expose thyself to feel what retches feel,
> That thou may'st shake the superflux to them,
> And show the heavens more just.[35]

Pausing before he stoops to enter a hovel and get in out of the storm that humanity must endure when facing nature without the benefit of arts, Lear is "pierced" by what Delia Bacon calls "the great lesson of state," that is, he begins to think about others, about the many who do not have even a hovel to enter:

> You, houseless poverty —
> Poor, naked wretches, wheresoe'er you are
> That bide the pelting of this pitiless storm —
> How shall your houseless heads and unfed sides,
> Your looped and windowed raggedness defend you
> From seasons such as these? O, I have taken
> Too little care of this.[36]

Lear's spirit is "dilated, and moved and kindling with its grandeur," Delia Bacon argues, because the poet has subjected him to an "ideal revolution," an "experimental 'change of places,' which the Poet recommends to those who occupy the upper ones in the social structure as a means of a more particular and practical acquaintance with the conditions of those for whom they legislate."[37] She recognizes that he is not the only member of the old order that undergoes this revolution. Indeed, she declares "it is never the custom of this author to leave the diligent student of his performances in any doubt whatever as to his meaning. It is a rule, that everything in the play shall speak and reverberate his purpose."[38]

To illustrate this assertion she points to the way Gloster's speech — Gloster, a blinded duke, led by a mad beggar — echoes Lear's prescription for rulers:

> Heavens, deal so still!
> Let the superfluous and lust-dieted man
> That slaves your ordinance, that will not see
> Because he doth not feel, feel your power quickly;
> So distribution should undo excess,
> And each man have enough[39]

Delia Bacon is careful never to reduce these speeches to a limited, specific political or economic program, although she readily sees and draws attention to their leveling tendencies. Instead, she insists that we hear in these speeches the results of a scientific study of society transmuted into poetry because "the sovereignty of mercy, the divine right of pity, the majesty of human kindness, the grandeur of the common weal" breathes from the poet's heart "like man new made" through the lips of his puppets of paper and ink.

How is it that the poet came to give voice to these marks of royalty that are not necessarily inherited with a title, wealth, or position in society? Delia Bacon answers that he was at once a "Radical of no ordinary kind" and the most "aristocratic" of poets, who wrote at a time when the conditions the play represents "could not endure much longer." She claims that he may well have then found "the rude surgery of the civil wars at last welcome." Despite this, she is convinced he would have viewed political revolution or civil war with as much foreboding as hope. Caught between these two positions, he remained a critic of the state. For him, politicians of all stripes are "scurvy" and only "seem to see" the things they do not. The tension of the poet's position caused him, she thinks, to place his hopes in the future, when his works would be read by a "freer age," but also caused him to express his most stringent critiques on the state through a mad king who has established a mad beggar and a fool as the representatives of law and order:

> Lear. Thou hast seen a farmer's dog bark at a beggar?
> Gloster. Ay, sir

Lear. And the creature run from the cur? There mightst
thou behold the great image of authority: a dog's
obeyed in office.[40]

It is impossible to summarize Delia Bacon on *King Lear*. She must be read in her annoy-
ing, illuminating entirety. What has been presented here should be sufficient to show the
originality and the profundity of her analysis. But it is worth considering, too, that when she
conceived and wrote this analysis, she felt the conditions the play represents were still unen-
durably present in her own time. After all, she repeatedly insists on what is, it must be admitted, obvious: that the lessons of Lear have not yet been learned and put into effect.

There had been much talk of "the parts of life, and their unions" in the New England
she had recently left. She must have been immersed in the arguments of the Abolitionists of
her homeland and they may have made her incline to welcome the "rude surgery" of Civil
War. But she, too, was no doubt torn between foreboding and hope by that prospect. Her
own madness, inaction, silence, and death may have been hastened by her inability to prevent the storm that was brewing for her country — the country where she expected the new
learning of the Elizabethans to ultimately work out its beneficent influence. Neither the private shocks of her affair with Alexander McWhorter nor the desire for a merely literary fame
drove her to suffer the privations required to produce her book. She subjected herself to that
suffering in order to urge the prescription of Lear on the rulers of her own time:

Take physic, pomp;
Expose thyself to feel what wretches feel.

Chapter 2

Shakespeare on the Mississippi:
Whitman, O'Connor, and Twain

Where America, the Indies?

Hawthorne expected Delia Bacon's book to receive better treatment in America than it did in England. She no doubt shared this expectation. If so, they were both disappointed. He could not keep from showing his contempt for the reception the book received:

> If any American ever wrote a word in her behalf, Miss Bacon never knew it, nor did I. Our journalists at once published some of the most brutal vituperations of the English press, thus pelting their poor countrywoman with stolen mud, without ever waiting to know whether the ignominy was deserved.[1]

This disappointment was not the only lingering problem that his assistance to Bacon caused him.

In his preface to her book, he leveled a charge against William Henry Smith, an Englishman who, in his "Letter to the Earl of Ellesmere," argued that Francis Bacon was the author of Shakespeare's plays. Smith's pamphlet caused a little stir and convinced Lord Palmerston and no doubt others.[2] But Smith did not mention Delia Bacon or her article in *Putnam's Monthly*, acknowledging her prior claim to having solved the problem. Hawthorne wrote of Smith in the preface that he "thought it was not inconsistent with the fair play on which his country prides itself, to take to himself this lady's theory, and favor the public with it as his own original conception." Hawthorne also gave the public Delia's characteristic reaction to the appearance of Smith's pamphlet:

> This has not been a selfish enterprise. It is not a personal concern. It is a discovery which belongs not to an individual, and not to a people. Its fields are wide enough and rich enough for us all; and he that has no work, and whoso will, let him come and labor in them. The field is the world's; and the world's work henceforth is it ... what matters it? says the philosophic wisdom, speaking in the abstract, what name it is proclaimed in, and what letters of the alphabet we know it by?[3]

Hawthorne should have sagely and silently nodded agreement. She spoke the plain truth. Who wrote the plays was not her primary concern. Smith's argument, brisk as a legal brief, did not really touch her approach to the subject at all. But Hawthorne seems to have been inspired to extremities of chivalry by Bacon and so declared in print, "Speaking on the author's behalf, however, I am not entitled to imitate her magnanimity; and, therefore, hope that the writer of the pamphlet will disclaim any purpose of assuming to himself, on the ground of a slight and superficial performance, the results of which she has attained at the cost of many toils and sacrifices."[4]

Hawthorne's stance brought him the added burden of correspondence with William Henry Smith, who declared, "I had never heard the name of Miss Bacon until it was mentioned in the review of my pamphlet in the *Literary Gazette*, September, 1856."[5] Presented with this declaration, Hawthorne withdrew his charge, responding to Smith, "I beg leave to say that I entirely accept your statement as to the originality and early date of your own convictions regarding the authorship of the Shakespeare Plays, and likewise to your ignorance of Miss Bacon's prior publication on the subject. Of course my imputation of unfairness or discourtesy on your part falls at once to the ground, and I regret that it was ever made."[6]

Despite the expense and concern Delia Bacon caused him, Hawthorne clearly continued to feel obliged to assist her and, later, her memory. It was with a well-earned sigh of relief that he was able to publicly pass this responsibility to a younger man:

> I believe that it has been the fate of this remarkable book never to have had more than a single reader. I myself am acquainted with it only in insulated chapters and scattered pages and paragraphs. But, since my return to America, a young man of genius and enthusiasm has assured me that he has positively read the book from beginning to end, and is completely a convert to its doctrine. It belongs to him, therefore, and not to me,—whom, in almost the last letter that I received from her, she declared unworthy to meddle with her work,—it belongs surely to this one individual, who has done her so much justice as to know what she wrote, to place Miss Bacon in her due position before the public and posterity.[7]

That lone reader and enthusiast was a fiery, young abolitionist writer, William Douglass O'Connor.

If the United States had contrived to peacefully abolish chattel slavery and wage slavery, a consummation that Bacon may have devoutly wished her book would bring about, O'Connor might have performed the service Hawthorne had passed on to him. He had a good, quick brain, a heart made for dedication to a cause, and a sprightly pen. His gift of invective made him a leading polemicist in an age of polemics. But the Civil War diverted the course of his career. As a result, his name is now more firmly tied with that of Walt Whitman than with Delia Bacon's. Nonetheless, he deserves a niche in the history of the Shakespeare authorship question as the first American to give support to Bacon's position in a relatively permanent form.

He was born in Boston in 1833. Although he had early hopes of becoming an artist, he was drawn into the antislavery movement and lent his pen in support of that cause as an associate editor of *The Commonwealth*. After that paper ceased publication, he became connected with *The Saturday Evening Post* in Philadelphia, where he remained until 1861.

While in Philadelphia, he read Bacon's article in *Putnam's Monthly* and then her book. He was the kind of reader she was looking for. He saw the strength and value of her work immediately and began defending her position in conversation and, apparently, in some of the newspapers of the day. He found a way of approaching the public on both of the causes that were dear to his heart by writing an abolitionist romance, *Harrington: A Story of True Love*, published in Boston in 1860. He met Whitman at the office of his publisher, in Boston, in that year. He appended a note to the novel that demonstrates how his wit was stirred when he felt moved to defend another. This note also shows that the attempt to discredit Bacon's work by associating it with her insanity was already underway within a single year of her death:

> The reader of the twelfth chapter of this book may already have observed that Harrington, if he had lived, would have been a believer in the theory regarding the origin and purpose of the Shakespearean

drama, as developed in the admirable work by
Miss Delia Bacon ... in which belief I should
certainly agree with Harrington.

I wish it were in my power to do even the
smallest justice to that mighty and eloquent volume, whose masterly comprehension and
insight, though they could not save it from
being trampled upon by the brutal bison of the
English press, yet lift it to the dignity, whatever
may be its faults, of being the best work ever
composed upon the Baconian or Shakespearean
writings. It has been scouted by the critics as the
product of a distempered ideal. Perhaps it is.

"But there is a prudent wisdom," says Goethe,
"and there is a wisdom that does not remind us
of prudence;" and, in like manner, I may say
that there is a sane sense, and there is a sense
that does not remind us of sanity. At all events, I
am assured that the candid and ingenuous reader
Miss Bacon wishes for, will find it more to his
profit to be insane with her, on the subject of
Shakespeare, than sane with Dr. Johnson.[8]

William Douglass O'Connor

The Civil War drew O'Connor to Washington. He became a clerk of the Lighthouse
Board and continued to serve that Board until 1874. The Civil War and Whitman changed
his life.

Justin Kaplan pictures O'Connor and Whitman discussing the Shakespeare issue this way:
"Whitman attended mildly and noncommittally as O'Connor railed against the fools and
knaves who for two and a half centuries had been crediting the immortal works of Francis
Bacon to a 'fat peasant' and 'third rate play-actor.'"[9] This scene is no doubt to some extent
accurate. O'Connor was certainly a master fulminator and tended to castigate the upholders
of the myth over the years. But that "noncommittally" seems to be a biographer's attempt to
protect his subject from the taint of a half-baked theory hatched by a woman who died in an
insane asylum — Kaplan's view of Delia Bacon's position. While it is true that Whitman never
publicly pushed the authorship question, he was deeply interested in the subject; and that
interest predates his first meeting with O'Connor and may have hastened and deepened their
friendship. Whitman's notebooks and recorded conversations tell that tale.

Ralph Waldo Emerson once claimed that Delia Bacon and Walt Whitman were "the sole
producers that America has yielded in ten years." This comment would have been enough to
cause Whitman to seek out her book. Of course, no such external motivation was required.
Part of Whitman's early poetic training consisted of chanting Shakespeare's lines within earshot
of the ocean, and he would no doubt have been eager to know more about the man who made
those lines. In any case, in 1857 he took the trouble to enter in his notebook words that show
he was then operating under the influence of Delia Bacon:

> I think it probable or rather suggest it as such that Bacon or perhaps Raleigh had a hand in Shake-
> speare's plays. How much, whether a furnisher, pruner, poetical illuminator, knowledge infuser —
> what he was or did, if any thing, it is not possible to tell with certainty.[10]

This is mild and noncommittal enough. But it is only the first in a series of notes that Whitman made over the next two years.

Whitman's next entry is a kind of chronology, combining dates of publication of Shakespeare's plays with events in the life of William Shakspere. It may have been an attempt to refute the mild proposition with which he began. But problems and puzzles rapidly emerge. "The printing of Shakespeare's dramas was without his instigation or assistance," he notes — certainly a strange circumstance from the point of view of a poet who set up and printed his own work himself. If Whitman runs into peculiarities when considering Shakspere as an author, he feels certainty when he thinks of him as an actor: "Queen Elizabeth no doubt often saw Shakespeare as an actor and applauded him."

At one point, Whitman seems to have convinced himself of the legend's authenticity. He writes, "It is evident to me beyond cavil that Shakespeare in his own day and at death was by many placed among the great masters and acknowledged." But even this positive statement is followed immediately by a qualification, "And yet the florid style of praise was applied to everybody and about everything in those times." In a footnote, Richard Bucke, Whitman's editor, tells us, "Later Whitman has put a ? to this paragraph."

This reflection on the language of praise in Elizabeth's time leads Whitman in a profitable direction. "'Gentle' is the epithet often applied to him," he notes; and then asks, "At that time was not its signification 'like a gentleman,' of high-blood bearing?" Such considerations cause him to contemplate the social attitude of the plays and its relation to the audience of Shakespeare's time:

> The character of the bastard Falconbridge — his gloating pleasure over the fact that he is the bastard of a King rather than the legitimate son of a Knight — what was this but either from a sentiment now repudiated or to please the aristocracy? Yet what was it also but a true depicting of those days? A true depicting also of thousands of men's minds these days?...
>
> Shakespeare put such things into his plays as would please the family pride of Kings and Queens, and of his patrons among the nobility. He did this for Queen Elizabeth and for James I. His renderings of man, phases of character, the rabble, Jack Cade, The French Joan, the greasy and stupid canaille that Coriolanus cannot stomach, all these fed the aristocratic vanity of the young noblemen and gentlemen and feed them in England yet. Common blood is but wash — the hero is always of high lineage. Doubtless in so rendering humanity Shakespeare strictly rendered what was to him the truth — and what was the truth.[11]

A report of the doings and lectures of William Henry Smith, the English Baconian, reached Whitman and provided him with additional matter for thought and his notebook, "Bacon, according to W. H. Smith, was most probably the real author — he goes on with his reasons, therefore, some of them very curious and plausible." Whitman soon breaks off and goes on to make notes on Spenser, Swedenborg, and others. But he repeatedly returns to Shakespeare and occasionally produces interesting jottings. For instance, "Shakespeare evidently did not anticipate the fame that was to follow him ? also was indifferent about fame."[12]

One of the earliest services that O'Connor performed for Whitman when they were in Washington was to help him land a job as a clerk in the Interior Department at $1,200 a year. When Whitman was fired from this post, O'Connor performed an even greater service. He wrote and published at his own expense a pamphlet, *The Good Gray Poet: A Vindication*, dated September 2, 1865, but published in 1866. The pamphlet was described by Wendell Phillips as "the most brilliant piece of controversial literature issued during the nineteenth century" and its author was described by Max Nordau as "an American driveller." O'Connor was polemicist enough not to dilute his defense of Whitman by tackling the Shakespeare question directly in the pamphlet. Calling Whitman "good" was heresy enough for one pamphlet to contain. But the Shakespeare question was always in his mind and it leaves traces even in this work.

O'Connor suggests to his fellow citizens that in the figure of Whitman they behold, if they could but see him from the vantage point of the future, "one of the greatest of the sons of men." Shakespeare is another member of this illustrious family, and consider what others thought of him: a "phantom whom the wits of the seventeenth century think not worth extraordinary notice, and the wits of the eighteenth century, spluttering with laughter, call a barbarian." But O'Connor's deep knowledge of the authorship question and Delia Bacon's point of view causes other unusual comparisons to come to mind as he considers and answers Whitman's critics: "I know, too, the inferences drawn by wretched fools, who, because they have seen him ... mixing freely and lovingly, like Lucretius, like Rabelais, like Francis Bacon, like Rembrandt, like all great students of the world, with low and equivocal and dissolute persons ... must needs set him down as a brute, a scalawag, and a criminal."

No doubt O'Connor would have been delighted to name at least one of those low and dissolute persons with whom Francis Bacon mixed. When O'Connor wishes to establish the nature, value, and quality of Whitman's intellectual influence, he again draws one of his comparisons from his reading of Delia Bacon's book: "His intellectual influence upon many young men and women.... I note as kindred to that of ... Raleigh upon the gallant young England of his day. It is a power at once liberating, instructing, and inspiring. — His conversation is a university." We can be sure that O'Connor was convinced that Shakespeare had attended the Elizabethan equivalent of Whitman's conversational university.

It is from the records of attendants on Whitman's talk that we gain a clearer idea of his mature view of the authorship question, a view no doubt developed through conversations with O'Connor. Edward Carpenter made more than one visit from England to the poet. He was 25 years Whitman's junior and a progressive in thought. His visits produced vivid reports on Whitman's way of life and opinions:

> I stayed to supper with Whitman in the little kitchen of his home,... Afterwards we sat in the front room ... Walt talked about Shakespeare, the Bacon theory, the greatness of the historical plays, the "dragon-rancours" of the barons, King Lear, &c. "I will not be positive about Bacon's connection with the plays," Whitman said, "but I am satisfied that behind the historical Shakespeare there is another mind, guiding, and far, far reaching, giving weight and permanent value to what would otherwise have been only two plays a year written for a wittily, alert, jocose audience — chiefly of young gallants."[13]

Ultimately, Whitman, the poet of democracy, delivered himself of an inspired guess, writing in his *November Boughs* (1888):

> We all know how much mythus there is in the Shakespeare question as it stands today. Beneath a few foundations of proved facts are certainly engulf'd far more dim and elusive ones of deepest importance — tantalizing and half suspected — suggesting explanations that one dare not put into plain statement. But coming at once to the point, the English historical plays are to me not only the most eminent as dramatic performances ... but form, as we get it all, the chief in a complexity of puzzles. Conceiv'd out of the fullest heat and pulse of European feudalism — personifying in unparallel'd ways the medieval aristocracy, its towering spirit of ruthless and gigantic caste, its own peculiar air and arrogance (no mere imitation) — only one of the "wolfish earls" so plenteous in the plays themselves, or some born descendent and knower, might seem to be the true author of those amazing works — works in some respects greater than anything else in recorded history.[14]

O'Connor's friends point to the draining requirements of his professional life as the reason he never fulfilled his literary promise. This no doubt also limited his contributions to the study of the authorship question. But he remained dedicated to the subject throughout his life, interesting many others in it through his conversation. He also devoted some paragraphs to it when he came to provide an introduction to his *The Good Gray Poet* for republication in an early life of Whitman. It is also said of him that his sympathy was greater than his ambition. One sign of this is that he roused himself to produce a full book touching the Shakespeare question in 1886, when he rushed to defend Mrs. Henry Pott from the attacks of a professional supporter of the Stratford legend, Richard Grant White. Mrs. Pott, an English woman who lived in London and raised a large family, was early attracted to the mixture of gravity and levity she found in the writings of Francis Bacon. She thoroughly immersed herself in his work and so was drawn to the Shakespeare controversy with his words ringing in her ears. An article by Lord Palmerston sent her to the writings of Delia Bacon and William Henry Smith. It seems likely that Delia Bacon's placement of Francis Bacon's prose side by side with Shakespeare's poetry confirmed what she already thought she had discovered. In any case, she set about a thorough study of the two writers' texts, drawing from them parallel thoughts and words on various subjects — horticulture, witchcraft, politics, and so on. This practice led to her publication, in 1883, of Bacon's *Promus*, said to be extracts from his commonplace book found in the Harleian manuscript collection, which she "illustrated" with, that is compared to, passages from Shakespeare.

Pott was clearly a bright and industrious woman who devoted immense labor to her task. The fruits of this immense labor, unfortunately, were often of the type that would delight convinced Baconians but evoke only groans or jeers from clingers to the tradition. For instance, Pott's work claims that the English tongue has been enriched by Francis Bacon through the plays by gracing it with such expressions as "Good day."[15] Even the most ardent anti–Stratfordian should no doubt be willing to grant that Will Shakspere could have gathered this phrase with his ears in the wilds of darkest Warwickshire. But Richard Grant White publicly groaned and jeered at Pott's work in a way which stirred William O'Connor to produce his *Hamlet's Notebook*: "this Bacon-Shakespeare notion," thundered White, "is ... a literary bee in the bonnets of certain ladies of both sexes." O'Connor was at his best when he not only had a victim to defend but also an enemy to attack. The auspicious conditions provided by Delia Bacon and White's attack on Pott produced what has been called one of the "brightest, keenest, and most vitriolic books in our literature." Although O'Connor brought to the argument his own comparison of the lives of Francis Bacon and William Shakspere, and his own discussion of the sonnets as the work of Raleigh, his genuine contribution to the subject was his tone. He made the Shakespeare authorship question the basis of a controversy by providing the ridiculed and ignored with a witty and effective champion. He was vastly outnumbered. He was never outgunned. "I'd rather hear O'Connor argue for what I consider wrong," Walt Whitman said, "than hear most people argue for what I think right: he has charm, color, vigor; he possesses himself of the field; he pierces you to the vitals and you thank him for doing it."[16]

I

Hawthorne overstated the case, of course, when he said that O'Connor had been the only reader of Delia Bacon's book. In fact, her words had worked their way to the Mississippi where they reached the young Samuel Clemens — probably at the time when he was contemplating his metamorphosis into Mark Twain, the nom de plume he drew from his days as a pilot. A river man named George Ealer, a devotee of Shakespeare and a defender of the Stratford cult, introduced Twain to Delia Bacon's book. Twain described this introduction in what is probably the funniest contribution to the literature of the Shakespeare authorship question, an essay entitled "Is Shakespeare Dead?"

Mark Twain. (Courtesy of the National Archives)

Twain writes of Ealer and his opinions this way:

> Did he have something to say — this Shakespeare-adoring Mississippi pilot — anent Delia Bacon's book? ... Yes. And he said it; said it all the time, for months — in the morning watch, the middle watch, and the dog watch; and probably kept it going in his sleep. He bought the literature of the dispute as fast as it appeared, and we discussed it all through thirteen hundred miles of river four times traversed in every thirty-five days — the time required by that swift boat to achieve two round trips.... He did his arguing with heat, with energy, with violence; and I did mine with the reserve and moderation of a subordinate who does not like to be flung out of a pilothouse that is perched forty feet above the water. He was fiercely loyal to Shakespeare and cordially scornful of Bacon and of all the pretensions of the Baconians. So was I — at first.[17]

He comically relates how this state of affairs could not last because Ealer needed someone to argue with and rapidly wearied of an agreeable disputant. Soon Twain was provoked into providing his master with the opposition he desired:

> Then the thing happened which has happened to more persons than to me when principle and personal interest found themselves in opposition to each other and a choice had to be made: I let principle go, and went over to the other side. Not the entire way, but far enough to answer the requirements of the case. That is to say, I took this attitude — to wit, I only believed Bacon wrote Shakespeare, whereas I knew Shakespeare didn't. Ealer was satisfied with that, and the war broke loose. Study, practice, experience in handling my end of the matter presently enabled me to take any new position almost seriously; a little later, utterly seriously; a little later still, lovingly, gratefully, devotedly; finally: fiercely, rabidly, uncompromisingly. After that I was welded to my faith, I was theoretically ready to die for it, and I looked down with compassion not unmixed with scorn upon everybody else's faith that didn't tally with mine. That faith, imposed upon me by self-interest in that ancient day, remains my faith to-day, and in it I find comfort, solace, peace, and never-failing joy.[18]

Despite all of the irony and humor of this, Mark Twain is serious. He's serious about the idea that "war broke loose" in this way. He's suggesting that wars and religious disputes of all types emerge from humanity's delight in violent differences of opinion. He's also serious about the way new faiths can be formed — they can be "imposed ... by self-interest." More importantly, though, he is serious about his faith itself. He devotes the rest of his lengthy essay to defending it by arguing against what he calls the "Stratfordolators" and giving the basis for his belief that Bacon wrote the plays. He begins his onslaught on the Stratford legend with a statement that deserves to be quoted fully:

> For the instruction of the ignorant I will make a list, now, of those details of Shakespeare's history which are facts — verified facts, established facts, undisputed facts....

He was born on the 23rd of April, 1564.

Of good farmer-class parents who could not read, could not write, could not sign their names.

At Stratford, a small back settlement which in that day was shabby and unclean, and densely illiterate. Of the nineteen important men charged with the government of the town, thirteen had to "make their mark" in attesting important documents, because they could not write their names.

Of the first eighteen years of his life nothing is known. They are a blank.

On the 27th of November (1582) William Shakespeare took out a license to marry Anne Whateley.

Next day William Shakespeare took out a license to marry Anne Hathaway. She was eight years his senior.

William Shakespeare married Anne Hathaway. In a hurry. By grace of a reluctantly granted dispensation there was but one publication of the banns.

Within six months the first child was born.

About two (blank) years followed, during which period nothing at all happened to Shakespeare, so far as anybody knows.

Then came twins — 1585. February.

Two blank years follow.

Then — 1587 — he makes a ten-year visit to London, leaving the family behind.

Five blank years follow. During this period nothing happened to him, as far as anybody actually knows.

Then — 1592 — there is mention of him as an actor.

Next year — 1593 — his name appears in the official list of players.

Next year — 1594 — he played before the queen. A detail of no consequence: other obscurities did it every year of the forty-five of her reign. And remained obscure.

Three pretty full years follow. Full of play-acting. Then

In 1597 he bought New Place, Stratford.

Thirteen or fourteen busy years follow; years in which he accumulated money, and also reputation as actor and manager. Meantime his name, liberally and variously spelt, had become associated with a number of great plays and poems, as (ostensibly) author of the same.

Some of these, in these years and later, were pirated, but he made no protest.

Then — 1610–11 — he returned to Stratford and settled down for good and all, and busied himself in lending money, trading in tithes, trading in land and houses; shirking a debt for forty-one shillings, borrowed by his wife during his long desertion of his family; suing debtors for shillings and coppers; being sued himself for shillings and coppers; and acting as confederate to a neighbor who tried to rob the town of its rights in a certain common, and did not succeed.

He lived five or six years — till 1616 — in the joy of these elevated pursuits. Then he made a will, and signed each of its three pages with his name.

A thoroughgoing business man's will. It named in minute detail every item of property he owned in the world — houses, lands, sword, silver-gilt bowl, and so on — all the way down to his "second-best bed" and its furniture.

It carefully and calculatingly distributed his riches among the members of his family, overlooking no individual of it. Not even his wife: the wife he had been enabled to marry in a hurry by urgent grace of a special dispensation before he was nineteen; the wife whom he had left husbandless so many years; the wife who had had to borrow forty-one shillings in her need, and which the lender was never able to collect of the prosperous husband, but died at last with the money still lacking. No, even this wife was remembered in Shakespeare's will.

He left her that "second-best bed."

And not another thing; not even a penny to bless her lucky widowhood with.

It was eminently and conspicuously a business man's will, not a poet's.

It mentioned not a single book.

Books were much more precious than swords and silver-gilt bowls and second-best beds in those days, and when a departing person owned one he gave it a high place in his will.

The will mentioned not a play, not a poem, not an unfinished literary work, not a scrap of manuscript of any kind.

Many poets die poor, but this is the only one in history that has died this poor; the others all left literary remains behind. Also a book. Maybe two.

If Shakespeare had owned a dog — but we need not go into that: we know he would have mentioned it in his will. If a good dog, Susanna would have got it; if an inferior one his wife would have got a dower interest in it. I wish he had had a dog, just so we could see how painstakingly he would have divided that dog among the family, in his careful business way.

He signed the will in three places.

In earlier years he signed two other official documents.

These five signatures still exist.

There are no other specimens of his penmanship in existence. Not a line.

Was he prejudiced against the art? His granddaughter, whom he loved, was eight years old when he died, yet she had had no teaching, he left no provision for her education, although he was rich, and in her mature womanhood she couldn't write and couldn't tell her husband's manuscript from anybody else's — she thought it was Shakespeare's.

When Shakespeare died in Stratford it was not an event. It made no more stir in England than the death of any other forgotten theater-actor would have made. Nobody came down from London; there were no lamenting poems, no eulogies, no national tears — there was merely silence, and nothing more. A striking contrast with what happened when Ben Jonson, and Francis Bacon, and Spenser, and Raleigh, and the other literary folk of Shakespeare's time passed from life! No praiseful voice was lifted for the lost Bard of Avon; even Ben Jonson waited seven years before he lifted his .

So far as anybody knows and can prove, he never wrote a letter in his life.

So far as any one knows, he received only one letter during his life.

So far as any one knows and can prove, Shakespeare of Stratford wrote only one poem during his life. This one is authentic. He did write that one — a fact which stands undisputed; he wrote the whole of it; he wrote the whole of it out of his own head. He commanded that his work of art be engraved upon his tomb, and he was obeyed. There it abides to this day. This is it:

> Good friend for Iesus sake forbeare
> To digg the dust enclosed heare:
> Blest be ye man yt spares thes stones
> And curst be he yt moves my bones.[19]

This list of facts that Mark Twain made is worth attention because it is so much more than a list of facts. It is a devastating argument masquerading as a list of facts. For instance, Twain lists Shakspere's birthday as a fact even though it isn't. The fact is that scholars conjecture about the birth date from baptismal records and grant it consensus. Twain let that pass, no doubt, as unimportant. On the other hand, Twain leaves out Shakspere's bequest of rings to fellow actors who were involved in the publication of the First Folio. That the bequests appear as interlineations in the will indicate that they were at best after-thoughts and at worst additions made after Shakspere's death. Either way, the record of the bequests exists and Twain must have known that. He did not want to have to deal with the connection between the will and the First Folio. The second-best bed of which he makes so much — almost a short story within the list of facts — is also an interlineation. But the most peculiar things that Twain leaves off this list are that a number of plays originally were published anonymously and that Shakspere did not spell his name "Shakespeare." Twain probably did not raise these matters because he was already building his case that "William Shakespeare" was a pen name and they would have confused the issue and, perhaps, weakened the case. As Huck Finn said of Mark Twain, "He told the truth — mostly."

Part of Twain's point is that the best any of us can do is to tell the truth mostly. His opposition to the Stratford legend is based on the fact that its upholders fail to do even that. They fill in all the gaps and enlarge on this meager list of facts, as he says, this way:

It is the very way professor Osborn and I built the colossal skeleton brontosaur that stands fifty-seven feet long and sixteen feet high in the Natural History Museum, the awe and admiration of all the world, the stateliest skeleton that exists on the planet. We had nine bones, and we built the rest of him out of plaster of Paris. We ran short of plaster of Paris, or we'd have built a brontosaur that could be set down beside the Stratford Shakespeare and none but an expert could tell which was biggest or contained the most plaster.[20]

The Shakespearean biographer's equivalent of plaster of Paris is surmises, guesses, probabilities, all presented as almost as sturdy as the few facts that provided them with bones because of the assumption that their subject wrote Shakespeare's works. But Twain realized that, with no manuscripts, with no documentary evidence, anyone interested in Shakespeare was forced to make some assumptions. It was for this reason that he tilted toward the Baconian position without taking it up.

In terms that are reminiscent of Whitman's mature position Twain states: "In the Assuming trade three separate and independent cults are transacting business. Two of these cults are known as the Shakespearites and the Baconians, and I am the other one — the Brontosaurian."[21] What he means by this is that he is willing to side with the position that strains reason the least — but he wants it fully understood that reason is still being strained. In order to support his position, he considers Shakespeare as a writer, a craft Twain certainly knows something about. He says that when a writer uses the language of a trade or profession, members of that trade or profession can judge whether the man uses the language because of real experience of the trade or profession or because he has merely worked the jargon up from without. For this reason, he accepts the verdict of numerous attorneys that Shakespeare must have practiced law. And he sees the attempts of some of Shakespeare's biographers to assume that Shakspere did so as too incredulous to merit serious consideration.

Twain plainly states that nobody knows whether Francis Bacon wrote Shakespeare's works. "We cannot say we know a thing when that thing has not been proved," he elaborates. "Know is too strong a word to use when the evidence is not final and absolutely conclusive." So what has he been about and at a good deal of length in this essay? He has been probing humanity's capacity to swallow improbabilities, he has been trying to determine where knowledge stops and faith begins. He puts it this way:

Am I trying to convince anybody that Shakespeare did not write Shakespeare's Works? Ah, now, what do you take me for? Would I be so soft as that, after having known the human race familiarly for nearly seventy-four years? It would grieve me to know that any one could think so injuriously of me, so uncomplimentarily, so unadmiringly of me. No, no, I am aware that when even the brightest mind in our world has been trained up from childhood in a superstition of any kind, it will never be possible for that mind, in its maturity, to examine sincerely, dispassionately, and conscientiously any evidence or any circumstance which shall seem to cast a doubt upon the validity of that superstition. I doubt if I could do it myself. We always get at second hand our notions about systems of government; and high tariff and low tariff; and prohibition and anti-prohibition; and the holiness of peace and the glories of war; and codes of honor and codes of morals; and approval of the duel and disapproval of it; and our beliefs concerning the nature of cats; and our ideas as to whether the murder of helpless wild animals is base or is heroic; and our preferences in the matter of religious and political parties; and our acceptance or rejection of the Shakespeares.[22]

Despite his humor and efforts to appear cynical, Mark Twain is dealing with an important subject. The Shakespeare authorship question is important to him because it demonstrates humanity's willingness to make a godling out of next to nothing. The Stratford cult is an embarrassment to Twain because it offers evidence of humanity's unreason. He is left with nothing to do but mock the cult. But there is bitterness mixed with the laughter:

We are The Reasoning Race, and when we find a vague file of chipmunk-tracks stringing through the dust of Stratford village, we know by our reasoning powers that Hercules has been along there. I feel that our fetish is safe for three centuries yet. The bust, too — there in the Stratford Church. The precious bust, the priceless bust, the calm bust, the serene bust, the emotionless bust, with the dandy mustache, and the putty face, unseamed of care — that face which has looked passionlessly down upon the awed pilgrim for a hundred and fifty years and will still look down upon the awed pilgrim three hundred more, with the deep, deep, deep, subtle, subtle, subtle, expression of a bladder.[23]

Twain compares his own celebrity with that of the putative Shakespeare. He never points out that his reputation could be confused, to some extent, because of his own use of a pen name. Nonetheless, that notion rests just beneath the surface of the essay because he puts so much emphasis on a writer's experience and the relationship of that experience to the writer's language. Early in the essay, while comparing the sources that exist for various stages in his own career with the absence of such sources for Shakespeare's career, he gives the origin of his own pen name: "there are still findable ... several deck-hands who used to heave the lead for me and send up on the still night air the 'Six — feet —*scant!*' that made me shudder, and the 'M-a-r-k —*twain!*' that took the shudder away."[24] It is this indirect reference to his pen name and its source that gives his conclusion real authority. After all, if a would-be biographer had cornered those old deck-hands and asked them about Mark Twain, they probably would have scratched their heads in bafflement, laughed at the feeble attempt to pull their legs, or feasted their listener with a dissertation on the depth of the Mississippi at various locales. They certainly would not have drawn out their memories of S. L. Clemens for the inquirer. He concludes by saying of Shakespeare,

he hadn't any history to record. There is no way of getting around that deadly fact. And no sane way has yet been discovered of getting around its formidable significance. Its quite plain significance ... is, that Shakespeare had no prominence while he lived, and none until he had been dead two or three generations. The Plays enjoyed high fame from the beginning; and if he wrote them it seems a pity the world did not find it out. He ought to have explained that he was the author, and not merely a nom de plume for another man to hide behind. If he had been less intemperately solicitous about his bones, and more solicitous about his Works, it would have been better for his good name, and a kindness to us. The bones were not important. They will moulder away, they will turn to dust, but the Works will endure until the last sun goes down.[25]

II

At this point, it will be worthwhile to briefly survey the various methods that had been applied to the Shakespeare authorship question and the way that the results of those methods were disseminated. Delia Bacon's method continued to stand alone. No one besides her delved so deeply into what the plays meant, the outlook they contained, and used that meaning and outlook to argue that it was necessary to jettison the traditional attribution of the plays to William Shakspere of Stratford. She also initiated the practices of seeing characters in the plays as spokesmen for the poet, and suggesting that some characters are modeled on contemporaries of the author. Simultaneously with her, William Henry Smith argued the way a lawyer does in court, making a case, an argument, based on facts and reasonable inferences that could be drawn from the facts, that William Shakspere did not write the plays and that Francis Bacon did. These can be said, between them, to constitute the two primary approaches to the question: as a cultural riddle of the first importance; and as a who done it, a literary mystery.

Whitman's friend, O'Connor, introduced the use of fiction as a way to popularize the question and also helped to make it a controversy in the press because of his skills as a polemicist. Mrs. Henry Pott developed and expanded a technique first applied by Bacon, the use of parallels drawn from two texts by two writers. Pott used this technique primarily to determine the name of the individual who wrote the plays, but necessarily drew attention to what they contained by the very nature of the technique. She did not, however, like Bacon, argue that the meaning of the plays contained lessons that modern humanity had not yet learned or applied. O'Connor clearly had a sense of this when he described the effect of Raleigh's academy as "liberating, instructing, and inspiring." Whitman limited his pursuit of the problem to private notes and conversations. But these scant materials show that he realized the question was of importance, because how we view Shakespeare's nature and purpose determines the way we think about the relation between a writer and his work and shapes our understanding of the writer's age, audience, and society.

Twain combined the techniques of the courtroom with the humor, irony, and sarcasm of the polemicist but for a reason that Delia Bacon would have understood. He wanted to establish the boundary between knowledge and faith; and he felt humanity degraded itself, and caused itself severe problems, when it pretended to know what it merely believed. A cult based on this kind of self-deception merited and received his scorn.

Because all of these methods display a respect for what passes among us as reason, they should have established the authorship question as a legitimate subject for inquiry. They did not. Instead the "thugs," as Mark Twain jokingly called them, who devoted themselves to the maintenance of the Stratford cult, poured such scorn and ridicule on the relatively few who took up the question that the movement was given an air of absurdity. Eventually, members of the movement themselves provided its enemies and critics with additional ammunition.

Chapter 3

The Great Cryptogrammatist: Ignatius Donnelly

All that glistens is not gold.

By the time Ignatius Donnelly's *The Great Cryptogram: Francis Bacon's Cipher in the So-Called Shakespeare Plays* appeared in 1888, an anti–Stratfordian and pro–Baconian "movement" actually existed. Baconian societies had sprung up in England and this country. A feverish network of researchers were in constant contact, sharing information. A pioneering bibliography of the Baconian literature, published in 1884, listed 255 titles. One measure of the movement's impact was the heavy, patronizing ironies of Richard Grant White in the respected and respectable pages of *The Atlantic Monthly*.

White declared the identification of Shakespeare with Bacon

a lunacy, which should be treated with all the skill and the tenderness which modern medical science and humanity has developed. Proper retreats should be provided, and ambulances kept ready, with horses harnassed; and when symptoms of the Bacon-Shakespeare craze manifest themselves, the patient should be immediately carried off to the asylum, furnished with pens, ink, and paper, a copy of Bacon's works, one of the Shakespeare plays, and one of Mrs. Cowden-Clarke's Concordance (and that good lady is largely responsible for the development of this harmless mental disease, and other "fads" called Shakespearean); and the literary results, which would be copious, should be received for publication with deferential respect, and then — committed to the flames. In this way the innocent victims of the malady might be soothed and tranquilized, and the world protected against the debilitating influence of tomes of tedious twaddle.[1]

Donnelly could have assured White, "You ain't seen nothing yet!" Because Donnelly's hefty tome, an odd mixture of sound reasoning and lively twaddle, was destined to establish him as both one of the outstanding advocates of the Baconian movement and one of its unintentional wreckers. His cockamamie cipher was the movement's kiss of death. Gelett Burgess, remembered mainly for his "The Purple Cow" and other nonsense rhymes, pronounced the eulogy when he said that the arguments of the Baconians blew up through the spontaneous combustion of their cryptograms.

I

Ignatius Loyola Donnelly was born on November 3, 1831, in Philadelphia, Pennsylvania. He shed the "Loyola" when he dropped the Roman Catholicism in which he was reared. His father, Philip, an Irish immigrant, became a physician in this country, studying at the

Philadelphia College of Medicine while his wife, Catherine Gavin Donnelly, met the growing family's needs by running a pawn shop. Donnelly's father died of typhus after practicing medicine for only two years and soon after the birth of his sixth child, Eleanor. Donnelly's widowed mother is said to have "cultivated the talents" with which her children "had been so richly endowed" with "solicitous assiduity."[2] Eventually, Ignatius shared these cultivating labors, especially with sister Eleanor — encouraging her poetic precocity. She published her first verses at the age of nine and developed into a religious poet. All four of Donnelly's other sisters became teachers.

Donnelly himself was intellectually precocious. He attended the public schools of Philadelphia and eventually entered the famous Central High School there, then equivalent to a college or university. What appears to have been his first published work was a Shakespearean sonnet entitled "Life" in the school's literary magazine. He published "A Mourner's Vision" in 1850, a lament for the failed liberal revolutions of

Ingatius Donnelly. (Photo courtesy of the Minnesota Historical Society)

1848 in Europe, and sent it to Oliver Wendell Holmes. After graduating from the Central High School he became a lawyer by reading law in the office of Benjamin Harris Brewster, later attorney-general of the United States. His intelligence and eloquence ably fitted him for the legal profession. This combination of poetry and the law no doubt destined him to identify with Francis Bacon as he came to view him.

His legal knowledge, oratorical abilities, and love of justice led him to become active in politics. He naturally joined the Democratic Party of the early fifties, taking immigrants as the constituency that needed his voice. In 1852 he attacked Horace Greeley publicly, using phrenology to analyze his character. This tendency to read and interpret deep realities from the surface appearances characterizes Donnelly's outlook. He somehow came to the conclusion early that what is written off as inconsequential can be a fundamental source of enlightenment. A corollary to this viewpoint was that everything, literally everything, is a reflection of actuality — a distorted reflection, perhaps, but a reflection all the same. It is this outlook that gives his work its substance and importance. It also led him into blind alleys.

He married Kate McCaffrey in September 1855. There seems to have been a good deal of tension between his wife and his mother and this may have contributed to his decision to move west. He also became active in the management of cooperative building associations and was, apparently unjustly, accused of fraud. The cloud that descended on him in Philadelphia stayed with him and could well have caused him to think hard about the differences that can innocently exist between a man's reputation and the actual facts of his life. He settled in St. Paul, Minnesota, and eventually became a partner of John Nininger. Donnelly invested in and worked to promote Nininger City — a kind of secular paradise for immigrants who fled Europe in 1848. He lost what was expected to be a fortune in the panic of 1857 and converted what were to be city lots into wheat fields. Though he traveled widely, he repeatedly returned to Nininger City and thought of himself as a farmer.

He supplemented his farming with the practice of law, public lecturing, and political activism. One sign of his restlessness is the political shifts he went through. These could appear to be opportunistic, but his shifts were based on principle — an honest attempt to find a party that really represented him. Opportunism would have caused him to become the obedient hack of a party that could guarantee him public office — something he clearly craved. Instead, he shifted from the Democrats to the Whigs, back to the Democrats, to the antislavery Democrats, and became a Republican in 1858. As a Republican, he was elected lieutenant governor of the State of Minnesota and then served three terms in the United States House of Representatives, between 1863 and 1869. He joined the Radical Republicans in Washington and it is possible that he became friendly with William Douglas O'Connor then. Throughout the period just prior to and during the Civil War his writing and speaking earned him a good deal of acclaim. It may well be that the hopes he had for America following the catastrophe of the Civil War contributed to his revitalization of the catastrophic view of human history.

His opposition to the Republican policy of protective tariffs caused him to criticize the party in characteristically frank terms: "The Republican Party of the nation must chose between the people and the capitalists," he wrote in March 1870. He had clearly already chosen and he began another political odyssey, aligning himself with parties that later paved the way for the Populists — the Liberal Republicans, the Grangers, and the Greenback Democrats, and serving in the state senate.

Despite this largely public, active life, he continued to write poetry, although no longer for publication. His bouts of journalism also helped him to develop a clear, readable, and forceful prose style. In 1882 he published a book in which he used that prose style to argue for the reality of Atlantis, the lost continent. He used what had been considered myths, legends, fables, and stories as evidence — a brilliant idea that would not now provoke the hoots it did then. Unlike the typical "freethinkers" of the nineteenth century, he did not discard the stories of the Bible as legends merely made up. He had the view that humanity never merely makes things up but rather tries to tell its story. He would have understood clearly Hamlet's idea that plays are the "abstracts and brief chronicles" of their time.

Even though only cultists now take seriously his belief in the actuality of Atlantis, his method and ingenuity are worthy of study and respect. More than that, his cultural conclusions served as a check on the naive idea of progress prevalent in his time. Despite that, he was always writing in order to stimulate progress. His *Ragnarok: The Age of Fire and Gravel*, published in 1883, begins in an almost homely way:

> Go out with me where yonder men are digging a well. Let us observe the material they are casting out.
>
> First they penetrate through a few inches or a foot of surface soil; then they enter a vast deposit of sand, gravel, and clay. It may be fifty, one hundred, five hundred, eight hundred feet, before they reach the stratified rocks on which this drift rests. It covers whole continents. It is our earth. It makes the basis of our soils; our railroads cut their way through it; our carriages drive over it; our cities are built upon it; on it we live, love, marry, raise children, think, dream and die; and in the bosom of it we will be buried.[3]

David D. Anderson, a sympathetic but critical biographer of Donnelly, writes of this passage: "After this attention-capturing, sensational, relevant opening, Donnelly modestly poses the question, 'Where did it come from?'" Donnelly had a kind of genius for asking obvious, but neglected and vital, questions. His legal training and political oratory caused him to put these questions clearly and seek to answer them by marshalling evidence and presenting it in a dramatic, convincing but at times, misleading way.

The publication of these two books indicates what Donnelly brought with him to the Shakespeare authorship question — a fascination with origins, a wish to be a benefactor of the human race, legal and oratorical skills, wide learning, but also a reputation as a fantasist, someone given to mistaking fiction for fact, and having a penchant for self-dramatization.

II

That penchant for self-dramatization quickly shows itself in his *The Great Cryptogram*. The reader has the sense that it was not simply commercial motives that caused the title page to be blazoned with the fact that Ignatius Donnelly is the author of *Atlantis: The Antediluvian World* and *Ragnarok: The Age of Fire and Gravel*. These titles do not simply reflect pride of authorship either; they immediately suggest that the book in hand deals with momentous matters, matters that take in and affect whole worlds and ages. The title page reinforces the advanced publicity that had appeared. Donnelly did not announce that he was preparing a contribution to the Shakespeare authorship question. Others had done that. He announced a discovery, the discovery of a cipher that would settle the issue once and for all and disclose the secret history of Bacon's time.

The self-imposed pressure caused by this public stance shows itself in the book's length — it runs to just under 1,000 pages — and in the introduction, which opens immediately with an attempt to put off doubts: "The question may be asked by some, Why divide your book into two parts, an argument and a demonstration? If the Cipher is conclusive, why is any discussion of probabilities necessary?" He answers his question this way:

> In answer to this I would say that, for a long time before I conceived the idea of the possibility of there being a Cipher in the Shakespeare Plays, I had been at work collecting proofs, from many sources, to establish the fact that Francis Bacon was the real author of those great works. Much of the material so amassed is new and curious, and well worthy of preservation. While the Cipher will be able to stand alone, these facts will throw many valuable sidelights upon the story told therein.[4]

Donnelly is here making a myth, a legend, a fable of his own. It is a myth that springs from a faith, as Mark Twain defined faith — "believing in what you know ain't so." At some, no doubt unconscious level, Donnelly knew that the Cipher would not stand alone or with the props he had provided for it. But he wanted to convince himself and his public that it would — and so distorted actuality that people could not see what was valuable in his book, the first part of it, the evidence he had gathered and the argument he presented against the Stratford citizen as the author of the plays and poems. What he considered a mere sidelight should in fact be placed center stage. His arguments for Bacon as the author, his parallelisms, his Cipher, and his speculations on the multitudinous other works that Bacon-Shakespeare authored are too dim to be considered even sidelights, although they are all presented in his lively way and nuggets of unrefined truth can be sifted from the masses of fool's gold. The book is in fact organized in descending order of importance. This organization may well be his unconscious better judgment tripping up the deluded would-be raveller of epoch-making riddles of his conscious self. Few readers would be patient enough to trudge through the massive volume. But if they stayed with him for just over one hundred pages, the section entitled

"William Shakspere Did Not Write the Plays," they would go away with the best he had to offer. There is little that is original in this section. It is based largely on the work of others. Donnelly's energy, style, and power to persuade is what makes it so effective.

Fundamentally, this first section of the book is an elaboration of two points first made by Delia Bacon. First, that the scholarly and critical literature on Shakespeare describes two separate and distinct Shakespeares — author of the plays and poems and the man from Stratford-on-Avon. Second, that an understanding of Shakespeare's life and work requires an understanding of the differences that exist between the culture of the sixteenth century and that of the nineteenth century. These differences arise largely from the differences in the means of communication and their impact on learning. Donnelly elaborates these two basic points into a devastating case against William Shakspere of Stratford as the author. Two things strengthen his case: the new material that has been brought to light by the patient, painstaking, and honest work of James Halliwell-Phillipps; and Donnelly's deft handling of hostile witnesses. In short, he shows that Shakspere could not have written the plays using the words, arguments, and documents of the Stratford man's adherents.

He makes his purpose clear at the outset by using an assertion as the title for this part of his work: "William Shakespere Did Not Write the Plays." He proceeds to establish this negative proposition by comparing the characteristics of the author as they have been established by scholars and critics with what has been determined about the life of William Shakspere. The first of these comparisons is between the learning contained in the plays with what is known of William Shakspere's education. In Donnelly's hands, this procedure produces unanswerable results.

For instance, consider the way Donnelly tracks down a single quotation in order to establish the author's classical learning:

> Alexander Schmidt, in his lexicon, under the word Adonis, quotes the following lines from Shakespeare:
>> Thy promises are like Adonis' gardens,
>> That one day bloomed and fruitful were the next.
> Upon which Schmidt comments;
>> Perhaps confounded with the garden of King Alcinous in the Odyssey.
> Richard Grant White says:
>> No mention of any such garden in the classic writings of Greece and Rome is known to scholars.
> But the writer of the plays, who, we are told, was no scholar, had penetrated more deeply into the classic writings than his learned critics; and a recent commentator, James D. Butler, has found out the source of this allusion.
> He says:
>> This couplet must have been suggested by Plato (Phaedrus, p. 276). The translation is Jowett's — that I may not be suspected of warping the original to fit my theory:
>> Would a husbandman, said Socrates, who is a man of sense, take the seeds which he values and which he wishes to be fruitful, and in sober earnest plant them during the heat of summer, in some garden of Adonis, that he may rejoice when he sees them in eight days appearing in beauty? Would he not do that, if at all, to please the spectators at a festival? But the seeds about which he is in earnest he sows in fitting soil, and practices husbandry, and is satisfied if in eight months they arrive at perfection.
> Here we clearly have the original of the disputed passage:
>> Thy promises are like Adonis' gardens,
>> That one day bloomed and fruitful were the next.[5]

Donnelly's arrangement of these citations and his brief comments perform two functions at once. First, they settle a rather obscure, scholarly issue. Second, they establish that the traditional authorities on Shakespeare are led astray by their theory of the authorship of the plays. They feel free to leap to the conclusion that Shakespeare is in error, misunderstood something, or simply made things up because they do not expect him to know any better. On the other hand, persistent inquiry with the right kind of author in mind can clarify and illuminate even the most obscure passages in the Shakespearean texts.

By piling up citations and examples, Donnelly establishes Shakespeare's learning, in ancient and modern languages, beyond a reasonable doubt and concludes, "We commence our argument, therefore, with this proposition: The author of the plays, whoever he may have been, was unquestionably a profound scholar and most laborious student.... We pass, then, to the question, Did William Shakspere possess such a vast mass of information?— could he have possessed it?"[6] Unlike many students of the authorship question, Donnelly does not seek to answer this question by pointing to how little we know about Shakspere. Instead, he makes the most of what has been discovered not only about him personally but also about his time, place, and station in life. He tackles this task as if he were Hercules preparing to cleanse the Augean stables and begs his readers not to think he is too hard on Shakspere and his family, "I trust my earnestness will not be mistaken for maliciousness."[7]

He again begins with a general assertion that he will seek to establish through the presentation of heaps of minute particulars. He describes the conditions of the time, place, and class from which Shakspere emerged this way: "The agricultural population and the yeomanry of the smaller towns were steeped to the lips in ignorance, rude and barbarous in their manners, and brutal in their modes of life."[8] He draws attention to the fact that Shakspere would have been raised speaking a dialect that could barely be interpreted in London. He narrows his vision to the Stratford of Shakspere's childhood and youth. "The lives of the people," he asserts, "were coarse, barren, and filthy," and quickly calls the frank Halliwell-Phillipps to the stand:

> The sanitary condition of the thoroughfares of Stratford-on-Avon was, to our present notions, simply terrible. Under-surface draining of every kind was then an unknown art in the district. There was a far greater amount of moisture in the land than would now be thought possible, and streamlets of water-power sufficient for the operation of corn-mills meandered through the town. This general humidity intensified the evils arising from the want of scavengers, or other effective appliances for the preservation of cleanliness. House-slops were recklessly thrown into ill-kept channels that lined the sides of unmetaled roads; pigs and geese too often reveled in the puddles and ruts, while here and there were small middens, ever in the course of accumulation, the receptacles of offal and of every species of nastiness. A regulation for the removal of these collections to certain specified localities, interspersed through the borough and known as common dung-hills, appears to have been the extent of the interference that the authorities ventured or cared to exercise in such matters. Sometimes when the nuisance was thought to be sufficiently flagrant, they made a raid on those inhabitants who had suffered their refuse to accumulate largley in the highways. On one of these occasions, in April, 1552, John Shakespeare was fined the sum of twelve pence for having amassed what was no doubt a conspicuous sterquinarium before his house in Henley Street, and under these unsavory circumstances does the history of the poet's father commence in the records of England. It is sad to be compelled to admit that there was little excuse for his negligence, one of the public stores of filth being within a stone's throw of his residence.[9]

Having established, through the words of a convinced Stratfordian, that Shakspere's environment was redolent of something other than Adonis' gardens, Donnelly again narrows his focus and considers the education of Shakspere's family.

Donnelly's energy is demonstrated not only in his tireless gathering of evidence but also in his ability to summarize. He characterizes the Shaksperes of Stratford as if he were vigorously drawing conclusions before a jury:

Shakspere's whole family were illiterate. He was the first of his race we know of who was able to read and write. His father and mother, grandfathers and grandmothers, aunts and cousins — all signed their names, on the few occasions when they were obliged to sign them, with crosses. His daughter Judith could not read or write. The whole population around them were in the same condition.... It would indeed be a miracle if out of this vulgar, dirty, illiterate family came the greatest genius, the profoundest thinker, the broadest scholar that has adorned the annals of the human race. It is possible. It is scarcely probable.[10]

What makes it possible, at least, is the assumption — there is no evidence to support it — that Shakspere attended the Free School of Stratford. Donnelly whittles away at this shred from which the possibility remains suspended.

Because there are no documents establishing that William Shakspere attended the school in Stratford, many students of Shakespeare, no matter who that name refers to, have ignored the question of the kind of education that must have been dispensed there. Donnelly, on the contrary, takes this question to be a vital one and seeks to answer it from a range of sources. He quotes Roger Ascham and *The Compleat Gentleman* of 1634 on the low quality of the schoolmasters of the period. He resorts again to Halliwell-Phillipps as the authority on the Stratfordian background, "There were a few persons at that time at Stratford-on-Avon capable of initiating" Shakspere into such "preparatory accomplishments" as could be gleaned from "the horn-book and the A, B, C."[11] Donnelly again stands before the jury and summarizes the situation by quoting from an authority who has declared the authorship question a species of mental illness, "It will be readily conceded that in such a town, among such a people, and with such a school, Shakspere could have learned but little, and that little of the rudest kind. And to this conclusion even so stout a Shakesperean as Richard Grant White is driven. He says, 'when, at twenty-two years of age, he fled from Stratford to London, we may be sure that he had never seen half a dozen books other than his horn-book, his Latin accidence and a Bible. Probably there were not half a dozen others in all Stratford.'"[12] With this Donnelly's negative case is virtually made, and he exults in the rhetorical question, "Where, then, did he acquire the vast learning demonstrated by the plays?"

But Donnelly is, if nothing else, patient and thorough. He gradually, from records, traditions, and the opinions of the accepted authorities on the subject, builds up a portrait of William Shakspere as a usurer, a liar, a tightwad, a toper, a poor son and worse father, with no feeling for the sufferings of others or any wish to alleviate those sufferings, who is nonetheless pretentious — one who seeks through fraud to obtain a coat-of-arms and the status of a gentleman and has the effrontery to use these external trappings even when they are denied him.

It is a fascinating portrait of a man that may well have indicted the doggerel on Thomas Lucy that is attributed to him by tradition, but who could not conceivably have written the works of Shakespeare. Having rendered the improbable impossible, he proceeds to the peculiarities of the publication of the First Folio and, thus, makes another valuable contribution to the authorship question.

Characteristically, Donnelly begins with a statement of the proposition that he intends to prove: "The whole publication of the Folio of 1623 is based on a fraudulent statement." He is referring to the statements that appear in the front matter of the Folio, the testimony of Heminge and Condell, those names of actors that flit between the lines of Will Shakspere's will, and the testimony of Ben Jonson. Donnelly gives the preface addressed by Heminge and Condell "to the great variety of readers" at some length and reasonably concludes that four points are asserted in it. He gives those points this way:

1. That the Folio was printed from the original copies.

2. That Heminge and Condell had "collected" these copies and published them in the Folio.

3. That the quarto editions were "stolne and surreptitious copies, maimed and deformed."

4. That what Shakespeare wrote was poured from him, as if by inspiration, so that he made no corrections, and 'never blotted a line,' as Ben Jonson said.[13]

To show the fraudulence of the actors' assertions, Donnelly places unassailable facts beside them. For instance, he writes, "Some of the finest thoughts and expressions, distinctively Shakespearean, and preeminently so, are found in the quarto editions, and not in the Folio." He supports this statement with the quotation of passages from the quarto edition of Hamlet that do not appear in the Folio and argues:

> It follows, then, that Heminge and Condell did not have the "true original copies," or they would have contained these passages. It follows, also, that there must have been some reason why portions of the quarto text were omitted from the Folio. It follows, also, that, in some respects, the "stolne and surreptitious" copies of the quarto are more correct than the Folio, and that but for the quartos we would have lost some of the finest gems of thought and expression which go by the name of Shakespeare.[14]

He also takes up the question of whether or not Shakespeare revised, of whether he poured out torrents of words in final form or rewrote like most mortals must do. He first shows that Ben Jonson contradicts the idea of the poet presented to the world by the actors in his introductory verses, which read in part:

he

Who casts to write a living line must sweat
(Such as thine are) and strike the second heat
Upon the Muse's anville, turn the same
(And himself with it) that he thinks to frame,
Or for the laurel he may gain a scorne.[15]

Donnelly insists that Shakespeare did not merely rework lines but also whole plays — *Romeo and Juliet, Henry V, The Merry Wives of Windsor,* and *Hamlet* all exist in short acting versions and in enlarged versions, almost twice the length of the pieces meant for staging.

The prosecution ready to rest, Donnelly concludes, "False in one thing, false in all.... If the playactor-editors thus falsified the truth, or were themselves the victims of an imposition, what confidence is to be placed in any other statement they make?" He has done valuable work here indeed. He shows that the primary documents that defenders of the legend inevitably point to in order to buttress the traditional attribution of the Shakespearean works to William Shakspere are self-contradictory and fraudulent. If the attribution is, as he has shown, impossible, and the primary documents supporting it are suspect, how can it continue to be maintained?

III

When arguing for the identification of Bacon with Shakespeare, Donnelly becomes as self-contradictory as the front matter of the Folio. David D. Anderson says truly and well of Donnelly as a writer, "A piece of writing — a novel, a tract, a scientific treatise, or a political essay — was to Donnelly an argument, to be like a legal brief, presented as logically, rationally, and eloquently as possible. It should have a purpose, a pragmatic point; and the task of the writer was to persuade his readers to accept it." This wish to persuade at times overrode Donnelly's respect for facts but his frankness kept him from trying blatantly to deceive. He provides his readers with the basis of his own undoing.

For example, early on he convincingly argues that the motive of the dramatist to write the plays in the first place could not have been profit. Nonetheless, when he comes to claim the Shakespeare crown for Bacon, he states that Bacon must have written the plays for pay. His readers are necessarily with him when he mocks the early commentators who said that Shakespeare was a natural, rustic poet who sang the way a bird does. Yet when he comes to write of Bacon as Shakespeare he waxes romantically eloquent, shouting that he sang because he had to, the way a bird does. Worst of all, Bacon was of course still alive when the First Folio appeared. Donnelly is forced to make his idol the perpetrator of the falsehoods he exposed in the Folio and twists the plain meaning of Jonson's words to indicate that the playwright was still alive at the time when Jonson was writing. Carried away by his faith, he seems oblivious to the contradictions and problems he poses to the reader. But much worse was yet to come. Finally, on page 505 of the book, he was ready to unveil the Cipher—the Cipher to which he had found the key on September 23, 1882. Gone are the level-headed propositions that he set out to prove, the hosts of authorities he patiently called as witnesses, the unanswerable summations. Instead, Donnelly himself takes center stage. He tells a personal narrative and calls the first chapter, "How I Came to Look for a Cipher."

What not only baffled but haunted Donnelly was how the playwright could have dissociated his own name from his work. Granted that there were powerful political and social reasons for not being connected with the plays in his own time, but could Bacon have possibly been content not to be credited with the works by posterity? He admits to having been "greatly troubled" by this question: "Would the writer of such immortal works sever them from himself and cast them off forever?" He searched the plays and poems to determine the author's attitude toward his work and the value he placed on it. He returned from that search with these conclusions: "There was, as it seems to me, no doubt: 1. That Bacon wrote the Plays; 2. That he loved them as the children of his brain; 3. That he estimated them at their full great value.... The question then arose,... How could he divest Bacon of this great world-out-living glory to give it to Shakspere? This thought recurred to me constantly, and greatly perplexed me."[16]

Chance intervened to relieve him of his perplexity and condemn him to years of futile labor. "One day," he writes, "I chanced to open a book, belonging to one of my children, called *Every Boy's Book....* I found a chapter devoted to 'Cryptography,' or cipher-writing, and in it I chanced upon this sentence: 'the most famous and complex cipher perhaps ever written was by Lord Bacon.'"[17] Soon he was reading everything that Bacon wrote on ciphers and then took up the plays because stumbling on this book for boys had produced, as he writes, "a pregnant association of ideas."

It is hard to resist the idea that Donnelly was myth making again here, reflecting an actuality in a way that distorted it. After all, he knew Delia Bacon's work and knew that she drew attention in it to the Elizabethan fascination with and need for anagrams and enigmas. He in fact quotes her eventually on this very subject: "It was the time in which the cipher, in which one could write 'omnia per omnia,' was in request; when even 'wheel ciphers' and doubles were thought not unworthy of philosophic notice ... with philosophic secrets that opened down into the bottom of a tomb, that opened into the Tower, that opened on the scaffold and the block."[18]

It seems likely that here, rather than in a book for boys taken up by chance, Donnelly's quest for the cipher began. He produced the whole first section of his book drawing heavily on the work of other Baconians, especially Nathaniel Holmes and Mrs. Henry Pott, but he did not openly borrow from or mention Delia Bacon there. He honored Delia Bacon by giving her pride of place in a collection of biographical sketches in the back of the book and even told "Delia Bacon's Unhappy Story" in the *North American Review* (1889), after his book had been published. Donnelly, perhaps because of his frustrations as a politician, seems to have wanted to be the sole discoverer of the cipher. After all, Delia Bacon, publicly at least, never suggested that this Elizabethan fascination meant any more for Shakespeare's works than that their lines had been filled to overflowing, offering double and triple meanings to listeners and readers with ears to hear and eyes to see. Donnelly would go beyond that and solve the authorship by finding a literal cipher in the plays.

Literal is certainly the approach he took. He describes the cipher in such terms that the reader would expect it would take a master unraveller to be able to find and decipher it. But when he starts his hunt he does so in a most mundane and obvious way, laboriously poring over the plays, not "for delight," as he says, but marking every time the word "bacon" occurs, every time the name "William" appears, each use of "shake" or "spear" or, just in case, "spur," and so on. He marks all of the Nicholases, Bacon's father's name, all of the St. Albanses, the name of Bacon's home, and locates Francis, Francisco, and Frank. This heady occupation stirs such giddiness in him that he starts looking for the names of other writers of the time in cryptic forms. An example: "The full name of Christopher Marlowe appears in The Taming of the Shrew. Thus: Christopher Sly. (Induction) 'I did not bit you mar it.' (Act iv, 3) "a low, submissive reverence.' [19] (Induction) In none of the other plays is such a combination found, for the word Christopher occurs in no other play." What the possible significance of these scattered syllables could be he does not pause to say. Instead, he hurries ahead to find the name of Bacon's home, Gorhambury, divided into syllables and scattered over three different scenes of Romeo and Juliet. Again, no clue as to the significance of this anatomization and burial of a word is given. At the same time, no thought is given to the possibility that the subject on which the playwright wrote might cause him to use "gore" in one act and "bury" in another without once thinking that posterity might locate them and yoke them from their contexts to make of them the name of someone's home.

This is the kind of evidence Donnelly presents to show how he became convinced the plays contain a cipher. Gone is the logician, the patient compiler of evidence, the convincing summarizer. He has been replaced by a fevered mind suffering from delusion. Despite that, the results are not without interest. For instance, he finds a whole fistful of Williams in an extraneous scene in *The Merry Wives of Windsor*. William is a boy who has not progressed well in his studies and is comically quizzed about his Latin. Donnelly is so busy looking for "bacons" and "franks" that he does not see Shakespeare depicting Shakspere before his eyes.

Convinced that the plays contained a cipher, Donnelly sat surrounded by his list of names, words, and bits of words, and tried to reduce them to a kind of order based on a rule. This was a mammoth task and he pursued it diligently. Counting the number of words down a column until he reached "bacon," say, then counting the words from the bottom of the column to the same spot, he would then check to see if either or both of these numbers were multiples of the page number on which the columns appeared. He went through this exercise and variations of it endlessly. Peculiarly, these frustrating pursuits seem to have never forced him to consider that he might be wrong about the existence of the cipher in the first place. Instead, he grew more convinced of the existence of the cipher and the importance of the secrets it would reveal. After all, he had found, for instance, the words "found out" tucked into the plays. Every plain word and phrase seemed to resonate for him with potential revelations. The cipher existed. The question was, did he have the wit to crack it?

Eventually it dawned on him that the locations of the words on the page would vary from edition to edition. He had his ideas about how and why the First Folio was produced and it struck him that the cipher might be broken if he worked with that text. Of course, use of the key required that he sometimes count hyphenated words as one word and at other times as two. He also had to learn that such things as "beacons" really had to be read Bacon's. Further, he had to assume that there were some uncorrected typographical errors in the Folio, but all errors in pagination were of intentional importance to the solution of the puzzle he had set himself, placed there for a reason, not errors at all. Finally, he could not even begin to contemplate how dramatic poetry could be written to the demands of such a system. At one point he comes close to this issue, commenting on a passage by Shakespeare, "this reads as forced and unnatural." It is possible that these words represent the judgment of Donnelly's better self on the concoction he himself was brewing. Listen to the kind of result all this toil yielded:

> We saw, in the first instance, that her Grace is furious and hath sent out; we come now to finish that sentence. What was it she sent out? As we counted downward all the words below the first word of the second subdivision of column 1 of page 75, so we count upwards all the words above the last word in the first subdivision. There are in that first subdivision 193 words; hence 192, the number of words above the last word, becomes, in the progress of the Cipher, a modifier, just as we have seen 253 to be. Let us again take the root-number 505, from which we have worked out thus far all the words given, and after deducting from it the modifier 50, we have left 455, which, it will be remembered, produced the words furious, is, hath and out. If from 455 we deduct 192, we have as a remainder 263, and if we carry this up the next column (2d of 75), we find that the 263d word is the 246th word, soldiers. Her Grace is furious and hath sent out soldiers.[20]

Enough. David Kahn in his *The Codebreakers* devotes a chapter to what he calls "The Pathology of Cryptography." There he writes: "Of Donnelly's 'system' it may be remarked that nothing like it has appeared in cryptology before or since. And with good reason, for the system is no system at all; there is neither rhyme nor reason to the choice of numbers that leads to the result."[21] Donnelly clothed the nakedness of his results in dramatic trappings. He worries about whether or not the discovery is protected by copyright even if he has made errors in its application. He has letters verifying the authenticity of the facsimiles of the Folio printed in the book. He reproduces the facsimiles themselves. But it's no good. There is no cipher in the plays and wishing will not place one there.

All of this would have been bad enough if Donnelly had simply quit after reporting what he had achieved. But he felt compelled, no doubt through his desire to produce original discoveries, to write a section called "Other Masks of Francis Bacon." To write Bacon's works and Shakespeare's plays and poems might be quite enough for anyone, especially a courtier, lawyer, and politician who had other things to do. Donnelly did not think so. He went on to claim for Bacon every anonymous piece of dramatic writing that any critic had ever thought might have been Shakespeare's. Even that would not suffice — the works of Marlowe, Robert Burton's *Anatomy of Melancholy*, the essays of Montaigne! Donnelly found Bacon's hand at work in all of them. He does not even feel the need to make a case, eventually. It is as if for the discoverer of the cipher it is enough merely to assert a piece of writing is by Bacon to make it so.

IV

Donnelly's critics, as the advanced publicity for the book assured they would, concentrated on the nonexistent cipher. There was an uproar in both England and America. Wits on both sides of the Atlantic used his "method" to show that the cipher in the plays announced that Shakspere was the true author or that Donnelly was a mountebank. The strength of his perfectly rational argument against the traditional attribution of the plays was lost in a cloud of hoopla and abuse.

The book was not a financial success. Donnelly sailed to England where he was lionized by Baconians, reeled in a few converts, and lost debates at Oxford and Cambridge. Eventually, he returned home — returning to politics, lecturing, and fiction. His friends in Minnesota called him the "Sage of Ninninger." There is an air of accuracy about this nickname. He had something of the "village explainer" about him and, as Gertrude Stein said of Ezra Pound, that is all very well if you are a village. His enemies called him "The Prince of Cranks." That is less accurate. Donnelly was large enough to house a democratic prince and an aristocratic crank. We hear the prince protest when the crank asserts that Montaigne's essays were the handiwork of Francis Bacon, "This is midsummer madness!" It is and would have been as harmless as moonshine if it had not made the authorship question ridiculous for decades to come.

Sir Sidney Lee, looking down on Donnelly from the critical heights attained by one with the sensibility to decide that Shakespeare's sonnets were literary exercises manufactured to win the patronage of courtiers, enunciated the establishment's verdict:

> The author pretended to have discovered among Bacon's papers a numerical cypher which enabled him to pick out letters appearing at certain intervals in the pages of Shakespeare's First Folio, and the selected letters formed words and sentences categorically stating that Bacon was author of the plays. Many refutations have been published of Mr. Donnelly's arbitrary and baseless contention.[22]

There was no pretending about it on the part of the author. He was convinced that he saw, found, and deciphered what was not there. Late in life he issued a pamphlet at his own expense, "The Cipher in the Plays and on the Tombstone." In it he argued that Bacon wrote *Don Quixote*!

His contribution to the Shakespeare authorship question is an ambivalent one. He did much solid work to strengthen the case against the Stratfordian theory. In fact, if he had modestly limited himself to that effort he could have rendered the doddering figure of the Stratford citizen a knockout blow. But he was not made to be content with that humble role. In his efforts to be an original — an explorer and discoverer bringing enlightenment to suffering humanity — he set back for years to come the cause he sought to serve. His work on the cipher established in the public mind the idea that anyone who took up the authorship question was a crank. Worse, his example led many students of the question to take up the cryptogrammic approach or to seek out even more works to claim as Shakespeare's or Bacon's. Exceedingly few readers have had the patience to separate what is valuable in the book from the wads of nonsense it contains. Nonetheless, those few who have done so went away well rewarded. As a result of Donnelly's work, the faith in the Stratford legend was permanently shaken and a solution to the authorship question was closer than it had ever been before.

Chapter 4

The Birthplace: Joseph Skipsey and Henry James

... and give to airy nothing
A local habitation and a name.

One aspect of the Shakespeare authorship question is the repeated feeling by visitors to Stratford that there is something rotten in the state of things there. When John Aubrey, that seventeenth century gossip columnist, stirred himself to gather information on Shakspere for his *Brief Lives*, he returned with this illuminating memorandum: "His father was a Butcher, and I have been told heretofore by some of the neighbors that when he was a boy he exercised his father's Trade, but when he kill'd a Calfe he would doe it in a high style, and make a speech. There was at this time another Butcher's son in this Towne that was held not at all inferior to him for a naturall witt, his acquaintance and coetanean, byt dyed young."[1]

Aubrey looked back at Shakspere from the other side of a vast divide, the Civil Wars. He was born ten years after Shakspere's death and lived until 1697. He never doubted that the person he asked about was the author of Shakespeare's work; and what he turned up was compatible with the Restoration's notion of a wit and author of dramatic comedies.

As far as we can judge from Aubrey's notes, Shakespeare's tragedies did not exist for him. He was even able to add to the corpus of Shakespeare's writings, he thought, by recording one of his poems that had gone unpublished:

> One time as he was at the Tavern at Stratford upon Avon, one Combes, an old rich Usurer, was to be buryed. He makes there this extemporary Epitaph:
>
> > Ten in the Hundred the Devil allowes,
> > But Combes will have twelve he sweares and vowes:
> > If anyone askes who lies in this Tombe,
> > Hoh! quoth the Devill, 'Tis my John o' Combe.[2]

This minor work has the true ring of the master who composed the doggerel that was chiseled on Shakspere's own tomb and clearly displays his "naturall witt." If Aubrey had compared this piece with the sonnets or the songs in the plays, the authorship question might have been taken up sooner than it was.

Stratford did not become a destination for pilgrims and a tourist trap until after the eighteenth century actor, David Garrick, staged his jubilee there. Garrick's time could not take Shakespeare straight, but had to "correct" him — they provided a happy ending for King Lear,

The original Shakespeare monument in Stratford-upon-Avon's Holy Trinity Church as pictured in Sir William Dugdale's *Antiquities of Warwickshire* (1656).

for instance. Garrick efficiently dealt with this problem at his jubilee by having not a single line of Shakespeare's read in Stratford on that occasion. The praises of Shakespeare were heard — including lines written by Garrick — but not Shakespeare himself.

Washington Irving, the American writer, visited Stratford sometime after Garrick's jubilee had done its good work. A pilgrim with a clear eye and sense of humor, Irving described his visit this way:

> I had come to Stratford on a poetical pilgrimage. My first visit was to the house where Shakspeare was born, and where, according to tradition, he was brought up to his father's craft of wool-combing. It is a small mean-looking edifice of wood and plaster, a true nestling-place of genius, which seems to delight in hatching its offspring in by-corners. The walls of its squalid chambers are covered with names and in-scriptions in every language, by pilgrims of all nations, ranks, and conditions, from the prince to the peasant; and present a simple, but striking instance of the spontaneous and universal homage of mankind to the great poet of nature.
>
> The house is shown by a garrulous old lady, in a frosty red face, lighted up by a cold blue anxious eye, and garnished with artificial locks of flaxen hair, curling from an exceedingly dirty cap. She was peculiarly assiduous in exhibiting the relics with which this, like all other celebrated shrines, abounds. There was the shattered stock of the very matchlock with which Shakspeare shot the deer on his poaching exploits. There, too, was his tobacco-box; which proves that he was a rival smoker of Sir Walter Raleigh; the sword also with which he played Hamlet; and the identical lantern with which Friar Laurence discovered Romeo and Juliet at the tomb! There was an ample supply also of Shakspeare's mulberry-tree, which seems to have as extraordinary powers of self-multiplication as the wood of the true cross; of which there is enough extant to build a ship of the line.[3]

Late in the nineteenth century, the English poet Joseph Skipsey and his wife were made the custodians of the birthplace, complete with all of the relics and traditions that Irving gently mocked. And thereby hangs a tale — two tales, one fact and one fiction.

I

Joseph Skipsey was born on March 17, 1832, in Northumberland, a region of coal mines in the north of England, the youngest of eight children.[4] His father, Cuthbert Skipsey, a miner married to Isabella Bell, was shot to death in a labor dispute when Joseph was still an infant. Skipsey had no schooling and went to work in the pits at the age of seven. Nonetheless, he taught himself to read at an early age and pored over the only book on which he could lay hands until he was fifteen years old, the Bible. Later, he obtained works by Shakespeare, Milton, and Burns, as well as poems in translation, especially those of Heine. As Charles Wisner Barrell has noted, "he cultivated the divine spark by constant practice and study, Blake being his most admired master."[5]

At the age of 20, he made his way to London, largely on foot. He found construction work on the railroads there for a time and married the landlady of the rooming house where he stayed. They returned to the north where he went back to work in the mines. He published his first book of poems, no doubt at his own expense, in 1859. The editor of a newspaper felt greatly impressed by the book, made contact with its author, and found Skipsey a job as an under storekeeper at an industrial plant in Gateshead. His life a little easier, Skipsey's literary work progressed.

His *Poems, Songs, and Ballads* appeared in 1862 and the following year he moved with his family to Newcastle-on-Tyne to fill an assistant librarian's position at the literary and philosophical society. His duties or colleagues there were not to his taste and he again worked in the mines near Newcastle from 1864 until 1882. His collections of verse continued to appear periodically and attract favorable attention.

The Pre-Raphaelites and their circle took him up and offered him support and encouragement. The painter Edward Burne-Jones helped him obtain a pension of ten pounds a year from the civil list in 1881. Lady Burne-Jones described Skipsey as "a noble-looking man, with extremely gentle and courteous manners." Ernest Rhys thought of him as a modern incarnation of a bard, sprung from the ranks of the people. He became general editor of the Canterbury Poets in 1884, writing biographical and critical essays for the series on Burns, Shelley, Poe, and Blake.

Penelope Fitzgerald, in her biography of Burne-Jones, writes that the painter "hated the idea that Skipsey (or anyone else) might feel he was being patronised. Not money, but 'the upper air' was needed. With George Howard's help, he got Skipsey the job of caretaker at Shakespeare's house at Stratford."[6] In fact, Skipsey had the support of many well-wishers in obtaining this post — a post they no doubt thought would be congenial to the collier-poet — Browning, William Morris, Rossetti, Tennyson, and others.

They must have been surprised when, on October 31, 1891, he resigned the job. Skipsey and his wife headed north and spent the rest of their days there, living on a rotating basis with their various children. He died at Gateshead in 1903.

What caused this gentle poet and laborer, whose lecture on "The Poet as Seer and Singer" was published in 1890, to flee the vicinity of Stratford where he held what could have been a cushy and interesting sinecure? Integrity. "All things considered," wrote Charles Wisner Barrell, "Skipsey was completely out of place in the synthetic, catch-penny atmosphere of the doubtful 'Birthplace.' Although he very badly needed the perquisites of the caretaker's office at that time, his innate honesty could not tolerate the situation, fraught with charlatanism, as it was, and he seems to have made more friends than he lost by resigning."[7]

Skipsey gave the reasons for his resignation in a letter to a friend, J. Cuming Walters, dated May 12, 1893:

> I had gradually lost faith in the so-called relics which it was the duty of the custodian to show, and, if possible, to explain to the visitors at the birthplace. This loss of faith was the result of a long and severe inquiry into which I was driven by questions from time to time put to my wife and me by intelligent visitors; and the effect of it on myself was such as almost to cause a paralysis of the brain.... That our Shakespeare was born in Henley street I continue fully to believe, and that the house yet shown as the Shakespeare House stands on the site of the house in which he was born I also believe (and it was sacred to me on that account); but a man must be in a position to speak in more positive terms than these if he is to fill the post of custodian of that house; and the more I thought of it the more and more I was unable to do this. As to the idle gossip, the so-called traditions and legends of the place, they are for the most part an abomination and must stink in the nostrils of every true lover of our divine poet.[8]

II

Henry James no doubt knew that the house on Stratford's Henley Street was latched onto as "Shakespeare's birthplace" when the politicians of Stratford were faced with an offer from P.T. Barnum to buy the thing. Barnum planned to take the place apart, ship it to New York, and put it together again as an exhibit in his museum. Once word of the plan reached the British people, an effort was made to preserve the shrine. John Payne Collier, who showed his devotion to scholarship by forging references to Shakespeare in biographical and historical documents, and his Shakespeare Association raised the funds to snatch the bogus birthplace from the clutches of the American showman. When James heard the story of Skipsey's experience, he immediately saw its possibilities for fiction.

While James may have first learned of how the Skipseys bolted from Stratford from Burne-Jones, as Ernest Rhys records, James made the following entry in his notebook on June 12, 1901:

> The other day at Welcombe (may 30th or 31st) the Trevelyans, or rather Lady T., spoke of the odd case of the couple who had formerly (before the present incumbents) been for a couple of years — or a few — the people in charge of the Shakespeare birthplace — which struck me as possibly a little donnee. They were rather strenuous and superior people from Newcastle, who had embraced the situation with joy, thinking to find it just the thing for them and full of interest, dignity, an appeal to all their culture and refinement, etc. But what happened was that at the end of 6 months they grew sick and desperate from finding it — finding their office — the sort of thing that I suppose it is: full of humbug, full of lies and superstition imposed upon them by the great body of visitors, who want the positive impressive story about every object, every feature of the house, every dubious thing — the simplified, unscrupulous, gulpable tale. They found themselves too "refined," too critical for this — the public wouldn't have criticism (of legend, tradition, probability, improbability) at any price — and they ended by contracting a fierce intellectual and moral disgust for the way they had to meet the public. That is all the anecdote gives — except that after a while they could stand it no longer, and threw up the position. There may be something in it — something more, I mean, than the mere facts. I seem to see them — for there is no catastrophe in a simple resignation of the post, turned somehow, by the experience, into strange sceptics, iconoclasts, positive negationists. They are forced over to the opposite extreme and become rank enemies not only of the legend, but of the historic donnee itself. Say they end by denying Shakespeare — say they do it on the spot itself — one day — in the presence of a big, gaping, admiring batch. Then they must go. That seems to be arrangeable, workable — for 6000 words.[9]

James published his satiric tale in his book *The Better Sort* and called it "The Birthplace."

In the writing of it, James's tale grew much more elaborate and cunning than this promising notebook entry suggests. Morris and Isabel Gedge, the characters loosely based on the Skipseys, do not in fact deny Shakespeare publicly at the birthplace, forcing their removal from the shrine. Morris achieves the mental outlook of an iconoclast and feels tempted to declare publicly the views he has come to hold. The mere lack of enthusiasm, hesitation, and attempt to temper the legend with hedges if not truth, is sufficient to cause a representative of the birthplace's governing body — the man who obtained the position for the Gedges — to indicate that Morris's job is in jeopardy. This threat heightens his anxiety and he resolves to give the public and his masters what they want — with a passion. He becomes a parody of a dedicated priest of the Stratford cult — a bombastic showman who can dismiss falsehoods, doubts, and questions with his well-polished barker's spiel. As a result, the governors of the birthplace decide to not only keep the Gedges on but increase their salary! In James's hands, the little tragedy of the Skipseys becomes an intellectual comedy on the gilded age's limitless gullibility.

James's theme is integrity, but his subject is its opposite — fragmentation, disintegration of the actual self and the manufacture of a fraudulent public self, a protective mask. In short, his subject is a symbolic rendering of the Shakespeare authorship question. Morris Gedge, the caretaker of the birthplace, carries the burden of James's theme by undergoing two metamorphoses — metamorphoses based on the attempt to maintain his integrity, to make a unity of his personal beliefs and his public conduct.

Before assuming his new post, Morris becomes thoroughly familiar with the writings of the genius of the birthplace. Morris conceives of the author in a personal, individual way, as a result of this familiarity, and becomes devoted to "Him" — the reverential being whose name cannot be pronounced. Once he becomes caretaker of the birthplace, however, he finds nothing whatsoever there that connects with the author he has deduced from affectionate readings of the works. Worse than that, he finds that he is pulled apart by divided loyalties — his loyalty to Him, his loyalty to his wife and their need to earn a living, his loyalty to Them, the vast public with its insistence on certainty, its appetite for legends, and yet another Them, the governors of the birthplace with their demand that he give the public what it wants.

He eventually tries to soften his presentations and urges his wife who has no doubts, no concern about the truth of the legend, to do the same, to keep from going "too far." "Too far for what?" Isabel demands.

> "To save our immortal souls. We mustn't, love, tell too many lies."
> She looked at him with dire reproach. "Ah, no, are you going to begin again?"
> "I never have begun; I haven't wanted to worry you. But, you know, we don't know anything about it." And then as she stared, flushing: "About His having been born up there. About anything, really. Not the least scrap that would weigh, in any other connection, as evidence. So don't rub it in so."
> "Rub it in how?"
> "That He was born —" But at sight of her face he only sighed. "Oh dear, oh dear!"
> "Don't you think," she replied cuttingly, "that he was born anywhere?"
> He hesitated — it was such an edifice to shake. "Well, we don't know. There's very little to know. He covered His tracks as no other human being has ever done."[10]

This attempt at compromise, to let the legend live while knowing it is without basis, leads to the threat of dismissal — "You know, Mr. Gedge, that it simply won't do." In order to keep his position and preserve his integrity, in an ironic, comic, and inverted way, he had to give up his private conception of the author and give up his critical sense. James clearly defines what the Stratford cult demands of its adherents when he has Gedge confess to his wife how and where he gave up his "critical sense." "'I killed it just now,' he tells her. 'There in the other place — I strangled it, poor thing, in the dark. If you'll go out and see, there must be blood. Which, indeed,' he added, 'on an altar of sacrifice, is all right. But the place is forever spattered.'"[11] The place Gedge refers to is the room in which it is said that Shakspere was born.

Having killed his "critical sense," Gedge becomes a kind of English P.T. Barnum. An American couple who had learned of his doubts about the legend on their first visit return to see him again because word of his enthusiastic performances has reached them. They are eager to learn how he manages it. He gives them a sample of the part he plays for the benefit of the foolish pilgrims to the birthplace:

> It is in this old chimney corner, the quaint inglenook of our ancestors — just there in the far angle, where His little stool was placed, and where, I dare say, if we could look close enough, we should find the hearthstone scraped with His little feet — that we see the inconceivable child gazing into the blaze of the old oaken logs and making out there pictures and stories, see Him conning, with curly bent head, His well-worn hornbook, or poring over some scrap of an ancient ballad, some page of some such rudely bound volume of chronicles as lay, we may be sure, in His father's window-seat.[12]

What is most remarkable about this hilarious parody is that it is simply what had been seriously taught by experts for years. James causes his character to raise Mark Twain's Shakespearean Brontosaurus with mere words before our very eyes. And with what result?

Truth, at least on this subject, is not to be determined by the conscience of an individual. A much more objective measure is required. It is to be determined instead, James shows, by the cash register — by popular success and the money that attracts. Gedge, fearful that he is giving himself away by overplaying his part, learns that his impassioned repetitions of tall tales have lured increasing numbers of pilgrims to the birthplace. The edifice's governors report that "the receipts" speak "volumes. They tell the truth."[13] Gedge earns a raise in salary by turning himself into a gifted and polished liar.

James never uses the name Shakespeare in "The Birthplace." But the story reflects his own point of view. He wrote to Violet Hunt on August 26, 1903, the year in which the story was published:

> I am "a sort of" haunted by the conviction that the divine William is the biggest and most successful fraud ever practised on a patient world. The more I turn him round and round the more he so affects me. But that is all — I am not pretending to treat the question or to carry it further. It bristles with difficulties, and I can only express my general sense by saying that I find it almost as impossible to conceive that Bacon wrote the plays as to conceive that the man from Stratford, as we know the man from Stratford, did.[14]

Others were reaching similar conclusions.

Chapter 5

An Agnostic and Two Rebels: Greenwood, Samuel Butler, and Frank Harris

O, learn to read what silent love hath writ.

Mark Twain did not write "Is Shakespeare Dead?" because of nostalgia for his early days on the Mississippi. He felt moved to see into print his ideas on the Shakespeare authorship question in the year before his death, he reports, because a book refired his interest in the question he had pondered for more than half a century. That book was Sir George Greenwood's *The Shakespeare Problem Restated*, published in 1908.[1]

Greenwood decided to commit himself to print on the authorship question for three reasons. First, he had a clear and shrewd understanding of how the question then stood with the public. He seems to have been one of those patient and industrious souls who slogged their way through Ignatius Donnelly's thick volume. He came away from that book with admiration for the strong case Donnelly made against the Stratfordian theory of the authorship but saddened by Donnelly's cryptogrammic antics and wild speculations. Second, as an experienced barrister, Greenwood was legitimately shocked by the tone and quality of argument used by the professional Shakespeare scholars against the advocates of Francis Bacon. Finally, he was clearly aware that Shakespearean studies were tumbling into chaos because of the inability or unwillingness of the scholars to face the authorship question squarely. He thought he could help ameliorate all of these conditions by maintaining an "agnostic" stance with regard to Shakespeare and urging that point of view on others. By Agnosticism Greenwood meant that he was convinced that William Shakspere of Stratford was not the author of the plays and poems but that he did not know the true author's identity.[2]

He states that he held "no brief for the Baconians, though, like Mr. Gladstone, 'I have always regarded their discussions as perfectly serious and to be respected.'"[3] Because of the turn the Baconian case had taken as a result of Donnelly's work and that of the little cryptogrammatists who sprang up in his footprints, Greenwood felt duty bound to further qualify his position this way:

> But I am quite free to admit that some of the extreme advocates of that "heresy" have done much harm by putting forward wild, ridiculous, and fantastic theories. It has been truly said that the worst enemies of good causes are those who try to support them by bad arguments, and thus it is that the way of the rational doubter as to the Stratfordian authorship is blocked by quite unnecessary obstacles. He is classed with "cranks" and "fanatics," and finds himself involved, quite

unjustly, in the cloud of prejudice and ridicule which attaches to ciphers that failed and cryptograms that will not bear the light. But I beg the reader of "candid and open mind" to put aside all such prejudices, and to bestow upon the question the fair consideration which is due from every honest and impartial inquirer.[4]

Greenwood did not expect the Shakespeare scholars of his time to behave like "honest and impartial" inquirers. At the beginning of the twentieth century, a darkening pall of professionalism was gathering over literary studies. Soon to be gone were the days when writers wrote for "the common reader" and literary judgments could be made by any reasonable and literate individual. Instead, professional students of literature were rapidly becoming established as authorities — people who by training and years of study had qualified themselves to proclaim definitive statements on literary

Francis Bacon.

matters. Everyone else could simply accept these and not worry their heads. Greenwood clearly did not wish for this priesthood to achieve a monopoly.

For one thing, their use of language suggested that they did not deserve the authority they claimed for themselves and strove to enjoy. Sidney Lee, who had recently produced what was taken to be the age's standard life of Shakespeare, described the Baconian movement as a "foolish craze," and stated that its adherents suffered from an "epidemic disease" and, therefore, they were "unworthy of serious attention from any but professed students of intellectual aberration." Similarly, John Churton Collins, a Shakespeare scholar who had inadvertently placed a stout arrow in the Baconian quiver through his explorations of Shakespeare's debt to classical literature, characterized the Baconian theory as a "ridiculous epidemic" with "many of the characteristics of the dancing mania of the Middle Ages." Greenwood accurately described the attitude of the experts as "that petulant spirit which cannot examine an argument with calmness, or discuss it with moderation of language."[5] Without descending to the name calling of his adversaries, Greenwood showed that the professional authorities on Shakespeare were producing an environment in which the authorship question could not be reasonably pursued.

This unnecessary stridency on the part of the experts arose, it seemed to Greenwood, from their lack of expertise. That is, they themselves disagreed violently on basic issues despite a century and more of Shakespearean scholarship. He writes:

> The pundits of the Stratfordian temple are at loggerheads among themselves. Upon such questions, for instance, as the authorship of *Titus Andronicus*, the trilogy of *Henry VI*, or the old plays of *The Troublesome Reign of King John* and *The Taming of the Shrew*, they are hopelessly at variance. In fact, to do justice to these various and multifarious differences of opinion I should require to devote a whole volume to the subject. When, therefore, the "heretics" are assailed by the "orthodox" with such extraordinary exuberance of epithet; when they are told that they are fit subjects

for "the student of morbid psychology," and bidden to seek shelter in a lunatic asylum; the words which the late Sir Leslie Stephen addressed to the theologians always come back to my mind: "Gentlemen, wait till you have some show of agreement amongst yourselves!"[6]

Having in this way shown that there is an authorship question even for traditional scholars, Greenwood is prepared to produce his restatement of the problem. He modestly limits himself to the subject of the first part of Donnelly's book — that is, to a demonstration that William Shakspere of Stratford was not William Shakespeare the author. The method he uses is a method in which he can claim more expertise than the Shakespearean scholars. As he says, "it is just as a matter of evidence and reasonable probabilities that I have considered, and should desire the reader to consider, the question."[7]

Greenwood's arguments are not basically new. He follows closely the case against the Stratford man that Ignatius Donnelly made. For instance, he contrasts "The Schooling of Shakspere" with "The Learning of Shakespeare." What Greenwood injects into the controversy is a cool head and lucid prose that is pleasurable to read. He also goes further than Donnelly did in arguing that Shakespeare must have been thoroughly familiar with the law, that he knew it the way a practitioner does — an argument that convinced Mark Twain. But Greenwood ends his book by taking a new direction. He examines the vexed question of the possible early composition of some of Shakespeare's plays — a position held by some Stratfordians as well as Baconians. Greenwood displays his even-handedness in that chapter by returning to the Stratfordians an argument that he could have used against them.

By the reckoning of some students of the subject, as many as 13 of Shakespeare's plays were said to be written before 1592. Baconians used these arguments to strengthen the case against Will Shakspere as the author of the plays — most commentators agree that he did not leave Stratford much before 1587. Stratfordians urge these early dates of composition, despite the strain it places on their theory of the authorship of the plays, because they do not wish to surrender some of the references to Shakespeare that have been found. Greenwood carefully examines the arguments for assigning early dates of composition to two of these plays, *Hamlet* and *King John*. He concludes that in both cases there were early plays, not by Shakespeare, whoever he was, and that these old plays were extensively reworked and "transmuted" by Shakespeare.[8] This willingness to examine evidence carefully, weigh it soberly, and go where it leads even if it weakens his own argument, shows what Greenwood contributed to the authorship question: he raised the level of the debate to such an extent that pursuit of the question should have regained the respectability it had lost. In fact, he should have established the legitimacy of the inquiry even for Shakespearean scholars. Nonetheless, as he had predicted, "The High Priests of Literature" treated his sober logic with "frigid and contemptuous silence."[9]

II

The most extreme case of assigning an early date of composition to work by Shakespeare was made by Samuel Butler, the author of *Erewhon* and *The Way of All Flesh*, and a writer very different from Greenwood. Butler confined himself to a study of the Sonnets. His work remains readable and helpful, but he severely limited himself by accepting the Stratfordian theory of authorship. Despite that, he was viewed as a rebel by the authorities on Shakespeare. In fact, he goes further than Greenwood did in demonstrating the intellectual bankruptcy of the professional Shakespeareans by surveying the various views of the Sonnets held by Sidney Lee.

Butler was a man of letters who made a career out of considering problems or riddles, solving them to at least his own satisfaction, and publishing the results. He did not feel at all shy about entering such diverse fields as evolution, theology, and classical studies. Unexamined expert opinion on any question meant less than nothing to him. In this respect, he brought to his study of Shakespeare's Sonnets a reputation not unlike that of Ignatius Donnelly. Butler had helped to revitalize the Lamarckian or catastrophic view of evolution when Charles Darwin's theory was dominant. He was responsible for the theory that Homer's *Odyssey* was written by a woman and argued his position convincingly. He was, in short, an unconventional and independent intellect who was not only willing but eager to give old evidence a new look. The results of such a mind contemplating Shakespeare's Sonnets were necessarily quirky and brilliant — a refreshing combination.

Butler's single most important contribution to our understanding of Shakespeare's work is his realization that the Sonnets are, in effect, letters — private letters never intended for publication at all. As a result, if the Sonnets are to be read with understanding it is necessary to imaginatively reconstruct the context in which the letters were written — when they were written, the order in which they were written, the persons to whom they were written, and the circumstances surrounding the individuals involved. Butler feels the lack of documented biographical facts with which to check his imagination and writes that he is shocked by the number of times he must resort to the phrase "I imagine" or its equivalent. Nonetheless, like Greenwood, he makes clear what we do know and what we can reasonably conjecture as a result of that, but he does not try to confuse guesswork with knowledge. He also demonstrates that Sidney Lee repeatedly tried to present guesswork as knowledge.

At the very start of his study Butler asserts that he does not expect a warm reception from the Shakespeare scholars and professors: "I am not sanguine about the reception of my conclusions by eminent Shakespearean scholars. One might as well try to convince an anti–Dreyfusard French general of the innocence of Dreyfus ... as to make a Herbertite, Southamptonite, Impersonalite, or Baconian devotee give up his own particular heresy."[10] What is unusual about this is that he lumps the eminent Shakespearean scholars and the Baconians together. They all, Butler suggests, deal with Shakespeare from a prejudiced position. But who are these Herbertites, Southamptonites, and Impersonalites? Sidney Lee can stand as an example of all three.

These three warring factions among the professoriat all held various views on the identity of Mr. W.H., otherwise known in the literature as the fair youth of the Sonnets. The question of the identity of Mr. W.H. arises from the dedication of the 1609 quarto edition of Shakespeare's or, rather, "Shake-speares," Sonnets. (The name is hyphenated, with no apostrophe, on the title page.) The dedication is signed T.T. and reads: "To. The. Onlie. Begetter. Of. These. Insuing. Sonnets. Mr. W.H. All. Happiness. And. That. Eternitie. Promised. By. Our. Ever-living. Poet. Wisheth. The. Well-wishing. Adventurer. In. Setting. Forth." T.T. has been identified as Thomas Thorpe, a publisher and trader in literary wares. Mr. W.H. remains something of a mystery.

Even the reason for the dedication to him is a matter for debate and speculation. The earliest commentators, especially the pioneering but still valuable Malone, assumed he was the subject or addressee and inspirer of the vast majority of the Sonnets. Later commentators conjectured that Mr. W.H. merely obtained the poems for Thorpe — that he was the "onlie begetter" of the Sonnets because he was their procurer, rather than their inspirer. Either way, people were eager to identify him because his identity could deepen our understanding of Shakespeare. The Herbertites identified him as William Herbert, Earl of Pembroke. The

Southamptonites identified him as Henry Wriothsley, Earl of Southampton, to whom the dedications of "Venus and Adonis" and "The Rape of Lucrece" were addressed. The Impersonalities identified him with nobody, arguing that the Sonnets were artificial works of the imagination that had been manufactured by Shakespeare to fit a fad of the time — the Elizabethan sonnet sequence. Sidney Lee at different times held each of these positions and Butler enjoyed surveying these critical permutations.

Lee declared himself a Herbertite in 1891 when he wrote the article on William Herbert for the *Dictionary of National Biography*. Butler writes:

> Mr. Lee, after more than ten years' study of Elizabethan literature, then wrote: "Shakespeare's young friend was doubtless Pembroke himself, and 'the dark lady' in all probability was Mary Fitton. Nothing in the Sonnets directly contradicts the identification of W. H. their hero and 'onlie begetter' with William Herbert, and many minute details directly confirm it."
>
> This is very confident, and proceeding to Mr. Lee's article on Shakespeare written for the Dictionary of National Biography in 1897, I was surprised to read: "Some phrases in the dedication to 'Lucrece' so clearly resemble expressions that were used in the sonnets to the young friend as to identify the latter with Southampton."[11]

As Butler says, a man may certainly change his mind, but he was nonetheless startled to find Sidney Lee writing in 1898 in the preface to his *Life of William Shakespeare*, "The Pembroke theory, whose adherents have dwindled of late, will henceforth be relegated, I trust, to the category of popular delusions."[12] To be fair to his readers, Lee might have admitted that he had been a popularizer of this particular delusion at one time.

It is in his *Life of William Shakespeare* that Lee appears as an Impersonalite. While he continues to allow that some of the poems were addressed to Southampton, this statement does not mean what it once did. Lee states, "My conclusion is adverse to the claim of the sonnets to rank as autobiographical documents." In reaction to this statement and others like it, Butler defines the nature of the Sonnets:

> If by "autobiographical" Mr. Lee means the intentional and deliberate record of one's own history for the delectation of other people, which we commonly associate with the word "autobiography," all readers will agree with him in holding that Shakespeare's Sonnets are not autobiographical. No one supposes that Shakespeare had any idea of writing his own life. If, on the other hand, Mr. Lee means that the Sonnets were not dictated by actual facts and feelings — that they did not grow out of actual occurrences — I prefer the view which he took after only more than seventeen years' study of Elizabethan literature, to the radically different one which a single additional year has ... revealed to him.
>
> The Sonnets are a series of unguarded letters in verse, written as the spirit moved a young poet who has just discovered his own gift, and was glorying in the pride of flight without much either forecast or retrospection. Such letters inevitably record varying phases of the writer's mind, and must occasionally afford a clue to incidents of his life.[13]

This is well said and immediately shows both the strength and the weakness of Butler's analysis. The strength of it lies in the clarity with which Butler saw and sensed the reality of the Sonnets. His method, rational enough although it would have struck Sidney Lee as mystical or fanciful, probably, was to prepare to reconsider the Sonnets by memorizing all of them.[14] This procedure led him to suggest a rearrangement of the Sonnets and also to show that some of them are not part of the series at all — mere appendages or show pieces. This procedure also must have impressed on Butler's mind with force the actuality behind the great bulk of the poems. The weakness of his analysis lies in his insistence that the writer was "a young poet."

There are two primary reasons for this position of Butler's — and neither of them has to do with the style of the Sonnets or the skill displayed by their author. He never classifies the Sonnets as juvenilia. But he was one of the earliest critics to detect a bisexual streak in Shakespeare's nature and to deal with it in a frank way. He insists on the youth of the poet because he is convinced of the nobility of Shakespeare's character — he says that the nobility of his character is an article of faith with him — and he can not believe that the love for a young man expressed in the Sonnets could have occurred when Shakespeare was mature. He also finds internal evidence to support an early date of composition for the poems. He convincingly argues that the following sonnet gives voice to a national sense of relief after the defeat of the Spanish Armada and he therefore dates the poem "about August 8" of 1588:

> Not mine own fears, nor the prophetic soul
> Of the wide world dreaming on things to come,
> Can yet the lease of my true love control,
> Suppos'd as forfeit to a confin'd doom.
> The mortal Moon hath her eclipse endur'd,
> And the sad Augurs mock their own presage;
> Incertainties now crown themselves assur'd,
> And peace proclaims Olives of endless age.
> Now with the drops of this most balmy time
> My love looks fresh, and Death to me subscribes,
> Since, spite of him, I'll live in this poor rhyme,
> While he insults o'er dull and speechless tribes:
>   And thou in this shalt find thy monument,
>   When tyrants' crests and tombs of brass are spent.

If Butler is right about the dating of this sonnet — and his arguments are strong — and Will Shakspere wrote it, he did so when he was 24 years old. Because this poem comes late in the sequence and because of other internal evidence, Butler argues that the earliest of the Sonnets was written in the spring of 1585 — that is, when Will Shakspere celebrated his twenty-first birthday, when his twins were born, and two years before most commentators can legitimately conjecture that he had left Stratford for London. The idea that Will Shakspere, as he stands in the record, could have been attracted to a young man in London and obsessed with a mistress there while producing and raising a family in Stratford is doubtful. The idea that he could have been emotionally involved in this way and expressed himself in the language of the Sonnets is unthinkable.

Because of his adherence to the Stratfordian theory of the authorship, Butler paddles himself into even deeper water. He is at his best when he shows that words mean precisely what they say and more, perhaps, but never less. In other words, his strongest arguments are based on the precision of Shakespeare's language. For instance, numerous Herbertites and Southamptonites state that line 5 in the sonnet quoted above refers to the death of Queen Elizabeth and place the date of its composition in 1603. By merely pointing to the word "endur'd" and not permitting the critics to wish it from the page, Butler shows the fallacy of that interpretation. But when he comes to consider the age of the poet, he is forced to distort the language of the Sonnets himself. Plain references to the poet's age, including the famous lines beginning "That time of year thou mayst in me behold," drive Butler to write: "One of my own earlier friends was of the same year as myself at Cambridge, but being three or four years (if so much) older than most of us, we always called him 'the old one.' He was more active and youthful than many of his juniors, but he accepted the name without demur, and rather gloried in it. It is one of the commonest affectations of youth to think itself old — as it is of age to imagine itself still young."[15] Wit and anecdotes cannot conjure away the testimony of the poems.

Herbertites, Southamptonites, and Impersonalites all agree that Mr. W.H. was vastly superior to Shakespeare in social rank. Butler is on strong ground when he attacks this assumption. His concluding example will suffice to show the uncommon sense with which he dealt with the issue. He quotes the closing lines of sonnet 125:

> No, let me be obsequious in thy heart
> And take thou my oblation, poor but free,
> Which is not mixed with seconds, knows no art,
> But mutual renders, only me for thee.
> > Hence, thou suborned Informer! a true soul
> > When most impeached stands least in thy control.

Butler's comment on this passage reads: "It is impossible to follow the train of thought that was passing in Shakespeare's mind, and which enabled him to offer his friendship frankly if his friend would take it on equal terms, and in the following couplet to call that friend a 'suborned informer' and to defy him — but it is even more difficult to understand how either the offering or the defiance could be addressed to a man of greatly higher rank than that of the writer."[16] Butler was not one for making impossibilities even more difficult. In the end, he supported the conjecture of early commentators which identified Mr. W.H. as "a person named William Hughes, or Hewes, or Hews, as the name was very commonly spelt at the close of the sixteenth century." He does not insist on this conjecture, based on puns in the Will sonnets and on the word hue, and is content to call the inspirer of many of the Sonnets Mr. W.H. When considering the rank of the recipient of most of the Sonnets, Butler came close to advancing the authorship question. The possibility that both writer and recipient of the poems were of high social rank seems not to have occurred to him.

The importance of Butler's work is his realization of the need to place the Sonnets in a concrete context. He made a valiant effort to do so but failed largely because he was hindered by the Stratfordian theory of authorship. The concrete context he produces is much less concrete than it should and could be. He makes no attempt to identify Shakespeare's mistress, the so-called dark lady. He does not refer to Shakspere's wife or children. He is well aware of the private nature of the poems, but does not try to explain why Shakspere, a man of means in Stratford in 1609 who hauled neighbors into court for petty debts, took no action and made no statement when a pirated edition of his work appeared. He was clearly limited because the known facts of Shakspere's life simply do not tally with the reality of the Sonnets.

On the other hand, Butler is exceedingly good on the value of the Sonnets, the relationship between the Sonnets and the plays, and Shakespeare's style. He says of these matters:

> In the Plays there is a veil at all times over the face of their author. He looms large behind it as the Armada behind sonnet 107Q; we feel the mightiness of his presence, but we never see him. In the Sonnets we look upon him face to face; there is no let or hindrance to our gazing on the millions of strange shadows that play round him, nor on the millions of shadows that he can lend. We see the man whom of all others we would most wish to see, in all his beauty, in all his sweetness, in all his strength, and, happily, in all his weakness — for in the very refuse of his deeds there is a strength and warrantise of skill which it were ill to lose.[17]

At this point, near where Samuel Butler ends, another rebel, Frank Harris, begins. Harris believes it is possible to remove that veil from the face of the author in the plays — or, rather, to demonstrate that the veil is transparent.

III

Frank Harris was a literary journalist who shocked a simpler age with his autobiography, *My Life and Loves*. His book *The Man Shakespeare* (1909) grew out of a series of articles he wrote for *The Saturday Review* in England. His book is a heroic attempt to reconcile the facts and chronology of Will Shakspere's life with the sense of the actual author that readers of the plays come away with. That the effort was doomed to failure because these two individuals, Shakspere and Shakespeare, are poles apart and cannot be merged, does not at all negate the value of the book. If it is a failure, it is a magnificent failure. Harris saw the true author clearly and only goes far astray when he is forced to do so by his adherence to the Stratford legend.

Harris's work was not designed to persuade an academic audience. Like Greenwood and Butler, he by-passed the academy and took his message directly to the people, those "common readers" who are said to have walked the earth before World War I. Not only that, he was a lively, immodest, and roaring writer who delighted in tweaking the noses of the professional Shakespeareans — calling them by Dickens' names, Dryasdust and Gradgrind. Here is his summary of more than two hundred years of Shakespearean scholarship and criticism:

> I do not wish to rail at my forerunners as Carlyle railed at the historians of Cromwell, or I should talk, as he talked, about "libraries of inanities ... conceited dilettantism and pedantry ... prurient stupidity," and so forth. The fact is, I found all this, and worse; I waded through tons of talk to no result. Without a single exception the commentators have all missed the man and the story; they have turned the poet into a tradesman, and the unimagineable tragedy of his life into the commonplace record of a successful tradesman's career. Even to explain this astounding misadventure of the host of critics is a little difficult. The mistake, of course, arose from the fact that his contemporaries told very little about Shakespeare; they left his appearance and even the incidents of his life rather vague. Being without a guide, and having no clear idea of Shakespeare's character, the critics created him in their own image, and, whenever they were in doubt, idealized him according to the national type.[18]

Harris noted three primary exceptions to his blanket condemnation of the travesty foisted on the public by the commentators — Ben Jonson, Goethe, and Coleridge, all of them writers, or, as Harris prefers to say, "artists." This frontal attack on the critics and these exceptions to it suggest what Harris was about. He was convinced that the only critics of art worth heeding were themselves artists and he placed himself in their ranks. But being an artist in itself was not enough to qualify as a critic. An artist could recognize a fellow artist — hear his voice in the work, see his face in it — but the critic must move on from there and also be a scientist, describing and classifying "as a scientist would do it: for criticism itself has at length bent to the Time-spirit and become scientific."[19]

One of the purposes of Harris's book was to wrest criticism from the establishment of professional commentators and make of literary criticism a combination of art and science that would be worthy of the attention of adult humanity. When he connects this dream of a new criticism with his vision of the age, his eloquence ignites a revolutionary fervor:

> The wonderful age in which we live — this twentieth century with its X-rays that enable us to see through the skin and flesh of men, and to study the working of their organs and muscles and nerves — has brought a new spirit into the world, a spirit of fidelity to fact, and with it a new and higher ideal of life and of art, which must of necessity change and transform all the conditions of existence, and in time modify the almost immutable nature of man. For this new spirit, this love of the fact and of truth, this passion for reality will do away with the foolish fears and futile hopes which have fretted the childhood of our race, and will slowly but surely establish on broad foundations

the Kingdom of Man upon Earth. For that is the meaning and purpose of the change which is now coming over the world.[20]

Only five years after these words were published, the sounds of trench warfare and the stench of nerve gas defined the meaning and purpose of the change which was coming over the world. Perhaps Harris's rhetoric was a way of whistling in the dark. If so, we should be grateful to him for the increased understanding of Shakespeare that resulted from his whistling.

Harris's method is basically to accept as given the facts and chronology of Shakspere's life and deduce from Shakespeare's work a story, an emotional biography, that will cause a reinterpretation of those facts and that chronology. While he paradoxically argues that the plays are more biographical than the Sonnets, simply because Shakespeare has the protection of the dramatis personae he speaks through and is therefore less circumspect, less self-conscious, he finds the key to this emotional biography in the Sonnets. He is a self-confessed Herbertite and apparently unaware that Sidney Lee has pronounced this theory, initially promulgated by James Tyler, a popular delusion. He is convinced that Mr. W.H. is William Herbert, the Earl of Pembroke, and that "the dark lady" is Mary Fitton, one of Queen Elizabeth's maids of honor and sometime mistress of Lord Herbert. This triangle is the basis for Shakespeare's tragedy as Harris sees it.

This theory of the Sonnets gives them a relatively late date — Harris stretches the usual 1598–1601 to argue that the series began in 1597, the year before Francis Meres published a reference to sonnets by Shakespeare circulating privately in manuscript. Shakspere was then 33 or 34 years old. The problems this dating cause Harris are the same ones that Samuel Butler tackled, and they revolve around Shakespeare's sexuality and social class and what these suggest about his personality. If the poems to the fair youth express homoerotic or homosexual love, an early date permits the interpretation that this love existed between social equals and near equals in age and was outgrown by the poet. A late date combined with the Herbertite identification of Mr. W.H. demands that this affection existed between a mature poet and a youth of superior social standing.

Harris denies that the Sonnets to the fair youth express any sincere feeling whatsoever. He insists that they are the flowery and hyperbolic effusions of an inordinate snob who is devoted to toadying and currying favor. In other words, because of the Stratford legend Harris is forced to describe Shakespeare as either a potential pederast or a flagrant flunkey and he chooses the latter. Harris insists that this is not a choice on his part so much as his reading of the evidence and there is no reason not to believe him. He convinces himself that Shakespeare was no philosopher and not much of a thinker on any subject other than his self-centered self. He claims that the poet swallowed wholesale the widespread truism of his time that friendship between males was nobler and more important than the love between a man and a woman — a kind of Neo-Platonism popularized. The Sonnets to the fair youth were versifications of this doctrine intended to lead to patronage and position for the poet.[21] Harris even turns aside to denounce the Earl of Pembroke for not making the poet Master of the Revels as a reward for his toil. In addition, Harris claims that the fair youth made no imprint on the plays. The "dark lady" who betrayed the poet, on the other hand, was the love of his life and she appears in play after play.[22]

This suggestions leads Harris to make some real and valuable discoveries. Like Georg Brandes and Sidney Lee, he recognizes in the Rosalines of *Romeo and Juliet* and *Love's Labours Lost* a reflection of the dark lady of the Sonnets. He argues that Shakespeare rarely gives physical details of any of his characters but that these Rosalines are clearly described in terms that echo the Sonnets. Harris takes Romeo and Biron to be self-portraits of the author, and he thinks he finds in these plays the early stages of a potential love affair between Shakspere and the 19-year-old maid of honor. Harris's interpretation of the Sonnets is that Shakespeare sent Lord Herbert to Mary Fitton to commend him to her and that she wooed and won the young Earl. He sees this tiny plot repeated in *Two Gentlemen of Verona*, introduced as a sidelight in *Much Ado About Nothing*, and again repeated in *Twelfth Night*.[23] Harris is convinced that Shakespeare's loss and need to mourn both friend and beloved drove him to madness and exhaustion. In *Antony and Cleopatra*, a play Harris is tempted to rank as Shakespeare's greatest, he detects the despairing voice of the author in Antony's cry, "Whither hast thou led me, Egypt?" Cleopatra is again reasonably identified with the "dark lady."[24]

These identifications and emotional links — and a host of others like them — are valuable because they throw new and clear light on the author and the way he worked. Harris can also do a great deal with them in reinterpreting the facts and dates of Shakspere's life. For instance, it was not necessary to be either a Baconian or an Agnostic to find the idea that Shakspere retired to Stratford after making a financial killing in London ludicrous. The Stratfordians had made Shakespeare the first great writer to simply retire from the craft once it had served its financial purpose. Harris argues that broken health, resulting from his despair and madness, sent him home. Again, the traditional chronology of the plays has Shakespeare going from the heights of *King Lear* and *Hamlet* and *Antony and Cleopatra* to produce some pretty thin stuff. Harris argues that Posthumous is a pale reflection of Hamlet because of the author's poor health and exhaustion, again attempting to explain in a rational way an apparent fact that runs against the grain of what we would ordinarily expect. But these speculations, earnest as they are, become unintentionally funny. Harris, for instance, is well aware of and accepts the malodorous descriptions of seventeenth century Stratford, yet he says that the native air caused Shakspere's health to improve after he had roused himself to compose *The Tempest* a few years before his death. More importantly, the tradesmen of letters were not merely making a godling in their own image when they described Shakspere's life in Stratford and at New Place. They were sticking closer to the documents than Harris does. He insists that Shakespeare was open-handed and generous in the extreme, a despiser of money-grubbing, but he does not attempt to explain the records that document Shakspere's attempts to recover relatively minor debts through the courts, his dealing in malt, and so on.

Harris is at his weakest when he discusses Shakspere's rank in society and his attitude toward the social classes of his time. He describes him as an "aristocrat born" — meaning a natural aristocrat, not one by birth at all.[25] This fact frustrated Shakspere, made him hate and vilify ordinary people, while repeatedly imagining himself as a prince or a king in his works. Harris says that Shakespeare knew and understood only the extremes of Elizabethan society, the top and the bottom — the courtiers Shakspere served and envied, and the Bottoms and Snugs he was forced to dwell among and despise. He claims that Shakespeare knew nothing of the middle class — the very class Shakspere demonstrably struggled to rise into, an ambition he can honestly be said to have achieved on his return to Stratford — whether that return was inspired by a weariness with writing masterpieces or by broken health. Time and again Harris produces brilliant flashes of insight about the author of the plays but inevitably makes hash of them by trying to force them to fit the life of the Stratford rustic.

His most important contribution to our understanding of Shakespeare is his recognition of the poet as a conscious artist, a conscious artist who gave himself away most clearly when he produced what appear to be lapses in art. These lapses, Harris contends, are faults introduced by strong personal feeling and thus throw light on Shakespeare's personality and life.

He passionately hunts the plays for these clues to character and shows that the author was aristocratic, kind, gentle, generous, impulsive, reclusive, anxious to be a man of action but destined to learn that he was not suited for the part, unhappy in marriage, unlucky in love, and prone sympathetically to identify with the world's failures. Harris even reasonably argues that late in life Shakespeare grew stout and scant of breath. He demonstrates in a convincing way that Slender in *The Merry Wives of Windsor* was as clearly based on an enemy to the author as Rosaline reflected an actual woman who had bewitched him. This compelling accumulation of flashes builds a concrete and believable portrait of the author. That portrait, however, does not mesh at all with the portrait of Will Shakspere that accumulates in the documentary evidence of his life.

As the twentieth century began, the Shakespeare authorship question stood unresolved. Greenwood's restatement of that question was thorough enough and tempered enough to convince anyone. At almost the same time, two sound critics, Samuel Butler and Frank Harris, did their level best to do what Emerson in 1850 said he could not do — that is, marry the facts of Shakspere's life to Shakespeare's verse. Neither Butler nor Harris could satisfactorily do it — despite their willingness to rebel against the critical establishment, their ingenuity, their flashes of insight, and their obvious goodwill toward the author. The body of work written by "Shakespeare" remained unfixed, undefined. The dates of composition for the works remained at best guesswork and at worst distortions of the facts to fit a theory. While the Agnostics and Rebels struggled to comprehend the actual author and the reality behind his works, the professional commentators resuscitated the notion that there is no relation between the life and the work, making a mockery of the idea of integrity. As a result, Charlie Chaplin became a more trustworthy guide to Shakespeare than the professional scholars and critics. Chaplin announced his agnostic creed in *My Autobiography*:

> I am not concerned with who wrote the works of Shakespeare, whether Bacon, Southampton or Richmond, but I can hardly think it was the Stratford boy. Whoever wrote them had an aristocratic attitude. His utter disregard for grammar could only have been the attitude of a princely, gifted mind. And after seeing the cottage and hearing the scant bits of local information concerning his desultory boyhood, his indifferent school record, his poaching and his country-bumpkin point of view, I cannot believe he went through such a mental metamorphosis as to become the greatest of all poets. In the work of the greatest of geniuses humble beginnings will reveal themselves somewhere — but one cannot trace the slightest sign of them in Shakespeare.[26]

Chapter 6

Many Candidates: Marlowe, Rutland, Derby, and So On

Very like a whale.

Many investigators were not content to say with Greenwood and Chaplin that William Shakspere of Stratford could not be legitimately identified with William Shakespeare, the poet and playwright, and let it go at that. No doubt like Butler and Harris they had a sense of an actual author behind and in the work, and they wanted to name him and know him. It was not just a question of solving a mystery—at least, not for the best of them. The identity of the author should clarify the work, increase our understanding of the Elizabethan age, aid our insights into the way lasting literature comes to be written, and enhance our understanding of ourselves. Few of the readers who went in search of the true author read the plays and poems because they were assignments that had to be trudged through or because they were entertainments that could provide some diversion. They, like Greenwood and Butler, Harris and Chaplin, loved Shakespeare and wanted to become even more familiar than they were with the work and the man. This purpose did not keep them from making mistakes and false starts, of course. As Henry James had acknowledged, the question bristles with difficulties.

It was perhaps inevitable that some would search for the author among the other known playwrights of Shakespeare's time. It is not, therefore, surprising that Christopher Marlowe, perhaps the best of Shakespeare's contemporaries, should have been proposed as a candidate. The suggestion that Marlowe was Shakespeare seems to have been made first in 1895, in a work of fiction by an American attorney named Wilbur Gleason Zeigler. He called his novel *It Was Marlowe: A Story of the Secret of Three Centuries*. This title immediately suggests one of the problems that served to discredit the Marlowe claim from the start—its adherents tend to concentrate on the "whodunnit" aspect of the authorship question and, thus, fail to see the vast differences in style and outlook that exist between Marlowe's work and that of Shakespeare. Nonetheless, Zeigler's book presented some straight-faced arguments as well as fiction and seems to have convinced at least one reader, Dr. Thomas Corwin Mendenhall, a professor in Ohio.

Dr. Mendenhall launched a project that seems to have provided a prototype for some of the enterprises of the Modern Language Association, that trade union for literature professors, as they were described by Edmund Wilson in his pamphlet, "The Fruits of the MLA." Mendenhall took a statistical approach to literature, even in the days before computers. He hired women to count words and the number of letters in words in various texts in order to chart the frequency of words of different lengths. The raw data accumulated by these women enabled Mendenhall to reduce the vocabularies of different writers to graphs. He published his findings in 1901, in *Popular Science Monthly*, and argued that the graphs demonstrated that samples of Marlowe's work agreed with samples of Shakespeare's. The fact that this agreement was achieved by counting, rather than reading, words points to another problem that has haunted the Marlowe candidacy and the authorship question generally — a lack of interest in the less melodramatic aspects of literature.

Bronson Feldman wrote that Mendenhall discovered that Shakespeare's

> "word of greatest frequency was the four-letter word" (a discovery made in entire innocence of the euphemism "the four-letter word" has become). At the same time he announced that Marlowe had a predilection for words of the same number of letters. The industrious doctor's discoveries were made in the unwavering belief that both Shake-speare and Marlowe used the spelling of Mendenhall's schooldays.[1]

Max Beerbohm's caricature, "William Shakespeare, His Method of Work." (Courtesy of Mrs. Eva Reichmann)

Another attraction the Marlowe case holds for some readers is that Marlowe was a homosexual, and a later upholder of the Marlowe candidacy, Calvin Hoffman, offers the readers of his *The Murder of the Man Who Was Shakespeare* (1955) a rather heady mixture of sex and violence, a tale fit to compete with the thrillers of Ian Fleming.

Of course the biggest obstacle to Marlowe's candidacy and the source of the thriller element in it is the fact that Marlowe was murdered in Deptford, at a tavern owned by Eleanor Bull, on May 30, 1593. Marlowe was only 29 years old. The facts and documents surrounding the murder case have been published. They do raise questions and call for careful analysis. But there is nothing in them to support Hoffman's wild conjecture that the murder of an anonymous victim was committed and the body palmed off on authorities as Marlowe's corpse. The upshot of this dark plot was to permit Marlowe to flee to the continent, escaping the long arm of the Privy Council who had him under a kind of arrest requiring him to appear before them daily, where he could travel, write Shakespeare's work, and eventually return to England, clandestinely.[2]

Now, there is no question that Marlowe was mixed up with spies and informers. It is also clear that his murder sheds light on the something that was rotten in the Elizabethan state. But his life and work cohere as we find them in the record. There is more tragedy in Marlowe's death than mystery. If a real, rather than a statistical, identity between the styles and outlooks of Marlowe and Shakespeare could be established, then there would at least be cause for speculation. No such identity exists and Calvin Hoffman's conjectures continue to appeal primarily to devotees of mystery stories with a taste for the outré.

If the style, nature, and outlook of Marlowe's work is a major stumbling block to his candidacy, the utter absence of work which can be compared with Shakespeare's causes problems for other candidates.

Roger Manners, Earl of Rutland, is one such candidate. Rutland traveled widely on the continent — a characteristic one would expect of the author of Shakespeare's plays — and it is perhaps for this reason that his candidacy was first urged by Europeans. He was, in addition, a friend of the Earl of Southampton, the man perpetually described by professional Shakespeare scholars as Shakespeare's patron because of the dedications to him of "Venus and Adonis" and "The Rape of Lucrece." Rutland seems to have been first proposed as Shakespeare or, rather, half of him, by Peter Alvor in a book entitled *Das neue Shakespeare-Evangelium*. Alvor, *nom de plume* of Burkhard Herrman according to Joseph S. Galland's definitive *Digesta Anti-Shakespeareana*, apparently suggested that Rutland wrote Shakespeare's comedies while the rest of the plays were the work of Southampton himself.[3] News of Alvor's position seems to have reached England in a review by R.M. Theobald in a 1907 issue of *Baconiana*. The most fetching evidence in support of the Rutland candidacy is his personal acquaintance with Denmark generally and Elsinore Castle in particular.

It was this fact of Rutland's life and others like it that led Celestin Demblon, of the University of Brussels, to put forward in a serious way the Rutland claim. His *Lord Rutland est Shakespeare* appeared in 1912 and was followed in 1914, the year of catastrophe in Europe, by his *L'Auteur d'Hamlet.*[4] Demblon's case has attracted few whole-hearted adherents. The greatest shortcoming of the case for Rutland is the total absence of any literary remains left by the Earl that could be compared with Shakespeare's works. Rutland's dates also tend to argue against him, although the dates of composition assigned to Shakespeare's works are largely the results of guesswork. Still, Rutland was only 16 when "Venus and Adonis" was published. Despite all this, the fact that a serious student of French literature proposed Rutland as the author of *Hamlet* helped move the authorship question forward for those who could not rest content with Agnosticism and for whom the Bacon case was dead. The point of view of the plays, as Delia Bacon had concluded more than half a century before, is from the Court to Arden and Eastcheap, not the other way around. A courtier with a solid education, foreign travel, and incidents in his life seemingly mirrored or echoed in the plays made a reasonable candidate to propose as the true author. If Rutland left no poems or plays, he did leave more samples of his writings than Will Shakspere's six signatures.

A stronger case was made for William Stanley, Earl of Derby. His candidacy has its beginnings in the early 1890s when an English antiquary, James Greenstreet, found two statements in the Calendar of State Papers, Domestic, written by George Fenner, a Jesuit who is said to also have been a spy. The statements, dating from June 1599, describe Derby as busied only in "penning Comedies for the commoun players." Greenstreet was moved by these statements to look further into Derby's life. He learned that the Earl had other theatrical connections — his elder brother, Ferdinando, Lord Strange, had been patron to a company of players that could have included Will Shakspere for a time. Derby had been educated at St. John's College,

Oxford, and had traveled in Europe. Greenstreet published articles on his findings but not a book.[5]

His earliest disciple seems to have been an American, Robert Frazer, who published *The Silent Shakespeare* in 1915.[6] This title is a clue to the major problem with the Derby candidacy. While there is one piece of documentary evidence to establish that Derby was a playwright, there is no body of work available by him to compare with the Shakespeare plays and poems. Unlike Bacon, there is not even any work to show him as a thinker — merely some letters on mundane matters.

Nonetheless, Derby found a champion in Abel Lefranc, a Frenchman, whose *Sous le masque de William Shakespeare* appeared in 1919.[7] Lefranc is a scholar, a student of the Renaissance in France, with a wide knowledge of the literature, history, and thought of the period. He has published respected work on these subjects. He is sober and brings to the plays a detailed knowledge of some of their ostensible settings. Like the supporters of Rutland, Lefranc was able to find apparent reflections of Derby's life in the plays. Unlike the supporters of Rutland, he did not have any extraordinary difficulties imposed by his candidate's youth — Derby was born in 1561 and lived until 1641. Derby had many of the qualifications one would expect to find in the author of Shakespeare's plays, but the absence of literary work definitely known to be by Derby meant that the best anyone could say for the case was "not proved" — exactly what by 1919 should have been said about the Shakspere candidacy.

The pioneers of these theories have not been fortunate with their followers. Especially in the twentieth century, there has been a strong tendency to try to prop what should be rational arguments and literary judgments with technological supports — more sophisticated equivalents of cryptograms. We have seen that the Marlowe case was rendered in charts and graphs. A supporter of the Derby advocacy, a chemistry professor at the University of Liverpool, Dr. Titherley, has brought modern genetics and handwriting analysis to the case. These tools seem to have led him into a fantasy of royal politics and intrigue, adding something of Calvin Hoffman's spice to the Derbyite stew.[8] Once the severe limitations of the theories have been established, it would be well to abandon them or try and overcome the limitations. The Elizabethan period remains a happy hunting ground of unexamined documents. It is certainly possible that poems or plays by Derby or Rutland or both could still be found and identified. In addition, full-blown biographies of these Earls, based on contemporary documents, would inevitably add to our knowledge of the period if not to the authorship question. For some reason, these approaches fail to attract the energies of some of the people drawn to the question. As a result, many enthusiasts inadvertently render pursuit of the question ridiculous.

Next to the Stratfordians, the authorship question's greatest enemies have been the anti–Stratfordians. There have been hosts of other candidates, of course, ranging from John Florio, the translator of Montaigne, and Robert Burton, the author of the *Anatomy of Melancholy*, to Queen Elizabeth and King James.[9] All of these candidates fail because they do not meet the test established by Emerson long ago, the desire to marry the life and the verse. If the candidate's life in some way seems to match the Shakespeare who is sensed behind the plays and poems, either the candidate's work is alien to Shakespeare's or the candidate has left no work at all. On the other hand, if there seems to be some similarity between the candidate's work and Shakespeare's, the candidate's documented life does not match what we would expect to find in the life of Shakespeare. In many cases, of course, neither the life nor the work of the candidate displays any connection with Shakespeare at all. The entire case seems spun from mere vanity and vexation of spirit. None of this, of course, diminishes the importance of the question or the ability of some to pursue it soberly. All the same, the sheer number of untenable candidates has given the professional supporters of the Stratfordian theory reason to hoot and jeer.

Some people have tried to overcome the failings of various candidates by combining them through group theories of authorship. Like those professional Shakespeare scholars and critics who have become known in the literature as "disintegrationists," fragmenters of Shakespeare's work who parcel out bits to other hands, the supporters of group theories seem unable to see Shakespeare as a single, solitary individual. In this respect, they clash violently with the unified emotional or psychological portrait of the author found in the work by Frank Harris. Greenwood, it will be recalled, followed the disintegrationists and thus showed that there was an authorship problem even among professional Stratfordians. His position demonstrates the limitations of Agnosticism. If we do not know who the author is, our scholarship and criticism will necessarily crumble into the chaos already produced by the professionals. The reason for the chaos, its source, after all, is the absence of fixed dates and a documented life that can be seen as that of the author of the plays and poems without placing unreasonable demands on our reason, without straining our credulity beyond the breaking point. Fortunately, just such a documented life, one that could serve as a contribution to and check on future interpretations of Shakespeare's plays and poems and also provide a framework for the future discovery of documents, was found. The discovery resulted from a fresh approach to the question, a new method, and was announced in a book published in 1920.

Chapter 7

"Shakespeare" Identified: J. Thomas Looney

Is not this something more than fantasy?
What think you on't?

J. Thomas Looney, a schoolteacher at Newcastle-on-Tyne in the north of England, as part of his professional duties, found it necessary to read one of Shakespeare's plays, *The Merchant of Venice*, repeatedly. This long and intense familiarity with the play "induced," Looney reports, "a peculiar sense of intimacy with the mind and disposition of its author and his outlook upon life."[1] Looney was a remarkable specimen of a once rare and now all but extinct species: a teacher who refused to outrage his own conscience by telling lies to children. "The personality which seemed to run through the pages of the drama I felt to be altogether out of relationship with what was taught of the reputed author," he writes, "and the ascertained facts of his career."[2] This crisis of conscience launched him on a mental voyage of exploration that ended with the discovery of "Shakespeare's" identity.

It did not take him long to map out how the authorship question stood at the time of his own investigation. He found in Frank Harris's *The Man Shakespeare* a close approximation of his own sense of the author's "mind and disposition," but warped and wrecked by Harris's attempt to house that mind in the native of Stratford. He also found that although Ignatius Donnelly's cryptic cryptogrammic utterances caused critics to ridicule the question, "the full force of the first hundred pages of his first volume has not yet been fully appreciated."[3] For Looney, what made those pages so valuable is that they scotched the Stratford theory of Shakespearean authorship in an unanswerable way by bringing together a mass of material from Stratfordians themselves — the recognized authorities on Shakespeare. Looney writes of Donnelly, "To allow a justifiable repugnance to his 'cryptogram' work to stand in the way of a serious examination of the material he has brought together from untainted sources, like Halliwell-Phillipps and others of recognized capacity and integrity, is to fall behind the time in the spirit of dispassionate scientific research."[4]

More than that, Donnelly's first 100 pages by no means stood on their own by the time Looney took up the question. Quite the contrary, he found a growing skepticism concerning the identity of Shakespeare. This growing skepticism resulted from the work of "writers of the caliber of Lord Penzance, Judge Webb, Sir George Greenwood, and Professor Lefranc."[5] Looney did not believe that the Stratfordians could continue to dismiss the question and those who raised it with "contemptuous expressions." Instead, the history of the question and the quality of the case that had been made against William Shakspere as the author had "raised the problem to a level which will not permit of its being airily dismissed without thereby reflecting adversely on the capacity and judgment of the controversialists who would thus persist in giving artifice instead of argument."[6]

In short, Looney found himself at one with Greenwood the Agnostic to this extent — the Stratford myth was gone forever but none of the attempts to replace it was satisfactory. He clearly knew Greenwood's work thoroughly and admired its shrewd realization that the strident tone of the Stratfordians showed a lack of faith in their own position. Looney's resolve to attempt to settle the question may have been strengthened by Greenwood's words, "I have made no attempt to deal with the positive side of the question. I leave it to others to say, if they can, who the great magician really was."[7]

Looney was so convinced that the Stratford theory had been exploded that he initially planned to ignore it in his book, *"Shakespeare" Identified* (1920), and deal exclusively with "the positive side of the question." Friends convinced him, however, that it was still necessary in a book aimed at the general public to rummage yet again through the bones and

John Thomas Looney (1870–1944). Reprinted, with permission of Ruth Loyd Miller's heirs, from *"Shakespeare" Identified* by J. Thomas Looney, third edition, Volume I. Edited by Ruth Loyd Miller (Jennings, La.: Minos Publishing Co., 1975). Copyright renewed.

plaster of Paris of the Shakespearean Brontosaurus. It is a good thing they did. Because Looney's point of view shifts the emphasis placed on some vital issues and adds to our understanding of the impossibilities that Stratfordians are required to swallow.

I

As Looney was the first to admit, he had no new evidence or even arguments to bring to the examination of the Stratford myth. So far as he was concerned, the writings of Donnelly, Greenwood and others had satisfactorily disposed of the traditional point of view. But he did see more clearly than any of his predecessors two outstanding anomalies of the Stratfordian theory: the chronology the theory had erected to support itself and the theory's dependence on an irrational view of the way a poet develops. He therefore focused on these two aspects of the case.

William Shakspere's life as it has been recorded, Looney realized, naturally divides into three periods. The early and late periods place him primarily in Stratford. The middle period places him in London. Of the early period, little is known except that he was born, married, and produced three children. Of the late period a good deal is known, relatively speaking, because there are records of his business affairs and legal activities. These records establish him as a fairly prosperous resident of the town who traded in land and commodities and sought the recovery of debts through the courts. The middle period, in London, is a matter of reputation more than documentation — his name, or a variation of it, appears as the signer of dedications to two poems to the Earl of Southampton, for instance, and begins to appear on the title pages of published plays in 1598.

What makes this division of his life at once natural and anomalous is the question of the duration of each period. There is no evidence that firmly places William Shakspere in London before 1592. On the other hand, there is evidence that does place him in Stratford again as early as 1597, when he purchased New Place, the house that remained his primary residence until his death in 1616. In short, the documentary evidence can reduce the middle or London period to five years — and it can be seen to end the year prior to the first appearance of his name on the title page of a published play. Looney does not at all insist that Shakspere's life in London must be limited to this five year period. He, of course, recognizes that he could well have come to London long before any document reflects the fact. He also recognizes that he could well have traveled back and forth to London after the purchase of New Place in Stratford. Nonetheless, the fact remains that his dominant interests were primarily elsewhere when his great period of reputation as a dramatist is supposed to have begun. It will be worth giving in full Looney's summary of the middle period of William Shakspere's life, the London period:

1. He was purely passive in respect to all the publication which took place under his name.

2. There is the greatest uncertainty respecting the duration of his sojourn in London and the strongest probability that he was actually resident at Stratford whilst the plays were being published.

3. Nothing is known of his doings in London, and there is much mystery concerning his place of residence there.

4. After Greene's attack and Chettle's apology the "man" and the "actor" was [*sic*] ignored by contemporaries.

5. Before the printing of the dramas began in 1598 contemporary references were always to the poet — the author of "Venus" and "Lucrece" — never to the dramatist.

6. Only after 1598, the date when plays were first printed with "Shakespeare's" name, are there any contemporary references to him as a dramatist.

7. The public knew "Shakespeare" in print, but knew nothing of the personality of William Shakspere.

8. The sole anecdote recorded of him is rejected by the general consensus of authorities, and even the contemporary currency of this anecdote is consistent with the idea of his being personally unknown.

9. He has left no letter or trace of personal intercourse with any London contemporary or public man. He received no letter from any patron or literary man. The only letter known to have been sent to him was concerned solely with the borrowing of money.

10. Edmund Spenser quite ignores him.

11. Although the company with which his name is associated toured frequently and widely in the provinces, and much has been recorded of their doings, no municipal archive, so far as is known, contains a single reference to him.

12. There is no contemporary record of his ever appearing in a "Shakespeare" play.

13. The only plays with which as an actor his name was associated during his lifetime are two of Ben Jonson's plays.

14. The accounts of the Treasurer of the Chamber show only one irregular reference to him three years before the period of his greatest fame, and none at all during or after that period.

15. The Lord Chamberlain's Books, which would have furnished the fullest records of his doings during these years, are, like the "Shakespeare" manuscripts, missing.

16. His name is missing from the following records of the Lord Chamberlain's company in which other actors' names appear:

>   (1) The cast of Jonson's "Every Man out of his Humour" in which all the other members of the company appear.
>   (2) The record of proceedings respecting the Essex Rebellion and the company.
>   (3) The company's attendance on the Spanish Ambassador in 1604.
>   (4) The company's litigation in 1612.
>   (5) The company's participation in the installation of the Prince of Wales.
>   (6) References to the burning of the Globe.

17. Even rumour assigns him only an insignificant role as an actor.[8]

Will Shakspere is conspicuous by his absence where Shakespeare's biographers lead us to expect him — and he pops up where Shakespeare's biographers would not have us look for him.

Similarly, the absence of any juvenilia, any youthful attempts at poems or plays that can be identified as William Shakspere's apprentice handiwork, makes the torrent of masterpieces attributed to him not only anomalous but literally unbelievable. Looney is above everything else rational, and he simply calls for the application of common sense to the origin and composition of Shakespeare's plays:

> Drama, in its supreme manifestation, that is to say as a capable and artistic exposition of many-sided human nature and not mere "inexplicable dumb shows and noise," is an art in which, more than in others, mere precocity of talent will not suffice for the creation of masterpieces. In this case genius must be supplemented by a wide and intense experience of life and much practice in the technical work of staging plays. Poetic geniuses who have not had this experience, and have cast their work in dramatic form, may have produced great literature, but not great dramas. Yet, with such a general experience as these few facts illustrate, we are asked to believe that a young man — William Shakspere was but twenty-six in the year 1590, which marks roughly the beginning of the Shakespearean period — began his career with the composition of masterpieces without any apparent preparation, and kept pouring out plays spontaneously at a most amazing rate.[9]

Looney's new emphases on the Stratford theory and his sense of the author's mind and outlook on life induced by his familiarity with *The Merchant of Venice* combined to cause him to take a fresh approach to the authorship question. It is in his approach that he stands apart from every other investigator. Before describing that approach, he clearly defines the problem and explains the past approaches taken to its solution. He writes that "our first task must be to define precisely the character of the problem that confronts us. Briefly it is this. We have before us a piece of human work of the most exceptional character, and the problem is to find the man who did it."[10]

Having defined the problem as he saw it, he summarizes the previous attempts at its solution in this way:

> Even up to the present day the problem has hardly passed definitely beyond the negative or sceptical stage of doubting what is called the Stratfordian view, the work of Sir George Greenwood being the first milestone in the process of scientific research. The Baconian view, though it has helped to popularize the negative side, and to bring into prominence certain contents of Shakespeare's

works, has done little for the positive aspect except to institute a misleading method of enquiry: a kind of pick-and-try process, leading to quite a number of rival candidates for Shakespeare honours, and setting up an inferior form of Shakespearean investigation, the "cryptogram." Amongst all the literature on the subject, we have so far been able to discover no attempt, starting from an assumed anonymity of the plays, to institute a systematic search for the author. Yet surely this is the point towards which the modern movement of Shakespearean study has been tending; and once instituted it must continue until either the author is discovered or the attempt abandoned as hopeless.[11]

II

What marks Looney most is a rare combination of self-assurance, even boldness, and extreme modesty, even humility. There is very little of the razzamatazz and bravado that accompany some attempts to settle the authorship question in his book. A sincere understanding of the gravity of the task he has undertaken causes him to almost apologize for his own preparation for the task and the method he decided to apply to it. While he is no blind or romantic believer in the Zeitgeist, he states his conviction that tendencies in the society of his time in general and in the attempt to answer the authorship question in particular were bound to bring about a solution, offsetting to a large degree any purely personal credit for accurately identifying Shakespeare.

Nonetheless, there are qualities in Looney beyond the clarity of his thought and writing that had prepared him for the task. It has been previously pointed out that the work on the Shakespeare question parallels what was called the "higher criticism" — the analysis of the composition of the Bible, the search for the historical Jesus, and the attempt to resolve the conflict between science and religion that dominated the thought of the nineteenth century. Looney was not untouched by this movement and these tendencies. Quite the contrary, his life was radically changed by them. This radical change was what prepared him to tackle and satisfactorily answer the Shakespeare authorship question through an uncommon combination of confidence and humility. He described his personal background of education and preparation in a letter to Charles Wisner Barrell, dated June 6, 1937.

Born on August 14, 1870, at South Shields, Looney was raised in what he describes as a "religious and strongly evangelical environment."[12] The sect his family was associated with was known as the Methodist New Connexion, but his work is reminiscent of the critical writing of his contemporary, Allen Upward, who had been raised among Plymouth Brethren and in his maturity applied his mind to literary and social questions. Anyway, one result of his upbringing was that he decided at the early age of 16 to become a minister. He seems to have begun studies in preparation for that vocation as soon as the decision was made and eventually attended the Chester Diocesan College. The very studies required to qualify him to be a minister derailed his professional plans and set his life on an altered course. He writes that "by the age of 19 I found that I could not go forward under the conditions originally planned; and by the age of 22 I was obliged, as a consequence of the conclusion to which I had come, to abandon all thought of a religious vocation, though without any definite plans or prospects for the future."[13]

Just as he was not content later to rest with the Shakespearean Agnosticism of Greenwood, he relied on thought and study to solve the problem that confronted him through the loss of the traditional faith in which he had been reared. While this period of his life, extending to the age of 26, included attending college and taking examinations, he looked for a firm outlook on life on his own — reading voraciously, stating problems briefly and clearly, seeking solutions to them that were in tune with reason and the dictates of his conscience, and meeting or corresponding with some of the most learned men in England at the time.

The authors who meant most to him were "Channing, Carlyle, Emerson, John Stuart Mill, & Herbert Spencer."[14] The subjects on which he most concentrated his efforts included "mathematics, general science, philosophy, history & social & moral science." These interests were not pursued to the exclusion of literature, though. "Throughout these years," he writes, "the greater poets, Shakespeare, Wordsworth, Tennyson, Byron & Burns were my constant companions."

He was looking for a philosophy of life, an outlook that would give him a firm footing because, for him, "the old philosophy of the Christian faith" had "been broken down during the preceding 10 years." Under these conditions, by way of John Stuart Mill, Looney was introduced to the writings of August Comte, the French Positivist philosopher and the father of sociology. One of Looney's outstanding traits as a thinker is his desire for unity, integrity, wholeness — traits no doubt embedded in him by his Methodist parents and environment and which he felt duty-bound to retain even without the prop provided by traditional Christianity. This desire for unity and integrity extended very much to society as a whole and was not merely a private matter concerned with personal salvation. His early impulse to be a minister was no doubt a reflection of an impulse to eliminate or ameliorate the anomalies he saw around him in English society leading up to World War I. The teachings of Comte and Looney's conversations and correspondence with Comte's leading followers in England — Dr. Richard Congreve, the friend of George Eliot, and Dr. J. K. Ingram, described by Gladstone as "the distinguished fellow of Trinity College" — provided him with an outlook that could replace his early Christian point of view while meeting the demands of his reasoning faculties and conscience. This is not at all to say that Looney merely accepted another's outlook. Far from it. Instead, Looney "came to realize" that Comte's teachings "presented the point of view towards which for the past ten years" he himself "had been spontaneously moving."[15]

This statement clearly echoes Looney's point of view on how the Shakespeare authorship question came to be solved. Numerous individuals, working on their own, were attempting to work out a crisis, a loss of faith — a loss of faith that was slight compared with the tremors caused by the loss of faith in traditional religion, a faith that bound society together and provided it with a generally agreed upon moral code, a guide to conduct. Despite this comparative slightness, the nature of the crises was the same and therefore their solution could be achieved along similar lines. Looney's crisis of conscience as a teacher was a pale recurrence of the crisis he had earlier experienced while preparing for the ministry — a crisis that had led him to a new understanding of humanity and the world through study and thought. This second crisis was no doubt for him a test of his Positivist principles, an attempt to see if his new philosophy of life could solve a problem he was forced to face by replacing an exhausted faith with knowledge. "Without Positivism I might possibly have solved the Shakespeare problem," he wrote, "but without it, and the influence it brought to bear upon me, my treatment of it would have been wholly different."[16] This statement should be kept in mind as we examine the method he used.

Looney's method evolved from his determination to treat Shakespeare's works as if they were anonymous and an application of what he called "the usual common-sense method of searching for an unknown man who has performed some particular piece of work."[17] Before beginning the search at all, he decided on a brief statement of the lines the investigation should follow. He gives that statement in full this way:

1. As a first step it would be necessary to examine the works of Shakespeare, almost as though they had appeared for the first time, unassociated with the name or personality of any writer; and from such an examination draw what inferences we could as to his character and circumstances. The various features of these would have to be duly tabulated, the statement so arrived at forming the groundwork of all subsequent investigation.

2. The second step would be to select from amongst the various characteristics some one outstanding feature which might serve best as a guide in proceeding to search for the author, by furnishing some paramount criterion, and at the same time indicating in some measure where the author was to be looked for.

3. With this instrument in our hands the third step would be to proceed to the great task of searching for the man.

4. In the event of discovering any man who should adequately fulfill the prime condition, the fourth step would be to test the selection by reference to the various features in the original characterization; and, in the event of his failing in a marked degree to meet essential conditions, it would be necessary to reject this first selection and resume the search.

5. Supposing the discovery of some man who should in a general way have passed successfully through this crucial test, the next step would be to reverse the whole process. Having worked from Shakespeare's writings to the man, we should then begin with the man; taking new and outstanding facts about his performances and personality, we should have to enquire to what extent these were reflected in Shakespeare's works.

6. Then, in the event of the enquiry yielding satisfactory results up to this point we should next have to accumulate corroborative evidence and apply tests arising out of the course of the investigation.

7. The final step would be to develop as far as possible any traces of a personal connection between the newly accredited and the formerly reputed authors of the works.[18]

Two points follow directly from this method. First, the question of Shakespeare's identity is not fundamentally a literary question and, therefore, is not to be left totally in the hands of literary scholars. In fact, the question is identical in nature to questions that must be answered by juries, made up of ordinary citizens. The implication of this is that it is up to ordinary citizens, common readers, rather than specialists and professional experts, to reach a decision on Shakespeare's identity — although it will be necessary to rely in part on the testimony of experts. Second, the nature of the evidence that will result from this method is circumstantial rather than documentary. This should not be surprising because it is the very lack of documentary evidence that caused the question to arise in the first place, that brought on the need to consider Shakespeare's works as if they were anonymous. All the same, Looney feels compelled to discuss circumstantial evidence and thus indicate how his case is to be judged:

> Such evidence may at first be of the most shadowy description; but as we proceed in the work of gathering together facts and reducing them to order, as we hazard our guesses and weigh probabilities, as we subject our theories to all available tests, we find that the case at last either breaks down or becomes confirmed by such an accumulation of support that doubt is no longer possible. The predominating element in what we call circumstantial evidence is that of coincidence. A few coincidences we may treat as simply interesting; a number of coincidences we regard as remarkable; a vast accumulation of extraordinary coincidences we accept as conclusive proof. And when the case has reached this stage we look upon the matter as finally settled, until, as may happen, something of a most unusual character appears to upset all our reasoning. If nothing of this kind ever appears, whilst every newly discovered fact adds but confirmation to the conclusion, that conclusion is accepted as a permanently established truth.[19]

III

Looney drew up two sets of identifying characteristics for the author of Shakespeare's work. These characteristics were based on the nature of the problem at hand, the established conclusions of recognized authorities on the nature and content of the works, and a fresh reading of the works themselves with a mind as free as possible of preconceived notions concerning the name, personality, or circumstances of the author. Repeatedly, in asides to the reader, Looney urges rereading of Shakespeare's plays and poems — to such an extent that it is possible to say that one of the requirements of judging his method is a thorough familiarity with the work. This, too, sets him apart from many others who took up the authorship question and deflected attention from what Shakespeare's works are and mean with word counts or biographical flights of fantasy.

His first set of characteristics are stated as general features of the author:

1. A matured man of recognized genius.
2. Apparently eccentric and mysterious.
3. Of intense sensibility — a man apart.
4. Unconventional.
5. Not adequately appreciated.
6. Of pronounced and known literary tastes.
7. An enthusiast in the world of drama.
8. A lyric poet of recognized talent.
9. Of superior education — classical — the habitual associate of educated people.[20]

From these general features Looney becomes more and more specific and personal, generating an additional set of special characteristics by citing authorities and quoting chapter and verse, or rather act, scene, and line from the plays. He performs this operation by showing the characteristics of the author in opposition to the characteristics attributed to William Shakspere. He is perhaps at his best when considering the author's attitude towards money — one of the concerns that had originally attracted Looney to the authorship question through his readings of *The Merchant of Venice*.

He begins by asserting a general proposition: "Nothing could well be clearer in itself, nor more at variance with what is known of the man William Shakspere than the dramatist's attitude towards money." He immediately follows this general assertion with a multitude of particulars. The hero of *The Merchant of Venice*, he points out, is a man who "pulls down the rate of usuance" in Venice. The hero's friend, Bassanio, is a spendthrift and a heavy borrower who has "disabled his estate" and sustains his flagging fortunes through wedlock. On the other hand, Looney shows, it is Shakespeare's villains who urge care and control of money. Iago counsels "put money in thy purse" and it is "the contemptible politician, Polonius, who gives the careful advice 'neither a borrower nor a lender be.'"[21]

From these and other particulars from the plays Looney moves to contrast the traditional motives attributed to the author with what he himself wrote and, it reasonably follows, thought and felt. He quotes Sidney Lee who said that Shakespeare's "literary attainments and successes were chiefly valued as serving the prosaic end of providing permanently for himself and his daughters."[22] Setting this statement by a professional authority on Shakespeare beside a speech from *Henry IV*, part 2 —

> For this the foolish over-careful fathers
> Have broke their sleep with thoughts, their brains with care,

Their bones with industry;
For this they have engrossed and piled up
The canker'd heaps of strange achieved gold.

permits Looney to conclude "the Stratfordian view requires us to write our great dramatist down as a hypocrite." Looney goes even further than this. Having asserted a general proposition, supported it with particulars from the text, compared it with a general proposition of the Stratfordians and stated the conclusion toward which that comparison necessarily leads, he steps back and makes a larger general statement that leads from the plays and the Shakespeare authorship question into the world and how life is lived:

> Money is a social institution, created by the genius of the human race to facilitate the conduct of life; and, under normal conditions, it is entitled to proper attention and respect. Under given conditions, however, it may so imperil the highest human interests, as to justify an intense reaction against it, and even to call for repudiation and contempt from those moral guides, amongst whom we include the great poets, who are concerned with the higher creations of man's intellectual and moral nature. Such, we judge, was the dramatist's attitude to money.[23]

While it would be neither necessary nor profitable to consider each of the characteristics that Looney identified in this detail — his case must be read and reflected on in its entirety — this sample clearly shows what he was up to. His interest goes well beyond the identity of the author of Shakespeare's plays and poems, although he cast his work along the lines of a "whodunnit."

What he does with each of these special characteristics is to show that the plays and poems scatter new light on old problems that confront humanity — light that has been dimmed or even blotted out by the interpretations produced in accordance with the Stratfordian view of the authorship. All the special characteristics that Looney treated in this way are:

1. A man with Feudal connections.
2. A member of the higher aristocracy.
3. Connected with Lancastrian supporters.
4. An enthusiast for Italy.
5. A follower of sport (including falconry).
6. A lover of music.
7. Loose and improvident in money matters.
8. Doubtful and somewhat conflicting in his attitude toward woman.
9. Of probable Catholic leanings, but touched with scepticism.[24]

At this point, Looney again insists on the lack of originality in his work. Just as Ignatius Donnelly's destructive criticism of the claims made on behalf of the citizen of Stratford was based in large part on the testimony of professional scholars and critics, so Looney freely admits that the general and specific characteristics he has derived from the works to form a positive likeness of the mind of the author are derivable in good measure from the professional authorities on Shakespeare — and this only serves to strengthen the validity of the characteristics. "The various points are, indeed," he concludes, "the outcome of the labours and criticisms of many minds spread over a number of years, and it may be that the only thing original about the statement is the gathering together and tabulating of the various old points."[25] He is too modest.

What is original about his compilation and discussion of these 18 characteristics is its effect on the reader. The blinders drop from our eyes and we see the point of view of Shakespeare more clearly than ever before — despite the strenuous and commendable efforts of Delia

Bacon and Frank Harris. When Looney takes us in search of the author we are no longer looking for an anonymity, but for an actual person who merely lacks a name.

IV

Part of Looney's stated method was to select from the characteristics of the author one which could serve as a predominant identifying characteristic, something that would be at the crux of the matter and offer a standard for judging potential candidates. He decided that the feature that would fulfill these requirements best was the eighth of the general features, that is, "A lyric poet of recognized talent." The lyric poetry of the Elizabethan period is a verbal haystack in which Looney determined to find a needle. Nothing about him or his method permitted him to merely run through that literature with an ear open for echoes of or, rather, premonitions of Shakespeare's work. Instead, he narrowed the search by allowing himself to be guided by the verse form Shakespeare used when he first emerged from obscurity and became associated with a polished and sophisticated poem, "Venus and Adonis." The stanza used in that poem consists of six lines of iambic pentameter that rhyme a, b, a, b, c, c,— equivalent to the concluding stanza and couplet of the English or Shakespearean sonnet. Looney searched an anthology of sixteenth century lyrics for poems that employed this form prior to its appearance in "Venus and Adonis" (1593).

He reports this search with a candor that earns him the faith of his readers even though it provides an opening for hostile criticism. He writes: "They turned out to be much fewer than I had anticipated. These I read through several times, familiarizing myself with their style and matter, rejecting first one and then another as being unsuitable, until at last only two remained. One of these was anonymous; consequently I was left ultimately with only one: the following poem on 'Women,' by Edward de Vere, Earl of Oxford."[26] It will be best to give the poem in full:

> If women could be fair and yet not fond,
>   Or that their love were firm not fickle, still,
> I would not marvel that they make men bond,
>   By service long to purchase their good will,
> But when I see how frail these creatures are,
> I muse that men forget themselves so far.
>
> To mark the choice they make, and how they change,
>   How oft from Phoebus do they flee to Pan,
> Unsettled still like haggards wild they range,
>   These gentle birds that fly from man to man,
> Who would not scorn and shake them from the fist
> And let them fly, fair fools, which way they list?
>
> Yet for disport we fawn and flatter both,
>   To pass the time when nothing else can please,
> And train them to our lure with subtle oath,
>   Till, weary of their wiles, ourselves we ease;
> And then we say, when we their fancy try,
> To play with fools, Oh what a fool was I.[27]

Looney frankly states that if he had met this poem outside the special context that he had established, he could well have missed its power and peculiar characteristics. But part of his method was to bring a particular context to each of the poems he used in this initial stage of his search. That context caused him to fix "provisionally" on this poem and therefore "follow up the enquiry along the line it indicated until that line should prove untenable."[28]

He could have legitimately proceeded at this point to explore the life of Edward de Vere to see how it matched the other features he had established as identifying traits of Shakespeare. Instead, he wished to have his selection first confirmed by expert opinion on the literature of the period. He found some information in the books he had at hand that indicated that at least some of the other traits could be found in the Earl of Oxford — he was born in 1550 and died in 1604, and so would have been 40 when the plays began to appear and lived through the period of the production of most and the best of Shakespeare's work even using the traditional chronology. He also found an indication that Oxford had at one time been a Catholic. But he found little information in general about Oxford and nothing by a literary scholar or critic to confirm his reputation as an Elizabethan lyric poet. He turned to the *Dictionary of National Biography*. It is not difficult to imagine the sheer delight he must have felt when he realized that the article on Oxford had been written by the editor of the reference work and the author of the then standard life of Shakespeare, Sir Sidney Lee. This was an extra gift that he could not have foreseen, almost an additional test for the validity of his method and the choice he had made as a result of it: if Lee confirmed Oxford's lyric talent few could quarrel with it. Lee did so and more — his article provided evidence that Oxford reflected almost all of the identifying characteristics of Shakespeare that Looney had established. But Lee was particularly strong on Oxford as an Elizabethan poet of recognized merit among his contemporaries. Looney gives three quotations:

"Oxford, despite his violent and perverse temper, his eccentric taste in dress, and his reckless waste of substance, evinced a genuine taste in music and wrote verses of much lyric beauty."

"Puttenham and Meres reckon him among the best for comedy in his day; but though he was a patron of players no specimens of his dramatic productions survive."

"A sufficient number of his poems is extant to corroborate Webbe's comment, that he was the best of the courtier poets of the early days of Queen Elizabeth, and that 'in the rare devices of poetry he may challenge himself the title of the most excellent amongst the rest.'"[29]

Looney writes with justice of these quotations: "If only such of those terms as are here used to describe the character and quality of his work were submitted without name or leading epithet to people, who only understood them to apply to some Elizabethan poet, it would be assumed immediately that Shakespeare was meant."

By consulting additional reference works and becoming familiar with Oxford's verses it was possible for Looney to show that Oxford directly and personally matched all but one of the identifying characteristics he was seeking — the Lancastrian sympathies. Even this trait, however, could be reasonably said to belong to Oxford because of the sympathies of his ancestors — a remarkable record of adherence in spite of real suffering to the "cause of the red rose." Having found someone who met all the conditions he had originally established, Looney devotes a chapter to a comparison of Oxford's verse with the early work of Shakespeare, a tour de force of literary and historical analysis which in some ways anticipates the procedures of the "new criticism." He demonstrates time and again how Oxford's poetry provides the juvenilia that Shakespeare has been lacking for so long. This dove-tailing of the two sets of work, along with the fact that Oxford meets all of the criteria established early, causes Looney to conclude the chapter this way: "It has become impossible to hesitate any longer in proclaiming Edward de Vere, Seventeenth Earl of Oxford, as the real author of 'Shakespeare's' works."[30]

V

It is impossible to do justice in a summary to the accumulation of evidence Looney gathered or the effect of its presentation once he proceeds to piece together the story of Oxford's life and compare it with both Shakespeare's work and the life of William Shakspere as it is described by the best authorities. All of the anomalies that originally caused Looney to take up his search disappear and we are presented for the first time with a rational account of the origin and composition of Shakespeare's plays and poems.

Oxford's life, like Shakespeare's, naturally divides into three periods. The early period of his life runs from his birth in 1550 to 1576. During this period he was raised at his family's ancestral home of Castle Hedingham in Essex where his father was known as a sportsman, a hunter and falconer, given to lavish entertainments. His father died when Oxford was 12 and he became a royal ward, like Bertram in *All's Well That Ends Well*. Oxford's relationship with his mother seems to have become strained, if not severed, on the death of his father — much as Hamlet's was. As a royal ward he was under the care of William Cecil, later Lord Burghley, recognized by Looney but also by Stratfordian authorities as the model for Polonius. Oxford's uncle, Arthur Golding, the translator of Ovid's *Metamorphoses*, traveled to live with his nephew in London, to look after his interests and education. Golding prepared at this time the translation of Ovid that Shakespeare is said to draw on constantly. Oxford was provided with the best tutors and education his age could provide. He married Cecil's daughter, Anne, a girl who had the character of Ophelia and, at the time of their wedding, was the same age as Juliet. Oxford, like Bertram, longed for a military career but was prevented from pursuing one and was kept at court — dancing. He also longed for foreign travel and finally gained permission to fulfill this wish — writing his father-in-law to sell his lands, like Timon, in order to pay his debts, including those incurred in Venice. On his return from the continent, he, like Othello, was deceived by his receiver, an Iago-like figure, about the fidelity of his wife, who had given birth to their daughter, Elizabeth; and they lived apart. Most if not all of the verses attributed to him by Grosart, that indefatigable diver among Elizabethan literary remains, were written during this early period. In 1573, Oxford "commanded" and no doubt paid for publication of *Cardanus Comforte*, translated by his friend Sir Thomas Bedingfield. Some Shakespearean scholars have argued that this work was Hamlet's book, the one he carries with him on stage and from which he gleans some of his philosophy.

Oxford's middle period, from 1576 to 1590, finds him associated with many of the writers Shakespeare is said to have learned or stolen from. John Lyly was Oxford's private secretary when he wrote his Euphues novels and began to write plays. He also acted as manager for a company of players, "Oxford's boys." Anthony Munday, another playwright to whom Shakespeare is said to have been indebted, describes himself as a servant of the Earl of Oxford. Robert Greene, too, dedicates one of his books to Oxford.

Edmund Spenser was early associated with Oxford. He has a dedicatory sonnet to him in his *Faerie Queen* and, as Looney cogently argues, Spenser reflected the literary, political, and personal rivalry that existed between Oxford and Sir Philip Sidney in his "The Shepherd's Calendar." Oxford arguably appears as "Willie" and Sidney as "Perigot" in the eclogue for August. This identification helps to solve another Elizabethan puzzle. Looney quotes three stanzas from Spenser's poem "The Tears of the Muses," published in 1590, and makes a strong case for identifying "our pleasant Willie" with Oxford. This Willie is connected by Spenser with "the Comic Stage" and is said to have issued "large streams of honey" from his pen. Now, instead, Willie "doth choose to sit in idle cell." It was at this time, after Oxford's participation

Castle Hedingham, Edward de Vere's ancestral home. (Published, According to Act of Parliament, April 1796)

in the defeat of the Armada and after the death of his wife, with whom he had been reconciled, that Oxford seems to all but disappear from the Elizabethan literary scene.

Looney does not neglect to link Oxford's middle period with that of William Shakspere. The Earl of Oxford's servants, a company of players, toured the provinces as well as taking an active part in the dramatic life of London. In 1584, his company visited Stratford-on-Avon. Looney writes:

> William Shakspere was by this time twenty years of age and had been married for two years. There has been a great deal of guessing respecting the date at which William Shakspere left Stratford-on-Avon, and it is not improbable that it may have been connected with the visit of the "Oxford Boys." As it is the birth of twins, early in 1585, which furnishes the date from which the time of his leaving Stratford has been inferred, the latter half of 1584 may indeed have been the actual time.[31]

Oxford's final or what Looney calls his "Shakespearean" period is spent to a large extent in seclusion. He remarried in 1592, to Elizabeth Trentham, a marriage that, like Bassanio's, seems to have helped restore the resources, the money and estates he had spent to a large extent on literary men, musicians, and theatrical companies. (Ruth Loyd Miller has shown that Oxford in effect financed the English Renaissance.)[32] He did not retire to the country, however. He lived in London or one of its suburbs, Hackney, "where," Looney points out, "he would be in direct contact with the theatre life of Shoreditch," the veritable birthplace of the Shakespeare plays.[33] The records Looney found of his life between his remarriage and his death were all but blank. Looney argues that Oxford spent this time writing and revising plays that he eventually issued, beginning in 1598, under the name of William Shakespeare. This period does not only coincide with the flood of Shakespearean work that appeared, but it also coincides with Will Shakspere's sparsely documented life in London — during which he accumulated enough wealth to buy New Place and engage in commercial activities. Furthermore, with Oxford's death there is a distinct hiatus in the publication of Shakespeare's works and Will Shakspere, so far as commentators can determine, is once again ensconced, all but permanently, in Stratford.

Part of the evidence Looney gathers for this period derives from the Sonnets. Most scholars and critics agree that the Sonnets urging the young man to marry date from about 1590 and are addressed to the Earl of Southampton. Southampton had been engaged by William Cecil to Elizabeth Vere, Oxford's daughter. Southampton broke the engagement and Elizabeth married William Stanley, Earl of Derby, another proposed candidate for Shakespearean honors. *A Midsummer Night's Dream* is said by no less a critic than E.K. Chambers to have been performed at their wedding celebration. The latest date assigned by Shakespearean scholars for the end of the series of Sonnets is 1603. The Sonnets were published in 1609 and the publisher in his dedication describes the author as "our ever-living poet," a term that is traditionally applied to one who is dead. Will Shakspere and Derby both lived well beyond 1609 without either commenting on the publication of these personal poems or adding a single sonnet to the literature of the period. Looney plainly states that of all the leading candidates proposed as Shakespeare — Shakspere, Bacon, Rutland, Derby, and now Oxford, only Oxford was dead by 1609.[34]

VI

Where Looney runs most strongly against the Stratfordian current is in his treatment of the plays that have been assigned a late date of composition — those plays said to have been written after Oxford's death in 1604. The "late" plays have been a problem for scholars all along. Some see them as early work. Others argue that they were early plays by Shakespeare taken up and revised or completed by others. Frank Harris, it will be recalled, rejected the traditional notion that Shakespeare retired but believed instead that illness and exhaustion caused the falling off in his last years. But Harris argued that Shakespeare pulled himself together to produce a final masterpiece as a farewell to the stage, *The Tempest*—a farewell prompted by approaching death rather than the urge to shuffle off to New Place, Stratford.

It is Looney's position on *The Tempest* that has given his admirers and detractors alike the most problems. He could have easily ducked the issue by simply pointing out that traditional authorities on Shakespeare date the composition of the play between 1596 and 1613 and, therefore, Oxford could certainly have written it before his death in 1604.[35] It is in fact the case that one of the reasons for the late dates of some of the plays is to try and make it humanly possible for Will Shakspere to have had the time to write them all. But ducking issues was not what Looney was about. He was less interested in making a case that would convince others than in determining the truth for himself. His education and Positivism caused him to spend his life "facing definite problems, attempting their solutions by the methods of science, and accepting the necessary logical conclusions, however unpalatable & inconvenient these might prove."[36] *The Tempest* presented itself as a problem to him not because it seemed to threaten his theory of the authorship but because it stood outside what he had come to mean by the term Shakespearean. He analyzed the work and concluded that it is distinctively un–Shakespearean.

Most of Shakespeare's plays, at least the best of them and those that most people associate readily with his name, seem to have evolved from playable sketches or entertainments into what Looney calls "literature"—works that are intended to be read and re-read, thought about and discussed, rather than provide an evening at the theater. What makes every production of *Hamlet* different is the way the director decides to cut it—because cuts there will be if it is to be squeezed onto the stage for a bearable length of time.

No such problems confront the director of *The Tempest*. It was made for the stage—next to the very early *Comedy of Errors* it is Shakespeare's shortest play and the one with the most detailed stage directions. It, like the *Comedy of Errors*, also observes the unity of time, a nod if not an obeisance in the direction of Aristotle's authority. Professional scholars and critics conjecture that Shakespeare wanted to prove to his rival, Ben Jonson, that he could successfully operate within this classically circumscribed limit. Looney's view of this is: "That 'Shakespeare' should do this at any time seems highly improbable; it is contrary to the free spirit of his genius, and it is an illustration of that 'tongue-tying of art by authority' which he explicitly repudiates. To think of his submitting to such unwholesome restriction at the extreme end of his career would require some extraordinary explanation."[37]

He says that the traditional dating of *The Tempest*, placing it "between the group which contains such a tragedy as *Pericles* and the nondescript historical play *Henry VIII*," makes it look "like a play that had wandered away and fallen into bad company. Its natural associate, *A Midsummer Night's Dream*, is separated from it by almost as wide an interval as the Shakespearean period will permit. Under any theory of authorship this work occupies an anomalous position."[38]

It is the language and thought of the play that makes it most anomalous. His approach to these subjects can perhaps best be seen in his discussion of two of the most famous lines in the play—

> We are such stuff as dreams are made on, and
> Our little life is rounded with a sleep.

Looney laments the lack of an objective standard for judging literary matters and then declares, "Although, then, we are assured that these words are eminently Shakespearean, we make bold to say that they appear to us as un–Shakespearean as any utterance with which 'Shakespeare' has been credited."[39] He then explains why. He finds in Shakespeare an unwillingness to be fuzzy. He has the sense that Shakespeare always has "clear and definite conceptions" in mind and "imparts" these to readers in crisp, precise language. Even when Shakespeare deals with abstractions or unknowns, Looney argues, he does so in terms of clear realities. Looney finds none of these traits in the two famous lines from *The Tempest*:

> Abandon for a moment the practice of squeezing into or squeezing out of these words some philo-sophic significance, and attempt the simpler task of attaching a merely elementary English mean-ing to the terms and placing these meanings into some kind of coherent relationship to one another. We are stuff: the stuff of dreams: dreams are made on (or "of"?): life rounded with a sleep — we will not say that Shakespeare never gives us such "nuts to crack," but we can say with full confidence that they are not characteristically Shakespearean. So far as we can get hold of the general drift of the metaphors, it seems that the present life of man is likened to dreams: "We are stuff, etc.," and that he brings his dreams to an end by going to sleep. In common with Shake-speare and the majority of mankind, however, we are accustomed to associate our dreams with our actual time of sleep.[40]

Looney follows this criticism with an analysis of the play's vocabulary — words common in other Shakespearean plays appear rarely in *The Tempest*— and then considers the versification in the play. Here, as with vocabulary, he believes he has an objective measure that can be applied, and takes as a standard the versification of *Hamlet*. He says the blank verse of *The Tempest* "jogs and jolts" to such an extent "that it is impossible to preserve for any length of time that sense of rhythmic diction which gratifies the sub-conscious ear in silent reading of the other plays."[41] The blank verse of the play again suggests that its success comes from its rhetorical and dramatic qualities, rather than as literature that has been written to be read. He finds the causes — or a cause — of this jogging and jolting in the grammatical closeness of the words at the ends of lines with what follows in the next line. Each line of blank verse, Looney argues, necessarily produces a slight pause. If the meaning of the final word in a line denies the reader the ability to take that pause, the lines become awkward, clumsy, and jumpy. *The Tempest*, he shows, is full of words at the ends of lines that deny the pause — auxiliary verbs, conjunctions, and so on — while these do not appear once in the blank verse of *Hamlet*. He points to the "and" which ends the first of the two lines analyzed above as one exam-ple, although he compiles many others, too."[42]

Looney is clearly convinced that *The Tempest* is not by "Shakespeare." But he is willing to leave the question open for others to pursue and concludes, "For the time being, it is inter-esting that the pivotal date on which even orthodox opinion turns as to the composition and authenticity of *The Tempest* is 1604 — the year in which Lord Oxford died and William Shakspere, it is said, 'retired.'"[43]

VII

In his *"Shakespeare" Identified* (1920), Looney presided over that marriage of Shakespeare's life and verse that Emerson had called for in 1850. As a result, he forces us to reverse many of the things we have been taught about Shakespeare, Elizabethan literature, and the history or evolution of the Elizabethan stage. We no longer have to wonder how the transition from miracle plays, *Everyman*, and *Ralph Roister Doister* to Lyly and Marlowe, Peele and Greene, occurred: Oxford, that is, Shakespeare, provides the bridge, the missing link. Looney's work renders a world figure a nonentity and transforms a forgotten courtier into a leading light of humanity's intellectual life. Shakespeare emerges from his pages as an originator, rather than an imitator; and as a conscious and conscientious craftsman who contrived to find the time, free of distractions, to work out his destiny in pen and ink, revising his work and lavishing on it the attention and care that made of it literature of lasting value. He also emerges as a thinker of the first order, with a distinctive point of view that is reflected in his work. Looney is almost uncanny in his ability to clarify what Shakespeare thought and felt on a host of subjects. One example will suffice.

Looney no doubt knew that many of his fellow schoolteachers taught their students that "Shakespeare's" philosophy was embodied in Polonius's advice to Laertes in *Hamlet* and some of them even required students to memorize the lines — as teachers continued to do years later. It may well be, in fact, that this was one of those lies that Looney refused to tell children for fear of stunting their moral and intellectual growth. What makes this likely is the heat and the uncharacteristic descent into slang that this subject provokes in him. Looney, of course, knew that Shakespeare did not simply "make up" this speech. It is carefully patterned on a series of precepts written out by Lord Burghley for the edification of his son. How William Shakspere could have had access to these private papers of Burghley's no one has been able to say. In any event, Looney clearly wanted to short-circuit Burghley's continuing educational effort. His analysis of the famous passage reads:

> The spirit of the closing words of Polonius's speech, the words beginning, "Unto thine own self be true," seems to us to be generally quite misunderstood. These words bring to a close a speech which, throughout, is a direct appeal in every word to mere self-interest. Is, then, this last passage framed in a nobler mould with a high moral purpose and an appeal to lofty sentiment? We think not. The bare terms in which the final exhortation is cast, stripped of all ethical inferences and reinterpretations, are as direct an appeal to self-interest as everything else in the speech. They are, "unto thine own self"; not unto the best that is in you, nor the worst. Consistently with his other injunctions he closes with one which summarizes all, the real bearing of which may perhaps be best appreciated by turning it into modern slang: "be true to 'number one.' Make your own interests your guiding principle, and be faithful to it."
>
> This is quite in keeping with the cynical egoism of Burleigh's advice, "Beware of being surety for thy best friends"; but "keep some great man for thy friend." And, of course, it does "Follow as the night the day" that a man who directs his life on this egoistic principle cannot, truly speaking, be false to any man. A man cannot be false to another unless he owes him fidelity. If, therefore, a man only acknowledges fidelity to his own self, nothing that he can do can be a breach of fidelity to another. On this principle Burleigh was true to himself when he made use of the patronage of Somerset; he was still true to himself, not false to Somerset, when he drew up the articles of impeachment against his former patron. Bacon was true to himself when he made use of the friendship with Essex; he was still true to himself, not false to Essex, when he used his powers to destroy his former friend.
>
> This philosophic opportunism was therefore a very real thing in the political life of those days. And the fact that Shakespeare puts it into the mouth not of a moralist but of a politician, and, as we believe, into the mouth of one whom he intended to represent Burleigh, serves to justify both the very literal interpretation we put upon these sentences, and the identification of Polonius with Elizabeth's chief minister. Needless to say, one who like "Shakespeare" was imbued with the best ideals of feudalism, with their altruistic conceptions of duty, social fidelity and devotion would never have put forward as an exalted sentiment any ethical conception resting upon a merely personal and individualist sanction. For his admiration of the moral basis of feudalism would enlighten him in a way which hardly anything else could, respecting the sophistry which lurks in every individualist or self-interest system of ethics.[44]

What caused Looney to see this clearly and buck the prevailing philosophic wind this vigorously was his own philosophy of life, his brand of Positivism. Years after his book had appeared, people who found it convincing urged him to write more on the subject. He declined because he wished to deal with other interests that had occupied him for years. "Those who can read between the lines of *'Shakespeare' Identified,"* he wrote to Eva Turner Clark on August 10, 1928,

> will not have much difficulty in detecting the direction, at least, of these other interests — though, naturally, I have avoided, in the main, using ... my Shakespeare writings ... for ventilating other matters.... To put it briefly, then, I have for very many years had a settled sense of our own age as one of increasing social and moral disruption tending towards complete anarchy, and my great wish has been to make some kind of contribution towards the solving of a problem much vaster, and more serious in its incidence, than the "Shakespeare," or any merely literary problem, could possibly be.[45]

Looney took care to identify the branch of English Positivism to which he adhered, as we have seen, by referring to Dr. Richard Congreve and J.K. Ingram. These men were leaders of the group of Positivists that retained the religious aspect of the movement, Comte's "religion of humanity," following a split in the movement that took place in 1879. This religious element provided a moral angle of attack to the rationalistic and scientific approaches to the problems of humanity, of society, that these Positivists took. Sociology was intended as a way of coordinating all of the sciences by placing them at the service of the human race at large.

One concrete result of this outlook for Dr. Congreve, a scholar and teacher who became a physician as a result of his Positivist outlook, was to urge peaceful solutions to potentially violent conflicts through generosity. He called, for instance, for England's voluntary withdrawal from Gibraltar and India. He also wrote a book that may have contributed to Looney's view of Elizabethan history — *Italy and the Western Powers, and Elizabeth of England.*[46]

J. K. Ingram, described by some as "well nigh" the best educated man of the age, first made a striking impact on the public life of his time through the publication of an anonymous poem, "The Memory of the Dead," which became a rallying cry and ballad for Irish Nationalists. (The poem begins with the words, "Who fears to speak of Ninety-eight?") But Ingram's own brand of nationalism, independence, was pacific, rather than violent or revolutionary, and he ultimately established his name in a wide range of fields — mathematics, economics, or what was then called political economy, especially, as well as literature. Following Comte, Ingram insisted that political economy should be viewed as a branch of sociology. He also followed Comte in considering society as an organism that should be, in effect, governed by "the consensus of the functions of the social system." He actively opposed the Boer War; and one of his best known sonnets is on the death of a British major that recognizes the individual courage of the man while denouncing the cause in which he died as "foul oppression."

Ingram was also the first professor of Trinity College, Dublin, with the responsibility for teaching English literature, a supplement to his duties as Erasmus Smith professor of oratory. He gave a lecture, later published, on the relationship between the chronology of Shakespeare's plays and the development of their versification. Another paper by him on "weak endings" in Shakespeare was published in 1874. Both of these could have been of use to Looney when he took up the dates and versification of works by Oxford both under his own name and as "Shakespeare."[47]

When Looney is seen in this tradition of wide and deep learning applied to problems that plague the human condition, it becomes likely that his composition of *"Shakespeare" Identified* during the First World War was an attempt to maintain and strengthen civilization when it was being overwhelmed. He said as much in a letter to Eva Turner Clark, dated November 10, 1939:

> This is where our interest in Shakespeare and all the greatest poets comes in. In the centuries that lie ahead, when the words Nazi and Hitler are remembered only with feelings of disgust and aversion and as synonyms for cruelty and bad faith, Shakespeare, Wordsworth, Tennyson & Shelley will continue to be honoured as expressions of what is most enduring and characteristic of Humanity.
>
> Amidst the darkness of the present time we shall do well therefore to make a special effort to keep alive every spark of interest in their work. More even than in normal times we need them today, however incompatible they may seem with the tragedy that overshadows us. My own work *"Shakespeare" Identified* was largely the result of an attempt to do this during the last war: a refusal to be engulfed by an untoward environment even when suffering most poignantly from the loss of many who were dear to me.
>
> This then is part of our share in the present day struggle: to insist, even in the slaughter and distress of battle-fields and bombardments by sea and air, on the supremacy of the things of the human soul.[48]

He died at Swadlincote, near Burton-on-Trent, where he temporarily made his home because of the heavy bombing in the area of Gateshead-on-Tyne, on January 17, 1944. All of the unsold copies of his books on Shakespeare were destroyed in the bombing of London.[49]

Chapter 8

Professionals, Amateurs, and the Question of Authority

Thou art not for the fashion of these times,
Where none will sweat but for promotion.

The best trained and most highly respected professional students of Shakespeare in the colleges and universities of England and America contemplated the seemingly seamless argument presented in *"Shakespeare" Identified* and quickly discovered a flaw in it. The book was written by a man with a funny name. They found their arguments against Looney where they had found their arguments in favor of William Shakspere — on a title page. Fortunately, others knew better.

Frederick Taber Cooper of Columbia University wrote of the book, "Here at last is a sane, dignified, arresting contribution to the abused and sadly discredited Shakespeare controversy.... Every right-minded scholar who seriously cares for the welfare of letters in the bigger sense should face the problem that this book presents and argue it to a finish."[1] Right-minded scholars were exceedingly few in number, at least among the professional ranks of the academic world. John Galsworthy, the novelist, though, declared the book "the best detective story I have ever read," bought up copies to circulate among his friends, and eventually worked the book and its subject into his fiction.[2]

While the book was gradually making its way, Looney once again set to work. He was convinced that the support his identification needed was a greater familiarity with Oxford's poems, most of which were then available only in a rare edition. He prepared a new edition and took the opportunity to write an introduction and explore the reevaluation of the chronology and tradition of Elizabethan poetry that his conclusions concerning Shakespeare's identity prompted.

I

Looney draws attention to an anthology of lyric poems, now best known as *Tottel's Miscellany* but originally entitled "Songs and Sonnetes written by the right honorable Lord Henry Haward, the late Earle of Surrey and Others," that was published in 1557, when Oxford was seven. The book contained work not only by Surrey but also Sir Thomas Wyatt and Lord Vaux. The Earl of Surrey had married Oxford's father's sister, and was therefore Oxford's uncle by marriage. Surrey's life was associated with Windsor Castle, where Oxford had been brought to court as a royal ward in 1562. In the first act and scene of *The Merry Wives of Windsor* these

words appear: "I had rather than forty shillings I had my Book of Songs and Sonnets here."
Looney writes:

> The play which furnishes the most precise Shakespearean topography gives not the environment of
> William Shakspere's early poetic life, but of Edward de Vere's, and the poetry to which direct ref-
> erence is made is not of William Shakspere's period, but of the period of the Earl of Oxford.[3]

More than that, the first Elizabethan anthology, *The Paradise of Dainty Devices*, published in 1576, contains work by Oxford and others, including Lord Vaux, whose poems had
been bound with those of Surrey in 1557. Vaux died in 1562 — the year of Oxford's father's
death and the year Oxford had come to court. By poetic practice, family ties, and political
outlook, Oxford provides a link between the court poets of the previous reign and the earliest of those under Elizabeth. This link finds concrete expression in *Hamlet*, where a song by
Lord Vaux is adapted and inserted as the gravedigger's song.

Looney concludes:

> Its insertion in such a place, forty years after the death of the poet, is not only an act of honour to
> his memory, but links on the great Shakespearean drama to a period of Oxford's life very far
> removed from the time usually associated with the writing of the play. Hamlet, too, is a drama of
> court life written by an Englishman who has shown himself intimate with Windsor. Elsinore is
> but Windsor thinly disguised. The introduction of this particular song connects this play also with
> the Windsor of Oxford's early days. The age of Hamlet himself, it has been pointed out, varies at
> different parts of the drama; which marks it both as the product of very many years, and also as a
> special work of self-revelation on the part of the dramatist.[4]

The Oxford theory takes us far from the atmosphere of traditional, professional scholarship
and criticism. Bound by the Stratfordian theory, the scholars have rendered Shakespeare as a
hack, rummaging through the work of others, to hammer together a serviceable piece of stage
business for the players. Such a theory cannot account for *Hamlet*.

Looney also provisionally attributes to Oxford some of the songs in John Lyly's plays —
placing them in a separate section of his edition of Oxford's poems and identifying their
source. These songs were not published in Lyly's plays until 1632 — years after Oxford, Lyly,
and William Shakspere were dead. Lyly had been Oxford's private secretary and the manager
of one of his companies of players. He dedicated his second novel, *Euphues and His England*,
to Oxford. The similarity between some of Shakespeare's songs and those of Lyly is clear.
Since Lyly did not on other occasions demonstrate a lyric gift, it is more likely that Oxford,
that is, "Shakespeare," provided the songs for Lyly's plays than that Will Shakspere was
influenced by, that is, copied from, Lyly.

In his edition of Oxford's poems, Looney showed what Oxfordian or Shakespearean
studies would look like if his theory were accepted. It would bring order where there had been
chaos, shed light on dark corners of the Elizabethan period, and continue to corroborate the
initial case made in *"Shakespeare" Identified*. Others soon joined in this work.

The Shakespeare Fellowship was organized in England, in 1922, with Sir George Greenwood as its president. Greenwood never shed his Agnosticism to become an Oxfordian, but
he respected Looney's method and tone. The Shakespeare Fellowship was not an Oxfordian
organization, but was instead open to all who wished to pursue the authorship question and
its consequences in a serious way. This conglomeration of viewpoints led to a vogue in group
theories — suggesting that Oxford, Derby, Rutland and others wrote the plays together. Group
theories continue to rely on the traditional disintegrationists, a viewpoint that has by and large
been discredited. Nonetheless, most of the Fellowship's members were Oxfordians and the
moving force behind its formation was Colonel B.R. Ward. Ward published his *The Mystery*

of Mr. W.H. in 1923, the result of a remarkable discovery that provided yet another link in the chain of circumstantial evidence that supports the hypothesis that "Shakespeare" was the Earl of Oxford.

Ward's work shows the way that traditional Shakespearean research and the Oxfordian hypothesis can be fruitfully joined. No evidence to link any of the people proposed as Mr. W.H.— William Hewes, William Herbert, Earl of Pembroke, or Henry Wriothesley, Earl of Southampton — with William Shakspere of Stratford exists. As a result, students of the subject began to favor the idea that Mr. W.H. obtained the Sonnets for the publisher, Thomas Thorpe, rather than inspiring the poet to write them. Charlotte C. Stopes, the author of the standard biography of Southampton, during a five years' search, could establish no connection between the subject of her book and William Shakspere, beyond the two signed dedications to Southampton from Shakespeare, and concluded that Mr. W.H., in Thorpe's words, "the onlie begetter" of the Sonnets, had merely provided the publisher with the manuscript. She also suggested that the dedication read like a wedding wish. Sir Sidney Lee, in his *A Life of William Shakespeare*, devotes an appendix to Thomas Thorpe and "Mr. W.H." In that appendix he argues that Mr. W.H. was William Hall, "an humble auxiliary in the publishing army" who "flits rapidly across the stage of literary history." Despite this rapid flitting, Lee is able to make these points concerning him:

> No other inhabitant of London was habitually known to mask himself under those letters. William Hall was the only man bearing those initials who there is reason to suppose was on familiar terms with Thorpe. Both were engaged at much the same period in London in the same occupation of procuring manuscripts for publication.[5]

Of course, no one could explain how William Hall had obtained the manuscript of "our ever-living poet," a term, as Looney argued, that suggested the poet was dead. Ward formulated a hypothesis based on these seemingly divergent points. If Hall obtained the manuscript near the time of his marriage and following Oxford's death, where and when would this have occurred? Oxford died at King's Place, Hackney, in 1604, and his widow was winding up his affairs in 1608 and 1609, before selling their home. Ward decided to look for a record of the marriage of William Hall in Hackney. He writes:

> I went to the Register to confirm the hypothesis that The Sonnets had been found at King's Place, and that William Hall was a Hackney man. Judge, therefore, my delight when I came across the following entry:
> "William Hall and Margery Gryffyn were joyned in matrymonye on the 4th August 1608."[6]

Subsequently, to confirm his find, Ward went through more than twenty volumes of records, trying to locate other William Halls that by date of birth, marriage, or death could fit the case. There were only four — one birth record, two death records, and only one additional marriage. Ward concludes:

> Two important points should, however, be noticed. First, that no entry so completely fulfils all the conditions as the record of William Hall to Margery Gryffyn at Hackney on August 4, 1608. And secondly, that my theory or working hypothesis guided me straight to the right Parish Register.
> The book called *Shakespeare Sonnets* was entered in the Stationers' Register on May 20, 1609. William Hall had been married just nine months before. What more suitable wedding present for him than the volume of sonnets which open with the quatrain:
>
> > From fairest creatures we desire increase
> > That thereby beauty's Rose might never die,
> > But as the riper should by time decrease,
> > His tender heir might bear his memory?

And what more suitable wedding wish than the one inscribed on the page just preceding this very sonnet:

To Mr. W. H. all happiness and that eternitie promised by our ever-living poet?[7]

Needless to say, the professional scholars and critics did not feel compelled to consider Ward's work—it was the work of an amateur, albeit an intelligent, interested individual who looked into it for the love of learning, from the desire to know. On the other hand, the professional scholars could not even produce a working hypothesis to explain how William Hall could obtain a manuscript of personal poems from William Shakspere of Stratford.

Ward's finding and argument first appeared in the *National Review*. If the professionals averted their gaze, others found it fascinating and felt drawn to try their hand at contributing to the reevaluation of the Elizabethan period that Looney had begun. Looney was delighted and in 1938 recalled the earliest Oxfordian scholarship by referring to Ward's book and others that soon followed:

> Hot-foot upon its publication, came a work of an entirely different and strikingly original character, entitled *Shakespeare Through Oxford Glasses* by Rear-Admiral H. H. Holland, C.B. Starting from the assumption that Oxford was the author of the plays, and that the first drafts of them were therefore written much earlier than the recognized Shakespeare period, Admiral Holland, who possessed an exceptional knowledge of the passing events of those days, studied the plays from the standpoint of topical allusions, and found that whilst, as is generally acknowledged, they contain but few allusions to the times of their publication or supposed date, they are full of allusions to affairs of an earlier time, both in England and abroad. In thus supplying historic evidence of the early composition of the dramas, he placed on very sound foundations what in *"Shakespeare" Identified* had been treated mainly as a strong a priori assumption.[8]

Looney urged that if William Shakspere's reputation would necessarily change as a result of his identification, Oxford's would have to also. He showed that Oxford's reputation had been determined largely by his enemies—the "new men" of the Elizabethan period who had been enriched by the confiscation of Church property and elevated to the nobility by service to the state, that is, by political maneuvering. Oxford's ancestry, extravagance, and sarcastic tongue were not likely to earn him accolades from the politicians of the period. On the other hand, his generosity, wit, and interest in the arts and sciences did win him the praises of writers, musicians, scientists, and thinkers. A serious attempt to reconcile these divergent contemporary opinions and produce the first full-length biography, based on original documents, appeared in B.M. Ward's *The Seventeenth Earl of Oxford* (1928).

Ward, an army captain and the son of B.R. Ward, was well aware of the academic hostility to the scholarship of the amateurs of the Shakespeare Fellowship. As a result, he wrote Oxford's life as a straight, scholarly biography, based on the thorough examination of masses of documents and letters, and confined his consideration of the connection between Oxford's life and Shakespeare's work to separate, clearly identified supplements to the life proper. This tactic was to some extent successful. His book remains the standard biography. He contributed scholarly articles to such respected, professional journals as the *Review of English Studies*. *The Shakespeare Pictorial*, published in Stratford-on-Avon, opened its pages to regular contributions from members of the Shakespeare Fellowship in 1930. Simultaneously, Ward had placed in the hands of Oxfordians the kind of full, documented life they needed to seriously explore Shakespeare's work.

In 1930, Canon Gerald Rendall, B.D., Litt.D., LL.D., drawing on Looney's edition of Oxford's poems, B.R. Ward's work on William Hall, and B.M. Ward's *The Seventeenth Earl of Oxford*, wrote his useful *Shakespeare's Sonnets and Edward de Vere*. Because Oxford did have a documented connection with Southampton, Rendall was content that the bulk of the Sonnets were addressed to him. He also was content to accept the order of the Sonnets as they were published. What he brought to the Sonnets, in addition to a documented life and literary tradition to serve as their context, was skill as a literary critic. For example, he explains Shakespeare's rejection of the Italian or Petrarchan Sonnet this way:

> Guided by a true instinct for the purposes to which he applied it, Shakespeare preferred the triple quatrain, with the concluding distich, to the more elaborate and rigid structure of the octave balanced by the sestet. There are gains and losses; the unity ceases to be monumental, but it becomes vertebrate and supple, the appropriate vehicle for the sonnet of personal reflection and address. The quatrorzain handling was not his own invention. The French had experimented in it, and metrically it was the form to which the Earl of Surrey inclined, adopting it in more than half the Sonnets to which his name is attached in *Tottel's Miscellany*. Other poets — among them Edward de Vere — with minor variations followed in his wake. Its danger lies in tedium and prolixity, in lack of effect; few can sustain a dominant idea at a high grade of poetic tension and expression through fourteen continuous lines. Sonneteering was a favorite game of skill with Elizabethan wits and poets; but a perusal of the output even of the best exponents is the true index of the unrivalled excellence of Shakespeare in this field of craftsmanship. This is due not only to grace of imagination, to the music of sound, and the magic of phrase, but above all to sincerity of appeal and manipulative skill in the use of his material.[9]

By 1930, Oxfordians, drawing on the work of traditional scholars, had solved a number of the problems with the Sonnets that had plagued Shakespearean scholars. Samuel Butler's suggestion that the Sonnets were, in effect, "unguarded letters" could be confirmed while maintaining his position that they were written by and to social equals — from an earl to an earl. Butler's "early" date for Sonnet 107 — 1588 — could be maintained without either twisting Oxford's life or doing violence to the chronology of the Shakespearean works. On the contrary, the one point made by Butler that rings false, that the Sonnets are the work of a very young poet who was just beginning to practice the craft, could be reasonably dropped. Oxford was then 38 years old and poems by him had appeared in print 12 years earlier.

Sigmund Freud was delighted with Rendall's book and, in 1932, wrote a correspondent: "There lies in front of me a book by Gerald H. Rendall, *Shakespeare's Sonnets and Edward De Vere*, that puts forward the thesis that those poems were addressed to the Earl of Southampton and written by the Earl of Oxford. I am almost convinced that none other than this aristocrat was our Shakespeare. In the light of that conception the Sonnets become much more understandable."[10]

Not everyone, of course, was as open-minded as Freud. In 1965, more than thirty years after Rendall wrote, A.L. Rowse published his *Shakespeare's Southampton*. He had found no more evidence than Charlotte Stopes had of a connection between William Shakspere of Stratford and Southampton. What he had found was the audacity to drop Charlotte Stopes's honesty and write as if the connection and relationship were thoroughly documented. He had also found no other explanation for the Sonnets than the one espoused by Frank Harris — that is, that they were by one of humble origin seeking the patronage of a peer. What Rowse had found was the wisdom to soft-pedal Harris's frankness — his description of Shakespeare as a fawning snob. Rowse puts a much better face on it: "Shakespeare, much encouraged by being received as the young peer's poet, naturally has more ambitious endeavors in mind."[11] While the "amateurs" who followed Looney made progress, the professionals who followed self-interest continued to march in place or trudge in circles.

In the same year that Rendall's book appeared, the first significant contribution by an American to Oxfordian scholarship was published. Eva Turner Clark's *Shakespeare's Plays in the Order of Their Writing* appeared in England in 1930 and was published in the United States the next year as *Hidden Allusions in Shakespeare's Plays*. Just as B.M. Ward had pieced together Oxford's life from original sources, Clark had the idea that the revised chronology for Shakespeare's plays suggested by Looney might have documentary support. If early drafts of Shakespeare's plays had been written by Oxford, they could have been performed at court or elsewhere in the late 1570s and the 1580s; and records of these performances might exist. Holland had shown that some of Shakespeare's plays contained references to historical events of that period. Ward's biography made it possible to find allusions to Oxford's personal circumstances, too.

What shows Clark's method most clearly is the record of a play performed at court on Tuesday, January 1, 1577: "the historie of Error [was] showen at Hampton Court on Newyeres daie at night, enacted by the Children of Powles." Clark argues that this play was an early comedy by Oxford that became known much later and much revised as *The Comedy of Errors* by "William Shakespeare."[12] Professional Shakespearean scholars, of course, knew of this reference. Some used the style of *The Comedy of Errors* and the "long, hobbling verses" they found in it to argue that it was an early play of Shakespeare's. Others realized that even early work, by the traditional chronology, would not explain the presence of lines like these in the play. They concluded that these verses were actual remnants of the "old Court-drama, of which Shakespeare made as much use as answered his purpose." In short, in this case, too, traditional scholarship could only account for its findings by postulating a Shakespeare who takes from others and revises their work. The Oxfordian position, on the other hand, places the beginning of the Shakespeare work when "long, hobbling verses" would have been the routine practice of the poet, provides for a constant development, allows enough time for the revision and reworking of plays by the author, and explains the presence of personal and historical allusions in the works. What was once extolled as the mysterious product of sheer genius, and later denigrated as the hack work of a handy man around the theater, becomes a rational subject for study and discussion — a subject that can benefit from research rather than be hindered by it: the facts found now fit the subject.

Within a single decade of the publication of *"Shakespeare" Identified*, a group of scholars had performed prodigious amounts of research and writing, established their credibility, and solved a number of problems relating to Shakespeare and the Elizabethan period at large. Looney had said that a case based on circumstantial evidence must stand or fall depending on whether it finds corroboration by turning up more and more coincidences that fit the established pattern or runs into a dead end by turning up facts that undermine the case. The work of the earliest Oxfordians strengthened his case by finding supporting evidence in times and places associated with Oxford while the professional scholars found either nothing or damaging evidence to their position in the times and places associated with William Shakspere of Stratford. Looney wryly noted that one result of this situation was "a tendency amongst Shakespeare scholars of late years to assign to the plays an earlier date than formerly. An outstanding example is a work by a perfectly orthodox scholar (Dr. A. S. Cairncross) assigning to the Shakespeare Hamlet so early a date (1588) that it is difficult to see how it could be reconciled with orthodoxy."[13]

II

The first popular presentation of the case for Oxford in the United States was "Elizabethan Mystery Man" by Charles Wisner Barrell, a journalist and photographic expert, in the

May 1, 1937, issue of *The Saturday Review of Literature*. Like William Douglass O'Connor in the preceding century, Barrell was impatient with the silence or jeers that greeted the serious scholarship of the Oxfordians and brought to the cause a cool head and a warm pen. "Smart Aleck detractors and reviewers," he wrote, "seized upon the Looney cognomen for purposes of ridicule. But the documentary facts and many hundreds of 'coincidences' connecting the mysterious Earl of Oxford with the plays and poems which the author of '*Shakespeare*' *Identified* presents in his dossier are not to be laughed off so easily."[14]

He was overly optimistic. Soon bombs were falling on London, bringing research to a halt and drowning out the roar of scholarly controversy. When the *News-Letter of the Shakespeare Fellowship* was forced to shut down, Eva Turner Clark, Louis Benezet of Dartmouth College, and Barrell organized an American Branch of the Fellowship and began to produce a newsletter, ably edited by Barrell, in this country.[15] At the end of the war, the English publication reappeared, edited first by Percy Allen and then by William Kent. But a change had come over the world. The growth of a massive system of higher education altered the way scholarship was conducted. The amateur scholar, who had been a respected and an important contributor to nineteenth century thought, who had been tolerated and able to continue between the wars, became an oddball — neither respected nor granted access to the means of communication. The hoots, snickers, and jeers that had been aimed at Looney and his early followers by academics found permanent expression in the books of professional Shakespearean scholars.

In 1964, Professor S. Schoenbaum stood in the Collegiate Church of the Holy Trinity in Stratford where he "could barely make out the monument and bust in the shadows of the north chancel."[16] Professor Schoenbaum had gone to Stratford "to attend an international conference honoring the quatercentennial of Shakespeare's birth," but "the learned papers on the bear in *The Winter's Tale*, and on *Hamlet* without words" had left him in something of a funk.[17] That brand of the blues that was peculiar to American academics in the 1960s, the sense of being or becoming "irrelevant," seems to have descended on him.

He tried to shake off this attack by conceiving a book that would be published in 1970 and entitled *Shakespeare's Lives*. What gave Professor Schoenbaum an Olympian's-eye view of the attempts to write Shakespeare's life was his cynical realization that Shakespeare's biographies were peculiar kinds of autobiography. This may well be true of all biography, Professor Schoenbaum considered, but saw clearly that it is especially true of Shakespeare's biographers because "the sublimity of the subject ensures empathy and the impersonality of the life record teases speculation!"[18]

The exclamation point is a sign that Professor Schoenbaum is warming to his subject, but also a sign that the world has entered a new age. "Impersonality" is hardly the word to describe "the life record" of William Shakspere of Stratford, as the scholars of the nineteenth century well knew. Generations of illiteracy, dung heaps, and getting and spending constitute a life record that is exceedingly personal. Professor Schoenbaum's phrase, "teases speculation," is a late twentieth century rendering of "demands explanation."

Despite a cynical, live-and-let-live way of looking at Shakespearean biography, Professor Schoenbaum knows a line must be drawn, a limit set — and he knows where to draw it and set it. His outlook permits — in fact, delights in — dealing with those scholars who have forged Shakespeareana — these will "comprise part — a fascinating part — of the story."[19] But beyond the forgers "one must reckon with the amateurs, the eccentrics, the cranks with theories. Of these the worst would be the heretics, alert to conspiracies, who saw a sinister plot to take away the plays from their true progenitor, Bacon or Marlowe or some Earl or other, and bestow them instead on the Stratford boor."[20] In his preface he has already defined "the worst" — the heretics.

Professor Schoenbaum's reference to "conspiracies" and "a sinister plot" helps us to understand why he felt irrelevant in 1964 and why he compiled a tome of more than 800 pages to tell the story of the attempts to tell Shakespeare's life story. Credibility and traditional authority were given a severe shock for Americans following the assassination of President Kennedy in November 1963. Enormous amounts of evidence were gathered and published in a series of thick volumes to assure the public that the president's murder was not the result of a conspiracy. A lone amateur, a lone eccentric, a lone crank with a theory was responsible for the murder, officialdom proclaimed. Nonetheless, doubters flourished and there was a brisk trade in books and articles that denounced this rush to judgment as a fraud. That Professor Schoenbaum saw some relation between these events and his own official, authoritative, professional view of Shakespeare became clear when he was interviewed for a PBS *Frontline* show on the authorship question in 1989. During that interview he said that he found no "grassy knoll" in Shakespeare — a reference to the site in Dallas from which, witnesses said, shots were fired, a site far from where Lee Harvey Oswald is said to have had his sharpshooter's roost.

It is probably for this reason that Professor Schoenbaum eventually jettisoned the term "heretics" for the doubters of the Shakespeare myth as antiquated and gave them a new label that better reflected the modern, massive, therapeutic state. He calls their positions "deviations," implying that they are deviationists. He harps on the therapeutic by introducing Delia Bacon's madness on the first page of his preface. By the time he considers the Oxfordians the machinery of his approach is well-oiled and the sneers click into place: "The book, '*Shakespeare' Identified*, appeared in 1920, and initiated the Oxford movement, which has given the Baconians a run for their madness."[21] It is not the competition between Baconians and Oxfordians that has caused Professor Schoenbaum to let so much ink. He is quick to point out that Looney "makes a virtue of amateurism" and it is this that has moved the professional Schoenbaum to write. Of course, no one knows what Shakespeare's life was. Every attempt to find out throws light on the person who makes the attempt rather than on Shakespeare. But books and articles must be written and published; *something* has to be taught in high schools, colleges, and universities. Professor Schoenbaum writes in support of the proposition that what is to be published and taught on Shakespeare should be determined by professionals.

It is for this reason that he does not analyze or refute the case Looney made. Instead, he associates Looney with madness, defines him as an amateur, and then patronizes him: "Without the advantages of historical or literary training, Looney had now to find the candidate who met all the general and special requirements."[22] Professor Schoenbaum, if he read Looney at all closely, would know that he concluded that Shakespeare was an aristocrat with feudal connections and Lancastrian sympathies by his study of the plays and gathering the views of professional Shakespearean scholars. He ignores all that and laments: "It is difficult to escape the conclusion that snobbery led Looney, a gentle retiring soul, to seek a Shakespeare with blue blood in his veins."[23] How hard did Professor Schoenbaum try to escape this conclusion? He could have energetically demonstrated, for instance, why William Shakspere of Stratford should have gone out of his way to protect the reputation of Robert de Vere, the earl of Oxford, who was a favorite of the historical Richard II, in his play on Richard. As Looney writes, "Shakespeare, whoever he was, had evidently some special reason for screening the Earl of Oxford. He had not overlooked him, for at the end of the play the Earl is mentioned as having been executed for supporting the King; possibly the only thing in his favor that could be recorded." In a footnote, Looney draws attention to the fact that the name "Oxford" was replaced in the First Folio edition of the play.[24] Professor Schoenbaum does not even consider any of this.

Professor Schoenbaum is quick to admit that he has not reached all of his conclusions on his own. He acknowledges his debt to previous historians of the upholders of "deviations." For instance, he is clearly indebted to the patter of Frank W. Wadsworth, the author of *The Poacher of Stratford* (1958).[25] Wadsworth predictably introduces Looney's name into his account with the parenthetical explanation to the reader, "not to be confused with the Baconian, George M. Battey."[26] Wadsworth, perhaps following Professor Oscar J. Campbell, misrepresents the work of Charles Wisner Barrell on "Shakespeare" portraits. Barrell used x-ray and infrared photography to demonstrate that three portraits of "Shakespeare" were done over paintings of portraits of the Earl of Oxford. Barrell's article on the subject in *Scientific American* clearly shows that he undertook this work as an Oxfordian — that is, as a possible additional source of circumstantial evidence in support of Looney's theory, a chance to turn up more coincidences. Much of his article is a brief restatement of that case and a tracing of the provenance of the paintings, much of which had been accomplished earlier by members of the Shakespeare Fellowship. Wadsworth, apparently secure in the knowledge that few of his readers would know this background or bother to look it up, felt free to ignore the context and concludes that while "orthodox Shakespeareans praise Mr. Barrell for the brilliant discovery of a long-lost Oxford painting, they insist with old-fashioned logic that the mere fact of some nineteenth century hack's having painted the Lord over with a likeness of the actor proves no more than that their man had an even higher market value than a seventeenth earl."[27]

Wadsworth knows that the market is the determiner of value, but it is strange that he refers to Shakspere here as an actor rather than an author — the issue under discussion. Old-fashioned logic is of no avail without old-fashioned honesty. If the major premise is a lie, the conclusion can be true only by accident. It is likely that Wadsworth is less guilty of misrepresentation than of merely copying. Professor Campbell's critique of Barrell's work seems to be the source of all the subsequent misrepresentations of it. For that reason, Looney's response can serve to answer not only Campbell, but also Wadsworth, and H.N. Gibson, author of *The Shakespeare Claimants*, who is described by Professor Schoenbaum as "the most recent authority," obviously a professional, but who so incompetently copies someone that Barrell appears in his book as Mr. Charles Russell.[28] Schoenbaum, too, merely resorts to misrepresentation to dismiss Barrell.

Looney writes:

> I accuse him [Campbell] of a deliberate attempt, not to present the Oxford case fairly and squarely, as honest opponents of ideas do with the cases they controvert, but to set it forth so flimsily, and even grotesquely, that hardly anyone but an imbecile could very well believe in it if it rested on nothing more substantial. This is the kind of argumentation one associates with political maneuvering rather than a serious quest for the truth on great issues and it makes one suspect that he is not very easy in his own mind about the case.[29]

It is this belief in the existence of the truth and humanity's ability to find it that separates Looney and his followers from the professional scholars and critics. They, like the other statists abroad in the world, the adherents of various isms of one kind or another, believe that truth does not exist and that the vacuum left by its absence must be filled by a kind of ideology made up of the mere assertions of authorities, professional authorities, qualified authorities — authorities who will not examine but only repeat the statements of other authorities. They are not scholars at all, in the usual sense of the word — people with the leisure to pursue and discover truths, and make those truths known so that others can examine them, probe them, accept, reject, or modify them. They are instead professional bureaucrats, servants of the state's cultural apparatus, who inform the people of the currently fashionable brand of truth by asserting it, repeatedly, and at great length.

Despite this growing presence of noxious gas in the cultural atmosphere, Oxfordians went about their work. One of the major losses in the record that accompanied the dismissal of Barrell with a misrepresentation was the failure to recognize that his work on the portraits was a mere sideline to his more traditional and valuable contributions to our knowledge of Shakespeare — particularly his tour de force of glossing a previously impenetrable Elizabethan text, Thomas Nashe's *Epistle Dedicatorie to Strange News*, which showed that Nashe addressed Oxford as "Gentle Master William."[30] Barrell also fixed the identify of Sir Edward Vere, a Jacobean scholar and soldier, as the illegitimate son of Oxford and Anne Vavasour, the Oxfordian candidate for "the dark lady." This identification had eluded the great Elizabethan scholar E.K. Chambers when he wrote of Sir Edward Vere in his biography of Sir Henry Lee, the Queen's champion.[31]

Other Oxfordians showed the strain of working in isolation and making little headway. Percy Allen in England conjectured that Southampton was Oxford's son by Queen Elizabeth — a conjecture prompted by his reading of the Sonnets prior to Barrell's discoveries concerning Oxford's private life. Baconians had entertained similar conjectures. Allen later thought he had solved the Shakespeare problem with the assistance of spiritualism. Two leading American Oxfordians, Dorothy and Charlton Ogburn, in their *This Star of England* (1952), an exhaustive examination of Shakespeare's work in the context of Oxford's life, independently decided that Oxford and Elizabeth were Southampton's parents. Wadsworth thinks it possible to discredit their work by reducing their argument in this way: "Central to this thesis is the Ogburns' respect for the Elizabethan pun. Fair Youth, Vere Youth — Q.E.D.!"[32] Setting out to ridicule what appears to be ridiculous is easy but rarely illuminating. Wadsworth's approach to this far-fetched theory must be compared with that of Gerald W. Phillips, an Oxfordian scholar. His comments, published in 1953, will be quoted at length in order to show the clear difference, in method and tone, between scholarly debate and misrepresentation and abuse:

> The authors of this book maintain that a son was born to the Earl of Oxford and the Queen in June 1574, either at Havering or some place unknown. They support this chiefly by inferences from poems, especially Gascoigne's, and from plays.
>
> The direct evidence offered (beginning at p. 821) is contained in Allen and Ward's pamphlet, to which reference should be made. They interpret it thus. In May 1574, the Queen's anxiety was due, not to "grave matters of State," as recorded, but to expectation of the birth of a child. She went to Havering of the Bower for the purpose of concealing that birth; and (they say) we do not know how long she stayed there, nor where she was until 28th June. Oxford's flight to the continent before 18th July was due, they think, to fear of the consequences of misbehavior.
>
> Due consideration of the evidence, however, will show that the Queen's movements were, in fact, as follows:
>
> MAY Leicester told Shrewsbury that the Queen had, for many days, been much troubled about some weighty causes of State, and was doubtful what to do about them.
>
> MAY 10TH Talbot wrote to Shrewsbury that on Saturday week (i.e. 19th–22nd May) the Queen was to go to Havering of the Bower, meaning to stay there till she began her progress to Bristol.
>
> In the latter end of May she passed six days in retirement at Havering, and was meditating a longer progress.
>
> MAY 24TH There was some talk of a progress to Bristol, but there was great opposition to her going so far. Hatton, being ill, wanted to go to "the Spawe" instead.

JUNE She returned to Court. This is evident, because (a) Talbot, "here at courte" wrote to Shrewsbury that "Her Matie styrreth litell abrode." He could not say this if she was in Essex or on a progress; (b) Talbot and Leicester wrote, from Court, that she remained sad and pensive during the month of June. They could not know this if she was absent; (c) She was afraid of some danger (to the State, presumably) arising during her absence, and therefore told Burghley, through Walsingham, not to wait upon her at Woodstock, as she had intended, but to stay in London; (d) Hatton now got leave to go to the Spaw, with Dr. Julio. If the Queen was away, he could not have done this; (e) She now dealt with a suit by Oxford, which she did not favour, "and hereupon his behavior before her gave her some offence." Talbot, at Court, could know this only if the Queen and Oxford were also there. Probably the suit was for leave to travel. (To go from Essex to Bristol, it would in any case be necessary to pass through London, and certainly it would be from Havering, which is just beyond Romford.)

JULY She began her progress to Bristol, and arrived there on 14th August.

AUGUST 5TH Oxford, returning, from his unlicensed absence abroad, joined her on her progress.

AUGUST 7TH He was pardoned, and attended her till 16th September.

The matter, therefor, is quite simple. The Queen went to Havering for a short rest from her worries, and then returned to her duties till July. There is no vestige of evidence of the birth of any child, or of any connection of Oxford with the Queen, except that she refused his suit.[33]

To the uninitiated, this careful gathering and analysis of evidence might look like professional scholarship and the rapid-fire quips of Wadsworth might look like amateurish antics. Professor Schoenbaum fares even worse than Wadsworth on the Ogburns. He makes again Wadsworth's point about the pun on Fair Youth and then strikes out on his own, forced to deal with a book that appeared after Wadsworth wrote. "Without once referring to *This Star of England*," Professor Schoenbaum fumes, "the Ogburns warmed over their stew as *Shakespeare: The Man behind the Name* (1962), which has at least the merit of comparative brevity."[34] Confusing names seems to be an occupational hazard with professional Shakespearean scholars. In this case, Professor Schoenbaum must have failed to consult that

Edward de Vere, Seventeenth Earl of Oxford. (From the portrait attributed to Marcus Gheeraedts, formerly in the collection of His Grace, the Duke of St. Albans. Portrait image reproduced by permission of the portraits owners, Bonner Miller Cutting, Minos Miller III and James Valcour Miller, and its copyright owner Minos Publishing Company, a wholly owned division of Ruth Loyd Miller, A Professional Law Corporation, Jennings, LA 70546–1309. All rights reserved under U.S., International, and Pan-American Copyright Conventions. Copyright: 1980, 1981, 1984, 1988, 1990, 1992, 1994, 1997. Minos Publishing Company, Jennings, LA 70546–1309.)

sturdy source of Shakespearean evidence, the title page. The Charton Ogburn who coauthored *This Star of England* was Charlton Ogburn, Sr., Dorothy Ogburn's husband. Dorothy Ogburn and her son, Charlton Ogburn, Jr., coauthored *Shake-speare: The Man behind the Name*. If Professor Schoenbaum had gone beyond the title page, he would have found more merits in the latter book than just brevity. It is a sober, concise, and lively introduction to the Oxford case, not a warmed over version of *This Star of England*.

When Professor Schoenbaum is not leaping to conclusions himself, he copies the conclusions that others have leapt to before him. This leads him far astray on the work of Dr. A. Bronson Feldman. He writes: "Inevitably, some of Freud's followers stumbled after him into the Oxfordian bog; most notably Dr. A. Bronson Feldman, who in a series of articles has explored the workings of de Vere's unconscious in *The Comedy of Errors*, *Othello*, and the Sonnets."[35] How does Professor Schoenbaum know that Feldman became an Oxfordian by following Freud? The answer is not far to seek. He found it in a book, Professor Norman Holland's *Psychoanalysis and Shakespeare* (1966).

Professor Holland, like Professor Schoenbaum, knows down deep somewhere that scholarship and criticism are not what they once were. They know that these endeavors once produced results that had the look, at least, of progress. The problem they face is how to continue pursuing these endeavors once they have reached a dead end. Professor Schoenbaum found an escape hatch in writing the story of Shakespeare's biographers. Professor Holland saw that psychoanalysis could provide a way of dispensing old wine in new bottles. But Professor Holland had an additional problem. Not everyone in the academic world respects Freud's theories and the jargon of psychoanalysis. Worse than that, Freud had been more than hospitable to Looney's answer to the authorship question and had said so in print. Professor Holland devised two strategies, to use the language of the modern academic world, for separating Freud from his beliefs about Shakespeare so that he, Holland, would be free to apply Freud's theories to literature, including Shakespeare. First, he would use Freud's theories to explain the master's aberration, his faith in Looney's theory. Second, he would pummel the lone Freudian writer who was also an Oxfordian, A. Bronson Feldman, by arguing that, no doubt for psychological reasons, he had blindly and wrong-headedly followed where Freud had led him. Neither of these strategies is supported by any evidence at all.

Professor Schoenbaum uses psychoanalysis as a weapon against all Oxfordians, including Freud, by relying on the authority of Professor Holland. "According to Norman Holland," he writes, "Freud's urge to dethrone Shakespeare stems from his view of 'the artist as a kind of totem whom he both resented and emulated.'"[36] This tells us nothing about Freud and less about Shakespeare. All it tells us is that Norman Holland's urge to dethrone Freud stems from his view of the father of psychoanalysis as a kind of totem whom he both resented and emulated. That Professor Holland had the bad taste to emote in this way in public is his business. But Professor Schoenbaum found Holland's speculations useful — with them he could get rid of Freud on Shakespeare and go on to explain away the Oxfordian position as "manifestations of filial ambivalence," but in terms that show his underlying concern, defending his professional status against rank amateurs: "The heretic's choice of de Vere, courtly amateur rather than professional man of letters, confirms his identification with his idealized choice, for the Oxfordians are, almost to a man, dilettante scholars."[37]

It is this point that makes plain why he must follow Professor Holland into the bog of falsehood about Dr. A. Bronson Feldman. Feldman was not a "dilettante scholar." His professional credentials were at least as good as those of Professors Schoenbaum and Holland. He became a Freudian after he had been an active Oxfordian scholar and after he had earned the Ph.D. in English literature at the University of Pennsylvania. He had written his doctoral dissertation there on the impact of the Dutch wars on the Tudor stage, under respected Elizabethan scholars including Conyers Read.

As early as 1947 Feldman had demonstrated that Robert Armin, known to professional scholars as "Shakespeare's Jester," was, when he was with the Lord Chamberlain's Players, and later the King's Men, a self-declared servant of the Earl of Oxford.[38] Feldman's thoroughly documented article, adding yet another pertinent coincidence to an ever-lengthening chain of coincidences, appeared in *The Shakespeare Fellowship Quarterly* when he was an instructor in English at Temple University and before be became a Freudian analyst. There is nothing Freudian about the article. It is a straightforward piece of literary and historical scholarship by one who had been through the requisite training. Feldman's skepticism towards Freudian analysis was in part overcome because Freud had the clarity to see the truth and value of the case presented by Looney in *"Shakespeare" Identified*.

Looney, in fact, answered all the professional scholars who sought to protect their livelihoods and respectability, to protect their authority, by attacking him and his followers with misrepresentations and ridicule. He wrote: "I have felt singularly indifferent to it [the ridicule] from the first; perhaps because that, feeling so confident that the truth was clear, I felt some pity for minds that could not see it."[39]

III

Two very different monuments of Shakespearean scholarship by Americans were published in 1975. One, as Professor Schoenbaum would certify, was by a professional scholar, the other by an amateur. One maintained the position that William Shakspere of Stratford was "Shakespeare"; the other that the Earl of Oxford was the man who used the "Shakespeare" pen name. Both are lavishly illustrated, printed, and bound; and each constitutes a kind of summing up of their respective positions.

The first is Professor S. Schoenbaum's *William Shakespeare: A Documentary Life*. The other is Ruth Loyd Miller's two volume edition of Looney's *"Shakespeare" Identified*. These two publications curiously illustrate how things stood with the Shakespeare authorship question as the twentieth century moved into its final decades.

In the first paragraph of his Preface, Professor Schoenbaum goes on the defensive: "I am conscious that to some my undertaking may seem improbable. What documents? Which records?"[40] He admits that no one attempted to gather the materials for a proper literary biography of Shakspere when eye witnesses and personal documents might still have been obtained. "Nevertheless," he writes,

> we do well to resist luxuriating in a sense of deprivation. Time scattered the Shakespeare papers like leaves before the wind, destroying a number (how many we cannot say), but tucking some safely away in odd corners, and preserving others under the kindly dust of the muniments room. Then, at first tentatively but soon gaining momentum, the movement to recover these relics got under way.[41]

Would the "Shakespeare" papers have been transformed into "relics" if they were not associated with the author of the plays and poems? Not likely. But these relics do not grant us entry into the life of the writer or even a writer, but rather, as Professor Schoenbaum writes, they "enable us to enter into the quotidian life of a vanished age."[42] How is it that these documents can be associated with the writer of Shakespeare's plays and poems? Professor Schoenbaum says they are. By the fourth paragraph of the Preface he says that Shakspere's father's "rise to civic eminence" appears in the documents, and we "see his poet son marrying under awkward circumstances, turning to the courts for the recovery of petty debts, and acquiring social respectability."[43] What is the basis for the description of John Shakspere's son William as his "poet son"? There is none. It is a mere assumption. It is a conclusion that has been reached by a leap that the documents do not support. Professor Schoenbaum has shown that his professionalism permits him to copy the mistaken assumptions and conclusions of others about his own contemporaries. There is no reason to think he is incapable of making the same kind of mistake with regard to a person who has been dead for more than three hundred years. Despite that, he moves on to even surer ground in the same paragraph by introducing a quotation from *Hamlet*. Having assumed that William Shakspere was a poet, Professor Schoenbaum pretends to know what he wrote, and the identification of the man whose documentary remains he has gathered and published with the author of *Hamlet* is complete. Two leaps and home free. Neat, no?

Despite Professor Schoenbaum's concern for the sparseness of the record, he does not reproduce all of the documents that relate to Will Shakspere's life. He has room to reproduce a section of Richard Hathaway's last will and testament. He provides his readers with picturesque views of Stratford in the eighteenth century. But he neither mentions nor provides the documents associated with two actions that involved William Shakspere — or, at least, some William Shakespeare, perhaps not the citizen of Stratford.

Ruth Loyd Miller's edition of "*Shakespeare" Identified* at least mentions both of these incidents and does reproduce part of the documentary evidence concerning one of them. Looney writes of William Shakspere that "the single money transaction which connects him with London during these years, the recovery of a debt of 7 pounds from John Clayton in 1600, might easily be the result of a short visit to the metropolis, or merely the work of an agent."[44] What Looney fails to point out is that Shakspere, or, at least, some "Willelmus Shackspere" had loaned these seven pounds to John Clayton on May 22, 1592, in Cheapside. The subject of Professor Schoenbaum's documentary life or someone with a similar name made a loan in May 1592, in London. If this someone is the subject of the professor's book, then the first thing he is known by the documents to have done in London is lend money. More than that, he would use the courts to recover the loan almost eight years later. Whether or not this is in keeping with the author of Shakespeare's works is beside the point. The transaction is certainly in keeping with what we know of William Shakspere of Stratford as the quotidian life suggested by the documents Professor Schoenbaum reproduces and discusses amply shows.

Why does he leave it out? Halliwell-Phillipps accepted the transaction as a documentary part of William Shakspere's life. It is no doubt because later professional scholars did not agree with Halliwell-Phillipps. E.K. Chambers agrees with Sidney Lee that there is no basis for identifying the party to this transaction with the dramatist and poet. It might be thought that the mere name of the man and the location of the transaction, Cheapside, would be enough of a basis for identifying the person who made this loan with William Shakspere of Stratford, even if it cannot be shown that he is the dramatist and poet. But no, the authorities have determined otherwise — for no apparent reason other than they do not want the record of William Shakspere's life in London to begin with him lending money. He can do that later, in Stratford, after he has made a killing as a poet and playwright. But if he is to be the Horatio Alger of English letters, he simply cannot start his London career in that way.[45] Professor Schoenbaum silently bows to these authorities and, thus, becomes an authority himself.

The other document that Professor Schoenbaum neither gives nor discusses in his documentary biography is the testimony of Thomasina Heminge Ostler that the "Willelum Shakespeare" who was a shareholder in the Globe Theater was dead in 1615, that is, the year before the death of William Shakspere, the subject of Professor Schoenbaum's book. Professor Schoenbaum is certainly aware of this legal document. He wrote of it in his *Shakespeare's Lives* this way: "In Ostler vs. Heminges (29 October 1615) the daughter of Shakespeare's old friend Heminges sued her father when he withheld the shares she expected to inherit after her husband's death."[46] This document does not demonstrate that William Shakspere was a writer, certainly, but it does connect him with the actors and the theater that are associated with Shakespeare's plays. Why does Professor Schoenbaum fail to reproduce the document? He quotes various authorities on the estimated earnings William Shakspere supposedly derived as a shareholder in the Globe. But why does he decline to even list the suit of Thomasina Heminge Ostler in his index?

It may be that between 1970 and 1975, that is, between the publication of his *Shakespeare's Lives* and the publication of his *William Shakespeare: A Documentary Life*, he realized that this document showed that either William Shakspere of Stratford was not a shareholder in the Globe or that he did not die as late as 1616. Professor Schoenbaum and all the world have documentary evidence that he died in 1616. What that leaves is the fatal conclusion that the shareholder in the Globe was not William Shakspere of Stratford, who is the subject of Professor Schoenbaum's documentary life.

Ruth Loyd Miller, following two Oxfordian scholars, Louis Benezet and Gwynneth Bowen, published the testimony of Thomasina Heminges Ostler "in the quaint Latin of medieval law" in her edition of *"Shakespeare" Identified* and writes:

> Thomasina is alleging Nicholaus Brend, a knight, leased the site [of the Globe] to Richard and Cuthbert Burbadge, gentlemen of London, and to Willelmo Shakespeare, Augustino Phillips and Thome Pope of London, *dead gentlemen*. The words used are generosis defunctis, and the first names of the three are in the dative case, in apposition with generosis. Willelmo Kempe, in the next line, is referred to as "a gentleman from London recently deceased. (Kemp is mentioned as dead in Heywood's *Apology*, circa 1608, and in Dekker's *Gull's Hornbook*, 1609.)
>
> According to Chambers, Augustine Phillips died in May of 1605, and Thomas Pope before February of 1604. Edward de Vere, Lord Oxford, who had been the sustaining force behind the acting acompanies [sic], died on June 24, 1604. But William Shakspere was still alive in Stratford when this suit was filed, c. 9 October, 1615.
>
> There was no advantage to be gained by Thomasina in misrepresenting a material fact in her pleadings.[47]

Miller's monument of Shakespearean scholarship is very different from that of Professor Schoenbaum. She does not begin with an assumption, but rather with Looney's carefully prepared and presented circumstantial case. She supplements that case with Looney's edition of Oxford's poems and healthy selections from the best Oxfordian scholars — the Wards, Holland, Rendall, Clark, Barrell, Feldman, Benezet, Bowen, and others. Finally, she also adds the results of her own research and illustrates the volumes with pertinent portraits and documents. In short, her work presents a documentary life of a poet and playwright.

Professor Schoenbaum's book results from a mistaken assumption supported by suppression of evidence. Miller's book results from a rational argument supported by circumstantial evidence. The first is the work of a professional scholar. The second is the work of a professional lawyer and an amateur scholar. Most importantly, the first is false and the second is true. Professor Schoenbaum felt compelled to defend the Stratford myth. Miller, on the other hand, has earned the right to say with Henry James that the Stratford myth is "the biggest and most successful fraud ever practiced on a patient world" and to proclaim with Shakespeare's Puck, combining infinite exasperation with unimpaired affection, "What fools these mortals be!"

Chapter 9

The Growing Oxfordian Challenge

And therefore as a stranger give it welcome.

An odd little volume with a paper cover the color of mustard appeared from an obscure publisher, Lovelore Press, in 1977. The book was entitled *Hamlet Himself* and its author was Bronson Feldman.

The book displayed none of the marks that are customary, even required, of a book that will be distributed and sold in bookstores. It had no ISBN, no listed price, no publisher's address, and no blurb — that wonderful word coined by Gelett Burgess and defined by him as "a noise made by a publisher." The book's cover had no illustration, just stark but sturdy sans serif type; and there was no photograph or biography of the author. In fact there was nothing to indicate directly that the author of this book was the Abraham Feldman who thirty years earlier had shown that Robert Armin, the actor known as Shakespeare's clown, was a self-confessed servant of Edward de Vere, Earl of Oxford.

Still, the book's dedication and introduction were enough to suggest that the author was a long-standing Oxfordian. The book was dedicated to two men, Gelett Burgess, the humorist, described as someone "whose immortality was thrust upon him by admirers of 'The Purple Cow,' Bromides and Blurbs, but who wanted to be known as the merriest of American champions of the Shakespeare-Oxford doctrine," and Charles Wisner Barrell, described as "the greatest American scholar, researcher and discoverer in the dramatic empire of Shakespeare." The introduction consists of four pages reprinted from the June 1951 issue of a journal of opinion called *The Critic and Guide*. Feldman had written and published those pages to attract readers of *The Critic and Guide* to the Oxford theory of Shakespeare authorship in celebration of the 401st anniversary of De Vere's birth. The pages offer a brisk retelling of Oxford's life with parallels to it found in Shakespeare's works. Feldman ended the piece by drawing attention to Ward's life of Oxford and J. Thomas Looney's *"Shakespeare" Identified*, and by stating that the anniversary of De Vere's birth "takes on poignant meaning to people who have delved into his life and paralleled it with the secret confessions called the comedies and tragedies of William Shakespeare."

In short, the dedication and introduction to Bronson Feldman's *Hamlet Himself* established the scholarly tradition of which the mustard-colored volume was a part, if not a culmination. It was a tradition that accepted Looney's identification of Shakespeare as a working hypothesis, a starting point, and went on from it to add evidence for that identification by digging up documents relating to De Vere's life and showing how that documented life fit and illuminated the plays and poems of Shakespeare. Feldman extended that tradition by applying its method and fulfilling its purpose in an exhaustive examination of Shakespeare's most popular and most self-revelatory play, *Hamlet*.

But that tabloidesque reference to "secret confessions" suggests the way in which Feldman veered from and broadened his tradition. He had supplemented his Ph.D. in Tudor Drama from the University of Pennsylvania by becoming a lay Freudian psychoanalyst. His analysis of *Hamlet* was as much a reaction against the traditional Freudian analysis of the play by the English analyst Ernest Jones who had no sympathy with Freud's acceptance of Looney's theory as it was an expansion of the scholarly tradition epitomized by the writings of Charles Wisner Barrell. The dedication of Feldman's *Hamlet Himself* is not unlike the ghost in *Hamlet*, a memory and an impulse that motivates the author to seek a new position that is indebted to but differs from the position maintained in the past, in 1951. As a result, *Hamlet Himself* is a monograph with a split personality, that is, it is divided into two major sections. Both sections deserve attention.

I

The first section of the little book, entitled "From the Sublime" begins with a survey of the shortcomings and incredulities caused by the traditional attribution of *Hamlet* to William Shakspere of Stratford and the theory of the play's composition based on that attribution. Feldman summarizes the problems caused by assuming the trigger for the writing of the play was the death of John Shakspere, who was buried on September 9, 1601. He makes fun of the rapidity with which the Stratford man must have written, for instance, and points out that William Shakspere's ability to write about deeply personal matters immediately after the triggering event flies in the face of the experience of such writers as Wordsworth and Stendhal. Finally, Feldman reminds his readers that companies of players opposed the printing of plays that were new — that had not yet become stale, flat, and unprofitable. The traditional theory of the composition of the play strains credulity beyond the breaking point.[1]

Even worse, there are clear contemporary references to *Hamlet* that predate John Shakspere's death by more than a decade. As a result of these early references to the play, traditional scholars decided there must have been an earlier play by someone other than Shakespeare that Shakespeare based his play on — the mythical but scientific-sounding *Ur-Hamlet* that high school and college students have been told about for almost a century as if there were good and substantial reasons for believing the play ever existed. More than that, traditional scholars who have no patience with the methods and efforts of anti–Stratfordians decided who wrote the *Ur-Hamlet*, Thomas Kyd, because of their faith that Kyd was the author of *The Spanish Tragedy*, one of the most popular Elizabethan plays of the 1580s. Feldman concludes that the demands that the traditional view of the authorship and date of composition of *Hamlet* make "on our credulity and common sense are too many and severe." He turns to an examination of *Hamlet* as a play written by De Vere originally in the 1580s and revised throughout his life as a far more rational and enlightening enterprise.

Basically, Feldman surveys chronologically the events, people, published works, and shreds of language that existed between 3 August 1562, the date of the death of De Vere's father, and 17 March 1584, the date Feldman suggests for the beginning of the original composition of *Hamlet*, which cast shadows or produce echoes in some version of the play. The result is rich with facts that help us understand Shakespeare, *Hamlet*, and ourselves. A few examples will serve to establish the value of Feldman's method.

Feldman cites a letter from William Cecil, Lord Burghley, the model for Polonius and

De Vere's father-in-law, in which he writes of Oxford, "there is much more in him of under-standing than any stranger to him would think." Feldman then writes:

> In copying that last remark, a line from the first printed version of Hamlet recurred to me, King Claudius's comment on the prince: "There's more in him than shallow eyes can see." Parallel to both opinions may be set the words of Polonius on the surprising sense that Hamlet revealed in the midst of his habitual riddling talk:" How pregnant sometimes his replies are! A happiness that often madness hits on."[2]

He shows how Shakespeare adapted his source material to perfectly fit the family life of the Cecils that Oxford had learned to know so well while living as William Cecil's ward:

> The reader has probably noticed a curious difference between the ballad of Jepthah as given by Bishop Percy and the song recited by Hamlet. Instead of "He had one only daughter and no more," he declaims: "One fair daughter, and no more." The model for Polonius had two daughters, Anne and Elizabeth. Only the elder seems to have won from observers the tribute of a pretty, attractive girl.[3]

Feldman also shows how the literary interests of the young De Vere made themselves manifest in *Hamlet*. For instance, Oxford published a translation by Thomas Bedingfield of a book known as *Cardanus' Comfort* in 1573. Some traditional Shakespearean scholars thought that this book of Italian philosophy was the book Hamlet is meant to read on stage, and Hardin Craig called *Cardanus' Comfort* "Hamlet's Book." The content of the book clearly influenced the author of *Hamlet*.[4]

These examples are drawn from just three of Feldman's pages. The cumulative effect of this piling up of parallels between a firm, knowable, documented life of the author and an imaginative work by that author is stunning and irresistible. It demonstrates why the play is very much alive even though the author has been dead for more than four hundred years. The author poured his life into his work.

Throughout this first section of the book, despite the psychoanalytic context in which it is set, Feldman basically uses the traditional methods of a literary historian and critic. He demonstrates a rigorous, scholarly conscience and an historian's respect for evidence through-out. When he conjectures, he does so within limits set by the documents and credibility, and he clearly informs his readers when they are reading speculation. This combination of thor-ough knowledge and restrained yet imaginative conjecture makes *Hamlet Himself* a feast of Shakespearean scholarship, a feast that would literally be impossible based on the traditional attribution and theory of composition of the play.

II

In the second section of the book, entitled "To The Subliminal," Feldman continues and completes his chronological survey of the life of De Vere as it is reflected in the play and then carries out a highly literate psychoanalytic case study. The prose still bristles with facts. One example will suffice.

The earliest public performance of *Hamlet* that has left a record that has been found is from 1594. Feldman uses this date as a way to gather facts from the life of De Vere, the his-tory of the companies of actors of the Elizabethan period, and the life of William Shakspere of Stratford, and then organize those facts in an attempt to describe a credible reality. The passage deserves to be cited at length to demonstrate his method:

> Earl Edward gave up the game of courtier and settled with his Countess in the suburb of Stoke Newington, near the playhouse where the Admiral's servants and the Chamberlain's men acted

Hamlet on June 8, 1594. This Chamberlain's company had been recently organized, round the nucleus of Lord Strange's troop. Strange became the Earl of Derby in September 1593 and the troop was called by his new title until April 1594 when he died. His brother William Stanley succeeded to the earldom and married Elizabeth Vere. But he did not take over the patronage of the Derby players. In May they obtained the status of servants with Henry Carey, the Chamberlain of the Queen.

The company included the enigmatic talent of William Shakspere of Stratford on Avon, whose name first appears in the records of the troop this year. No one knows when Shakspere, the son of a butcher, glover, and sterquinarian, became a member. Some time after the christening of his twins Hamnet and Judith in February 1585, he went to London to look for a job. The next we know of him (apart from a vague assertion by his father that in 1587 he had concurred in a Warwickshire trade in real estate) is that in 1592 he had enough funds to lend one John Clayton seven pounds in Cheapside, and enough theatrical fame to prompt a sneer from the scribbler of *Greene's Groatsworth of Wit* against his practice of usury and his pretense to literary skill. (Greene did not write the Groatsworth; the evidence of the text preponderantly indicates Henry Chettle as the culprit author.) A tradition of Shakspere's family hold that he earned his first fellowship in a cry of players by attracting the good-will of an unknown gentleman who rescued him from the wages of horse-holding at the door of a theater.

That Shakspere's benefactor and master was the Lord Chamberlain of England, you will readily understand when you see the affirmation of Robert Armin, the clown of the Chamberlain's company, about his instructor and lord. "I take my journey," Armin wrote in December 1599," (to wait on the right honorable good Lord, my Master whom I serve) to Hackney." Hackney was the village outside London where the Earl of Oxford moved in 1596, a short distance for a horse to his beloved theaters. He resided there, at "King's Place," until his death in June 1605.[5]

These few paragraphs, bulging with parentheses for the sake of completeness, serve to indicate how the literary history of the Elizabethan period would have to be revised if it were to be based on the facts as they have been collected throughout the nineteenth and twentieth centuries and how that revision would bring about a radical reevaluation of the reputations of two people, Edward de Vere, Earl of Oxford, and William Shakspere of Stratford-on-Avon.

This reevaluation clearly would not entail hero-worship or hagiography with regard to Oxford if it were up to Feldman. The vigor of his psychoanalytic analysis leaves little room for those all-too-human tendencies. "The truth is," Feldman writes, "Hamlet is radically immature and sick.... My own diagnosis of Hamlet's malady would place it in the category of hysteria, bordering on narcissic derangement or paranoia." Feldman derives this diagnosis by an analysis of De Vere's unconscious, a dark, weird, and subterranean region dominated by urges to lust and murder. As a result, Feldman is even willing to listen to and learn from Oxford's enemies.

For instance, Feldman's diagnosis is in part dependent on the recognition of a homoerotic streak in the make up of Oxford and, thus, Shakespeare. He points out that Oxford's enemies accused him of buggery and specifically mentioned Oxford's mistreatment of an Italian boy named Auratio. Feldman is able to suggest how what Oxford's enemies meant to be a sordid and discrediting incident potentially found a quite different meaning in *Hamlet*. "The memory of the Italian lad whom Oxford selected for one of his trials in pederasty may have given our dramatist the name of Hamlet's singular friend"—Horatio.[6]

In the end, Feldman shows that Oxford's disillusionment with the members of the old nobility and the Catholic party—basically Lord Henry Howard and his followers—through De Vere's discovery of their willingness to sell out their country, deeply affected the earl's life and outlook. There is a tendency among some Oxfordians to think of the earl as a romantic, nostalgic, reactionary, clinging to the ideals of the Feudal past.

Feldman shows Oxford's position was more complex than that. He describes Oxford as eventually "ethically alone," and argues that it was in this condition that the earl

rewrote *Hamlet*. He sang farewell to the ideals of his father and poured out his contempt for the economic cult of the future. The former he consigned to the dust of an impotent wintry ghost, and the cult of capital he damned to Osric's dirt and the clay where his clowns put Polonius. The reflection hurt him that the glorious bodies of Alexander and Caesar — not to mention saints and knights — might have gone a worse way. For a while he tried to retain the youthful confidence of his letter to Thomas Bedingfield preluding *Cardanus' Comfort*, in which he chanted: "For when all things shall else forsake us, and when our bodies fall into the bowels of the earth, yet that shall mount with our minds into the highest heavens." When he reached the final cadences of *Hamlet* and listened to the music of his adolescent fidelity in Horatio's epiphany of flights of angels singing the Prince to rest, he heard nothing more holy than a lullaby.[7]

Passages such as this one show why this little volume represents the culmination of a long tradition of Oxfordian scholarship — a line that can be traced from Looney and the Wards, through Holland and Allen, to Barrell and Feldman. But he also established himself as part of this tradition by adding to the store of primary documents relating to De Vere's life that have been published. He obtained a copy of the coroner's inquest on the death of Thomas Brinknell, in July 1567, an undercook in Burleigh's household who seems to have died by running onto the earl's sword. This death casts its shadow on the catastrophic ending of *Hamlet* and has its echo in the graveyard scene when one of the clowns declares, "It must be 'se offendendo'; it cannot be else." Feldman concludes his study of the document and of the play with these words:

In my belief we have here the confession of Edward de Vere, Earl of Oxford, that he was guilty of the abrupt death of Tom Brinknell; moreover, that he was responsible for shortening the life of Anne Cecil. He came to these conclusions by a road remote from coroner's inquest law, by the justice of the divine light in his head. But he could only endure the light by refracting it in his lone way, with laughter and various arts.[8]

Although Feldman's little book was issued outside the commercial mainstream, it reached many who were interested in and later wrote about the authorship question.

III

The lack of widespread acceptance of the Oxford theory led the history of the Shakespeare authorship controversy to start repeating itself. For instance, the publication of Charlton Ogburn's *The Mysterious William Shakespeare: The Myth and the Reality* in 1984 was in many ways a recapitulation of the publication of *This Star of England*, a book published by his parents in 1952. Both books constitute popular restatements of the case for De Vere in an encyclopedic way that was designed to attract media attention and so finally resolve the authorship question. The results were mixed.

There is no question Ogburn's book did attract widespread attention and did interest, if not convince, large numbers of people. One way in which his book differed from *This Star of England* is that it surveyed the treatment of earlier Oxfordians by journalists and academics. One result of this extensive survey of the tactics employed by the defenders of the traditional attribution of the plays and poems was to make it less likely that the same tactics would be wheeled out and used against Ogburn's book. If anything, the tendency was for reviewers to treat the book with respect, thus introducing a welcome shift in tone by the participants in the controversy.

One reason for this tone on the part of reviewers was the disarming "Foreword" by David McCullough, the popular and highly respected historian, then best known for his biography of Harry Truman and now best known for his life of John Adams. McCullough, like Nathaniel Hawthorne in the previous century, generously ran the risk of losing some of his own credibility by urging a fair hearing for what was generally taken to be the point of view of a crank. McCullough was actually far more enthusiastic and far less tentative than Hawthorne had been. McCullough wrote:

> This brilliant, powerful book is a major event for everyone who cares about Shakespeare. The scholarship is surpassing — brave, original, full of surprise — and in the hands of so gifted a writer it fairly lights up the sky.... Anyone who considers the Shakespeare controversy silly or a lot of old stuff is in for a particular surprise. This is scholarly detective work at its most absorbing. More, it is close analysis by a writer with a rare sense of humanity. The strange, difficult, contradictory man who emerges as the real Shakespeare, Edward de Vere, the 17th Earl of Oxford, is not just plausible but fascinating and wholly believable. It is hard to imagine anyone who reads the book with an open mind ever seeing Shakespeare or his works in the same way.[9]

More was no doubt accomplished to popularize the question through events that were spurred by discussions surrounding the book than through the book itself. For instance, just as a moot court was held following the publication of *This Star of England*, so a moot court on the authorship issue was scheduled for September 25, 1987, through the Washington Law School of American University in Washington, D.C. The big difference in the two moot courts was that now three Supreme Court justices would participate as judges — William J. Brennan, Jr., Harry A. Blackmun, and John Paul Stevens.

When Charlton Ogburn thanks people who have helped or encouraged him in the front of his book, he includes a reference to David Lloyd Kreeger, "whose contributions to the cultural life of the national capital in the fields of music, painting, and the theatre have been a major factor in its rise to artistic eminence."[10] David Lloyd Kreeger was also a trustee of American University and sponsored the moot court on "Who Wrote Shakespeare?" that took place in the National Methodist Church before an audience of about 1,000 in attendance and many more reached on television through coverage by C-Span. In addition, the event was widely covered by the print media.

The moot court was established to act like an appellate court in that briefs were prepared and presented by two law professors — James Boyle presented the case for William Shakspere of Stratford and Peter Jaszi took the side of Edward de Vere. More importantly, it was determined at the outset that the burden of proof would be on the Oxford side since it represented a challenge to a long-established tradition. As Justice Brennan, who served as Chief Justice, made clear, it would not be sufficient to show that William Shakspere was not the author of the plays and poems but it would be necessary to positively establish that Oxford was the author. In other words, the standard would be especially high for the Oxford side. Despite this, headlines in the press throughout the country seemed to contain a slight sigh of relief when they reported that the Justices came down unanimously on the side of the traditional attribution of Shakespeare's work.

The case that Professor Jaszi presented on behalf of Oxford's candidacy consisted mainly of the idea that the works reflect a highly educated author who was probably of noble birth. He also concentrated on parallels between Oxford's life and the plays — particularly *Hamlet*. Professor James Boyle, arguing on behalf of William Shakspere, asserted that the multiple theories put forward to explain why De Vere would want to conceal his authorship were "internally contradictory and collapsible." He also argued that the consensus of scholars on the dates of composition of the plays determined that at least one of them was written after Oxford's death — which supported the notion that he wrote none of them. He did admit that the life of William Shakspere of Stratford as suggested by all the relevant documents represents the "most troublesome aspect of the case," but argued that his attendance at the Stratford Grammar School was a "reasonable assumption" even if there are no records to support the assumption.

Both sides had the opportunity to present rebuttals to the opposition's presentation. Professor Jaszi argued the possibility of the Stratford man's attendance at the local grammar school could not be seen as the educational equivalent of Ben Jonson's documented grammar school education in London. He also wondered aloud why the literary remains of William Shakspere are so sparse compared with those of his contemporaries. Finally, Jaszi argued that the silence, the lack of tributes, at the time of Shakspere's death in 1616 was at best peculiar. Professor Boyle, on the other hand, argued that there was no evidence that Edward de Vere would use a pseudonym. He also argued that

U.S. Supreme Court Justice John Paul Stevens. (Library of Congress)

there are ample records to show that William Shakspere was the author, and that his background and likely education did not contradict the idea that he was the author.

Perhaps the best aspect of the moot court was the decision to follow the English rather than the American practice and let each of the judges describe his own position. Justice Brennan began by reminding his audience of the conditions concerning the burden of proof and used them to justify the decision in favor of William Shakspere. He also argued that since there are inaccuracies in the plays it could be that the author need not be so highly educated or so thoroughly conversant with certain skills as the Oxfordians suggest. Furthermore, he also thought it very likely that William Shakspere was not nearly so ignorant as the Oxfordians tend to depict him. As a result, there was no compelling reason to overturn a long-standing tradition. Justice Blackmun was not nearly so firm in his view. On the contrary, he argued that he supposed the decision in favor of William Shakspere represented "the legal answer," because of the burden of proof, but "whether it is the correct one causes me greater doubt than I think it does Justice Brennan."

Justice Stevens who has established himself on the court as an independent thinker who takes principled and well-reasoned dissenting positions spoke at the greatest length and with the greatest sympathy for the strength of the Oxford case. He started by affirming that it was necessary "to say that the prima facie case is made, that what the scholars have principally" believed over the years is the "correct answer." But he quickly went on to insist that "the contrary view is not totally frivolous," and admitted to having "lingering doubts about gaps in the evidence" — such as the absence of eulogies when Shakspere died in 1616 and the absence of references to Shakspere in the writings — letters and diaries — of the period.

It was clear that Justice Stevens had been taken by the case and he admitted that he had also been "very struck by much of the internal evidence that is assembled in great detail in Mr. Ogburn's book about the various skills that the man had." He went on to say "I would tend to draw the inference that the author of these plays was a nobleman; there are just too many places in which nobility is stressed as a standard. In Hamlet's 'To be or not to be' soliloquy, the standard is which 'is nobler in the mind.' There are all sorts of references to nobility and skills that are familiar to the nobility but unknown to most common people. So, you can't help but have these gnawing doubts that this great author may perhaps have been someone else."

What was no doubt most heartening for supporters of the case for Edward de Vere was Justice Stevens's admission that he was "persuaded that, if the author was not the man from Stratford, then there is a high probability that it was Edward de Vere. I think his claim is by far the strongest that has been put forward."[11]

The attention paid to the Ogburn book and the moot court produced a large audience with a desire to learn more about the authorship controversy in general and the case for De Vere in particular. In April 1989, the PBS show *Frontline* devoted a program to "The Shakespeare Mystery." People interested in the subject wrote letters to the editors of numerous newspapers in an attempt to draw the program to the notice of a large audience. Reportedly the program reached approximately five million viewers. The authorship controversy had finally reached a mass audience.

IV

The link between the moot court and the *Frontline* show was made as soon as Judy Woodruff, the host of *Frontline* (now a reporter on PBS's evening news show, *The News Hour with Jim Lehrer*), welcomed viewers to the Folger Shakespeare Library in Washington, D.C., by telling them that "The Shakespeare Mystery" has engaged a wide range of people — Sigmund Freud, Charles Dickens, and Supreme Court Justice Harry Blackmun, among them. What is perhaps most surprising about the program produced and directed by Kevin Sim and reported by Al Austin is the sympathy it shows toward the case for Edward de Vere. There is no sense that the makers of the show set out to tilt the scales in Oxford's direction. On the contrary, there is about the show a sense of a wish to be fair and balanced. But there is the undeniable impression hat what the makers of the show discovered about the documents, people, and places associated with the Oxford case had an air of authenticity while what they found about the documents, people, and places associated with the Stratford case had an air of mendacity.

In part, this was no doubt the result of treating the subject visually. Early on, an actor reads lines from Hamlet's final speech while sitting at Castle Hedingham, the ancestral home of the Earls of Oxford in Essex, and one of the oldest Norman keeps still standing in Europe. The words, the actor's costume, and the setting are all of a piece. There is no straining needed to connect them. In Stratford, on the other hand, on the day set aside to celebrate the birth of the small-town genius, there is a carnival atmosphere and the tour of "the birthplace" is conducted by a guide with the patter of a sideshow barker. A look at the face of the supposed likeness of William Shakspere in the church in Stratford necessarily calls up the ironic voice of Mark Twain drawing attention to the bust's "deep, deep, deep, subtle, subtle, subtle expression of a bladder."

The attempt to be balanced is supported by the number and type of commentators who were interviewed. The traditional attribution of the plays and poems is maintained by A.L. Rowse in England and Samuel Schoenbaum in the United States, two undisputed, internationally recognized authorities on Shakespeare. The speakers on behalf of the Oxford case or, at least, the doubters, are Enoch Powell, the English politician, and Charles Vere, Lord Burford, a descendant of the Earl of Oxford, in Britain, and Charlton Ogburn in the United States, people who are serious but amateurs in the sense that they are not academics or professional scholars. If the amateurs came off better, it was not because there could have been any certainty that they would do so in advance based on their selection.

Similarly, the visits to the Folger Shakespeare Library in Washington and the Public Record Office in London, to Castle Hedingham in Essex, and to Stratford-on-Avon in Warwickshire show an effort to be balanced. Where the show possibly did become skewed was when it spent time to set up and take gamma-ray photographs of the base of the monument in the church in Stratford to check on Charlton Ogburn's theory that the Shakespeare manuscripts might have been placed there. The film showed there was nothing there. But this devotion of time to a whim of an Oxfordian that proved fruitless did nothing to stack the deck against the case for the Stratford man. On the contrary, it simply finally put to rest one of the vagaries of the doubters that dates back to Delia Bacon haunting the church in Stratford. (Some critics of the show complained, with some justice, that this type of investigative reporting belonged to the Geraldo Rivera school of journalism.)

Still, it was remarkable how much ground was covered and how well it was covered in an hour-long show dealing with a highly specialized, relatively complicated subject. It also did so in a way that held the interest of ordinary viewers. If PBS received blasts from outraged adherents of the traditional attribution, doubters, Oxfordians, and many members of the public at large who were first introduced to the issue by the show were full of appreciation. It can still serve as a good introduction to the subject for students and others who are new to it.[12]

Like the moot court on "Who Wrote Shakespeare?," the *Frontline* show on "The Shakespeare Mystery" raised serious questions about what counts as evidence, how a writer's biography relates to his or her work, and the nature of genius with a large, mass audience. It is likely that it sent many people back to texts and performances of Shakespeare's plays. But it also sent large numbers of students into college classrooms with questions about the authorship of Shakespeare's work. Stratfordians felt compelled to respond.

Chapter 10

The Stratfordian Response

Seem to see the things thou dost not.

Broadcasting "The Shakespeare Mystery" on such an intellectually respectable network as PBS gave the English-speaking world some new images with which to think about the Shakespeare authorship controversy. If the relentless but futile bombarding of the Stratford monument with gamma rays could stand as a metaphoric representation of the activities of the doubters, A.L. Rowse pointing a finger at the penis of Al Austin while reciting Sonnet 20 provided a figure for the Stratfordian response. In time, of course, that response became far more substantial. The shift seems to have come when highly respected literary magazines opened their pages to serious treatments of the controversy.

I

In October, 1991, for instance, the cover story of the *Atlantic Monthly* was "Looking for Shakespeare," a story that devoted a good deal of space to rather dignified presentations of the cases for both Edward de Vere and William Shakspere or, to use the names the magazine used, for Oxford and Shakespeare. Even the use of these names in the titles of the articles suggests to some extent the approach taken.[1]

Tom Bethell, a Washington, D.C.-based writer connected to *The American Spectator*, made the case for Oxford. Although he is described as "partisan," he actually describes what Oxfordians think and feel from the outside — as if he has made himself familiar with their case but does not necessarily share it or represent it himself. One big advantage of this position is the shift in tone it permits. Bethell lacks the stridency that too often enters into debates on the identity of Shakespeare. He also does not feel obliged to maintain or defend every scholarly lapse or unintentionally funny fantasy of Oxfordians. While he seems to have been led to an interest in the subject by Joseph Sobran's review of Charlton Ogburn's book in the *National Review* and the moot court held in Washington, he has found his way to J. Thomas Looney's *"Shakespeare" Identified* and nicely gives it the position the book deserves in intellectual history: "If it is ever vindicated — as is still possible — it will far surpass Heinrich Schliemann's discovery of Troy in the annals of amateur scholarship."[2]

Bethell does not bring any new arguments or research to the case for Oxford, but he does bring a dignified if lively tone, objectivity, and a sense of humor. He makes the case well. He of course follows the by now traditional practice of using "'Shakspere' to denote the man from Stratford and 'Shakespeare' to denote the author of the plays, whoever he was." Bethell's worthy opponent, Irvin Matus, declines this gambit, and so, from the start, acts as if there is no need to make a case for Shakspere as Shakespeare.

Irvin Matus does share the new tone that Tom Bethell brings to the debate. He, too, remains relatively calm, cool, and objective. But he shows just a little heat when he parenthetically mocks the anti–Stratfordian's position on the use of names. He writes: "(And let it be understood that any reference by me to Shakespeare is always to that 'man from Stratford.')" The trouble is that this statement indicates Matus assumes that what he is supposed to demonstrate has already been proved, so he has no need to make a case. As a result, instead of presenting a case for Shakspere as Shakespeare, Matus gives himself an interesting but very different assignment. He writes:

> The major questions that have been raised and that will be addressed here are whether the contemporaneous record of the man and playwright is suspect; whether the "Soul of the Age" (as Ben Jonson called him) was the very heart of it as well; and, finally, whether Shakespeare was indeed a man of the theater.

In short, Matus takes a pass on attempting to answer the one really major question that must precede all others: Who was Shakespeare?

Despite that, Matus does add something to the debate by taking an historical approach as a way to explain why the controversy arose in the first place. Matus argues that Shakespearean scholarship generated an image of the author that he calls "the scholar's Shakespeare." This figure, he implies, is very different from "the actor's Shakespeare," a figure who can be understood in the context of the life of the Elizabethan and Jacobean theater. The actor's Shakespeare, Matus tells us, is "a fellow who wrote plum parts, often set to musically poetic verse." The scholar's Shakespeare, on the other hand, is "a highly educated man versed in law and classical literature, fluent in several languages, equally at home at court and on the Continent." In short, the authorship controversy derives from the image of Shakespeare generated by scholars, an image that has been rejected or at least severely modified by modern, contemporary Shakespeare scholars who are coming to understand "the actor's Shakespeare" by placing him in the context of the theatrical life of his time. Since Matus thinks the real debate about Shakespeare in our time is this contest of images, he need not make a case for William Shakspere of Stratford as Shakespeare so much as find fault with "Bardolatry," the cult of the scholar's Shakespeare, in general, and with one subdenomination of this cult, Oxfordianism, in particular.

He begins to find fault with the Oxford case by stating that we know as much or more about Shakespeare as we do about most if not all of his contemporary playwrights. From the start, the question is framed in terms of quantity rather than quality — as if a document showing that William Shakspere hoarded grain in time of famine helps to establish him as the author of Shakespeare's plays. In addition, unlike Tom Bethell, Irvin Matus does not go back to J. Thomas Looney for a statement of the Oxford case, but instead concentrates primarily on Charlton Ogburn's popularization — a book that served to bring the case to the notice of a new mass audience, but also a book with numerous faults, fallacies, and fantasies. Finding fault with Ogburn's book as a way to refute Looney is roughly equivalent to using arithmetical errors in the calculations of an eighteenth century astronomer as a way to refute Copernicus. The earth does not return to the center of the universe simply because someone forgot to carry the one.

On the other hand, Matus does have a chastening effect, drawing attention to the tendency among all anti–Stratfordians to be too careless in the presentation of the results of research and too reckless when indulging in speculation. For instance, Matus does an excellent job of showing that there is no reason to expect to find Shakespeare's name in Henslowe's Diary simply because Shakespeare was connected with a different company of players by the time any such reference might have occurred. Charlton Ogburn's suspicion that something is rotten in the state of Shakespeare studies because the playwright's name does not appear in the diary is therefore baseless.

Similarly, while it is certainly true that there is no record to show that William Shakspere attended the Stratford Grammar school, it is because there are no records with regard to any students from that time. Furthermore, Matus shows that there is nothing unusual about this absence of records from so long ago. He writes: "It so happens that no admission books from before 1715 survive for Westminster School either, and Westminster has been called 'the most fashionable school' in Tudor England." In this context, Ogburn's suggestion that, in any case, the Stratford school records "would have disappeared because they showed he [Shakspere] did not attend it" sounds merely silly.

Irvin Matus loses his objective tone, however, when he sets out to summarize what Oxfordians think: "in their scenario," he writes, "Shakespeare [sic] the bit actor had been packed off to Stratford in the late 1590s." It is certainly true that, unlike any other playwright of the age, William Shakspere was able to purchase one of the best houses in his home town a mere five years after he was first mentioned as active in the life of the London theater, and Oxfordians certainly point this out. They also show how documents support the idea that he had ongoing interests in Stratford, sometimes pursuing various legal matters there while he is said to be writing at the height of his powers in London, for instance. Instead of dealing with the problems and questions the documentary record of William Shakspere raises, Matus merely ridicules through misrepresentation the Oxfordian position.

If anything, Tom Bethell was perhaps too willing to accept Irvin Matus's corrections of Oxfordian errors. For instance, Matus mocks the suggestion that the Lord Chamberlain's men might refer to players in the service of the Lord Great Chamberlain of England, that is, to Oxford, rather than to the Lord Chamberlain of the Household, Lord Hunsdon. To refute this suggestion that has been held by some Oxfordians — although it is of course not central to the Oxford case — Matus cites a publication by Gilbert Dugdale, *The Triumph of Time*, which states that King James I "to the mean gave grace: as taking to him the late Lord Chamberlain's Servants, now the King's Actors." Matus writes of this quotation: "This could only be a reference to Hunsdon, who had died six months earlier. Oxford survived another three months." It is the "only" here that places Matus with Ogburn as someone who tends to overstate a case. The word "late" here could simply mean "former," referring to the name of the company of players rather than to the death of the Lord Chamberlain. Besides, there are problems with Matus's interpretation. First, if the Lord Chamberlain had been dead for six months before the King took up the patronage of the company, who was the patron in the interim? Second, as Bronson Feldman long ago showed, Robert Armin, the chief clown of "Shakespeare's company," that is, the Lord Chamberlain's men, stated in print that he served a Lord in Hackney and the only Lord then living in Hackney that Armin could have been referring to was Oxford. Whether Oxford was an official patron of the company or not, members of it acknowledged him as their master.

Matus is perhaps at his best in his demonstration that it is perfectly reasonable that the original manuscripts of Shakespeare's plays have disappeared. In fact, as Tom Bethell points out, Matus in a way strengthens the case for Oxford by showing that Sir Thomas Bodley, founder of the Bodleian Library at Oxford, described plays and other low, ephemeral publications as "riffraffs," things to which a nobleman could not devote himself, his time, and his energy without causing a scandal.

Matus ends the first section of his argument by showing that the reputation of Shakespeare's plays was not nearly so great during the Restoration as it became in the eighteenth century. He in fact dates the birth of "Bardolatry" from Samuel Johnson's edition of the plays in 1765 and argues that the split between the "scholar's Shakespeare" and the "actor's Shakespeare" dates from David Garrick's Jubilee in 1769 at Stratford-on-Avon. It is this split, really, on which Matus wishes to hang his hat. He writes:

> At the heart of the authorship controversy is not only what we would expect to find of the author in his own time but precisely what his special genius was. Was it essential that he have been a man deeply involved in the world of the theater (as Oxford was not)? Or could he have been, as Algernon Charles Swinburne contended, a learned belletrist who wrote for the studious future reader "who would be competent and careful to appreciate what his audience and fellow actors could not?"

Irvin Matus concludes his "The Case for Shakespeare" with an eloquent answer to these questions. He persuasively argues that Shakespeare wrote plays full of major and minor characters who live and breathe on the stage because of his long connection with the company of players who would perform them. This eloquent argument would carry much more weight if Matus had not inserted the parenthetical assertion that Oxford was not "a man deeply involved in the world of the theater." It would not have taken much effort to find he was the patron of companies of players, both boys and men, of tumblers, of musicians, and of playwrights. In fact, he also clearly had a contemporary reputation as a playwright himself, although no plays known to have been by him survive under his own name. It also would not have taken too much effort to learn that Shakespeare's clown was Oxford's servant. While deep involvement in the theater alone might not be enough to help us understand "precisely what [Shakespeare's] genius was," Oxford certainly meets that criterion.

Irvin Matus basically leaves the authorship controversy where it was when Delia Bacon started it by asking who is more likely to have written *Hamlet*, Hamlet himself, or one of the players he instructed on the art of acting?

II

Irvin Matus expanded his article in the *Atlantic Monthly* into a book, *Shakespeare, in Fact*, published in 1994. In his preface to that book, Matus describes how he has met numerous Oxfordians and other anti–Stratfordians and says that he "did not find them to be, as I have heard them called, 'kooks' or 'loonies' (except insofar as Oxford's supporters adhere to a cause founded by a J. Thomas Looney)." He goes on to say, "I have found those who dispute the authorship to be intelligent and thoughtful people, many of whom are interested in aspects of the English Renaissance and its theater beyond the confines of the authorship question."[3] On the other hand, these contacts, although pleasant and beneficial, have done nothing to change Irvin Matus's mind so far as the authorship controversy goes. In fact, he opens the book with a declaration of faith that makes clear why he did not and will not make a case for Shakspere as Shakespeare:

> Regarding the authorship of William Shakespeare's plays, I am satisfied that a glover's son, born in a market town in the English Midlands, having had nothing more than a grammar school education, was the William Shakespeare who wrote a number of the world's greatest literary works. If I cannot offer incontrovertible proof of his authorship, the smoking pen if you will, I did not find either that the evidence which is supposed to undermine his authorship, any more than the evidence that alleges to show another to be the most likely author, stands up to investigation.[4]

It is clear from the start that Irvin Matus's interest is less in the authorship question than in "the opportunity to view Shakespeare from a new perspective." His aim once again is to urge "the actor's Shakespeare" at the expense of "the scholar's Shakespeare," because of his sense that the Oxfordian's Shakespeare represents "the scholar's Shakespeare" carried to an extreme.

What is surprising is the extent to which Matus is willing to accept some of the Oxfordian conclusions about the Stratford man. For instance, he appears willing to accept, based on the testimony of an expert on literacy in the Elizabethan period, that William Shakspere's father probably was illiterate. He also seems willing to accept the notion that William Shakspere simply followed the custom of his time, place, and class by raising his daughters without teaching them to write. It is hard to believe that Matus can come to these conclusions without doubting that William Shakspere produced Juliet and Ophelia, Rosalind and Beatrice, Desdemona and Cleopatra. Still, he shows no sign of any such doubt.[5]

Matus is at his best when catching mistakes, misstatements, or exaggerations of Oxfordians. For instance, he corrects an argument by Ruth Loyd Miller that was accepted and repeated in Chapter 8 of this book. Miller argued, based on the expertise of translators she had hired, that the legal documents in the suit brought by Thomasina Heminges Ostler, a widow, against her father, John Heminges, in October 1615, showed that the William Shakespeare mentioned in the suit was then dead — months before William Shakspere of Stratford died. Matus corrects this view by citing the authority of an archival scholar who is "experienced in the translation of legal documents." This scholar, we are told, "recognized the importance of the phrase, 'the aforesaid William Shakespeare.'" According to this scholar, the important phrase exempts Shakespeare from the sentence of death that had been pronounced over him by Miller's translators. It is a difficult case for anyone other than an expert to settle, and it is possible that Miller has somewhere responded to Matus's correction in her work. It is in any case odd that Matus's expert insists on anonymity, but we are at least made aware of how easy it is to err when dealing with alien and ancient matters.

Matus himself is not above the human tendency to err. In his discussion of what is taken to be the first reference to Shakespeare in connection with the theater, the complaints against him attributed to the playwright Robert Greene, and published in a pamphlet entitled *Greene's Groats-Worth of Witte* in 1592, Matus writes: "In early August 1592, in the company of Thomas Nashe and other cronies, he [Greene] dined on Rhenish wine and pickled herring, fell ill and died on September 3, aged 34." This statement derives from Thomas Nashe who told of only one additional crony at the "fatal banquet," a man named Will Monox who turns up nowhere else, so far as anyone can tell, in the annals of the Elizabethan period. Oxfordians have argued that Nashe used the name Will Monox to refer to Oxford. Charles Wisner Barrell, the Oxfordian scholar, showed that on another occasion Nashe addressed Oxford as "gentle Master William." None of this appears in Matus's book to be either discussed or refuted. It is simply as if it does not exist.[6]

In fact, there is a tendency throughout to deal narrowly with specifics in the career of Shakespeare, the life of Shakspere, and the life of Oxford, without allowing things that might otherwise do so to link up. Matus takes up a good deal of space arguing that the actors of the King's Men were responsible for the publication of the First Folio along with the printers, but without the involvement of the noblemen to whom it was dedicated, the Earls of Pembroke and Montgomery. In fact, he often uses the Earl of Montgomery to shed light on the workings of the Jacobean theater. But Matus never mentions that the Earl of Montgomery was the husband of Susan Vere, the youngest daughter of the Earl of Oxford. This connection by marriage need not shift any of the evidence he presents at all, but the unwillingness to acknowledge the connection seems based solely on the wish to keep Oxford and his friends and family apart from Shakespeare's work.

Similarly, when Matus speculates on Shakspere's start in the theater, he suggests that it could have come through a local Warwickshire man, Sir Thomas Lucy. He goes on to say, "Like many of status and position in Elizabethan England, Lucy was the patron of an acting troupe. Notice of the company are found in the accounts of Coventry for 1583–84." Matus admits that most "modern scholars" leave this question with a more general answer: "at some time he made his way into one or another of the many playing troupes that, for want of a permanent home, toured the countryside and stopped at Stratford."[7] What Matus does not want to point out is that Oxford's Men, one of those playing troupes without a permanent home, played in both Coventry and Stratford in 1583–84, clearly providing as likely a start in the theater for William Shakspere as Sir Thomas Lucy's company did.[8]

This visit to Stratford by Oxford's Men is also not referred to in what Matus describes as the "entire history of Oxford's theatrical patronage." He also in this "history" strives to minimize Oxford's role in the performances of companies of boys at the Blackfriars. The source for the "Oxfordian" notion that Oxford played a central role is Joseph Quincy Adams, a respected historian of the Elizabethan theater, and a former director of the Folger Shakespeare Library in Washington, D.C. Adams wrote:

> The young Earl of Oxford, himself a playwright and the patron of a troupe of boy-actors, came to the rescue of the theatre [Blackfriars]. He bought the lease from Evans, and undertook to reorganize its affairs. To Hunnis's twelve Children of the Chapel he added the Children of St. Paul's Cathedral, making thus a company of adequate size. He retained Hunnis, no doubt, as one of the trainers of the Boys, and he kept Evans as manager of the troupe. Moreover, shortly after the purchase, probably in June 1583, he made a free gift of the lease to his private secretary, a young man who had recently won fame with the first English novel, *Euphues*.[9]

Adams goes so far as to suggest that Oxford took on this central role at the bidding of the Queen. Adams wrote before Looney published his hypothesis identifying the Earl of Oxford as "Shakespeare." Adams's authoritative view was then the generally accepted one.

Matus closes his book with eloquent statements on the power of Shakespeare to produce characters that live on the stage and in the memory. These statements apply to Shakespeare's plays no matter who the author of them is. What they lead to is a wish for "the actor's Shakespeare" rather than "the scholar's Shakespeare," as if these two cannot be reconciled. There is no question that the plays were written to be performed and to be enjoyed by contemporary audiences made of the democratic mass audience Matus describes. But that does not deny that they have a life beyond the stage and the contemporary audience. The texts, too, have power, life, and can be not only read with pleasure and profit, but re-read and in fact studied. Actors and directors have benefited from the work of scholars. Scholars have benefited from productions of the plays. There is no need to choose between them.

There is something sad about Matus's conclusion, his wish that "Shakespeare will cease to be studied some day, and be simply acted." He is convinced that "these new approaches to the plays," that is, reading them only as if they are scripts to be staged, performing them, or watching film or TV versions of them, will "bring about the end of the authorship controversy." In part he thinks this to be the case because the young people who enjoy taking up the texts as actors will not see "friendly Shakespeare" in "an aristocrat (and especially not in one so self-obsessed as the Earl of Oxford)." The book closes with these words, "It would be poetic justice indeed if the spear through the heart of the authorship controversy turns out to be the joy of his plays discovered on such as the stage of a modern-day Elizabethan theater." What Irvin Matus failed to realize is that the young people who will take part in that joy are now likely to giggle and roll their eyes if their teachers trot out again the stale tale of the glover's son who set out from his market town in the English Midlands and magically found fame and fortune in the big city.[10]

III

Matus's sense that Oxford's personality would turn away young potential lovers of Shakespeare's works is the key to Alan H. Nelson's treatment of Oxford in his full-length biography, *Monstrous Adversary* (2003). His aim from the start seems to have been to portray Oxford in such a light that nobody could possibly accept him as Shakespeare. His book is a piece of propaganda posing as scholarship.

In his introduction, Nelson acknowledges that his biography is a response to the popularity of Charlton Ogburn's book and the publicity events that it spurred. Nelson writes: "It has become a matter of urgency to measure the real Oxford against the myth created by partisan apologists, and all too often embraced without critical rigour by the popular press — even by justices of the United States Supreme Court."[11] (Justice John Paul Stevens followed up on his interest in the Oxford theory by using it as the basis for an article entitled "The Shakespeare Canon of Statutory Construction" published in the *University of Pennsylvania Law Review* for April, 1992.) The way Nelson handles three relatively minor characters in Oxford's life — George Brown, Orazio Coquo, and William Hunnis — will shed light on his own "critical rigour."

Nelson devotes a short chapter entitled "Murder" to the case of George Brown. Brown killed George Saunders of London and John Bean of Woolwich on March 25, 1573 close to Shooters-hill near Greenwich. Brown was soon captured and, after being tortured, confessed that he had fallen in love with the wife of George Saunders and, with the encouragement of a Mistress Anne Drury, he murdered Saunders in the hope of marrying Saunders's wife. Brown was convicted of the crime and hanged on April 20. The wife of George Saunders, Mistress Drury, and their accomplice, Roger Simms, known as "Trusty Roger," were hanged as accessories to Brown's crime on May 13. This bold case of a wife conspiring to have her husband murdered captured the popular imagination. Arthur Golding, Oxford's uncle and the translator of Ovid's *Metamorphoses*, produced a pamphlet on the murder entitled *Brief Discourse of the late murther of master George Saunders*. Another writer and playwright, Anthony Munday, a servant of Oxford's, reported on the case in *A View of Sundry examples. Reporting Many Straunge Murthers* (1580). In time, the murder case became the basis of an anonymous play, *A Warning for Fair Women* (1599) which was, as Nelson reports, "performed by the Lord Chamberlain's Men — Shakespeare's Company."[12]

The only connection between this murder case and Oxford is that William Cecil in a message to Walsingham describes George Brown as a man "who had served, and is put from my Lord of Oxford's service." This connection with Oxford leads Nelson to describe Golding's pamphlet, which was apparently published for the ostensible purpose of "avoiding of miscredite," as "damage control." Nothing in the testimony of Brown, Mistress Drury, Mistress Saunders, or Trusty Roger ever in any way mentions much less implicates Oxford. Nonetheless, Nelson writes as if Oxford is guilty of murders committed by someone Nelson describes as "Oxford's man." Worse, Nelson uses this guilt by association to harp again on a constant theme of his, that Oxford is protected from the consequences of his heinous crimes by others and therefore remains irresponsible throughout life. He begins his next chapter, alliteratively entitled "Mayhem," with these words: "Untouched by the crimes of his servant Brown, on 22 April Oxford received votes from ten of the twelve electors for the Order of the Garter, including Burghley in his first year of membership in the Order."[13] If all Elizabethan nobles were held responsible for all of the crimes of all of their servants, would any of them have escaped whipping?

As if this is not grotesque enough, Charles Arundel, after he had been accused by Oxford of Catholic and Spanish sympathies, in response said of Oxford, among other things, that he had been "greveid in conscience about the killing of (blank)." Nelson, apparently losing all touch with reality, makes the ludicrous suggestion that "we may guess the murder on Oxford's conscience was that of George Saunders, killed by George Brown in 1573."[14]

From the point of view of the authorship question, what is perhaps most interesting about this murder is its movement from fact to literature via Oxford's relatives and servants. What Nelson does not point out is that the anonymous play *A Warning of Fair Women* was not only performed by the Lord Chamberlain's men but it contains some of the evidence for an early date of *Hamlet*, as Bronson Feldman showed by quoting from the play in his *Hamlet Himself*. It is typical of Nelson's method that he dwells on this murder in order to connect Oxford with violence without justification while ignoring or slighting the clear and justifiable connections of Oxford with literature.

In his treatment of the case of Orazio Coquo, an Italian singer who returned to England from Italy with Oxford, Nelson does for sex what he did for violence in the case of George Brown.

Nelson establishes a context for Oxford's relationship with Orazio by introducing it with the words of Lord Henry Howard and Charles Arundel, the former friends who Oxford had exposed to the Queen by charging them with treachery. They responded with what are known as libels, attempts to discredit Oxford by smearing him with everything they could think of, from conjuring to murder and buggery. Nelson introduces the testimony of Lord Henry Howard by asserting, "Oxford's adventures in Italy were not only heterosexual, but homosexual and pederastic." Howard's words follow: "Touchinge buggerye Auratio the Italian boye complained howe horribly my Lord had abused him, and yet would not give him any thinge." Fearing this statement of Howard's isn't quite unpleasant enough on its own, Nelson inserts editorially in brackets these explanatory words, "by way of medical relief." When Nelson later quotes the same passage of Howard's in a fuller context, there is nothing to suggest that what Howard had in mind was medical relief.[15]

Charles Arundel asserted that the singer left Oxford's service because of this sexual abuse: "Auracio that came with him owte of Italie made it the quarrel of his departure." Nelson promises his reader that Orazio Coquo "will tell his own story," implying that it will be a story of perversity and sexual abuse. It is nothing of the sort.

The chapter entitled "Orazio Coquo" consists of two paragraphs by Nelson which frame two pages of testimony by Orazio Coquo before the Venetian Inquisition in August 1577, when the singer returned to Venice from England. The document itself is concerned with Orazio's travels, his practice of his religion, and the attitude of others in England toward Catholicism. We learn that Oxford urged the teenager to go with him to England after hearing him sing in the choir in the church of Santa Maria Formosa in Venice. In England, Orazio lived in Oxford's house as a page. Through Oxford, Orazio not only met and spoke with the Queen but also had the opportunity to sing for her. Orazio claims that the Queen wanted him to convert to the Church of England. Other Venetians in London encouraged him "to read prohibited books and to study the doctrine of the heretics." When he says that he left England at the urging of a Milanese in order to prevent his being corrupted, it is clear that the corruption refers to religious conversion rather than sexual perversion.

On the other hand, Orazio clearly states that Oxford never encouraged him to convert or interfered with his ability to live as a Catholic. On the contrary, there were others in Oxford's household who also were Catholics and were permitted to attend mass and observe dietary prohibitions. In fact, Orazio gives clear testimony on Oxford's religious tolerance, "He let each person live in his own way."[16]

In this testimony of a supposed victim of sexual abuse, there is not a single word about sexual abuse. In other words, the only testimony concerning Oxford's perversion comes from his political enemies who are known as masters of the poison pen and tongue, Lord Henry Howard and Charles Arundel. Bronson Feldman in his *Hamlet Himself*, a book that appears in Nelson's notes and bibliography, thought it likely that there was justification for the charge and even suggested that Hamlet's dear friend, Horatio, was named in honor of Orazio, a name given as "Horatius" by Nelson on the record of his interrogation in Venice. But mostly what we learn directly from Orazio himself is that Oxford was a tolerant, generous, lover of music who was fluent in both Latin and Italian. In other words, what we learn from Orazio's testimony is that Oxford was what we might well expect the young Shakespeare to have been.

Nelson admits that Orazio's traveling to England with Oxford probably saved his life. His parents urged him to go with the Earl, and they both seem to have died of the plague while he was in England.[17]

Oxford's interest in music comes up again with William Hunnis, a man who is mentioned in a document that Nelson quotes but otherwise plays no part in this biography of Oxford. The man's family name occurs in a document that discusses the lease of the Blackfriars Theatre. It reads, "she let the house to one Hunnis, and afterward to one Newman or Sutton, as far as I remember, and then to Evans, who sold his interest next to the Earl of Oxford (who made a gift of his interest to Lyly)."[18] In other, similar cases, Nelson does an excellent job of tracking down every name in a document and often producing mini-biographies of tenants or joiners to whom Oxford owed money. He shows no such interest in Hunnis, although Hunnis is in many ways far more interesting.

Joseph Quincy Adams in his discussion of the first Blackfriars Theatre says that Oxford no doubt retained the services of William Hunnis as a trainer of the boys of the combined acting troupe even though Evans was the manager and Lyly was involved as playwright and in other ways, eventually holding the lease himself. But Hunnis is also a poet and musician who has at least one other connection with Oxford's life. They were both contributors to *A Paradise of Dainty Devices* (1576), the first anthology of courtier poetry to appear during the reign of Elizabeth. Hunnis had been a loyal supporter of the Queen even when her Catholic sister, Mary Tudor, was on the throne. Elizabeth rewarded Hunnis for his loyalty by putting him in charge of her gardens at Greenwich when she came to power. Charlotte Carmichael Stopes, the Victorian Shakespearean scholar and the biographer of the Earl of Southampton, wrote a study of Hunnis entitled *William Hunnis and the Revels of the Chapel Royal: a Study of His Period and the Influences Which Affected Shakespeare*. It is unclear whether Nelson neglects Hunnis and his connections with Oxford because he wishes to avoid them or because he is unaware of them. In any case, the neglect shows the weakness of Nelson's scholarship.

Nelson's wish to establish Oxford as a "monstrous adversary" colors his approach to virtually every aspect of Oxford's life. Oxford fathered a natural son, Edward Vere, later Sir Edward Vere, by Anne Vavasour. The boy was born on March 21, 1581. Nelson writes on the only page that deals with the boy that "Oxford took no responsibility for his upbringing or education."[19] He gives no indication of the basis for this assertion. The mere fact that Oxford permitted the boy to use his name constitutes a kind of acknowledgement. As a young man, Edward Vere attended the University of Leyden and, in the absence of evidence to the contrary, the reasonable assumption is that Oxford paid his fees. Edward Vere certainly learned to be a soldier by serving with Oxford's cousin, Sir Francis Vere, in the Low Countries. In fact, in time, the boy became not only a member of parliament but also a captain of the army in the Low Countries. He died while serving there in 1629. John Hampden, the famous parliamentarian who died fighting in the Civil War, described Sir Edward Vere's character as "all summer in the field, all winter in the study." Vere was a translator of Polybius as well as a soldier. Nelson finds space for none of this in his life of Sir Edward Vere's father.

Nelson's treatment of Henry de Vere, the eighteenth earl of Oxford, Oxford's son by his second wife, Elizabeth Trentham, is, if anything, even less fair. He ends the book by asserting that, although there is no proof of it, "it is seems [*sic*] certain that the 18th earl by neglect consigned the mortal remains of both his parents in oblivion."[20] He also leaves the 18th earl in Venice at Carnival time, getting into trouble with the authorities for having a courtesan in his gondola, a circumstance that the earl did not realize was against the laws. Nelson does not bother to tell his readers that the earl returned to England, married Lady Diana Cecil, a beauty and heiress, and then died, like his half-brother Sir Edward Vere, fighting in the Low Countries, in 1625. In short, what is traditionally expected of a biographer is left out of *Monstrous Adversary* by Alan H. Nelson, while he devotes whole chapters to things that biographers would traditionally leave out, or mention in passing, or carefully put in context. The result is in fact worthless as biography and of little value as propaganda.

But this is not to say the book is valueless. On the contrary, Nelson deserves a great deal of credit for bringing to light additional documents that will eventually contribute to the understanding of Edward de Vere, Earl of Oxford, otherwise known as Shakespeare. It is simply that these materials will have to be treated as raw material by a future biographer of Oxford who will either have no axe to grind or who will be able to keep from distorting or suppressing evidence even though he or she has an axe to grind. The main lesson is that Oxfordians have failed to seek out, find, and publish all the documents relating to Oxford's life. It is unclear that even the letters that have been collected are now complete. (Nelson does not include Oxford's first letter that was written to William Cecil in French for some reason.) What is ultimately surprising is the extent to which Nelson, despite his best efforts, has left Oxford's reputation largely as it was before the authorship controversy began. It would be wrong to describe his book as a character assassination. It is far too clumsy for that. The book remains merely an attempted assassination.

By and large, the Stratfordian response to the growing popularity of the Oxfordian position has taken on two forms. First, Stratfordians have become more willing to examine Oxfordian scholarship, find fault with it, and argue that those faults constitute a refutation of the Oxfordian hypothesis. Second, Alan H. Nelson took up the task of trying to depict Oxford as a demon or a monster, thus hoping to convince people that he could not have been Shakespeare. Neither of these approaches stopped or stymied the Oxfordians, but rather generated yet more research and publications.

Chapter 11

The Rest Is Scholarship

A crown's worth of good interpretation.

The state of the authorship question early in the twenty-first century might best be described as eclectic or confused. There are serious Oxfordian scholars who have continued to add to the store of documents or of valuable interpretations that make up the case for Oxford, but there has been no decisive discovery or argument that has settled the question. One result is the sense that the history of the argument continues to repeat itself. There have been vigorous restatements of the agnostic position as well as arguments for yet more candidates for the true author. The general tendency of the argument seems to be toward an eventual acceptance of the question as one worthy of attention within the academic world. Both scholars and people associated with the theater seem able to join forces on this common ground, insisting that a love for and an interest in the works of Shakespeare imply a desire to know as thoroughly as possible the identify and the life of their author.

I

Nina Green and Peter Moore are two of the Oxfordians that Alan H. Nelson thanks for help in the "Acknowledgements" of his *Monstrous Adversary*. He says that Nina Green put him "on to so many documents that I have lost count, and asked (and still asks) questions which test both my memory and my complacency."[1] A sense of Peter Moore's contribution to the book can be gained by a consideration of Moore's own work.

Peter R. Moore's essay entitled "The Earl of Oxford and the Order of the Garter," first published in 1996 in the *Shakespeare Oxford Newsletter*, begins by stating that Moore originally suggested that Professor Nelson microfilm "the records of the elections to the Order of the Garter for the years 1569 to 1604 from the register in the British Library."[2] Nelson followed up on this suggestion and used the votes cast for Oxford in the elections as a kind of chorus in his book, a convenient way to sum up a period in Oxford's life. Oxford was never elected to the Order. Moore, on the other hand, does not simply report on results but also interprets the votes cast in an effort "to examine the tale that these elections tell about the standing of the Earl of Oxford during his adult years." The result is enlightening and serves as a kind of model of how scholars who hold divergent views on the authorship question can profitably cooperate.[3]

Moore shows that, so far as Garter elections are concerned, Oxford's career as a courtier consists of four phases: 1569–1580; 1581–1584; 1585–1588; and 1590–1604.[4] The earliest period represents a time of Oxford's popularity and prestige when he received relatively large numbers of votes for membership in the Knights of the Garter, although the Queen never awarded him the honor. The second phase is the period when he had the clash with Lord Henry Howard and Charles Arundel, and also the time when he fathered a natural son, Edward Vere, by Anne Vavasour, putting him on the outs with the Queen and at court. Votes for election to the Garter reflect this status. The third phase, a period of reconciliation with his wife, the fathering of additional children, and the defeat of the Armada, represents a time when Oxford once again received votes for election to the Garter. As Moore shows, the identities of the individuals who cast votes for Oxford in this third phase are enlightening. They included Henry Stanley, fourth Earl of Derby, Henry Herbert, second Earl of Pembroke, and Charles, the second Lord Howard of Effingham, the Lord Admiral. Moore points out that some marriages support the notion that these votes in Garter elections reflect a connection with Oxford. His main point is that the votes cast and marriages arranged suggest a faction at the court of Elizabeth made up of the nobles who were patrons of major acting companies.[5]

Although this analysis was published long before Nelson's biography of Oxford appeared, Nelson felt no need to refer to it or to refute it. He simply left the evidence that votes for election to the Knights of the Garter and marriages established a connection between Oxford and some of the other leading patrons of companies of players of the period out of his biography.

In a way, the fourth and final phase of Oxford's life with regard to votes for Garter elections is the most interesting. During the long stretch of years from 1590 to 1604, Oxford received only a single vote and that was cast in 1604, the year of Oxford's death, by his brother-in-law, Thomas Cecil, the second Lord Burghley. As Moore remarks, "Oxford's loss of his father-in-law's vote is easily explained by Anne Cecil's death in 1588, but his failure to get anyone else's vote seems to indicate that he was living under something of a cloud in this period."[6] Moore argues that "the least dramatic explanation of Oxford's disrepute would be his financial collapse around 1590," but he goes on to show that the poverty of other peers did not cause the same lack of votes in Garter elections.

Moore looks at the way earlier biographers of Oxford have treated his life in the same period. He points out that Ward described Oxford's life from 1589 onwards as one of mystery. Even though Oxford was at court early in this period, he appears to have been a pariah to the Knights of the Garter. Grosart, Oxford's first modern editor, hit the nail on the head when he wrote of Oxford, "An unlifted shadow lies across his memory."[7]

Moore is aware that his analysis of the pattern of votes received by and withheld from Oxford can be connected with the Shakespeare of the Sonnets. In an earlier essay, Moore had already used new material on Oxford's life that Professor Nelson had found to reinforce "the appropriateness of Shakespeare's self-description in Sonnet 37, 'lame, poor, [and] despised,'" as applied to Oxford. Moore had then cited Sir John Peyton's statement in 1603 "that Oxford lacked friends" to justify the application of the word "despised" to Oxford. Now, because of his analysis of the votes for the Garter, Moore is able to conclude that Oxford, like Shakespeare, was barred from "public honour and proud titles" and was "vile esteemed" because he had made himself "a motley to the view."[8]

Moore's careful interpretation of the record of votes cast for Oxford with regard to the Knights of the Garter connects the earl with both the theater and the personal statements made by the author of the Sonnets. They are far from being sufficient to identify the earl as Shakespeare, but at this point they do not need to do so. Instead, they simply help to make clear that everything new that is learned about Oxford reinforces and supports the hypothesis that he was Shakespeare.

On the other hand, Moore's article raises a question that has gone unanswered. Clearly expecting revelations to come as a result of Professor Nelson's research into Oxford's life, Moore leveled grave charges against respected biographers. "Both B. M. Ward and Conyers Read, biographers respectively of Oxford and Lord Burghley," Moore asserted, "concealed their knowledge of a memorandum in Burghley's hand showing that Lady Burghley carried off her daughter after she reunited with her husband upon his return from Italy."[9] Moore clearly expects Nelson's biography to dispel the myth "that Oxford cruelly rejected his wife in 1576" by making public this memorandum that previous scholars had suppressed.[10]

Nelson in fact reprints the memorandum, but introduces it by saying it consists of "complaints from Oxford" and follows it up with this statement: "Though Oxford objected to Lady Burghley's interference, she may well have acted to protect Anne from abuse. It can come as no surprise that the mother-in-law of such a son-in-law would have wished him dead." In short, Nelson uses the document to reinforce rather than dispel what Moore calls the "myth" of Oxford's cruel rejection of his wife. What is even more disconcerting is that when Moore wrote his detailed and devastating review of Nelson's *Monstrous Adversary*, a piece entitled *Demonography 101*, this question of Nelson's use of Lord Burghley's memorandum is not discussed. The result is a puzzle that awaits further clarification through yet more scholarship.[11]

A number of the documents Nina Green tracked down, transcribed or translated, and made public on her The Oxford Authorship Site, *www.oxford-shakespeare.com*, shed light on what Peter Moore called Oxford's "financial collapse." Green's article, "An Earl in Bondage," published in 2004, uses these documents to provide a careful and thorough analysis of the reasons for Oxford's financial problems. She shows in a detailed way that the reference in *All's Well That Ends Well* to Bertram's being a ward and, therefore, "evermore in subjection," is a precise "reflection of Oxford's unique personal experience after his father's death on 3 August 1562."[12] Green's view serves to dispel the myth that Oxford went through a massive inheritance merely through a combination of foolishness, pique, and extravagance. Another Oxfordian, Christopher Paul, has used Green's work as a springboard for a critique of an academic study of Oxford's finances by Daphne Pearson.

Daphne Pearson wrote a doctoral dissertation at Sheffield University on "Estates and Lawsuits of Edward de Vere." The dissertation served as the basis of a book entitled *Edward de Vere (1550–1604): The Crisis and Consequences of Wardship*. Pearson's stated aim is to use Oxford as the basis for a case study in economic history. The main single criticism of her work is that she overestimated the annual income Oxford inherited from the ownership of land passed on by his father. Pearson places this figure at 3,500 pounds per year. Nina Green, on her website, describes this figure as a myth. Christopher Paul, in his review of Pearson's book, states, "Oxford's inherited annual income was around £2,200, nowhere near Pearson's exaggerated figure of £3,500."[13]

While this difference of 1,100 to 1,300 pounds might sound insignificant to moderns, it represented a huge amount of money in Elizabethan times. The main point is that if Pearson is in fact wrong about this fundamental figure, she cannot be right about much else — because her entire case study is based on a false assumption. Worse, Alan Nelson relied to a large extent, if not exclusively, on Pearson's findings for his discussion of Oxford's finances. If Pearson is wrong, then Nelson is wrong, too. In short, Oxfordian critics have found that the two leading academic experts in our time on Oxford's life have produced works with fundamental flaws.

Part of the reason this slip in accounting is important is because it is in part the basis for judgments on Oxford's character. Neither scholar does anything at all to make clear what

Oxford spent his wealth on — and it is undeniable that he went through a fortune in his life-time even if there can be legitimate arguments over the amount of that fortune. At one point, Nelson tells us that Oxford was the patron simultaneously of a company of adult actors, a company of children actors, a company of musicians, and a company of tumblers, but he gives no idea whatsoever how much patronage of those four companies would cost. The point is no doubt best made in Christopher Paul's conclusion of his review of Daphne Pearson's book:

> In calling Pearson to account, one need not argue that Oxford was a financially savvy wizard or that he did not over-spend; that is beside the point.... Pearson is surely not far wrong when she reiterates that talk of revenue probably bored Oxford, but admits that one can only speculate what most of his money was spent on, vainly consigning it to "the black hole of [his] expenditure." However, because Oxford actually had a great deal less money than Pearson credits him with, this margin of speculation can be narrowed considerably, and even then, Spanish leather shoes can be discounted. Although there has been a great deal of controversial speculation about this particular earl of Oxford in modern times, there needn't have been when it came to his finances. Had Pearson presented the available material with forthright diligence and integrity, rather than with an appalling disregard for accuracy, her conclusions that Oxford's fiscal ruin was entirely his own doing and that the Queen's political neglect of him came about because of his financial reckless-ness, would (perforce) have been quite different.[14]

The two basic questions about Oxford's life are how he spent his time and how he spent his money. His modern academic biographers have left these questions unanswered. It is perhaps worth noting, however, that by dying basically broke Oxford shared the plight that was common to his fellow playwrights. Only William Shakspere of Stratford-on-Avon retired to his hometown to pursue business deals in relative comfort and security.

If academics have begun to study Oxford, Oxfordians have begun to enter the academy. Roger Stritmatter earned a Ph.D. in comparative literature at the University of Massachu-setts at Amherst in 2000 with a doctoral dissertation that analyzes the marginalia in a Geneva Bible that bears Oxford's family crest.[15] The case for Oxford as Shakespeare is based on cir-cumstantial evidence — a collection of facts that when fitted together point in a persuasive way toward what seems to be the truth. Oxford's Bible can be seen as the most recent addi-tion to a long chain of evidence that stretches back to the case first made by J. Thomas Looney. The fact that this analysis of a piece of Oxfordian evidence could serve as the subject of a doctoral dissertation is one measure of the progress the Oxford case has made. Another meas-ure of that progress is that Nina Green, an Oxfordian, is critical of Stritmatter's findings. She argues that it is not clear that the annotations are in Oxford's hand, and that the correlations between the markings in the Bible and passages in Shakespeare's work might be les significant than they seem. What is positive about this argument is that it is not partisan. Nina Green is as critical of Roger Stritmatter as she is of Daphne Pearson — and others will no doubt be similarly critical of her. It is in this way that errors will be caught and corrected, and the truth will eventually emerge: the rest is scholarship.

II

Elliott Baker, the novelist and screenwriter, finally made Nathanial Hawthorne's wish come true about one hundred and fifty years late. Baker edited Delia Bacon's book, *The Phi-losophy of Shakspere's Plays Unfolded,* and revealed its gist and juice while removing much of its repetition and its mesmeric passages of prose that simply arrested the argument. The sur-prising thing is that Baker was able to do this in a seamless way and by virtually adding no words of his own. The work in its sense and texture remains Delia's, but it is now far more accessible to readers than the original was and the reader's labor has been greatly diminished. Baker's title gives a sense of the shift in emphasis that is at the root of his surgical work as editor: *Shakespeare's Philosophy Unfolded.*[16]

Baker published his manuscript as a book in 2001, but it earlier appeared in a journal that has its own place in the history of the Shakespeare controversy — *The Elizabethan Review,* published by Gary Goldstein. The idea behind this journal was that it would be peer-reviewed like a traditional academic journal and be independent of any membership organization that might wish to impose its agenda. In other words, the publication represents another sign of the growth in respect and acceptance that the controversy had attained. Stratfordian academics and Oxfordian scholars and interested parties such as Elliott Baker could all share space in the journal's pages. In addition, because of this editorial open-door policy with regard to the authorship question — although most contributors clearly leaned in the direction of the Oxford theory — numerous college and university libraries not only in the United States but throughout the world became regular subscribers to the journal. There was a sense of aptness that Elliott Baker's valiant and sympathetic attempt to do justice to Delia Bacon's bold and pioneering work should appear first in a journal that dealt with the authorship question in a way that had earned some measure of respect and acceptance by traditional scholars.

If Baker's book sent the authorship question back to a reconsideration of its very beginnings, the appearance of other books early in the twenty-first century did so too. For instance, Diana Price's *Shakespeare's Unorthodox Biography: New Evidence of an Authorship Problem* took the agnostic point-of-view that was earlier associated with Greenwood — an honorable position and one that no doubt needed to be taken up again. Price acknowledges as her predecessors not only Greenwood but also Alden Brooks and J. Thomas Looney. But she brings something of her own to the controversy — a cool head and a strong sense of humor. She concludes her "Introduction" with these words — an ironic statement of purpose: "If you want to know whether there is anything of substance to the Shakespeare authorship question, then the following pages may help you make up your own mind. This review of Shakespeare's life story may convince you that not all anti–Stratfordians are lunatics or victims of misinformation."[17]

What Diana Price is especially good at is finding and analyzing contemporary references to William Shakspere of Stratford-on-Avon that depict him not as a great playwright but as he appeared to those who knew him. She writes in a chapter of her book that is dedicated to this subject entitled "The 'Poet-Ape,'"

> Writers satirized Shakspere in print, not as a budding playwright and not as "gentle Shakespeare," but as a braggart, opportunist, paymaster, or pretentious gentleman by purchase. Several allusions pointed to a paymaster or broker who traded in plays and costumes, including secondhand clothes or frippery. Some allusions further suggested shady dealings or callous conduct.[18]

Price helps to establish this contemporary portrait of William Shakspere by quoting and analyzing the source of her chapter's title, an epigram by Ben Jonson entitled "On Poet-Ape" — Jonson's only epigram that is written in the form of a Shakespearean sonnet. She establishes that there is a scholarly tradition that identifies Shakspere as the target Jonson had in his sights when he wrote the epigram. One of these scholarly commentators was Richmond Crinkley, a former director of programs at the Folger Shakespeare Library, who wrote, "William Shakespeare is being accused of passing off the writing of others as his own.... Among contemporaries who referred to him, there is a shared view that William Shakespeare appropriated the work of others."[19] Price is especially good at connecting this contemporary view of Shakspere with the view of modern Stratfordian scholars who have taken up, in Irvin Matus's words, "the actor's Shakespeare" as opposed to "the scholar's Shakespeare." Price begins her chapter with a relevant quotation from Jonathan Bate's *The Genius of Shakespeare*, "The image of the crow and the accusation 'beautified with our feathers' suggest that Shakespeare may even have been filching with his pen."[20] Price has pieced together a credible portrait of William Shakspere from references by contemporaries that parallels the portrait of the man sketched by Alden Brooks.

If Price is convincing in establishing what William Shakspere was actually like, she is even more convincing in establishing what he was not. She does this in a quantitative way that takes the form of a chart in an appendix that is entitled, "Chart of Literary Paper Trails." This chart considers 10 categories of evidence with regard to 25 writers, including William Shakspere. The categories of evidence are:

1. Evidence of education
2. Record of correspondence, especially concerning literary matters
3. Evidence of having been paid to write
4. Evidence of a direct relationship with a patron
5. Extant original manuscript
6. Handwritten inscriptions, receipts, letters, etc. touching on literary maters
7. Commendatory verses, epistles, or epigrams contributed or received
8. Miscellaneous records (e.g., referred to personally as a writer)
9. Evidence of books owned, written in, borrowed, or given
10. Notice at death as a writer

Of the 25 contemporary writers considered, William Shakspere is the only one who leaves no evidence at all of having been a writer — who produces a complete blank in every category of evidence.[21] This chart seems designed to dispel once and for all the notion that the remains of William Shakspere's life are typical of a writer of his time. The evidence is much stronger that he was a money-lender and jack-of-all-trades around the theater than that he was any kind of a writer at all.

Price's cool-headed and convincing demonstration that there still is an authorship problem appeared at a time when this sense was finding expression in more and more mainstream publications. One example is the article entitled "Who Was Shakespeare?" by William Rubinstein, the historian, in the August 2001 issue of the highly respected British journal, *History Today*. Rubinstein provides an overview of the history of the controversy, but starts where the controversy began, with the irreconcilable contrast between Shakspere's documented life and his ostensible work. Rubinstein writes:

> In striking contrast to the obscurity of his background there is the achievement of Shakespeare the writer. This son of an illiterate provincial butcher had the largest vocabulary of any writer in English in history, using about 37,000 different words in his works, twice as many, for instance, as the Cambridge-educated John Milton. Shakespeare coined hundreds of phrases (such as "into thin air," "time-honoured," and the "be-all and end-all"), which are widely imagined to be proverbial. He apparently also coined at least 1,500 English words, including "addiction," "alligator," "birthplace," "cold-blooded," "critic," "impede," and "amazement." Shakespeare was also, apparently, the first writer to use the word "its" as a third person possessive. He wrote convincingly of court life, foreign intrigues, and the affairs of kings and courtiers, subjects of which he could have had no direct knowledge. As well as law, his works reveal a mastery of science, of classical and European literature, and of other specialized fields, which seem utterly incongruous — indeed, inexplicable — in a poorly-educated country actor. It is this incredible incongruity which has led so many to question whether the Stratford man wrote the plays attributed to him — not, as is often alleged by orthodox scholars, snobbery on the part of proponents of other writers, who allegedly insist that

only a nobleman could have been England's national poet, not a commoner of humble background.[22]

The article makes clear that the popular imagination will not readily give up what Matus called "the scholar's Shakespeare."

Rubinstein's article is neutral with regard to the identity of Shakespeare, although he admits at one point, "Had the plays and poems been written anonymously, it seems likely that today Oxford would be the leading candidate for their authorship, and that no one would argue that Shakespeare of Stratford wrote the plays." Within a few years of the publication of this article, however, Rubinstein would be the co-author of a book that would make a case for a new candidate for the Shakespeare crown, Sir Henry Neville.

The book, published in 2005 and entitled *The Truth Will Out: Unmasking the Real Shakespeare*, and written by Brenda James and William D. Rubinstein, begins with a survey of the authorship controversy. It makes the by now traditional arguments against the traditional attribution of the plays and poems to William Shakspere, but also finds fault with some of the other candidates, especially Edward de Vere, the seventeenth Earl of Oxford. Much is made of the fact that Oxford died in 1604 — years before a number of the plays are said to have been written based on the traditional chronology. No doubt because of the influence of Alan H. Nelson's *Monstrous Adversary*, the authors write, "Some historians who have studied De Vere's life also believe that he was simply too violent, quarrelsome and moody to have written the plays ... and while his early verse shows talent, it lacks the complexity and intelligence we associate with Shakespeare."[23]

This fault-finding is of course neither a serious examination of the Oxford theory nor a refutation of it. It is instead an attempt to make room for yet another candidate. The authors also raise the question of what they call a "smoking gun" and what Matus wittily and more precisely called a "smoking pen." Since Judge Stevens's declaration that the prima facie case for William Shakspere of Stratford — the combination of the Stratford monument and the publication of the First Folio with an apparent reference to the Stratford monument — was made, there has been a restless sense that there should be documentary evidence to establish an alternative candidate. James and Rubinstein are in part moved by their sense that the chances of such evidence turning up for Oxford are growing relatively slim. They write, "As with Bacon, another major point against Oxford is the lack of any direct evidence that he wrote the plays: surely a clear-cut 'smoking gun' would have been found in the more than 80 years since De Vere was first proposed as a candidate, if it existed."[24] The use of the word "surely" here shows the rhetorical strategy of the authors.

They begin their argument by presenting what purports to be "documentary evidence," that is, an extract from what they call "the Tower Notebook" that describes a feast and the celebration of the coronation of Henry VIII. The authors argue that this material is parallel to stage directions and speeches in Shakespeare's *Henry VIII*, Act IV, scene i. It must be said at once that the parallels between the material in the Notebook and the play are neither striking nor unique. Beside that, there are other clearly established, published sources for the material in the play. Worse, the description of the provenance of the Notebook, while tracing its ownership to families tied to Neville, leaves some gaps:

Its provenance is unquestionably from Sir Henry Neville: he was a prisoner in the Tower in 1601–03, when he was freed by James I. At Neville's death in 1615, the notebook was inherited by his favourite daughter and her husband Sir Richard Worsley, who were ancestors of the family which became Baron Yarborough in 1794 and Earl of Yarborough in 1837. This family owned land in the Isle of Wight and in Lincolnshire, and in about 1954 donated the Tower Notebook and other associated material to the Lincolnshire Record Office. There it has remained, unnoticed and apparently little read, until it was discovered in the course of researching this book.[25]

The use of "unquestionably" here is roughly equivalent to the use of "surely" in the earlier passage. It is only after this provenance is traced that we learn the Notebook is not in Neville's handwriting. The authors write, "The fact that the tower Notebook does not appear to be in Neville's hand does not present a problem. The employment of scribes was entirely permissible for wealthy prisoners in the Tower, and Neville's long-time scribe, John Packer, was probably employed for this purpose."[26] The authors never assert that the Notebook is in Packer's hand. If this is a smoking gun, it has fired a blank cartridge.

In the end, the case for Neville has neither documentary evidence nor a strong circumstantial case to support it. What it reflects mostly is a continuing dissatisfaction with the traditional attribution of the plays and poems and the inability of any of the proposed candidates to achieve so far a decisive victory.

Yet another candidate has been proposed for the Shakespeare honors, Mary Sidney Herbert, the Countess of Pembroke. Robin P. Williams makes the suggestion in a light-hearted, non-dogmatic way. She seems to want to make the suggestion as a way to start an inquiry into the possibility of Mary Sidney Herbert's authorship rather than trying to make a definitive case that will settle the issue. Williams' *Sweet Swan of Avon: Did a Woman Write Shakespeare?*, published in 2006, raises rather than answers a question. The difficulty is that the case is not likely to even generate an ongoing interest in the candidacy unless it is because of an interest in female intellectuals of the Tudor period — a subject that is worthy of serious attention on its own without the need of a prop from the authorship controversy.

Williams follows the odd procedure of ending rather than beginning with the other candidates. Nonetheless, her consideration of the Oxford candidacy is idiosyncratic in its reliance on and interpretation of Alan Nelson's biography. Williams writes:

> In some minds, an issue against Oxford is that he was considered a rather despicable person in his time; very few scholars can refrain from using pejoratives whenever his name is mentioned. With Oxford's well-documented misogyny, it's difficult to claim that he thought highly enough of women to create the lengthy list of great women in the plays.[27]

The case in favor of the Countess of Pembroke as Shakespeare is at about the same level as the case against Oxford. For instance, Williams writes about the original elements in Shakespeare's *Much Ado About Nothing* in this way:

> No source has been found for Dogberry, the illiterate constable, one of two illiterate characters in the canon (both male). It is documented, however, that the constable in Wiltshire, the town where Mary Sidney lived, was illiterate.[28]

Dogberry's originality certainly rests with something other than his illiteracy — if that is an accurate description of his linguistic condition. In any case, it would no doubt be possible to beat the bushes and flush documented illiterate constables from numerous other parts of Elizabethan England — including Warwickshire and Essex.

Mary Sidney Herbert and the circle of writers who gathered around her deserve all the scholarly attention they will ever receive even if she did not write the works of William Shakespeare.

In general, the attempts to add to the number of candidates for the Shakespeare honors have failed. The contest mostly remains between the traditional attribution of the authorship and the case for Edward de Vere, Earl of Oxford.

Mary Sidney Herbert, Countess of Pembroke.
(Copyright National Portrait Gallery, London)

III

Popular restatements of the case for the Earl of Oxford as Shakespeare appear from time to time. Richard F. Whalen's *Shakespeare: Who Was He?*, published in 1994, was one relatively brief, popular presentation of the case. Joseph Sobran's *Alias Shakespeare*, published in 1997, concentrated most heavily on the Sonnets and the homoerotic relationship that Sobran argued existed between the author of the Sonnets and the young man who has traditionally been known as "the fair youth." Both of these no doubt derive in part from the interest in the Oxford candidacy aroused by Charlton Ogburn's *The Mysterious William Shakespeare: The Myth and the Reality*. Some people thought that book was if anything too long, and so, in a way, it made room for briefer, more popular treatments of the subject.

Mark Anderson's *"Shakespeare" by Another Name*, published in 2005, a contemporary equivalent of Charlton Ogburn's book—popular in that it is meant for a large audience, but also thorough in that it presents a full-blown biography of Oxford as Shakespeare, hence the book's subtitle, *The Life of Edward de Vere, Earl of Oxford, the Man Who Was Shakespeare*. More importantly, the book comes after Alan H. Nelson's *Monstrous Adversary*, so it can build on the documents concerning Oxford's life that Nelson found while also benefiting from the work of Peter Moore and others who showed how this new material supported the identification of Oxford as Shakespeare. Anderson's book can now be seen as the most complete and up-to-date statement of the Oxfordian hypothesis that is available. To sum up the current state of the authorship controversy, Anderson's book will be compared here with a very recent life of William Shakspere, Bill Bryson's *Shakespeare: The World as Stage*, published in 2007.

What sets Mark Anderson's book apart from other contributions to the Oxfordian case is that it feels no or, at least, little need to make a case. Instead, it mainly dismisses the authorship problem briefly in its Introduction and then proceeds to tell the story of Oxford's life while all but assuming that it has been established that Oxford was Shakespeare — or Shakespeare as Anderson prefers to spell the name, indicating by the hyphen that it is a pseudonym. The book starts with the assertion, "Every author's life tells a story." As a result, Anderson is less a polemicist, a debater, as the author of this book, than a story-teller, the maker of a narrative. There is a sense in which the time has come to test the circumstantial case that has been made to identify Oxford as Shakespeare by telling his story. Any anomalies, any false notes, any jarring confusions, that arise from the telling of Oxford's story will show the weaknesses in and potentially destroy the case for Oxford. On the other hand, if the case that Looney first made and that has been expanded by almost 80 years of scholarship can be told as a narrative without hitch — a narrative that fits together and reads credibly, the experience of reading the story should in itself provide support for and strengthen the case. As a result, the newness of Mark Anderson's approach and tone counts for more than the newness of any specific piece of evidence that appears in the book.

One thing that adds credibility to the tale Anderson has to tell is that he is able to supply a concrete context for suspected influences on Shakespeare. For instance, he shows that Oxford's father, John de Vere, the sixteenth Earl, was a patron of the Protestant playwright John Bale. Anderson writes:

> Bale's *King Johan* was a work of Protestant propaganda that had debuted before the court of Elizabeth's father twenty-five years before. Scholars have long noted Bale's likely influence on the Shake-speare play *King John*, even though Bale's *King Johan* was available only in manuscript and never, so far as is known, staged anytime after the early 1560s. If the young de Vere were not in the audience that night in Ipswich, he would at least have had access to Bale's manuscript, since Earl John had been one of Bale's longtime patrons.[29]

It is to a large extent Anderson's ability to replace the typical speculations of Shakespearean biography with facts and concrete details that makes the story he tells credible.

Anderson is still producing biography, however, and so must at times turn from storytelling to evaluate evidence. He picks his way well through the potential mine field of Oxford's earlier biographers — especially with regard to the controversial matter of the Howard-Arundell Libels:

> Arundel and Howard's slanders are at once the most revealing and also the most misleading documents from the whole of de Vere's life. De Vere's two previous biographers — B.M. Ward and Alan H. Nelson — have taken polar opposite views on these troublesome papers. The former finds little of any historical value in the entire Arundell-Howard docket, other than as sidelights on a nasty catfight. Nelson, on the other hand, essentially treats the Libels as statements of documentary fact.[30]

Anderson goes on to note that strikingly similar defamatory statements appeared a few years later in *Leicester's Commonwealth,* an anonymous 1584 pamphlet, charging the Earl of Leicester with "murder, conspiracy, incest, bigamy, lechery, and generally being 'overwhelmed and defamed in all vice.'" According to Anderson, it is likely that Arundell was the author of *Leicester's Commonwealth*. "Enmity to Leicester dating from Arundell's father's execution gives Arundell motive aplenty, and the style of writing and the intimate courtly knowledge the libel conveys all point strongly in Arundel's direction."[31]

In summary, Anderson offers this observation:

> Historians treat the anti–Leicester libels as "gross and malevolent": a "mass of misdemeanors and infamies"; and "not only scurrilous but dangerous, even treacherous." Yet, to D.C. Peck..., "in our investigations of individual charges, in this and the other libels against the earl [of Leicester], we find few to be entirely true, but few to be entirely false." The Elizabethan historian E.K. Chambers concluded that the bias of the anti–Leicester libels "is too strong to give ... unsupported statements much credence."
>
> So it goes with the Arundell-Howard Libels against de Vere. They cannot be wholly written off, but no responsible historian has cause to take them at face value either.[32]

This balanced, judicial and reasonable approach to controversial evidence leads the reader to follow Anderson when he compares Arundel's statements with those of Dogberry in *Much Ado about Nothing*. Anderson points out that Arundel said Oxford "perjured himself a hundred times and damned himself into the pit of hell." Anderson's sly comment on Arundell's assertion takes us back to Shakespeare's text: "Or as Dogberry puts it, 'Why this is flat perjury to call a prince's brother 'Villain.'... O villain, thou will be condemned into everlasting redemption for this!"[33]

As with most of the best books on the authorship question, Mark Anderson's *"Shakespeare" by Another Name* repeatedly sends readers back to Shakespeare's plays and poems. Bill Bryson's life of William Shakspere is far less likely to do so.

The Bryson book is part of a series of biographies. While Bryson admits the world does not need yet another life of Shakespeare, he asserts that the series, the Eminent Lives Series, needed one.[34] Bryson happily admits that Shakespearean biography has been largely conjecture simply because we know little about his life and that little is not the stuff of which biographies are traditionally made. He does not intend continuing that tradition, but rather describes his aim as "to see how much of Shakespeare we can know, really know, from the record." And he admits that his aim explains why his book is so "slender."[35]

While the result is readable, it is also disappointing. What makes it disappointing is the amount of material in the slender volume that is about the times, or social conditions, or the Armada, but never presented in a way that actually touches the life of William Shakspere of Stratford — unless it is to debunk one of the myths that has sprung up about him. For instance, here is Bryson on the notorious tale of the young poet as poacher:

> Formal education stopped for Shakespeare probably when he was about fifteen. What became of him immediately after that is unknown — though many legends have rushed in to fill the vacuum. A particularly durable one is that he was caught poaching deer from the estate of Sir Thomas Lucy of Charlecote, just outside Stratford, and prudently elected to leave town in a hurry. The story and its attendant details are often repeated as fact even now. Roy Strong, in the scholarly *Tudor and Jacobean Portraits*, states that Shakespeare left Stratford in 1585 'to avoid prosecution for poaching at Charlecote' and that he was to be found in London the following year. In fact, we don't know when he left Stratford or arrived in London or whether he ever poached so much as an egg. It is, in any case, unlikely that he poached deer from Charlecote, as it didn't have a deer park until the following century.[36]

This would be admirable if it were not so dreary. Why should anyone with any interest in Shakespeare wish to once again disentangle the ghastly tales that have gathered around the memory of William Shakspere? Worse, Bryson inserts the word "probably" in his sentence on the ending of Shakspere's education. He knows perfectly well that there is no evidence William Shakspere ever attended school much less any evidence to determine when he stopped going.

The myth of the Stratford man has the power to make a good, lively, and funny writer like Bill Bryson become dull. His writing comes to life in a footnote when he throws himself with relief on the real, documented life of an actual writer, John Stow, the historian of London. Despite Bryson's best efforts to try and make a biography of a poet and playwright from the facts of the life of the man from Stratford, he can't do it. It would be reasonable to guess that his experience would send him in search of the true author. But no. Bryson, like the experts he interviews in his journalistic approach to the authorship question, is convinced of only one thing, the words with which he concludes his book: "Only one man had the circumstances and the gifts to give us such incomparable works, and William Shakespeare of Stratford was unquestionably that man — whoever he was."[37] It is the use of the word "unquestionably" that makes this statement of faith at once pathetic, nonsensical, and deadly. At the beginning of the twenty-first century, it is a wonder that anyone still clings to it.

Just about a century ago, Mark Twain contemplated the Stratford Monument and decided that, based on the gullibility of the human race, it would probably stand for another three hundred years. Twain was right, and the Monument will no doubt continue to attract tourists for at least another two centuries. The big advantage now, however, is that lovers of Shakespeare have a far better chance than ever before of finding their way to the happy hunting ground of the Shakespeare controversy.

Chapter Notes

Introduction

1. See R.C. Churchill, *Shakespeare and His Betters* (Bloomington: Indiana University Press, 1958); Frank W. Wadsworth, *The Poacher from Stratford* (Berkeley: University of California Press, 1958); H. N. Gibson, *The Shakespeare Claimants* (London: Methuen, 1962); and Samuel Schoenbaum, "Part Six — Deviations," in *Shakespeare's Lives* (Oxford: Clarendon Press, 1970).

2. Lord Sydenham of Combe, "The First Baconian," *Baconiana*, February, 1933, pp. 143–150.

3. Allardyce Nicoll, "The First Baconian," *The Times Literary Supplement* (London), February 25, 1932, p. 128.

4. L. H. Butterfield, *Diary and Autobiography of John Adams* (Cambridge, Mass.: Belknap Press of Harvard University Press, 1961), vol. 3, p. 185.

5. Joseph C. Hart, *The Romance of Yachting* (New York: Harper, 1848), p. 213.

Chapter 1

1. Unless otherwise noted, the facts of Delia Bacon's life related here are drawn from Theodore Bacon, *Delia Bacon: A Biographical Sketch* (London: Sampson Low, Marston, Searle and Rivington, 1888); Irving Wallace, *The Square Pegs: Some Americans Who Dared to Be Different* (New York: Alfred A. Knopf, 1957); and Martin Pares, *A Pioneer: In Memory of Delia Bacon* (London: Francis Bacon Society, 1958).

2. Quoted in Pares, p. 15.

3. Pares, p. 15.

4. Delia Bacon, *The Philosophy of the Plays of Shakspere Unfolded* (1857; reprint, New York: AMS Press, 1970), p. lxv.

5. The influence of Margaret Fuller was first suggested by Irving Wallace, p. 180.

6. Mrs. John (Eliza) Farrar, *Recollections of Seventy Years* (Boston: Ticknor and Fields, 1866), p. 319.

7. Pares, p. 15.

8. *Ibid.*, p. 16.

9. Farrar, p. 320.

10. Quoted in Wallace, pp. 182–183.

11. *Ibid.*

12. Ralph Waldo Emerson, *Representative Men* (Boston: Phillips, Sampson, 1850), pp. 214–215.

13. Editor's note to Delia Bacon, "William Shakespeare and His Plays; An Inquiry Concerning Them," *Putnam's Monthly*, January, 1856, p. 1.

14. Quoted by Wallace, p. 197.

15. Nathaniel Hawthorne, *Our Old Home and English Note-Books* (Boston: Houghton Mifflin, 1894), vol. I, p. 141.

16. Quoted by Wallace, p. 170.

17. Putnam's Monthly, p. 2.

18. *Ibid.*, p. 1.

19. *Ibid.*, pp. 2–3.

20. *Ibid.*, p. 13.

21. *Ibid.*, p. 14.

22. *Ibid.*, p. 11.

23. *Ibid.*, p. 11.

24. Hawthorne, p. 141.

25. Pares, p. 5.

26. *The Philosophy of the Plays of Shakspere Unfolded*, p. xxii.

27. *Ibid.*, p. 190.

28. *Ibid.*, pp. 192–193.

29. *Ibid.*, pp. 192–193.

30. *Ibid.*, footnote on p. 194.

31. *Ibid.*, pp. 195–196.

32. *Ibid.*, p. 205.

33. *Ibid.*, p. 203.

34. *Ibid.*, pp. 203–204.

35. *Ibid.*, pp. 207–208.

36. *Ibid.*, pp. 224–225.

37. *Ibid.*, p. 224.

38. *Ibid.*, p. 226.

39. *Ibid.*, p. 227.

40. *Ibid.*, p. 294.

Chapter 2

1. Nathaniel Hawthorne, *Our Old Home and English Note-Books* (Boston: Houghton Mifflin, 1894), vol. I, p. 142.

2. Nathaniel Hawthorne, "Preface," in Delia Bacon, *The Philosophy of the Plays of Shakspere Unfolded* (1857; reprint, New York: AMS Press, 1970), pp. xii–xiii.

3. *Ibid.*, p. xiii.

4. *Ibid.*, p. xiii.

5. William Henry Smith to Nathaniel Hawthorne, quoted in Ignatius Donnelly, *The Great Cryptogram* (Chicago: R.S. Peale, 1888), p. 918.

6. Nathaniel Hawthorne to William Henry Smith, quoted in Donnelly, pp. 918–919.

7. Hawthorne, *Our Old Home*, p. 143.

8. William Douglass O'Connor, *Harrington: A Story of True Love* (Boston: Thayer & Eldridge, 1860); quoted in Donnelly, p. 924.

9. Justin Kaplan, *Walt Whitman: A Life* (New York: Simon & Schuster, 1980), p. 291.

10. Dr. Richard Bucke, ed. *The Complete Prose Works of Walt Whitman* (New York: G.P. Putnam's Sons, 1902), vol. 6, p. 70.

11. *Ibid.*, pp. 74–75.

12. *Ibid.*, p. 89.

13. Edgar Lee Masters, *Whitman* (London: Charles Scribner's Sons, 1937), p. 233.

14. Walt Whitman, November Boughs; quoted in *The Shakespeare Fellowship Quarterly*, July 1946, p. 46.

15. Ignatius Donnelly waxes enthusiastic about this point made by Mrs. Pott in his *The Great Cryptogram*, p. 931.

16. Justin Kaplan, p. 290.

17. Mark Twain, "Is Shakespeare Dead?" in *The Complete Essays of Mark Twain*, ed. Charles Neider, (Garden City, NY: Doubleday, 1963), p. 410.

18. *Ibid.*, p. 411.

19. *Ibid.*, pp. 415–418.

20. *Ibid.*, p. 420.

21. *Ibid.*, p. 423.

22. *Ibid.*, pp. 447–448.

23. *Ibid.*, pp. 448–449.

24. *Ibid.*, p. 427.

25. *Ibid.*, p. 452.

Chapter 3

1. Richard Grant White, "The Bacon-Shakespeare Craze," *Atlantic Monthly*, April, 1883, p. 521.

2. Unless otherwise noted, the facts of Ignatius Donnelly's life related here are drawn from the articles "Eleanor Cecilia Donnelly" and "Ignatius Donnelly" in *The Dictionary of American Biography*; and David D. Anderson, *Ignatius Donnelly* (Boston: Twayne Publishers, 1980).

3. Quoted by Anderson, p. 43.

4. Ignatius Donnelly, *The Great Cryptogram*, p. v.

5. *Ibid.*, pp. 16–17.

6. *Ibid.*, p. 26.

7. *Ibid.*, p. vi.

8. *Ibid.*, p. 27.

9. *Ibid.*, pp. 28–29.

10. *Ibid.*, pp. 29, 31.

11. *Ibid.*, p. 34.

12. *Ibid.*, p. 36.

13. *Ibid.*, p. 90.

14. *Ibid.*, p. 14.

15. *Ibid.*, p. 51.

16. *Ibid.*, p. 506.

17. *Ibid.*, p. 506.

18. *Ibid.*, p. 513.

19. *Ibid.*, p. 540.

20. *Ibid.*, pp. 664–665.

21. Quoted by Anderson, p. 64.

22. Sidney Lee, *A Life of William Shakespeare* (New York: Macmillan, 1898), p. 372.

Chapter 4

1. Oliver Lawson Dick, ed., *Aubrey's Brief Lives* (Ann Arbor: University of Michigan Press, 1962), p. 275.

2. Aubrey's Brief Lives, p. 275.

3. Washington Irving, *The Sketch-Book* (New York: Spencer Press, 1936), pp. 276–277.

4. Unless otherwise noted, the facts of Joseph Skipsey's life related here are drawn from the article "Joseph Skipsey" in *The Dictionary of National Biography*, Supplement, Jan. 1901–Dec. 1911, vol. 1 (Oxford University Press, 1912).

5. Charles Wisner Barrell first demonstrated that the experience of the Skipseys served as the germ for "The Birthplace" in his "Genesis of a Henry James Story," *The Shakespeare Fellowship Quarterly*, October 1945, p. 63.

6. Penelope Fitzgerald, *Edward Burne-Jones* (London: Hamish Hamilton, 1975), p. 187.

7. Barrell, p. 63.

8. J. Cuming Walters, "The Shakespeare Relics at Stratford," *The Times* (London), September 8, 1903, p. 5.

9. Leon Edel and Lyall H. Powers, eds., *The Complete Notebooks of Henry James* (New York: Oxford University Press, 1987), p. 195.

10. Henry James, "The Birthplace," in Leon Edel, ed., *The Complete Tales of Henry James*, vol. 11, 1900–1903 (Philadelphia: J. B. Lippincott, 1964), pp. 427–428.

11. *Ibid.*, p. 446.

12. *Ibid.*, pp. 451–452.

13. *Ibid.*, p. 465.

14. Percy Lubbock, ed., *The Letters of Henry James* (New York: Octagon Books, 1970), Volume 1, p. 424.

Chapter 5

1. Mark Twain, "Is Shakespeare Dead?" in *The Complete Essays of Mark Twain*, ed. Charles Neider, (Garden City, N.Y.: Doubleday, 1963), p. 408.

2. G. G. Greenwood, M.P., *The Shakespeare Problem Restated* (1908; reprint, Westport, Conn.: Greenwood Press, 1970), p. xviii.

3. *Ibid.*, pp. xv–xvi.

4. *Ibid.*, pp. xv–xvi.

5. *Ibid.*, p. ix.

6. *Ibid.*, pp. xii–xiii.

7. *Ibid.*, p. xviii.

8. *Ibid.*, pp. 500–514.

9. *Ibid.*, p. xxiii.

10. Samuel Butler, *Shakespeare's Sonnets*, in Henry Festing Jones and A.T. Bartholomew, eds., *The Works of Samuel Butler* (1925; reprint, New York: AMS Press, 1968), p. xix.

11. *Ibid.*, pp. 48–49.

12. *Ibid.*, p. 49.

13. *Ibid.*, pp. 51–52.
14. *Ibid.*, pp. xvii–xviii.
15. *Ibid.*, p. 109.
16. *Ibid.*, p. 76.
17. *Ibid.*, p. 142.
18. Frank Harris, *The Man Shakespeare* (New York: Mitchell Kennerley, 1909), pp. x–xi.
19. *Ibid.*, p. xiv.
20. *Ibid.*, p. xv.
21. *Ibid.*, pp. 229–238.
22. *Ibid.*, p. 212.
23. *Ibid.*, pp. 208–211.
24. *Ibid.*, p. 201.
25. *Ibid.*, pp. 229–230.
26. Charles Chaplin, *My Autobiography* (New York: Simon and Schuster, 1964), p. 364.

Chapter 6

1. Bronson Feldman, "The Marlowe Mystery," *The Bard*, vol. 3, no. 1 (1980): p. 1. This article clearly delineates the differences between Marlowe's style and outlook and those of Shakespeare.
2. See *ibid.*, pp. 43–46, for a new but much less melodramatic examination of the evidence in the Marlowe murder case.
3. Peter Alvor, *Das neue Shakespeare–Evangelium* (Hannover: Adolf Sponholtz, 1906). See also Joseph S. Galland, *Digesta Anti-Shakespeareana*, Part 1 (Ann Arbor: University Microfilms, 1949).
4. Celestin Demblon, *Lord Rutland est Shakespeare* (Paris: P. Ferdinando, 1912) and *L'Auteur d'Hamlet* (Paris: P. Ferdinando, 1914).
5. James Greenstreet's articles appeared in *The Genealogist*, vol. 7 and 8 in 1891 and 1892.
6. Robert Frazer, *The Silent Shakespeare* (Philadelphia: W.J. Campbell, 1915).
7. Abel Lefranc, *Sous le Masque de "William Shakespeare"* (Paris: Payot & Cie, 1918–1919).
8. A. W. Titherley, *The Sonnets and the Earl of Derby* (Liverpool: Phillip, Son and Nephew, 1943).
9. George Elliott Sweet in his *Shake-speare: The Mystery* (printed by Stanford University Press, 1956) makes a case for Queen Elizabeth as the author. S. Schoenbaum, *Shakespeare's Lives* (New York: Oxford University Press, 1970), pp. 620–629, surveys "Other Claimants" in an attempt to ridicule the authorship question generally. He calls King James the "Black Muslim candidate," for instance, because, while in prison, Malcolm X, when he was still Malcolm Little, argued in favor of the King as the author.

Chapter 7

1. J. Thomas Looney, *"Shakespeare" Identified*, 3rd ed., ed. Ruth Loyd Miller (Jennings, La.: Minos, 1975), vol. 1, p. 2.
2. *Ibid.*, p. 2.
3. *Ibid.*, p. 12.
4. *Ibid.*, pp. 12–13.
5. *Ibid.*, pp. 11–12.
6. *Ibid.*, pp. 11–12.
7. G. G. Greenwood, M.P., *The Shakespeare Problem Restated* (1908; reprint, Westport, Conn.: Greenwood Press, 1970), pp. xviii–xix.
8. Looney, pp. 64–65.
9. *Ibid.*, p. 76.
10. *Ibid.*, p. 71.
11. *Ibid.*, p. 78.
12. J. Thomas Looney to Charles Wisner Barrell, June 6, 1937, in "Discoverer of the True Shakespeare Passes," *The Shakespeare Fellowship Quarterly*, April, 1944, p. 20. Other biographical information is drawn from "John Thomas Looney (1870–1944)" by Percy Allen in *The Shakespeare Fellowship News-Letter* (London), May, 1944, pp. 2–4.
13. "Discoverer of the True Shakespeare Passes," p. 20.
14. *Ibid.*, p. 20.
15. *Ibid.*, p. 20.
16. *Ibid.*, p. 21.
17. Looney, *"Shakespeare,"* p. 80.
18. *Ibid.*, pp. 81–82.
19. *Ibid.*, p. 80.
20. *Ibid.*, p. 92.
21. *Ibid.*, p. 98.
22. *Ibid.*, p. 98.
23. *Ibid.*, p. 99.
24. *Ibid.*, p. 103.
25. *Ibid.*, p. 104.
26. Looney, *"Shakespeare,"* p. 108. Steven W. May in his "The Poems of Edward De Vere, Seventeenth Earl of Oxford," *Studies in Philology*, Early Winter, 1980, describes this poem as "possibly by Oxford." While praising the seriousness and contributions of Oxfordians, Professor May is quick to argue that his withdrawing from Oxford some lyrics that Grosart and others assigned to him weakens Looney's case. It does not. What his work does is render more incomprehensible than ever the contemporary praise of Oxford as a lyric poet and warn us all against certainty in an uncertain field — the attribution of Elizabethan literary works, including those attributed to "Shakespeare." Professor May rends literary works from their historical contexts and relies on such things as the tracing of initials in light ink on a manuscript with darker ink as evidence — a caricature of the application of scientific principles to literary and historic research compared with Looney's method.
27. Looney, *"Shakespeare,"* p. 108.
28. *Ibid.*, p. 109.
29. *Ibid.*, p. 112.
30. *Ibid.*, p. 112.
31. *Ibid.*, p. 257.
32. Ruth Loyd Miller, "The Earl of Oxford — A Patron of the English Renaissance," in *"Shakespeare" Identified*, 3rd ed., vol. 2, pp. 486–533.
33. Looney, "Shakespeare," p. 310.
34. *Ibid.*, p. 367.
35. J. Thomas Looney, "'Shakespeare': Lord Oxford or Lord Derby?" *National Review* (England), February, 1922.
36. "Discoverer of the True Shakespeare Passes," p. 21.
37. Looney, "Shakespeare," p. 426.
38. *Ibid.*, p. 415.

39. *Ibid.*, pp. 419–420.
40. *Ibid.*, pp. 420–421.
41. *Ibid.*, p. 431.
42. *Ibid.*, pp. 431–435.
43. *Ibid.*, p. 436.
44. *Ibid.*, pp. 402–403.
45. J. Thomas Looney to Mrs. Eva Turner Clark, August 10, 1928, in "Discoverer of the True Shakespeare Passes," p. 18.
46. See the article on "Richard Congreve" in *The Dictionary of National Biography*.
47. See the article on "John Kells Ingram" in *The Dictionary of National Biography*.
48. J. Thomas Looney to Mrs. Eva Turner Clark, November 10, 1939, in "Discoverer of the True Shakespeare Passes," p. 22.
49. Ruth Loyd Miller, "John Thomas Looney," in *"Shakespeare" Identified*, 3rd ed., vol. 1, p. 654.

Chapter 8

1. Frederick Taber Cooper in *The Forum*, Spring 1920; quoted in J. Thomas Looney, *"Shakespeare" Identified*, 3rd ed., edited by Ruth Loyd Miller (Jennings, La.: Mino, 1975), vol. 1, p. 655.
2. Ruth Loyd Miller, "John Thomas Looney," in *"Shakespeare" Identified*, 3rd ed., vol. 1, p. 648.
3. John Thomas Looney, "Poems of Edward De Vere," in *ibid.*, p. 544.
4. *Ibid.*, p. 546.
5. Sidney Lee, *A Life of William Shakespeare* (New York: Macmillan, 1898), p. 403.
6. B. R. Ward's book is quoted and supplemented in *"Shakespeare" Identified*, 3rd ed., vol. 2, pp. 211–225.
7. *Ibid.*, p. 218.
8. J. Thomas Looney to Will D. Howe, June 2, 1938, in "Discoverer of the True Shakespeare Passes," p. 22.
9. Gerald H. Rendall, *Shakespeare's Sonnets and Edward De Vere* (London: John Murray, 1930), p. 86.
10. Sigmund Freud to Dr. R. Flatter, 1932; quoted in *"Shakespeare" Identified*, 3rd ed., vol. 2, p. 268.
11. A.L. Rowse, *Shakespeare's Southampton* (New York: Harper & Row, 1965), p. 65.
12. Eva Turner Clark, *Hidden Allusions in Shakespeare's Plays*, 3rd rev. ed. (Jennings, La.: Minos, 1974), p. 15.
13. "Discoverer of the True Shakespeare Passes," p. 22.
14. Charles Wisner Barrell, *Elizabethan Mystery Man* (New York: August Gauthier, 1940), p. 3.
15. Eva Turner Clark, "To Members of the Shakespeare Fellowship," *The Shakespeare Fellowship Newsletter*, December, 1939, p. 1.
16. S. Schoenbaum, *Shakespeare's Lives* (New York: Oxford University Press, 1970), p. vii.
17. *Ibid.*, p. vii.
18. *Ibid.*, p. ix.
19. *Ibid.*, p. viii.
20. *Ibid.*, p. viii.
21. *Ibid.*, p. 598.
22. *Ibid.*, p. 599.
23. *Ibid.*, p. 598.

24. Looney, *"Shakespeare,"* vol. 1, p. 183, and footnote on the same page.
25. Schoenbaum, note on p. 530.
26. Frank W. Wadsworth, *The Poacher from Stratford* (Berkeley: University of California Press, 1958), p. 111.
27. *Ibid.*, p. 126.
28. H.N. Gibson, *The Shakespeare Claimants* (New York: Barnes & Noble, 1962), p. 248.
29. J. Thomas Looney, *The Shakespeare Fellowship Newsletter*, December, 1940, p. 2.
30. Charles Wisner Barrell, "New Milestone in Shakespeare Research," *The Shakespeare Fellowship Quarterly*, October 1944, pp. 49–66; reprinted in Eva Turner Clark, *Hidden Allusions*.
31. Charles Wisner Barrell, "Shakespeare's Own Secret Drama," *Shakespeare Fellowship Newsletter*, Dec. 1941-Oct. 1942; reprinted and supplemented in Looney, "Shakespeare," vol. 2, p. 70–106.
32. Wadsworth, p. 129
33. G.W. Phillips, "This Star of England," *The Shakespeare Fellowship News-Letter* (London), April 1953, pp. 8–9.
34. Schoenbaum, p. 605.
35. *Ibid.*, p. 611.
36. *Ibid.*, p. 612.
37. *Ibid.*, p. 612.
38. Abraham Feldman, "Shakespeare's Jester — Oxford's Servant," *The Shakespeare Fellowship Quarterly*, Autumn 1947, pp. 39–43. Excerpts of this article are reprinted in Looney, "Shakespeare," vol. 2, pp. 152–156. For Feldman's clarifying response to Norman Holland's attack, see his "Psychoanalysis and Shakespeare," *The Psychoanalytic Review*, 53 (1966).
39. J. Thomas Looney to Carolyn Wells, December 6, 1932, in "Discoverer of the True Shakespeare Passes," p. 19.
40. S. Schoenbaum, *William Shakespeare: A Documentary Life* (New York: Oxford University Press/The Scolar Press, 1975), p. xi.
41. *Ibid.*, p. xi.
42. *Ibid.*, p. xi.
43. *Ibid.*, p. xi.
44. Looney, *"Shakespeare,"* vol. 1, p. 44.
45. Alden Brooks drew attention to the importance of this transaction and the significance of its suppression by traditional scholars in his *Will Shakspere and the Dyer's Hand* (New York: Charles Scribner's Sons, 1943), pp. xii–xiv. Brooks did more than anyone else to show how William Shakspere appeared to his contemporaries. Brooks's own theory of the authorship goes awry by out-disintegrating even the most ardent of professional disintegrators. Nonetheless, Brooks's work aroused the enthusiastic interest of Maxwell Perkins, the editor, and Ernest Hemingway; and his books did much to popularize what Looney called the "negative" side of the question.
46. Schoenbaum, *Shakespeare's Lives*, p. 648.
47. Looney, "Shakespeare," vol. 2, pp. 281–282.

Chapter 9

1. This discussion is based in part on Warren Hope, "A Review: *Hamlet Himself*," in *The Bard*, Vol. 2, No.

4, 1980. Bronson Feldman, *Hamlet Himself* (Philadelphia: Lovelore Press, 1977), p. 3.

2. *Ibid.*, p. 23.
3. *Ibid.*, p. 22.
4. *Ibid.*, pp. 23–24.
5. *Ibid.*, pp. 71–72.
6. *Ibid.*, p. 100
7. *Ibid.*, pp. 110–111.
8. *Ibid.*, p. 126.
9. Charlton Ogburn, *The Mysterious William Shakespeare: The Myth and the Reality* (New York: Dodd, Mead & Company, 1984), p. x.
10. *Ibid.*, p. xiii.
11. This discussion is indebted to material available at: www.pbs.org/wgbh/frontline/debates.
12. This discussion of the *Frontline* program "The Shakespeare Mystery" is based on viewing the original telecast and the DVD of it that is available from PBS.

Chapter 10

1. "Looking for Shakespeare: Two Partisans Explain and Debate the Authorship Question," *The Atlantic Monthly*, Vol. 268, No. 4 (October 1991, 46–61. All quotations here are from the online version available at www.theatlantic.com/unbound/flashbks/shakes.
2. Joseph Sobran, review of "The Mysterious William Shakespeare: The Myth and the Reality," in *National Review*, April 5, 1985.
3. Irvin Leigh Matus, *Shakespeare, in Fact* (New York: Continuum Publishing Co., 1999), p. 9.
4. *Ibid.*, p. 13.
5. *Ibid.*, pp. 30–32.
6. *Ibid.*, p. 65. See also Mark Anderson, *"Shakespeare" by Another Name* (New York: Gotham Books, 2005), pp. 255–257.
7. Matus, p. 266.
8. Alan H. Nelson, *Monstrous Adversary* (Liverpool: Liverpool University Press, 2003), p. 246.
9. Joseph Quincy Adams, *Shakespearean Playhouses: A History of English Theaters from the Beginnings to the Restoration* (Cambridge: Riverview Press, 1917). The quotation here is drawn from an online excerpt available from www.theatredatabase.com/16th_century/first_blackfriars_theatre.
10. Matus, p. 293.
11. Nelson, pp. 1–2.
12. *Ibid.*, pp. 89–92.
13. *Ibid.*, p. 92.
14. *Ibid.*, p. 167.
15. *Ibid.*, p. 141.
16. *Ibid.*, p. 157.
17. *Ibid.*, pp. 155–157.
18. *Ibid.*, p. 248.
19. *Ibid.*, p. 266.
20. *Ibid.*, p. 442.

Chapter 11

1. Alan H. Nelson, *Monstrous Adversary* (Liverpool: Liverpool University Press, 2003), p. xviii.
2. Peter R. Moore, "The Earl of Oxford and the Order of the Garter," *The Shakespeare Oxford Newsletter*, Spring 1996. All quotations are drawn from the online version available at www.shakespeare-oxford.com.
3. *Ibid.*
4. *Ibid.*
5. *Ibid.*
6. *Ibid.*
7. *Ibid.*
8. *Ibid.*
9. *Ibid.*
10. *Ibid.*
11. See Nelson, pp. 146–147.
12. Nina Green, "An Earl in Bondage," *The Shakespeare Oxford Newsletter*, Summer 2004, p. 1.
13. Christopher Paul, "A Crisis in Scholarship: Misreading the Earl of Oxford," *The Oxfordian*, Vol. 9 (2006): 96.
14. *Ibid.*, p. 109.
15. See Roger Stritmatter, "The Marginalia of Edward de Vere's Geneva Bible: Providential Discovery, Literary Reasoning, and Historical Consequences," Ph.D. Diss. University of Massachusetts, 2001.
16. Elliott Baker, ed. *Shakespeare's Philosophy Unfolded* by Delia Bacon (Philadelphia: Xlibris, 2001).
17. Diana Price, *Shakespeare's Unorthodox Biography* (Westport, Conn.: Greenwood Press, 2001), p. xv.
18. *Ibid.*, p. 91.
19. *Ibid.*, p. 94.
20. *Ibid.*, p. 91.
21. *Ibid.*, pp. 302–305.
22. William Rubinstein, "Who Was Shakespeare?" *History Today*, August 2001, p. 30.
23. Brenda James and William D. Rubinstein, *The Truth Will Out* (New York: Harper Perennial, 2006), pp. 39–40.
24. *Ibid.*, p. 40.
25. *Ibid.*, p. 47.
26. *Ibid.*, p. 50.
27. Robin P. Williams, *Sweet Swan of Avon* (Berkeley, Calif.: Wilton Circle Press, 2006), p. 221.
28. *Ibid.*, p. 117.
29. Mark Anderson, *"Shakespeare" by Another Name* (New York: Gotham Books, 2005), p. 13.
30. *Ibid.*, pp. 167–168.
31. *Ibid.*
32. *Ibid.*
33. *Ibid.*, p. 169.
34. Bill Bryson, *Shakespeare: The World as Stage* (New York: Atlas Books, 2007), p. 21.
35. *Ibid.*
36. *Ibid.*, p. 39
37. *Ibid.*, p. 196.

PART II

Chronological
Annotated Bibliography

The literature devoted to the Shakespeare authorship question is immense. In 1884 W.H. Wyman's *Bibliography of the Bacon-Shakespeare Controversy* contained 255 references. By 1949 Joseph Galland's monumental manuscript *Digesta Anti-Shakespeareana* had 4,509 entries. The following bibliography contains the seminal works, much of the periodical literature of the past several decades, and a selection from the vast literature on the question that has appeared since 1728.

We do not include biographies of Shakespeare unless they contain significant material on the authorship question. Thus such well-received modern biographies as Park Honan's *Shakespeare: A Life* (1999), Peter Ackroyd's *Shakespeare: The Biography* (2005) and Stephen Greenblatt's *Will in the World* (2005) are omitted. Nor is the issue raised in Susan Cooper's excellent young adult novel, *King of Shadows* (1999), in which a modern teen travels through time to perform at the Globe under the tutelage of Shakespeare.

An Essay Against Too Much Reading. With the Whole Lives and Proceedings of Sancho and Peepo, at Aix la Chapelle in Germany and A True Account and Design of the Proceedings This Last Year in So Many Processions at Bath. London: A. Moore, **1728**. (Anonymous but Joseph Galland indicates it may be by Matthew Concanen.)

At the time of publication this cost 1 shilling. The authorship question emerges in "An Essay Against Reading, &c." on pages 12–15 with complaints about the deleterious effects of Shakespeare's reputation. He has frightened people from writing for fear they cannot measure up to his standards. "I will give you a short account of Mr. Shakespeare's Proceeding; and that I had from one of his intimate acquaintance. His being imperfect in some things, was owing to his not being a scholar, which obliged him to have one of those chuckle-pated historians for his particular associate, that could scarce speak a word but upon that subject; and he maintain'd him, or he might have starv'd upon his history. And when he wanted any thing in his way, as his plays were all historical, he sent to him, and took down the heads of what was for his purpose in characters, which were thirty times as quick as running to the books to read for it: Then with his natural flowing wit, he work'd it into all shapes and forms, as his beautiful thought directed. The other put it into grammar; and instead of reading, he stuck close to writing and study without book. How do you think, reading could have assisted him in such great thoughts? It would only have lost time. When he found his thoughts grow on him so fast, he could have write for ever, had he liv'd so long."

Lawrence, Herbert. *The Life and Adventures of Common Sense: An Historical Allegory*. London: Montagu Lawrence, **1769**. 2nd ed., London: J. Whiston and M. Lawrence, 1771. 2 vols.

Volume I, Chapter IX of the first edition: "At the time of my imprisonment in Florence, it seems my father, Genius and Humour made a trip to London, where, upon their arrival, they made an acquaintance with a person belonging to the playhouse; this man was a profligate in his youth, and, as some say, had been a deer-stealer, others deny it; but be that as it will, he certainly was a thief from the time he was first capable of distinguishing any thing; and therefore it is immaterial what articles he dealt in. I say, my father and his friends made a sudden and violent intimacy with this man, who, seeing that they were a negligent careless people, took the first opportunity that presented itself, to rob them of every thing he cold lay his hands on, and the better to conceal his theft, he told them, with an affected concern, that one misfortune never comes along.... As soon as he had got fairly rid of them, he began to examine the fruits of his ingenuity. Amongst my father's baggage, he presently cast his eye upon a common place book, in which was contained, an infinite variety of modes and forms, to express all the different sentiments of the human mind, together with rules for their combinations and connections upon every subject or occasion that might occur in dramatic writing. He found too in a small cabinet, a glass, possessed of very extraordinary properties, belonging to Genius and invented by him; by the help of this glass he could, not only approximate the external surface of any object, but even penetrate into the deep recesses of the soul of man — could discover all the passions and note their various oper-ations in the human heart. In a hatbox, wherein all the goods and chattels of Humour were deposited, he met with a mask of curious workmanship; it had the power of making every sentence that came out of the mouth of the wearer, appear extremely pleasant and entertaining — the jocose expression of the features was exceedingly natural, and it had nothing of that shining polish common to other masks, which is too apt to cast disagreeable reflections.

"In what manner he had obtained this illgotten treasure was unknown to every body but my mother, Wisdom, and Myself; and we should not have found it out, if the mask, which upon all other occasion it used to disguise, had not make the discovery. The mask of humour was our old acquain-tance, but we agreed, tho' much against my Mother's inclination, to take no notice of the robbery, for we conceived that my Father and his friends would easily recover their loss, and were likewise appre-hensive that we could not distress this Man without depriving his Country of it greatest Ornament."

Adams, John. "Notes on a Tour of English Country Seats, &C., with Thomas Jefferson, 4–10? April **1786**" in *Diary and Autobiography of John Adams.* Edited by L.H. Butterfield. Vol-ume 3. Cambridge, Mass.: Belknap Press of Harvard University Press, 1961.

When giants walked the earth, two of them, John Adams and Thomas Jefferson, toured the English countryside. Of Shakespeare's birthplace, Adams wrote: "Stratford upon Avon is interesting as it is the Scaene of the Birth, Death and Sepulture of Shakespear. Three Doors from the Inn, is the House where he was born, as small and mean, as you can conceive. They shew Us an old Wooden Chair in the Chim-ney Corner, where He sat. We cutt off a Chip according to the Custom. A Mulberry Tree that he planted has been cut down, and is carefully preserved for Sale. The House where he died had been taken down and the Spot is now only Yard or Garden. The Curse upon him who should remove his Bones, which is written on his Grave Stone, alludes to a Pile of some Thousands of human Bones, which lie exposed in that Church. There is nothing preserved of this great Genius which is worth knowing — nothing which might inform Us what Education, what Company, what Accident turned his Mind to Letters and the Drama. His name is not even on his Grave Stone. An ill sculptured Head is sett up by his Wife, by the Side of his Grave in the Church. But paintings and Sculpture would be thrown away upon his Fame. His Wit, and Fancy, his Taste and Judgment, His Knowledge of Nature, of Life and Character, are immortal." In *Thomas Jefferson and the New Nation* (New York: Oxford University Press, 1970), p. 344, Merrill D. Peterson records the reactions of Adams and Jefferson upon visiting Stratford. Jefferson merely noted the costs of guide, seeing the birthplace, tombstone, and entertainment plus remuneration for servants and transportation.

Wilmot, James. [Views delivered via James Corton Cowell.] At Ipswich Philosophic Society, February 7, **1805**. See: Nicoll, Allardyce (1932) and Sydenham of Combe, Lord (1933).

Disraeli, Benjamin. *Venetia.* **1837.** Republished, New York and London: M. Walter Dunne, 1904.

This is a two-volume novel by the British prime minister, the Earl of Beaconsfield. Venetia is based on Clara, Percy Bysshe Shelley's daughter. Lord Cadurcis is based on George Gordon, Lord Byron. On page 154 of Volume II: "'And who is Shakespeare?' said Cadurcis. 'We know of him as much as we do of Homer. Did he write half the plays attributed to him? Did he ever write a single whole play? I doubt it. He appears to me to have been an inspired adapter for the theatres, which were then not as good as barns. I take him to have been a botcher-up of old plays. His popularity is of modern date, and it may not last; it would have surprised him marvellously. Heaven knows, at present, all that bears his name is alike admired; and a regular Shakespearian falls into ecstasies with trash which deserves a niche in the Dunciad. For my part, I abhor your irregular geniuses, and I love to listen to the little nightingale of Twickenham.'" The "little nightingale" refers to Alexander Pope. We see that this is not so much a questioning of authorship as of Shakespeare's genius.

Dickens, Charles. *The Letters of Charles Dickens, 1833 to 1870.* Edited by Georgina Hogarth and Mamie Dickens. London: Macmillan, 1893. [**1847**]

Dickens' sister-in-law Georgina and eldest daughter Mamie include the June 13, 1847, letter to William Sandys. Paragraph two: "I have sent your Shakespearian extracts to Collier. [John Payne Collier] It is a Great comfort, to my thinking, that so little is known concerning the poet. It is a fine mystery; and I tremble every day lest something should come out. If he had had a Boswell, society wouldn't have respected his grave, but would calmly have had his skull in the phrenological shop-windows."

Hart, Joseph C. *The Romance of Yachting.* New York: Harper, **1848**.

Aboard the yacht *Restless* in Spanish waters, our author expounds (pp. 207–242), "Oh, Shakspeare — Immortal bard — Mighty genius — Swan of Avon — thou Unapproachable! Art there no more fish, no more krakens in that wondrous sea from which thou wert taken? Shall there be no more cakes and ale?" Hart reviews Nicholas Rowe's 1709 memoir and says that Ben Jonson was more honored than the Swan till Rowe. As for Shakspeare, a "destitution of authentic incidents marks every stage of his life." His background is presented. An interesting point: Shakespeare's obscenity exceeded other dramatists. A subconscious plug for the common Stratford man? Hart explains the origin of various works, e.g., *A Midsummer Night's Dream, Hamlet.* "Upon the same principle that the Shakspere series of plays selected by Rowe and Betterton are called Shakspeare's, might we call the rare old tracts and papers of the Harleian Miscellany, the Earl of Oxford's, because they were found in his library, and some of them copied in his hand-writing. If they had been buried a century or two, he certainly would have been their author with the commentators of the calibre of those, generally, who have written upon Shakspeare."

Emerson, Ralph Waldo. *Representative Men.* Boston: Phillips, Sampson, **1850**.

This includes "Uses of Great Men," "Plato; or, The Philosopher," "Plato: New Readings," "Swedenborg; or, The Mystic," "Montaigne; or, The Skeptic," "Shakspeare; or, The Poet," "Napoleon; or, The Man of the World," and "Goethe; or, The Writer."

Regarding Shakespeare's plays, "It is now no longer possible to say who wrote them first. They have been the property of the Theatre so long, and so many rising geniuses have enlarged or altered them, inserting a speech, or a whole scene, or adding a song, that no man can any longer claim copyright of this work of numbers." Extolling the men of the Elizabethan Age, Emerson finds it odd that "their genius failed them to find out the best head in the universe. Our poet's mask was impenetrable." Later, "the Egyptian verdict of the Shakspeare Societies comes to mind, that he was a jovial actor and manager. I can not marry this fact to his verse. Other admirable men have led lives in some sort of keeping with their thought; but this man, in wide contrast. Had he been less, had he reached only the common measure of great authors, of Bacon, Milton, Tasso, Cervantes, we might leave the fact in the twilight of human fate: but, that this man of men, he who gave to the science of the mind a new and larger subject than had ever existed, and planted the standard of humanity some furlongs forward into Chaos, — that he should not be wise for himself,-it must even go into the world's history, that the best poet led an obscure and profane life, using his genius for the public amusement."

"Who Wrote Shakespeare?" *Chambers's Edinburgh Journal*, August 7, **1852**, pp. 87–89. (This essay, according to Cochrane, 1916, and Wadsworth, 1958, was written by Dr. Robert W. Jameson.)

"With the exception of Homer, who lived before the time of written history, and Junius, who purposely and successfully shrouded himself in obscurity, there has, perhaps, been no great writer who has not in his life, his letters, or his sayings, more or less identified himself with the productions of his pen." There is a "skeleton biography" of Shakespeare but "his whole correspondence, if he ever wrote a letter, has sunk like lead beneath the dark waters of oblivion." According to this, "William Shakspeare, the man, was comparatively well known" and "at least from the time the plays commenced, never had to shift for his living: he had always money to lend and money to spend." Moreover, "What was to hinder William Shakspeare from reading, appreciating, and purchasing these dramas, and thereafter keeping his poet, as Mrs. Packwood did?" Anyway, Shakespeare's friends supported him, and he was well liked. "Take, besides, the custom of the age, the helter-skelter way in which dramas were got up, sometimes by half-a-dozen authors at once, of whom one occasionally monopolised the fame; and the unscrupulous manner in which booksellers appropriated any popular name of the day, and affixed it to their publications." He admits that the dedication of the "Venus" and the "Lucrece" to Lord Southampton does counter this line of argument. How come Raleigh and Bacon didn't know Shakspeare? When the poet died, the employer retired from London.

Carlyle, Thomas. *New Letters of Thomas Carlyle*. Edited and Annotated by Alexander Carlyle. London and New York: John Lane, The Bodley Head, 1904. Republished, Scholarly Press, 1970. [**1853**]

Volume II contains Carlyle's June 13, 1853, two-paragraph letter to his physician brother. Paragraph two: "For the present, we have (occasionally) a Yankee Lady [Delia Bacon], sent by Emerson, who has discovered that the 'Man Shakespear' is a Myth, and did not write those Plays which bear his name, which were on the contrary written by a 'Secret Association' (names unknown): she has actually come to England for the purpose of examining that, and if possible, proving it, from the British Museum and other sources of evidence. Ach Gott!"

Whitman, Walt. *The Complete Prose Works of Walt Whitman*. "Notes and Fragments Left by Walt Whitman." Edited by Richard Bucke. New York: G.P. Putnam's Sons/The Knickerbocker Press, 1902. "Part II. Memoranda from Books and from His Own Reflections — Indicating the Poet's Reading and Thought Preparatory to Writing 'Leaves of Grass.'" [Circa mid–**1850**s]

Note 27 begins, "I think it probable or rather suggest it as such that Bacon or perhaps Raleigh had a hand in Shakespeare's Plays. How much whether as furnisher, pruner, poetical illuminator, knowledge infuser — what he was or did, if anything, is not possible to tell with certainty." After jotting down what was known of the Stratford man, he writes, "Queen Elizabeth no doubt often saw Shakespeare as an actor and applauded him." Later, "Death, Shakespeare, Drayton and Ben Jonson had a merrie meeting, and, it seems, drank too hard, for Shakespeare died of a fever there contracted." Then, "It is evident to me beyond cavil that Shakespeare in his own day and at death was by many placed among the great masters and acknowledged [Later, Whitman put a ? to this paragraph]. And yet the florid style of praise was applied to everybody and almost everything in those times." Later, "'Gentle' is the epithet often applied to him. At that time was not its signification 'like a gentleman,' 'of high-blooded bearing?'" And "Shakespeare put such things into his plays as would please the family pride of Kings and Queens, and of his patrons among the nobility ... all these fed the aristocratic vanity of the young noblemen and gentlemen and feed them in England yet. Common blood is but wash — the here is always of high lineage." Whitman recalls the *Illustrated London News*, 25 October 1856, and the paper read by William Henry Smith, author of "Was Lord Bacon the author of Shakespeare's plays?"

Bacon, Delia. "William Shakespeare and His Plays: An Enquiry Concerning Them." *Putnam's Monthly*, January **1856**, pp. 1–19.

"In commencing the publication of these bold, original, and most ingenious speculations upon the real authorship of Shakespeare's plays, it is proper for the Editor of *Putnam's Monthly*, in disclaiming all responsibility for their startling view of the question, to say that they are the result of long and conscientious investigation on the part of the learned and eloquent scholar, their author; and that the Editor has reason to hope that they will be continued through some future numbers of the Magazine."

Author Delia Bacon is not mentioned by name in what initiated the controversy with a vengeance. She begins: "How can we undertake to account for the literary miracles of antiquity, while this great myth of the modern ages still lies at our own door, unquestioned?" Perhaps her most startling inference is that such a superhuman being as Shakespeare has become must be based on a common fellow because of the necessity for "this one mighty conjuror." Several paragraphs reveal her obsession with finding manuscripts. How could the writer be a clod? Didn't he have "experiences of some sort? Do such things as these, that the plays are full of, begin in the fingers' ends?" And, "Has there been no personal grapple with realities here?" So "it is only the work itself that we now know by that name-the phenomenon and not its beginning." Later, "The common sense cannot any longer receive it." Has any other English writer acted like this? "He [the author] carries the court perfume with him, unconsciously." "These men distinctly postpone, not their personal reputation only, but the interpretation of their avowed works, to freer ages." Was it the invention "of a stupid, ignorant, illiterate, third-rate play-actor"?

Smith, William Henry. "Was Lord Bacon the Author of Shakspeare's Plays? A Letter to Lord Ellesmere," in *The Panorama of Life and Literature*, January 1857, pp. 12–16. Originally published for the author by Woodfall and Kinder, 1856. Reviewed in the *Illustrated London News*, December 6, 1856.

Smith quotes Alexander Pope to the effect that perhaps some of Shakspeare's plays were pieces from unknown authors. Shakspeare's background at Stratford (the suggestion being that he was "removed from school at an early age") and in London is traced. "Seeing, then, that William Shakspeare was a man of limited education, careless of fame, intent upon money-getting, and actively engaged in the management of a theatre, are we, from the simple circumstance of his name being associated with these plays, to believe, at once, that he was the author of them?" Bacon is a better choice. "The history of Bacon is just such as we should have drawn of Shakspeare, if we had been required to depict him from the internal evidence of his works." Smith concludes by quoting an undated letter to Lord Viscount St. Alban [Bacon] from Tobie Matthew with this postscript: "The most prodigious wit that ever I knew of my nation, and of this side of the sea, is of your lordship's name, though he be known by another."

Bacon, Delia. The *Philosophy of the Plays of Shakspere Unfolded*. Preface by Nathaniel Hawthorne. London: Groombridge and Sons, 1857. Republished, New York: AMS Press, 1970.

Noncommittal regarding authorship, Hawthorne's preface commends Bacon's labor. "No man or woman has ever thought or written more sincerely than the author of this book." He concludes: "It is for the public to say whether my countrywoman has proved her theory. In the worst event, if she has failed, her failure will be more honorable than most people's triumphs; since it must fling upon the old tombstone, at Stratford-on-Avon, the noblest tributary wreath that has ever lain there." As Delia herself states early on, "The question of the authorship of the great philosophic poems which are the legacy of the Elizabethan Age to us, is an incidental question in this inquiry, and is incidentally treated here." What Delia attempts to demonstrate is that a cadre of people could see a brighter age for mankind in the future than the despotic age in which they labored. These "suppressed Elizabethan Reformers and Innovators" therefore hid identities and information that might be revealed in a more conducive age. This is almost subsidiary to her analysis of the plays, in particular *King Lear, Julius Caesar* and *Coriolanus*. The Introduction is 93 pages in length and is followed by Book I, "The Elizabethan Art of Delivery and Tradition," and Book II, "Elizabethan 'Secrets of Morality and Policy'; or, The Fables of the New Learning." There are 582 pages in the AMS edition.

Shackford, C.C. "Shakespeare in Modern Thought." *North American Review*, October 1857, pp. 490–514.

Shackford reviews and elaborates on material in four German books and Delia Bacon's *The Philosophy of the Plays of Shakspere Unfolded*. Most attention is given to the latter and to Von G.G. Gervinus' 1850 tome, *Shakespeare*. Shackford begins, "The appreciation of Shakespeare seems to be a test of the genius of an age or a people." As for Bacon as author, "The theory is a nullity, and will not bear the least serious handling." But he finds Delia Bacon's insights of exceptional perspicuity because her work contains "a spirit of subtle analysis, a deep moral insight, and a penetrating research." Nor can there be a group, for a coterie cannot produce art. "The very idea of this perfection of form, this unity of life, presupposes one creative mind, one inspiring, because inspired, genius, alone. There is no dualism or polytheism in creation of any sort."

O'Connor, William Douglass. *Harrington: A Story of True Love.* Boston: Thayer & Eldridge, **1860**.

A novel whose background is the Fugitive Slave Law, this was instrumental in bringing the authorship controversy to a broad audience. O'Connor dealt with the theory in nonfictional terms in *Hamlet's Notebook* (Boston: Houghton, Mifflin, 1886) and *Mr. Donnelly's Reviewers* (Chicago: Belford, Clarke, 1889).

Hawthorne, Nathaniel. *Our Old Home, and English Note-Books.* **1863**; reprinted, Boston: Houghton, Mifflin and Company, 1894. 2 vols.

This is a work whose "Recollections of a Gifted Woman" profiling Delia Bacon as Hawthorne journeys from Leamington to Stratford-on-Avon originally appeared in *The Atlantic Monthly* (January 1863, pp. 43–58). While Hawthorne does recognize Shakespeare's mysterious life, he does not agree with Bacon's interpretation. He describes her negotiations to open the grave, her "noble qualities," her books. He does not think Delia Bacon provided Shakespeare a benefit: "Her labor, while she lived, was of a nature and purpose outwardly irreverent to the name of Shakspeare, yet, by its actual tendency, entitling her to the distinction of being that one of all his worshippers who sought, though she knew it not, to lace the richest and stateliest diadem upon his brow." As for her book, "It was founded on a prodigious error, but was built up from that foundation with a good many prodigious truths." He did advocate its publication, but knew it required an editor who knew what to leave out. He reviews U.S. reprints of sharp criticism in England.

"Lord Palmerston." *Fraser's Magazine for Town and Country*, November **1865**, pp. 665–670.

This tribute to Prime Minister Lord Palmerston, who died on October 18, 1865, contains on page 666: "He was tolerably well up in the chief Latin and English classics; but he entertained one of the most extraordinary paradoxes touching the greatest of them that was ever broached by a man of his intellectual calibre. He maintained that the plays of Shakspeare were really written by Bacon, who passed them off under the name of an actor for fear of compromising his professional prospects and philosophic gravity. Only last year, when this subject was discussed at Broadlands, Lord Palmerston suddenly left the room, and speedily returned with a small volume of dramatic criticisms, in which the same theory (originally started by an American lady) was supported by supposed analogies of thought and expression. 'There,' he said, 'read that, and you will come over to my opinion.' When the positive testimony of Ben Jonson, in the verses prefixed to the edition of 1623, was adduced, he remarked, 'Oh, these fellows always stand up for one another, or he may have been deceived like the rest.' The argument had struck Lord Palmerston by its ingenuity, and he wanted leisure for a searching exposure of its groundlessness."

Farrar, Eliza Ware. *Recollections of Seventy Years.* 2nd ed. Boston: Ticknor and Fields, **1866**.

Mrs. John Farrar, as she is often listed, writes about Robespierre, Lady Hamilton, "The French State," Edinburgh and assorted other people and places with whom she was acquainted. Chapter 40 is "Miss Delia Bacon." Farrar describes Delia's outstanding history lectures and her "fancy," the authorship of Shakespeare, which Farrar and her friends thought wise not to mention in Delia's presence. Farrar reviews Delia's trip to England, her meetings with Carlyle, Emerson and Hawthorne, using letters from Delia to herself and a London meeting as references. "Her life of privation and seclusion was very injurious to both body and mind."

Holmes, Nathaniel. *The Authorship of Shakespeare.* **1866**. 2 vols. 4th ed., 1886. New and enlarged ed., Boston: Houghton, Mifflin, 1887. Reprinted, New York: AMS Press, 1976.

Bacon was the author. "The biography of William Shakespeare may now be considered as in the main settled and fixed for all time. Modern research has explored every forgotten corner in search of new facts; all discoverable archives and dusty repositories of lost books and derelict papers have been ransacked." As for genius, "School, or no school, without books and studies, we know that learning is impossible." Other chapters: "Preliminaries, Bacon, Further Proofs, More Direct Proofs, Models. In Volume 2: Philosophical Evidences, Spiritual Illumination, Conclusion, Index. Appendices.

Sedgwick, A.G. "Holmes's Authorship of Shakespeare." *North American Review*, January 1867, pp. 276–278.

    This reviews Nathaniel Holmes's 1866 book, *The Authorship of Shakespeare*. The reviewer does not buy Judge Holmes' argument that Bacon was the author, contending that Bacon could not have written *The Tempest* and that the legal terms in Shakespearean plays were commonly understood in their day.

"Literary Notices: The Authorship of Shakspere, by Nathaniel Holmes." *Harper's Magazine*, January 1867, pp. 263–264.

    The reviewer indicates that Holmes ingeniously argues his case (that the works were by Francis Bacon, not, as Delia Bacon intimated, by a group) but provides no real evidence to refute Shakespeare's authorship. So what if Bacon wrote sonnets in his youth, so did everyone else around the Virgin Queen's court.

Morgan, James Appleton. *The Shakespearean Myth: William Shakespeare and Circumstantial Evidence*. Cincinnati: R. Clarke & Co., 1881.

    Primarily a groupist, Morgan makes a good case against the Stratford man in this and numerous other books and articles, including *Digesta Shakespearianae: Being a Topical Index of Printed Matter, Other Than Literary or Aesthetic Commentary or Criticism, Relating to William Shakespeare, or the Shakespearean Plays and Poems, Printed in the English Language to the Year 1886* (New York: Shakespeare Society of New York, 1887).

Clarke, James Freeman. "Did Shakespeare Write Bacon's Works?" *North American Review*, February 1881, pp. 163–175.

    Clarke wonders how one man could write both the poetry and the prose associated with Shakespeare and Bacon, respectively. Perhaps a reversal is in order: what if we assume Shakespeare wrote Bacon? After all, Shakespeare was a philosopher as well as a poet; Bacon was no poet. Shakespeare picked up his knowledge from the play-houses of London as well as from his grammar school. And since he was in London for 11 years before his name was connected with a play, he had ample time to develop his skill. If it were Bacon, he'd advertise it because he was a proud man. Apparently Clarke had no qualms about the veracity of Shakespeare portraits. He claims they show a dome more capable of thought than Bacon's. Clarke refers to Delia Bacon, William Henry Smith, and Judge Holmes. He believes Holmes made "the most elaborate and masterly work" dethroning Shakespeare.

Halliwell-Phillipps, James Orchard. *Outlines of the Life of Shakespeare*. 1882; reprinted, New York: AMS Press, 1966.

    A preeminent 19th century Shakespeare scholar believes that "the number of the ascertained particulars of his [Shakespeare] life reached at least the average." In Elizabethan times the lives of authors were not of much account and "biographical indifference continued for many years." Thus there's no reason to expect personal correspondence or diaries. He admits that "In the absence of some very important discovery, the general and intense desire to penetrate the mystery which surrounds the personal history of Shakespeare cannot be wholly gratified." One must make a "critical study of the materials now accessible" but "avoid the temptation of endeavoring to decipher his inner life and character through the media of his works." The "dramas were not written for posterity, but as a matter of business, ... the products of an intellect which was applied to authorship as the readiest path to material advancement." As for chronology, "it is not likely that the exact chronological arrangements will be determined." Halliwell-Phillipps tries to sketch Shakespeare's life "strictly out of evidences and deductions from those evidences." He admits that "In no single instance have I at present found in any municipal record a notice of the poet himself." Shakespeare's parents were illiterate but obviously appreciated the importance of education "and the poet, somehow or other, was taught to read and write, the necessary preliminaries to admission into the Free School." And, "it may perhaps be assumed that, at this time, boys usually entered the Free School at the age of seven." Only 188 of the 703 pages are text. Appendices include "The Two Noble Kinsmen," "The Spurious Plays," "Shakespeare's Neighbours," and "Documentary Appendix." There is no contents table; there is a three-page index.

White, Richard Grant. "The Bacon-Shakespeare Craze." *The Atlantic Monthly*, April **1883**, pp. 507–521.

To White it matters not a whit who wrote Shakespeare's plays for that "affects in no way their literary importance or interest, their ethnological or their social significance, their values as objects of literary art, or their power as a civilizing, elevating influence upon the world." His article is chiefly an examination of Mrs. Pott's edition of Bacon's *The Promus of Formularies and Elegancies* and concludes with a general critique of the authorship question. A good point: if Bacon wrote the plays he must have written the Sonnets since we can't dispute the chronology of the latter [Francis Meres mentioned them in 1598]. As for Shakespeare, he was certainly a genius: "glowing with instant inspiration," and "one who, when he wrote, did not seem to have a self," and "the untaught son of the Stratford yeoman a miraculous miracle, that does not defy or suspend the laws of nature." Delia Bacon "was plainly neither a fool nor an ignoramus, she must be insane; not a maniac, but what boys call 'loony.' So it proved: she died a lunatic, and I believe in a lunatic asylum." Humorously, White says Baconians should be carted to a special asylum and cured. "As to treating the question seriously, that is not to be done by men of common sense and moderate knowledge of the subject."

Wyman, W.H. *Bibliography of the Bacon-Shakespeare Controversy with Notes and Extracts*. Cincinnati: Peter G. Thomson, **1884**.

There are 255 annotated entries, from Hart's *Romance of Yachting* (1848) to Appleton Morgan's "Whose Sonnets?" in the May, 1884, issue of *Manhattan*. There is an Index to Titles.

Black, Hugh. "Bacon's Claim and Shakespeare's 'Aye.'" *The North American Review*, October **1887**, pp. 422–426.

Using Bacon's *De Augmentis* to examine the Stratford epitaph, Black makes much of the large and small letters. "It is now clear that this epitaph was written by Bacon." As for Shakespeare's part — he consented.

Clark, Edward Gordon. "Bakon, Shaxpere — We." *The North American Review*, October **1887**, pp. 426–434.

Although he says he was never a Baconian, rather "an impartial literary expert," Clark supports Hugh Black's contention that Bacon had something to do with Shakespeare and carries the decipherment of the epitaph even farther. He concludes that there will be little difficulty bringing out "The Anagrammatic Biography of William Shakspere: By Francis Bacon."

Vinton, Arthur Dudley. "Those Wonderful Ciphers." *The North American Review*, October **1887**, pp. 555–562.

In light of the Hugh Black and Edward Gordon Clark articles, Vinton reviews four methods of decipherment. He says the authorship question began with the Reverend James Townley's 1759 Drury Lane farce, *High Life Below Stairs*, continued with Delia Bacon, Mrs. C.F.A. Windle's *The Discovery and Opening of the Cipher of Francis Bacon*, Lord Verulam, alike in his prose writing and in the 'Shakespeare' dramas, proving him the author of the dramas, Ignatius Donnelly, Herbert J. Browne, Black and Clark. He finds it odd that Bacon used ciphers for trifling revelations.

Donnelly, Ignatius. *The Great Cryptogram: Francis Bacon's Cipher in the So-Called Shakespeare Plays*. Chicago: R.S. Peale & Co., 1888, ©**1887**. 2 vols.

There are 998 pages in the two volumes. Book I: "The Argument." Book II: The Demonstration." Book III: "Conclusions." There are 15 illustrations, including Bacon, Shakspere, Jonson, Robert Cecil, William Henry Smith, William D. O'Connor, Nathaniel Holmes, Constance Pott, William Thomson and Thomas Davidson. In the first book Donnelly quotes from many sources to prove that the man from Stratford was an illiterate bumpkin incapable of writing that which is attributed to him. He maintains that the author was a lawyer and that Francis Bacon was indeed capable of producing poetry as he was of scientific literature. Why was his authorship concealed? "In the first place, he knows they are youthful and immature performances. In the second place, it will grieve his good, pious mother to know that he doth 'mum and mask and sinfully revel.' In the third place, the reputation of a poet will not materially assist him up those long, steep stairs that lead to the seat his great father occupied." Donnelly cites Sir Walter Scott as another who was secretive about some of his output. Concerning ciphers, Donnelly explains how he had much difficulty until he realized that he was working with common editions of the plays that had been "doctored, altered, corrected by the commentators." Procuring a facsimile copy of the 1623 folio, he found the cipher story purely arithmetical and "grows out of a series of root-numbers." Thus, "The proofs are cumulative. I have shown a thousand of them." This is all explained with diagrams. Book III begins with a discussion of Delia Bacon and is followed with chapters devoted to Baconians such as William Henry Smith. The final chapter is an apologia for misdeeds charged to Bacon. Joseph Gilpin Pyle countered this with *The Little Cryptogram: A Literal Application to the Play of Hamlet of the Cipher System of Mr. Ignatius Donnelly* (St. Paul, MN: Pioneer Press, 1888). One of several biographies of Donnelly is David D. Anderson's *Ignatius Donnelly* (Boston: Twayne, 1980).

Traubel, Horace. *With Walt Whitman in Camden (March 28–July 14, 1888)*. 1905; reprinted, New York: Rowman and Littlefield, 1961.

In several volumes Traubel recorded just about everything about a stay with Whitman. The Shakespeare question rears its head many times. For instance, in Volume I, on Friday, May 11, 1888, Whitman told Traubel, "Tom has been in today. He brought Donnelly's book along—*The Cryptogram*: I told him I wanted to look it over. It is a formidable book: I do not feel strong enough to say I will read it all through: that would be almost a dare-devil thing to promise: but I'm going to tackle it. The subject is attractive to me—I do not deny it—although I have only got along as far as its preliminaries.... I think both sides exaggerate the genius of Shakespeare—set it up too high, count it for too much (far, very far, too much). Do you suppose I accept the almost loony worship of Shakespeare—the cult worship, the college-chair worship? Not a bit of it—not a bit of it.... I do not know that I really care who made the plays—who wrote them. No—I do not think it a supreme human question though it is without doubt a great literary question.... I never met Donnelly, but he has written me. William O'Connor was a storm-blast for Bacon.... I am firm against Shaksper—I mean the Avon man, the actor: but as to Bacon, well, I don't know."

Bacon, Theodore. *Delia Bacon: A Biographical Sketch*. London: Sampson Low, Marston, Searle and Rivington, 1888.

Delia Bacon's nephew examines her childhood, personal tragedy, work in England, relationships with Emerson and Hawthorne, her theory and its reception. This 319-page biography is indexed.

Clark, Edward Gordon. "The Bacon 'Farce' a Tragedy." *The Cosmopolitan*, May 1888, pp. 225–232.

Clark is a doubter. "'Shakespeare,' I think, was a convenient, shrewdly-adopted nom de plume." Bacon claimed authorship via cipher, the counters of which "were cut on Shakspere's grave-stone in the guise of an epitaph." He discusses the varied gravestones at Stratford, citing Halliwell-Phillipps. Why did Bacon open his *Advancement of Learning* with a chapter on ciphers? Reference is made to Hugh Black's October 1887 *North American Review* article. Clark believes the apparent silliness of his translation of the gravestone cipher can be accounted for by Bacon's having used phonetic English spoken by the masses. Shakespeare is said to have died after drinking with Ben Jonson and Dick Drayton. Clark says Bacon poisoned him! This article is not as ridiculous as it may sound from this annotation.

Donnelly, Ignatius. "Delia Bacon's Unhappy Story." *The North American Review*, March **1889**, pp. 307–318.

Basically a review of Theodore Bacon's biography of his aunt, Donnelly points out that her nephew "has not the slightest sympathy with the cause for which she sacrificed her happiness and her life." So, "A biography of Delia Bacon can only be justified by a belief in the truth of the theory with which her life is identified. Anything less than that is to stir the dust of the lunatic dead for commercial purposes; it is to exhibit her, straight-jacket and all, to an unsympathetic public, for a pecuniary consideration." It is also an attack on the British. "Has not the time come for the New World to revise the prejudiced judgments of intolerant and unprogressive England?"

Stopes, Charlotte (Carmichael). *The Bacon-Shakespeare Question Answered.* London: Tuebner and Company, **1889**. Reprinted, New York: AMS, 1973.

Stopes put no credence in the Baconian theory, finding that its proponents have "specious arguments." On the other hand, it opens up new vistas of study of the Elizabethan age. She examines internal and external evidence and ciphers. Sections include "Some Introductory Dates," "Contemporary Biographical Dates," and "Contemporary Minor Dramatists." Stopes is the author of the definitive biography of Southampton.

Pott, Constance Mary (Fearon). *Francis Bacon and His Secret Society: An Attempt to Collect and Untie the Lost Links of a Long and Strong Chain.* Chicago: Francis J. Schulte and Co., **1891**. Reprinted, New York: AMS Press, 1975.

No one man could have done all that Bacon did, writes Pott, thus help came from such societies as the Rosicrucians and Freemasons. Secret societies use ciphers. Pott also wrote the 28-page *Did Francis Bacon Write "Shakespeare"? Thirty-Two Reasons for Believing That He Did* (London: W.H. Guest & Co., 1884; 3rd ed., 1908).

Zeigler, Wilbur Gleason. *It Was Marlowe: A Story of the Secret of Three Centuries.* Chicago: Donohue, Henneberry & Co., **1895**.

This novel's preface makes a good point that a man cognizant of the importance of the plays — "Not marble, nor the gilded monuments/Of princes, shall outlive this powerful rhyme" — will not forget them in his will. Zeigler cites Phillips, Collier, Dowden, Malone, Swinburne and Dyce to support his view that had Marlowe lived longer, he could have written the Shakespeare plays. "This belief was founded upon the striking similarity of the strongest portions of his acknowledged works to passages of the Shakespere plays; the tendency of each to degenerate into pomposity and bombast in passages of tragic pathos [note 7]; the similar treatment of characters, and the like spirit that pervades them." Zeigler does not carry this story as far as Calvin Hoffman, i.e., Marlowe certainly did not die in June, 1593, but wrote from afar.

Harris, C. Shirley. "Sir Anthony Sherley the Author of Shakespeare's Plays." *Notes and Queries*, March 13, **1897**, pp. 204–5.

The above title was a book by the Reverend Scott Surtees read by Mr. Harris, who thinks the seventy-sixth sonnet might bear investigation for the coincidences between Sir Anthony Shirley's life and the plays. For instance, Sherley had a headquarters in Venice in 1604 and 1605. The sonnet mentions Pota, which Harris thinks might be Pola, a seaport on the Adriatic.

Castle, Edward James. *Shakespeare, Bacon, Jonson and Greene.* **1897**; reprinted, Port Washington, NY: Kennikat Press, 1970.

There is no index but there are footnotes in this 352-page book whose primary goal is to show by inference that Bacon provided Shakespeare's legal background.

Schucking, Levin L. *The Meaning of Hamlet.* Translated from the German by Graham Rawson. Oxford: The Clarendon Press, **1897**. Republished, New York: Barnes and Noble, 1968.

For purposes of authorship, pages 9–10 of this 195-page analysis are illuminating. "The most surprising fact about Shakespeare is not, as is commonly supposed, the contrast between his education and his achievements, but rather his personality left so slight an impression on the times in which he lived.... How is it that the incomparable intellectual and creative power of this man, the richness of his imagination, his liberating humor, his fascinating wit, did not keep his name continually on their lips and make him a familiar figure in the life of his time? ... The only possible explanation is that he lived in a particularly secluded way, took little part in social life, and came into contact with the public chiefly through his profession as an actor. This is borne out by the fact that not a single laudatory poem by him has been preserved, although it was a customary proof of friendship among writers of the time to dedicate such compositions to one another, and for the recipients to print them at the beginning of their works."

Lee, Sidney. *A Life of William Shakespeare*. New York: Macmillan, **1898**.

A staunch Stratfordian, Lee "cannot promise my readers any startling revelations. But my researches have enabled me to remove some ambiguities which puzzled my predecessors, and to throw light on one or two topics that have hitherto obscured the course of Shakespeare's career." He does not believe the Sonnets are autobiographical. "Elizabethan sonnets were commonly the artificial products of the poet's fancy." In the first appendix, "The Sources of Biographical Knowledge," Lee traces the biographical knowledge back to 1662 and Fuller's *Worthies*, which he himself reckons poor. "Appendix II: The Bacon-Shakespeare Controversy" (pages 370–73) takes heretics to task. For him there is abundant "contemporary evidence attesting Shakespeare's responsibility for the works." Lee also wrote "Shakespeare, William" in Oxford University Press's *The Dictionary of National Biography* (vol. 17, "Robinson-Sheares"): 1286–1335. "The Bacon-Shakespeare Controversy," a "baseless contention," is discussed by this eminent Stratfordian on pages 1334 and 1335 of the 1964 edition.

Butler, Samuel. *Shakespeare's Sonnets*. The 1925 edition originally published in October **1899** as *Shakespeare's Sonnets Reconsidered*, and in part rearranged; with introductory chapters, notes, and a reprint of the original 1609 edition. New York: AMS Press, 1968.

Butler does not raise the authorship question but presents a workable method of literary criticism: "studying text much and commentators little." Of Sidney Lee he opines that he "has opened his mind so repeatedly, and at such short intervals, that he may well open it again." Shakespeare, Butler says, had nothing to do with the first (1609) publication of the sonnets.

Nietzsche, Friedrich. *The Will to Power*. **1901**. Edition translated by Walter Kaufmann and R.J. Hollingdale, and edited by Walter Kaufmann. New York: Vintage, 1968.

On pages 446–47, note 848 (Spring–Fall 1887), in the "To be classical" section is: "Is the highest personal value not part of it?'—To consider perhaps whether moral prejudices are not playing their game here and whether great moral loftiness is not perhaps in itself a contradiction of the classical?—Whether the moral monsters must not necessarily be romantic, in word and deed?—Precisely such a preponderance of one virtue over the others (as in the case of a moral monster) is hostile to the classical power of equilibrium: supposing one possessed this loftiness and was nonetheless classical, then we could confidently infer that one also possessed immorality of the same level: possibly the case of Shakespeare (assuming it was really Lord Bacon)."

James, Henry. Note from Lamb House, June 12th, **1901**. *The Complete Notebooks of Henry James*. Edited by Leon Edel and Lyall H. Powers. New York and Oxford: Oxford University Press, 1987.

In the note James mentions that Lady Trevelyan spoke of Joseph Skipsey and wife who'd been in charge of the Shakespeare birthplace in Stratford for a couple of years. James writes, "they were rather strenuous and superior people from Newcastle, who had embraced the situation with joy, thinking to find it just the thing for them and full of interest, dignity, an appeal to all their culture and refinement, etc." However, they found their office "the sort of thing that I suppose it is: full of humbug, full of lies and superstition imposed upon them by the great body of visitors, who want the positive impressive story about every object, every feature of the house, ever dubious thing — the simplified, unscrupulous, gulpable *tale.*" James finds material for a story of 6,000 words. "I seem to see them — for there is no catastrophe in a simple resignation of the post, turned somehow, by the experience, into strange skeptics, iconoclasts, positive negationists.... Say they end by denying Shakespeare.... Then they must go." His idea became "The Birthplace." (See 1903 James entries.)

Mendenhall, T.C. "A Mechanical Solution of a Literary Problem." *The Popular Science Monthly*, December, **1901**, pp. 97–105.

Apparently an unbiased bystander, Mendenhall hired several women to count words and the number of times words of, say, 2, 3 or 4 letters appeared in selected Elizabethan literature, to answer the question, "Can an author purposely avoid the peculiarities of style that belong to his normal composition?" Shakespeare's "word of greatest frequency was the four-letter word, a thing never met with before." Mendenhall became convinced that 100,000 words were necessary to give the characteristic curve of a writer and devised graphs. Not Bacon but Marlowe comes closest to Shakespeare.

Stephen, Leslie. "Did Shakespeare Write Bacon?" *National Review* (England) **1901**, pp. 402–406. Republished in *Men, Books, and Mountains.* Minneapolis: University of Minnesota Press, 1956.

Virginia Woolf's father was first a cleric, then an agnostic and frequently an essayist. In "Did Shakespeare Write Bacon?" he takes the novel — and satirical — approach that Shakespeare retired to Stratford because Bacon paid him to do so to write Bacon's *Advancement of Learning* and *Novum Organum.* Stephen makes fun of ciphers: "When Shakespeare's plays were collected after the author's death, Bacon we know got at the printers and persuaded them to insert a cryptogram claiming the authorship for himself."

Mendenhall, Thomas Corwin. "Did Marlowe Write Shakespeare?" *Current Literature* (February **1902**): 149–151.

Twenty years previous to this article Mendenhall developed an "almost purely mechanical" method to exhibit peculiarities of authorial style and composition. The expense of time and labor ("The operation is not one of thrilling interest,") prevented implementation until Augustus Heminway of Boston paid people to classify nearly 2 million words (number of letters in a word, number of words in a sentence, sentence structure). Analyzing Shakespeare, they discovered that average word length was a trifle under four letters while words of greatest frequency were of four letters, "the striking characteristic of his composition." Four hundred thousand of Shakespeare's words were counted and compared to 200,000 of Francis Bacon's in his *Advancement of Learning, Henry VII* and shorter essays. Counting was also conducted on works of Ben Jonson, Addison, Beaumont and Fletcher, Marlowe, Goldsmith, Lord Lytton and some moderns. Bacon's was not a very good match but if he didn't write Shakespeare, Augustus Heminway still inquired, "who did?" Marlowe was a better match for "it was discovered that in the characteristic curve of his plays Christopher Marlowe agrees with Shakespeare about as well as Shakespeare agrees with himself." There are three Figures (graphs).

Webb, Judge. *The Mystery of William Shakespeare: A Summary of Evidence.* London: Longmans, Green, and Company, **1902**.

Webb is a reasonable Baconian. He doesn't care for the cipher/cryptogram theories and admits objections to both sides, e.g., "neither of them [Shakespeare or Bacon] claimed to be the author." Shakespeare had a motive to claim authorship and Bacon had a reason to conceal — stage writers were not reputable. Webb cites Stratfordians like Sidney Lee and Halliwell-Phillipps, British objections from such as Lord Palmerston, and American idolaters like Holmes, Donnelly, and Reed. He wonders why it is so hard to believe in a pseudonym. After all, Jean-Baptist Poquelin used Moliere and Francois Marie Arouet used Voltaire. "Shaksperiolatry has become a religion" is Webb's prime objection — "The boundless admiration of the plays of Shakespeare which we now profess had no existence while he lived." He says Coleridge deified him. There is an excellent, informative index and Notes A–K ("Of Shakespeare and Sir Thomas Lucy," "Of Shakespeare as a Sportsman," "Of Money in the time of Shakespeare," "Of

Copyright in the Time of Shakespeare," "Of Shakes-Speare's Sonnets," "Of the Shakespeare Folio," "Of Bacon's Promus," "Of the Northumberland Papers," "Of Bacon's Apology," "Of Shakespeare's Knowledge of Ireland").

Irving, Sir Henry. "Third Trask Lecture." *The Daily Princetonian*, March 20, **1902**, p. 1.

Sir Henry Irving delivered his "The Shakespeare-Bacon Controversy" in Princeton's Alexander Hall on March 19. Before he'll believe in a hoax, Irving wants proof that Ben Jonson was a fool and that the literary men of the Elizabethan era formed a conspiracy. The article's author writes, "The Baconians say that there is no evidence that Shakespeare could write, but his contemporaries and the players who acted with him speak of him as one who 'wrote without a blot.'" Stressed is internal evidence against Bacon, who had no intimate knowledge of the stage. "The Shakespeare plays are written for the stage by a player." Baconians "have no sense of proportion or of the ridiculous, but seem to be moved only by an unjust prejudice against those engaged in the theatrical profession." Mention of the lecture and Irving's view is made in *The Princeton Alumni Weekly*, March 22, 1902, pp. 295–96.

Walters, J. Cuming. "The Shakespeare Relics at Stratford." *The Times* [London], September 8, **1903**, p. 5.

Walters quotes from a May 12, 1893, letter to him from Joseph Skipsey, one-time custodian of the Shakespeare birthplace in Stratford. Because of too many bogus artifacts, the trustees or a national trust," say, with Mr. Sidney Lee at the head," must disperse the legends. As for Skipsey, whose sojourn in Stratford provided the inspiration for Henry James' "The Birthplace" (1903), he wrote, "I must not conceal from you the fact that there was another reason [beyond a personal reason specified] why I should resign, and that was that I had gradually lost faith in the so-called relics which it was the duty of the custodian to show, and, if possible, to explain to the visitors at the birthplace. This loss of faith was the result of a long and severe inquiry into which I was driven by questions from time to time put to my wife and me by intelligent visitors; and the effect of it on myself was such as almost to cause a paralysis of the brain.... That our Shakespeare was born in Henley street I continue fully to believe, and that the house yet shown as the Shakespeare House stands on the site of the house in which he was born I also believe (and it was sacred to me on that account); but a man must be in a position to speak in more positive terms than these if he is to fill the post of custodian of that house; and the more I thought of it the more and more I was unable to do this. As to the idle gossip, the so-called traditions and legends of the place, they are for the most part an abomination and must stink in the nostrils of every true lover of our divine poet."

James, Henry. Letter to Miss Violet Hunt, August 26, **1903**. *The Letters of Henry James*. Selected and edited by Percy Lubbock. New York: Octagon Books, 1970, 2 vols.

"Dictated. Lamb House, Rye. Aug. 26th, 1903." In the middle of the letter: "I am 'a sort of' haunted by the conviction that the divine William is the biggest and most successful fraud ever practiced on a patient world. The more I turn him round and round the more he so affects me. But that is all — I am not pretending to treat the question or to carry it any further. It bristles with difficulties, and I can only express my general sense by saying that I find it almost as impossible to conceive that Bacon wrote the plays as to conceive that the man from Stratford, as we know the man from Stratford, did."

James, Henry. "The Birthplace." *The Better Sort* (London, **1903**), pp. 403–465. Republished in *The Complete Tales of Henry James*. Edited by Leon Edel. Vol. 11: 1900–1903. Philadelphia: J.B. Lippincott, 1964.

Mr. and Mrs. Morris Gedge became the live-in guides for pilgrims to the birthplace of a first-rate poet always referred to as He or Him. Mr. Gedge prowls the birthplace by night. He confesses to his wife: "It isn't him — nothing's about Him. None of Them care twopence about HIM. The only thing They care about is this empty shell — or rather, for it isn't empty, the extraneous, preposterous stuffing of it." Later, "There are no relics." His doubts about the morality of expounding on facts begin to split him into several people: "the keeper, the showman, the priest of the idol; the other piece was the poor unsuccessful honest man he had always been." And, "There's very little to know. He covered His tracks as no other human being has ever done." Americans have the most questions and a young American couple come and realize that Gedge is posturing. The man says, "'The play's the thing. Let the author alone.'" Gedge realizes, "They simply wanted it piled up, and so did everybody else; wherefore, if no one reported him, as before, why were They to be uneasy? It was in consequence of idiots brought to reason that he had been dealt with before; but as there was now no form of idiocy that he didn't flatter, goading it on really to its own private doom, who was ever to pull the string of the guillotine?" Thus the man who hired Gedge in the first place gives Gedge a raise for providing the people with what they want.

Stronach, George. *Mr. Sidney Lee and the Baconians*. London: Gay & Bird, **1904**.

A revised version of Stronach's letter to Lee in *Pall Mall Magazine* (November, 1903) this 24-page pamphlet assesses Lee's "so-called" *Life of Shakespeare*. "Mr. Lee has abused Baconians, but he has never argued with them."

Stotsenburg, John H. *An Impartial Study of the Shakespeare Title*. **1904**. reprinted, Port Washington, NY: Kennikat Press, 1970.

Stotsenburg dismisses ciphers and maintains a group theory involving Michael Drayton, Thomas Dekker, Anthony Munday, Henry Chettle, Thomas Heywood, John Webster, Thomas Middleton, Henry Porter and Francis Bacon. Philip Sidney wrote the Sonnets. No one man could have the 20,000+ word vocabulary evinced in the material. Best point: dethroning Shakespeare opens up a whole world of study for scholars of English literature. Stotsenburg believes impartial investigation will unmask the true authors. Superstition and false opinions will fall by the wayside. He calls Richard Farmer the first heretic, when in 1767 he wrote an essay questioning Shakespeare's learning. Joseph Hart, William Henry Smith, Delia Bacon, Appleton Morgan, and Ignatius Donnelly follow. Thus he misses *An Essay Against Too Much Reading* and *The Life and Adventures of Common Sense*. The ignorance of Shakespeare's children is offered as proof that their sire was not the author. He had no books! There is an index.

Smith, Francis A. *The Critics Versus Shakspere: A Brief for the Defendant*. New York: Knickerbocker Press, **1907**.

A lawyer wrote this 128-page pro–Stratford book. He believes that occasionally there is a glimpse of the Stratford man in the works. He says that courts have constantly ruled in that man's favor.

Greenwood, Granville George. *The Shakespeare Problem Restated*. London: John Lane, The Bodley Head, **1908**. Reprinted, Westport, CT: Greenwood Press, 1970.

This is one of the half dozen most important analyses of the authorship question, one to which many others refer. Greenwood himself takes no sides but merely explains why the author can't be the man from Stratford. He begins by drawing an analogy between Shakespearean and theological debates. There is a "Table of Dates." He contends that we do not know more about Shakespeare than his contemporary poets. He presents the Stratford man's background, discusses his signatures and his literacy, disputes Sidney Lee's facts, and demonstrates that Jonson, Marlowe, Robert Burns, John Keats, and Leonardo da Vinci had better educations. He examines conflicting Stratfordian views, i.e., was he cultured or was he not? Greenwood believes that whoever he was, he was the "most cultivated writer of his time." He contends that actors were not held in high esteem even if under the Queen's patronage they received some respectability. He shows that Sidney Lee finds no inconsistency in the money lender-businessman writing *Hamlet*. In his will there is no mention of books: "Would he have considered them of less importance then plate and linen, and jewels, and silver-gilt bowls?" And, "He left no books, and he left a daughter who could not read!" Why such a mundane epitaph? "Shakspere never during his life did or said anything to show that he claimed to be the author of the Plays and Poems or any of them." Actually we know too much of Shakspere, "If we knew nothing, we might imagine anything. What we do know is fatal to the case." How come such a prodigious scholar was not noticed during his days at school? Portraits are discussed as well as The First Folio, sixteenth-century copyright, legal acumen, and Jonson as a prop for the Stratfordian view. There are many notes and an index. No mention is made of Delia Bacon or the Earl of Oxford.

Beeching, Canon [Henry Charles]. *William Shakespeare: Player, Playmaker and Poet: A Reply to Mr. George Greenwood.* London: Smith, Elder and Company, **1908**.

"But the heresy, if I may call it so, which at the outset numbered but a few fanatical adherents, has of late made many converts among members of your profession [lawyers] ... most persons who have enough capacity to discuss the question at all, judge it as a question, not of evidence, but of the literary palate." And, "In one word then, if I am asked how we can get behind Shakespeare's writing to the man himself, I should say, we must ask ourselves what is the impression left on our mind after a careful reading of any play; because that will be Shakespeare's mind speaking to ours. And I cannot think the general impression we thus gather from the great volume of the poet's work is at all a vague one. We feel that the praise he gives to Brutus is still truer of himself. 'His life was gentle; and the elements/So mixed in him that Nature might stand up/And say to all the world, This was a man!'" Beeching's approach is none other than that of Oxfordian Looney: examine the work and what kind of author would be capable of it. They draw different conclusions.

Greenwood, Granville George. *In Re Shakespeare: Beeching v. Greenwood. Rejoinder on Behalf of the Defendant.* London: John Lane, **1909**.

Greenwood replies to Canon Beeching's attacks on his theories propounded in *The Shakespeare Problem Restated.* "He has put into my mouth arguments which I never uttered, and which I should not dream of uttering, and has proceeded to demolish them with great self-satisfaction and with the most entire success." He agrees that "The Baconian theory lends itself to ridicule. It has been brought into discredit by the extreme pretensions and absurdities of some fanatical enthusiasts. It is an American importation. And did not poor Miss Delia Bacon end her days, under restraint as a harmless lunatic?" Greenwood restates his agnosticism, contending only that he cannot accept the Stratford man as the culprit.

Twain, Mark. "Is Shakespeare Dead?" **1909**. In *The Complete Essays of Mark Twain.* Edited by Charles Neider. Garden City, NY: Doubleday, 1963.

Some Stratfordians know that Twain was influenced by Greenwood and say he wrote this tongue-in-cheek, but after talking about Greenwood's *The Shakespeare Problem Restated,* Twain says he's had a "fifty years' interest in that matter.... It is an interest which was born of Delia Bacon's book." He recounts riverboat days with George Ealer, with whom he argued the authorship question. Ealer "bought the literature of the dispute as fast as it appeared." Twain makes a parallel between Satan and Shakespeare: a poverty of biographical detail is common to both. He presents the facts of the Stratford man and writes of books. "Books were much more precious than swords and silver-gilt bowls and second-best beds in those days, and when a departing person owned one he gave it a high place in his will." Not Shakespeare. "Many poets have died poor, but this is the only one in history that has died this poor; the others all left literary remains behind. Also a book. Maybe two." In the same section: "So far as anybody actually knows and can prove, Shakespeare of Stratford-on-Avon never wrote a play in his life." The next section is "Conjectures" and Twain writes, "For experience is an author's most valuable asset; experience is the thing that puts the muscle and the breath and the warm blood into the book he writes." As for Shakespeare, "He is a brontosaur: nine bones and six hundred barrels of plaster of Paris." Next comes "We May Assume." Then Twain writes that the matter rests on legal knowledge and he quotes at length from Greenwood's 50 pages on "Shakespeare as a Lawyer." Bacon's credentials are reviewed. "It is the atmosphere we are reared in that determines how our inclinations and aspirations shall tend." Twain complains of the traditional scholars' use of "presumption." Finally, "I believed, and I still believe, that if he had been famous, his notoriety would have lasted as long as mine has lasted in my native village out in Missouri. It is a good argument, a prodigiously strong one, and a most formidable one for even the most gifted and ingenious and plausible Stratfordolater to get around or explain away." (Ealer but not the controversy is mentioned in Twain's *Life on the Mississippi.*)

Harris, Frank. *The Man Shakespeare and His Tragic Life Story.* New York: Mitchell Kennerley, **1909**.

Not an authorship book per se, this is nevertheless important for its biographical-psychological investigation that makes the man from Stratford fit the plays and sonnets. In short, Harris argues that literature reflects the writer. Harris neither wants to make Shakespeare a clod nor a superman though he considers his literature vastly more important than current British literature. He admits that "What is known positively about him, could be given in a couple of pages; but there are traditions of him, tales about him, innumerable scraps of fact and fiction concerning him which are more or less interesting and authentic; and now that we know the man, we shall be able to accept or reject these reports with some degree of confidence, and so arrive at a credible picture of his life's journey, and the changes which time wrought in him." There is a 10-page index.

Walcott, John. "Delia Bacon and After." *Putnam's Magazine*, August **1909**, pp. 619–624.

Walcott traces the controversy from Delia Bacon, whose challenge marks "the beginning of the most lively literary skirmish of our time." He is sympathetic to her aim to expound the meaning of the plays. He covers William Henry Smith, Nathaniel Holmes, Edwin Reed, and Judge Webb. He believes the latter was "unlearned in Elizabethan literature." He reviews new items on the topic: George Greenwood's *The Shakespeare Problem Restated*, H.C. Beeching, Mark Twain's "Is Shakespeare Dead?" ("a good deal of bland misstatement and careless deduction. It contributes nothing."), and Ignatius Donnelly. The cipher/anagram theories are discussed.

Durning-Lawrence, Edwin. *Bacon Is Shake-Speare*. London: Gray & Hancock, Ltd., **1910**.

This 286-page tome has many illustrations but no index. It includes Bacon's "Promus of Formularies and Elegancies" plus chapters on the "Shackspere" monument, bust, and Portrait, the signatures, correspondence, the Sonnets, Sidney Lee, and the meaning of "Honorificabilitudinitatibus." The author believes "There is also shewn in the plays the most perfect knowledge of Court etiquette and of the manners and the methods of the greatest of the land, a knowledge which none but a courtier moving in the highest circles could by any possibility have acquired." And, "The mighty author of the immortal plays was gifted with the most brilliant genius ever conferred upon men.... He had by study obtained nearly all the learning that could be gained from books." Thus, Bacon must be the author.

Wallace, Charles William. "New Shakespeare Discoveries." *Harper's Monthly Magazine*, March **1910**, pp. 489–510.

Wallace makes much of his and his wife's examination "through some million of documents" in London's Public Record Office. "No one prior to our search had ever examined them in the course of three centuries." Twenty-six relate to Shakespeare, a common, ordinary, business-oriented fellow as evidenced by the deposition in a Bellott-Mountjoy suit, a purchase-deed, a mortgage-deed and his will. Wallace explains that the shoddy signatures are attributable to a Gothic-like script common at the time. He deduces that the Ovid book given by W. Hall was from Wm. Hall "who in 1694 wrote Edward Thwaits, of Queen's College, Oxford, an interesting letter concerning a visit paid to Shakespeare's grave." He explains how Shakespeare may have met the boy John Milton. In conclusion, "The mystery that surrounds the personality of Shakespeare is, after all, made up largely of our own ignorance, much of which is inherited from dead books of large pretensions, but most of which is the result of our own perverse inclination to sit and fiddle in the dark rather than walk in the sun. The truth is, we have more documentary evidence about Shakespeare than about any other dramatist of his time.... There is also a mass of documentary evidence on his family, neighbors, associate actors, fellow-dramatists, and the theatres, more or less contributive to his biography." Finally, "It has sometimes been said that a man's last will and testament best expresses his character. Does it? Do we not rather know a man best from the simple act, look, or speech of daily life when the consciousness is unaware?"

Bostelmann, Lewis F. *Rutland: A Chronologically Arranged Outline of the Life of Roger Manners Fifth Earl of Rutland*. New York: Rutland Pub. Co., **1911**.

"The Stratford swindle must be stopped," writes Bostelmann in his introduction, and "common sense must, by legislation, if necessary, compel ordinary decency by the suppression of the Stratfordian propagation of that colossal fraud." According to him, Shaksper of Stratford was a dummy, or strawman for Rutland. Francis Bacon initiated the swindle and "Shaksper was instructed to neither admit nor deny his connection with anything that Rutland might thereafter wish to publish." There's a detailed chronology of Rutland's life. His continental travels are recounted. There are illustrations and short extracts of opinions on the authorship issue by various famous personages. There is also Bostelmann's "Roger of Rutland: A Drama in Five Acts," designed "to show the modus operandi of the creation of the Shake-Speare mystery." Sadly, Bostelmann fails to provide an index or bibliography. "Documentary evidence supporting this contention is in existence and will be produced when demanded by proper authority"(!). Another important Rutland book is Celestin Demblon's *Lord Rutland est Shakespeare: Le plus grand des Mysteres devoile Shaxper de Stratford hors cause* (Paris: Ancienne Maison Charles Carrington, 1912). It consists of 559 pages, has footnotes but is not indexed.

Lang, Andrew. *Shakespeare, Bacon and the Great Unknown.* London, **1912.** Reprinted, New
    York: AMS Press, 1968.

    This book, dedicated to Horace Howard Furness, has an index but no bibliography. Occasional notes are at page bottoms. There are eight illustrations, e.g., signature facsimile, monument at Stratford. Writing the plays was not a "physical impossibility," rather an "intellectual miracle." Lang does not believe a conspiracy was possible because of "the eager and suspicious jealousy and volubility of rival playwrights." Books that could have provided the author with background were available, including translations, writes Lang. "That Shakespeare was the very reverse of a dullard, of the clod of Baconian fancy, is proved by the fact that he was thought capable of his work."

Robertson, J.M. *The Baconian Heresy: A Confutation.* London: Herbert Jenkins Limited, **1913;**
    republished, St. Clair Shores, MI: Scholarly Press, 1971. 612p. (General index, index of words
    discussed, index of phrases discussed.)

    Robertson bemoans the lack of induction on the Baconian side and hopes to check the spread of the Baconian heresy caused by misinformation and zealous Stratfordians by stimulating scientific Shakespearean criticism. He wisely says, "It is very doubtful whether the Baconian theory would ever have been framed had not the idolatrous Shakespeareans set up a visionary figure of the Master." He discounts the cipher theory, notes that both sides have treated the other unfairly, states that there is just as much missing documentation on the lives of John Lilly, Thomas Dekker, Thomas Heywood, Thomas Kyd, Ben Jonson and Spenser as on Shakespeare, and examines in Chapter II "The Positions of Mark Twain." He believes Twain was misled by George Greenwood's books.

Baxter, James Phinney. *The Greatest of Literary Problems, the Authorship of the Shakespeare
    Works: An Exposition of All Points at Issue from Their Inception to the Present Moment.* Boston:
    Houghton Mifflin, **1915.** Reprinted, New York: AMS Press, 1971.

    In the prologue to this heavily illustrated, indexed, 686-page book, Baxter discusses the genesis of the controversy. Delia Bacon was "a woman of remarkable intellect, a profound scholar, and merits a high place among the literary women of America." He describes the Elizabethan age and discusses the Shakespeare portraits. Bacon had the time because contemporaries explained how he filled up each day. The Epilogue compares the lives of Bacon and Shakespeare chronologically. The bibliography runs from pages 635 to 664.

Greenwood, Granville George. *Is There a Shakespeare Problem? With a Reply to Mr. J.M. Robertson and Mr. Andrew Lang.* London: John Lane, **1916.**

    Greenwood replies to J.M. Robertson's objections to his previous efforts on behalf of the skeptics who Greenwood humorously says "are, really, not all amenable to the provisions of the Mental Deficiency Act." He disputes Robertson's analogies, condemning his citations as irrelevant. Greenwood also deplores the "indiscriminate abuse which is now constantly showered upon the memory of Francis Bacon by certain Shakespeariolaters." He maintains that his *Shakespeare Problem Restated* is not a Baconian tome. He believes much of the argument remains unexplored. He covers Shakespeare's legal acumen, his learning, the Elizabethan theater, Shakspere's will, that name, allusions to Shakespeare, Ben Jonson, the First Folio, the Stratford Monument and portraits of Shakespeare. There are appendices and an index.

"Shakespeare." *The Times Literary Supplement,* April 20, **1916,** pp. 181–182.

It's not really about the controversy, but this brief article is better than most long tomes and may be the best analysis to promote the man from Stratford as the plays' author. "But the desire to call the institutional Shakespeare Bacon is inevitable; for, if all these plays are perfect, if they always manifest omniscience, omnipotence, and the loftiest intentions, they must have been produced by a god; and we do know enough about Shakespeare to be sure that he was not at all like a god. We know that he was something of a hack, like Mozart and Tintoret. He wrote to earn his living, and did not care much what became of his plays after they had been acted." Furthermore, "Worldlings make the best saints, and Shakespeare is a worldling among all the great saints of poetry." And, "Shakespeare's problem was the problem of one who wrote for a living, of one who loved life as it was too well to empty it of content for artistic purposes." His was "a hand to mouth struggle."

Cochrane, R. "Who Wrote Shakespeare?" *The Times Literary Supplement,* April 20, **1916**, p. 189.

Writing from Edinburgh, Cochrane praises Sidney Lee's Shakespeare article in the *Dictionary of National Biography* as well as his "monumental volume on the same subject" but his main aim is to inform us that the author of "Who Wrote Shakespeare?" in *Chambers's Journal* (August 7, 1852) was Edinburgh journalist and author Robert W. Jameson. "His trained legal mind balances the evidence which had then emerged for and against the Shakespearian authorship, and he concludes 'that, whether by inheritance, purchase, or divine afflatus, the man who wrote Shakespeare was William Shakespeare.' Jameson's critical acumen and sense of humor kept him from the German-like stupidity of the Baconians." It is somewhat misleading to say that Jameson said "Shakespeare was William Shakespeare." See: "Who Wrote Shakespeare?" (1852)

Lefranc, Abel. *Sous le Masque de William Shakespeare: William Stanley, VI Comte de Derby.* Paris: Payot & Cie, **1918** (vol. 1), **1919** (vol. 2). Translated by Cecil Cragg and published as *Under the Mask of William Shakespeare.* Braunton and Devon: Merlin Books, 1988.

After 35 years of research and teaching about the sixteenth and seventeenth centuries, Lefranc determined that William Stanley, VI Comte de Derby, was the author. "Not the slightest link has it been possible to establish in all seriousness, I mean with the reassurance of sane elementary criticism, between this immortal drama and its author" (the Stratford man). It was not just material gain that prompted the dramas. "Is it really that the inspiration of a Dante, of a Rabelais, of a Shakespeare, when all is said and done, comes down to the lure alone of some pieces of gold?" In the Paris 1918–1919 edition, Lefranc cites Greenwood's tomes, Sidney Lee (1916), and Emerson, *The Nineteenth Century* (April 1918, p. 839, and April 1917, p. 883). There are signatures and illustrations of Shakespeare, portraits of De Vere and Derby.

Lee, Sidney. "Shakespeare Dethroned Again." *Illustrated London News,* January 25, **1919**, p. 108.

Lee reviews the candidates, especially Derby as proposed by Lefranc, who he says is developing James Greenstreet's proposals made regarding Derby in an 1890 *Genealogist* article. Lee says he has Greenstreet's papers. There is a portrait of Derby, five Shakespeare signatures, and a holograph from 31 October 1607.

Looney, J. Thomas. *"Shakespeare" Identified in Edward De Vere, Seventeenth Earl of Oxford and The Poems of Edward De Vere.* 3rd ed. Edited by Ruth Loyd Miller. London: C. Palmer, **1920**. Reprinted, Port Washington, NY: Kennikat Press, 1975. 2 vols.

Literary methods and expertise are not necessary to understand or examine the authorship question, argues Looney [1870–1944] in this, the most important argument for Lord Oxford as Shakespeare. Discounting Ignatius Donnelly's cryptogram, he praises the man's unappreciated first hundred pages and also commends Halliwell-Phillipps' biography as the most honest. Looney compares the lowly beginnings of Robert Burns to Shakespeare's. "Burns died at the age of thirty-seven, leaving striking evidence of his genius, but no masterpiece of the kind which comes from wide experience and matured powers. Shakspere, before reaching the age of thirty, is credited with the authorship of dramas and great poetic classics evincing a wide and prolonged experience of life." There are illustrations and appendices. Volume II contains analyses of various topics by Ruth Loyd Miller, Eva Turner Clark, J. Valcour Miller and others.

Lucas, R. Macdonald. "Did Lord Derby Write Shakespeare?" *National Review* (London), November **1921**, pp. 359–369.

> Drawing on three books (Henry Pemberton, Jr.'s *Shakspere and Sir Walter Raleigh*, J. Thomas Looney's *"Shakespeare" Identified*, Abel Lefranc's *Sous le Masque de Shakespeare: William Stanley, VI Comte de Derby*), Lucas reviews but downplays the Baconian theory and concentrates on Derby and Oxford. He believes that had Looney seen Lefranc's work before publishing his Oxfordian tome, he would have supported Derby. Lefranc's work "should be absolutely convincing." Dates make the Oxfordian theory "hopeless. There is no other word for it." Lucas also wrote *Shakespeare's Vital Secret* (Keighley, Yorkshire: Wadsworth, 1937).

Looney, J. Thomas. "'Shakespeare' Lord Oxford or Lord Derby?" *National Review* (London), February **1922**, pp. 801–809.

> After reviewing the genesis of his Oxfordian theory that was publicized almost simultaneously with Abel Lefranc's Derby theory, Looney deals with Lucas's objections to de Vere in the November, 1921, *National Review*. He believes that "one test of a new authorship theory must be whether or not it furnishes a key by which prototypes can be identified and the great dramas thus brought into line with the literary practices of the time." Most importantly, he deals with the "conjectural dating' of the plays. In short, "we have a proved interval of at least some thirty years between the actual writing and the publication of the plays" and "the 1597–1604 publication was an outpouring from a large accumulated stock, and when it stopped suddenly with the authorized *Hamlet* in 1604 there were still on hand many plays which had never been published." The First Folio is analyzed.

Smithson, E.W., and Greenwood, George. *Baconian Essays*. **1922**; Reprinted, Port Washington, NY: Kennikat Press, 1970.

> There are five [?] essays by Smithson ("The Masque of 'Time Vindicated,'" "Shakespeare — A Theory," "Ben Jonson and Shakespeare," "Bacon and 'Poesy,'") and two by Greenwood ("The Common Knowledge of Shakespeare and Bacon," "The Northumberland Manuscript"). Greenwood also contributes the "Introductory" and "Final Note." In his introduction Greenwood begins by quoting Henry James' view that "the divine William is the biggest and most successful fraud ever practiced on a patient world," then reviews the article "Hamlet and History" in *The Times Literary Supplement* (June 2, 1921) and that author's appeal to "relativity," which is helpful for "informing our judgments on men long gone, whether of their characters or their actions, or their sayings or their writings, we must ever bear in mind the views, the beliefs, the opinions, and the special circumstances of the time and the society in which they lived." To wit, literary deception in Elizabethan times was common. Many pens are believed to be at work in the 1623 Folio. Stratfordians are berated because "they have accepted without thinking the dogmas of the Stratfordian faith; they are impervious to reasoning and common sense." How could a Stratford lad write *Love's Labours Lost* and other such items within five or six years of hitting London? How could he have become a gentleman in so short a time? Knowledge of the Court of Navarre was needed. Cited is Professor Lefranc's *Sous le Masque de William Shakespeare*. Greenwood says he's an agnostic and has never sought to advance a candidate, then discusses wild as well as more reasonable Baconians. Smithson believes there were probably many concealed poets.

Ward, Bernard Rowland. *The Mystery of "Mr. W.H."* London: Cecil Palmer, **1923**.

> This is an extension of Ward's "'Mr. W.H.' and "Our Ever-living Poet" in the *National Review* (September, 1922): 81–93. Ward's research into Parish Registers for birth and death certificates bolstered the Oxford theory of authorship and gave the Shakespeare Fellowship a lift.

Connes, Georges. *Shakespeare Mystery*. Whitefish, MT: Kessinger Publishing, March 2003, ©**1927**.

This is comprised of the Shakespeare Fellowship's 1925 translated lectures. "Alas! we are all terribly anthropomorphic, we refuse to accept works that have fallen direct from heaven, in their stead we look for the man;" Chapter I: General Situation, Chapter II: The Days of Elizabeth, Chapter III: Shakespeare Is Shakespeare, Chapter IV: The Man Shakespeare, Chapter V: Shakespeare Is Not Shakespeare, Chapter VI: Bacon Is Shakespeare, Chapter VII: Rutland Is Shakespeare, Chapter VIII: Derby Is Shakespeare, Chapter IX: Oxford Is Shakespeare, Chapter X: Conclusion. In Chapter IV, attention is focused on Frank Harris and his *The Man Shakespeare and His Tragic Life Story*. Harris' analysis of the plays reveals that Shakespeare is Hamlet, *every* character is really Hamlet. The Sonnets are keys to the Stratford man's soul. In Chapter V, Mark Twain is quoted on Sidney Lee's Shakespeare, i.e., like a brontosaurus reconstruction of bone fragments and tons of plaster. Connes also cites Donnelly, Durning-Lawrence, Greenwood, Demblon, Lefranc, Baxter and Looney. He presents Looney's 17 reasons for doubting Shakspere. Why were there no odes and lamentations for Shakespeare when he passed away? Such were written for Spenser, Beaumont and Ben Jonson. The portrait and monument are discussed. As for Stratfordians who claim many writers spoke of Shakespeare, "it is invariably the author and never the man that is alluded to ... the man was completely ignored by his contemporaries." In Chapter VI it is argued that Bacon *was* a poet. The political opinions of Bacon and Shakespeare are the same, i.e., anti-rabble. They use similar expressions. Mrs. Pott's research is considered. Bacon's aim was "to be of use to posterity." Bacon *did* have time. In Chapter VII, Demblon's research on Rutland is summarized. Rutland traveled in Europe, including Denmark. He is Hamlet! In Chapter VIII, Lefranc's Derby studies are reviewed. Derby, whose family was interested in the theater, traveled in France, had a quick temper, was jealous, highly connected, and considered eccentric. Perhaps Mary Fitton was the Dark Lady of the Sonnets. Derby knew Rabelais enough to create Falstaff. Derby was at the Court of Navarre between 1582 and 1587, thus *Love's Labours Lost*. Shakespeare's plays are political, so Derby, not Shakspere, is Shakespeare. In Chapter IX, Looney's systematic investigation is examined. There is melancholy in Shakespeare. Oxford is "Willie" and "Will" to Edmund Spenser. "The Shakespeare work ... is far more suggestive of leisurely work than of hasty response to theatrical needs." And, "It is literature first and foremost, and only secondarily designed for the theatre." *The Tempest* is not Shakespeare or Oxford for it has none of their hallmarks. Oxford is indeed Hamlet. In conclusion, Connes claims not to have sought a solution or to reconcile all opinions. He says he did not use sarcasm or criticize Demblon, Lefranc or Looney. No alternative candidate is proven definitively to be Shakespeare. It would seem that Shakspere moved amongst the aristocracy and put his stamp of genius on what he found. Great actors have always enjoyed patronage. The epitaph of Shakspere's daughter Susanna Hall [died 1649] calls her a wit, thus people in Stratford recognized her father's past after all:

> Witty above her sex, but that's not all,
> Wise to salvation was good Mistress Hall,
> Something of Shakespeare was in that, but this
> Wholly of him with whom she's now in bliss.

Diagrams: The Tudor Dynasty, The Shakespeare Group. Three concluding pages provide the objects, membership qualifications, and studies of The Shakespeare Fellowship, George Greenwood being at that time its President with Lefranc and Looney two of the Vice-Presidents.

Galsworthy, John. *The White Monkey*. New York: Charles Scribner's Sons, 1928, ©1924.

Chapter VII ("'Old Mont' and 'Old Forsyte'") of Part I in this continuation of the Nobel Prize winner's Forsyte Saga begins with Soames remembering being "struck by the name Golding in a book which he had absently taken up at the Connoisseurs' Club. The affair purported to prove that William Shakespeare was really Edward de Vere, Earl of Oxford. The mother of the Earl was a Golding — so was the mother of Soames! The coincidence struck him; and he went on reading. The tome left him with judgment suspended over the main issue, but a distinct curiosity as to whether he was not of the same blood as Shakespeare. Even if the Earl were not the bard, he felt that the connection could only be creditable, though, so far as he could make out, Oxford was a shady fellow. Recently appointed on the board of the P.P.R.S., so that he passed the College [of Arms] every other Tuesday, he had thought: 'Shan't go spending a lot of money on it, but might look in one day.' Having looked in, it was astonishing how taken he had been by the whole thing. Tracing his mother had been quite like a criminal investigation, nearly as ramified and fully as expensive. Having begun, the tenacity of a Forsyte could hardly bear to stop short of the mother of Shakespeare de Vere, even though she would be collateral;

unfortunately, he could not get past a certain William Gouldyng, Ingerer, whatever that might be, and he was almost afraid to inquire, of the time of Oliver Cromwell."

Ward, Bernard Mordaunt. *The Seventeenth Earl of Oxford, 1550–1604: From Contemporary Documents*. London: John Murray, **1928**.

Ward quotes from a plethora of letters, diary entries, account books, travel accounts, church records, Dugdale's *Baronage* (1675), and more recent publications to flesh out Edward de Vere's life. (The Stratford man appears but briefly in one of Ward's "Interludes.") Future biographers would do well to consider many of Ward's conclusions, e.g., permitting the youth Oxford to spend a huge sum per year on clothes makes adult profligacy more understandable; Henry Howard's accusations were those of a mischief-making enemy; Gabriel Harvey's tribute to Oxford confirms Oxford's Latin literacy; the dismantling of Castle Hedingham's neglected outbuildings was entirely reasonable. Oxford is representative of Elizabethan courtiers: "first and foremost men of action, full of joie de vivre, ... over-grown schoolboys.... To them life, literature, and war were indissolubly mixed, and could only be enjoyed to the full after a liberal admixture of fun and adventure. No one who fails to appreciate this can catch the true spirit of Elizabethan England." And, "in Lord Oxford we are not dealing with a normal, humdrum man. His views, for example, on literature were sufficiently unorthodox to outrage the feelings of so conventional a man as Lord Burghley. We cannot doubt that, as his mind developed, he chafed more and more at his virtual imprisonment in Cecil House." Ward provides probable reasons for anonymity, e.g., "failure to obtain the Laureateship roused in him the determination never again to allow his name to appear in print. There can be no doubt that he continued to write and take a keen interest in poetry and the drama till the day of his death. Men like Harvey, William Webbe, Francis Meres, and others, are unanimous in testifying that he stood supreme from 1578 till 1598, both as poet and dramatist. But whether or no his writings still exist, it is abundantly clear that they were not printed under his name." Ward quotes Lord Lumley in *The Arte of English Poesie* (1589): "For as well Poets as Poesie are despised, and the name become of honorable infamous, subject to scorn and derision, and rather a reproach than a praise to any that useth it." Regarding Queen Elizabeth's grant of 1,000 pounds per year to Oxford, Ward notes that other favorites "worked hard for their presents." What did Oxford do? We don't know, and Ward doesn't buy the theory that the largesse was to "relieve him in his poverty." Ward explores the state of literature in England, including the Euphuists (Oxford and Lyly) and the Romanticists (Sidney and Spenser). Dedications to Oxford are made much of. And why did not Elizabeth famously object when Oxford married Elizabeth Trentham, a Maid of Honor? Other courtier assignations with the Maids had been dealt with severely. Includes illustrations (Edward de Vere; Thomas Radcliffe, the 3rd Earl of Sussex; Queen Elizabeth and the Earl of Oxford, with Windsor Castle in the Background; Autograph Letter of the Earl of Oxford to Sir Robert Cecil, July 1600; two maps (London and Westminster; Sketch Map of the [Scottish] Border; two Genealogical Tables; nine appendices: A: The Earl of Oxford and the house of Lords (1571–1601), B: The Earl of Oxford's Lands (1571–1603); C: The Earl of Oxford's Annuity (1586); D: "Willy" and the "Gentle Spirit" in Spenser's "Tears of the Muses" (1591); E: The Earl of Oxford's Tomb; F: An Elizabethan Court Circular; G: A London and Westminster Directory; H: Annotated Bibliography; K: "He is But a Little Fellow." [no Appendix I or J — printer's error?] Indexed.

Clark, Eva Turner. *Shakespeare's Plays in the Order of Their Writing*, **1930**. Republished as *Hidden Allusions in Shakespeare's Plays: A Study of the Early Court Revels and Personalities of the Times*. 3rd rev. ed. Edited by Ruth Loyd Miller. Port Washington, NY: Kennikat Press, 1974.

Clark examines the plays and compares them to Oxford's time. She draws on the work of Bernard M. Ward. There is an index and illustrations in this 973-page book. In 1926 Clark had written *Axiophilus or Oxford alias Shakespeare* (New York: Knickerbocker Press). In this she aimed to support Looney's work. Axiophilus is a double anagram. In 1933 Clark produced *Love's Labour's Lost: A Study* (New York: William Farquhar Payson). "My own theory is that the writing of the plays was begun in 1576 by the young Earl of Oxford who, in that year, at the age of twenty-six, returned home after sixteen months of travel on the Continent, having spent most of his time in Italy, where the dramatic art was then the best in the world."

Chambers, Edmund K. *William Shakespeare: A Study of Facts and Problems*. Oxford: Clarendon Press, **1930**. 2 vols.

Respected Shakespearean scholar Chambers admits in his Preface that "I collect the scanty biographical data from records and tradition, and endeavor to submit them to the tests of a reasonable analysis." There are maps and other illustrations, appendices ("Contemporary Allusions," "The
Shakespeare-Mythos," etc.), bibliography and index. In the "Shakespeare's Origin" chapter Chambers
disputes the dirtiness of Stratford, likening it to every other town and London, as well. "Nor was it
entirely bookless.... The Grammar School was probably of good standing."

Eagle, Roderick. *New Views for Old*. London: Cecil Palmer, **1930**.

"When the experts disagree, there is nothing left for the humble student but to think for himself." Eagle contends that it is silly to presume the plays were for playhouse youths; they wouldn't have
endured. "I cannot believe that Shakespeare's heroines were created for their interpretation by male
actors." He believes the poet must be judged by the works and what they reveal. Who is the poet? Bacon,
for he believed he was born to serve mankind and thus took "all knowledge to be his province."

Slater, Gilbert. *Seven Shakespeares: A Discussion of the Evidence for Various Theories with Regard
to Shakespeare's Identity*. London: Cecil Palmer, **1931**.

There are 316 pages, some footnotes, no bibliography. Slater's background is economics and economic and social history. He examines the claims of Bacon, Marlowe, William Stanley, Roger Manners, Oxford, the Countess of Pembroke, Raleigh and concludes that the Shakespeare canon emanated
from a group. There are prefatory chapters on the historical background of Elizabethan drama, the man
from Stratford, contemporary evidence, handwriting and spelling, and Shakespeare's landscape. In the
historical background chapter he demonstrates how England was a relatively weak power confronting
the Spanish Empire. It took all of a monarch's power to remain independent. Plays, therefore, could
be used as propaganda. "The drama, however, had an even more important function than that of
enhancing the attractions of the Court. It was also a channel by which the populace could be given an
education in political science, and popular emotions be stirred. Because membership in the group was
a State secret, it was never acknowledged that the plays were authored by other than the Stratford man.
Oxford was the group's organizer. "He came into contact, perhaps through Greene, with the young
actor from Stratford, was quickly impressed with his genius, and enlisted his help." The man from Stratford is not viewed as a dolt.

Douglas, Montagu W. *The Earl of Oxford As "Shakespeare."* London: Cecil Palmer, **1931**. Published as *Lord Oxford and the Shakespeare Group*. 3rd ed. Oxford: Alden Press, 1952.

There is a two-page index and a de Vere frontispiece in this 168-page book that includes "A Summary of Evidence" by J.T. Looney, Canon G.H. Rendall, and Gilbert Slater. "The object is to convey
a general impression of the case for the Earl of Oxford as Shakespeare, and, leader of a Group of dramatists responsible under his inspiration for the Plays." Quoted are Looney, Chambers, Ward, Greenwood,
Rendall, Percy Allen, Slater, Admiral H. Holland, and Eva Turner Clark. The 1931 edition contains
two appendices, the first an annotated list of 35 books written by members of The Shakespeare Fellowship, the second the order of the Sonnets.

Allen, Percy. *The Oxford-Shakespeare Case Corroborated*. London: Cecil Palmer, **1931**.

Allen complains that academics have failed to come to grips with the matter and thinks a court
case would corroborate Oxford. For instance, counsel would ask, "What is your explanation of the fact
that out of 47 separate quarto editions of Shakespearean plays published before the Folio in 1623, 13
are anonymous, and 15 show the hyphenated form 'Shake-speare'? Did the Stratford man ever sign his
name Shakespeare?" Ben Jonson is discussed. There are footnotes and a three-page index.

"Exit Shakespeare." *The Times Literary Supplement*, January 14, **1932**, p. 30.

Book reviews of Bertram G. Theobald's *Exit Shakspere*, Montagu W. Douglas' *The Earl of Oxford
As "Shakespeare,"* Gilbert Slater's *Seven Shakespeares*, George Frisbee's *Edward De Vere*, Percy Allen's *The*

Oxford-Shakespeare Case Corroborated, and Gilbert Standen's *Shakespeare Authorship*. The reviewer finds Bacon's claims receding, Oxford's in ascendance, while "the group theory holds the field at the moment." "If the reader accepts the assumption that the exercise of genius is impossible without high birth and high education (ignoring Keats, Burns and an army of other enigmas), then he can enjoy the ingenuity of these six demonstrations against the Stratford player, and even be half persuaded by the case for de Vere."

Nicoll, Allardyce. "The First Baconian." *The Times Literary Supplement*, February 25, 1932, p. 128.

Nicoll reveals that Joseph Hart's 1848 *Romance of Yachting* was not the first time the authorship was questioned. He describes a quarto volume among the books of the late Sir Edwin Durning-Lawrence that were donated to the University of London (35 pages worth). In it are two addresses, the first being "Some Reflections on the Life of William Shakespeare A Paper Read before the Ipswich Philosophic Society by James Corton Cowell February 7 1805 — Arthur Cobbold Esqre., President." Cowell didn't say who his source was then but later admitted it to be the Reverend James Wilmot, D.D., the Rector of Barton on the Heath, which is six or seven miles north of Stratford. He was born on March 3, 1726, and espoused the Baconian hypothesis about 1785. He had all his notes burned. Wilmot had searched neighboring private bookshelves without finding any book owned by Shakespeare.

Sydenham of Combe, Lord. "The First Baconian." *Fly-Leaves*, August 1932. Republished in *Baconiana*, February 1933, pp. 143–150.

Ben Jonson's "contradictory views" are examined, with Sydenham's opinion that Jonson knew the author was Bacon: "In his 'Scriptorum Catalogus,' Jonson gave a list of the great thinkers and orators of his time, placing Bacon at the head and omitting the dramatist described as the 'Soul of the Age' in the First Folio." He uses George Eliot as an example of acquiescence in a pseudonym by the reading public. Sydenham also believes that Shakespearean literature "had not attained the pinnacle of honor" it would later and was thus not on the mind of everyone else. So who was the first Baconian: not Hart or Delia but rather the Reverend J. Wilmot. Allardyce Nicoll's *Times Literary Supplement* piece on Wilmot is reviewed. Incidentally, the Plays contain 23 allusions to St. Albans, Bacon's home, none to Stratfordian countryside.

Theobald, Bertram G. "Who Was the First Baconian?" *Baconiana*, January 1935, pp. 1–9.

Theobald notes that the genesis of the Bacon-Shakespeare controversy is commonly dated from 1856, when William Henry Smith wrote his letter to Lord Ellesmere. However, Theobald says the first indications of dissatisfaction with the man from Stratford can be traced to Joseph Hall in 1597.

Spurgeon, Caroline F.E. *Shakespeare's Imagery and What It Tells Us*. New York: Macmillan, 1936, ©1935.

Established academic critic Spurgeon tackles Shakespeare through his literary images. "It enables us to get nearer to Shakespeare himself, to his mind, his tastes, his experiences, and his deeper thought than does any other single way I know of studying him." She believes the poet reveals himself, sometimes unconsciously, through his images. Knowing that Bacon is held to be the author by many, she examines Bacon's *Essays*, *Advancement of Learning*, *Henry VII*, and *New Atlantis*, concluding that besides differences in temperament and worldview, "on a study of their imagery alone other noticeable differences emerge." Spurgeon explains how *Timon of Athens* provides "an extraordinarily reliable test of authorship." Chapter XI is "Shakespeare the Man." There are illustrations, appendices and an index.

Barrell, Charles Wisner. "Elizabethan Mystery Man." *Saturday Review of Literature*, May 1, 1937, pp. 11, 12, 14–15.

Committed Oxfordian Barrell examines Looney's work on de Vere, drawing attention to *1586's A Discourse of English Poetrie*, 1589's *The Arte of English Poesie*, and Francis Meres' *Palladis Tamia* (1598), all of which establish Oxford's contemporary reputation as a poet and playwright. Much is made of the fact that John Lyly acted as a spy for Lord Burghley while spending 15 years in Oxford's home as private secretary. Sonnets are quoted.

Stoll, Elmer Edgar. "The Detective Spirit in Criticism." *Saturday Review of Literature*, May 8, **1937**, pp. 12, 14, 16, 17.

From the University of Minnesota, Shakespeare studies author Stoll discounts Barrell's views expressed in the May 1 issue. After covering the controversy and its main advocates and contenders, he concludes that Oxonians "are but Baconians brought up to date," and that this is just a historical or literary crossword puzzle for those with idle time. Like many others, he doesn't like the "snobbish" view of anti–Stratfordians. In his own opinion, a rustic from Stratford could indeed write the plays via alert intelligence, observation, hearsay and reading plus "transcendent genius." Stoll concludes with a general discussion of the "detective spirit" and criticism, external and internal evidence.

Brooks, Alden. *Will Shakspere: Factotum and Agent.* Round Table Press, **1937**. Republished, New York: AMS Press, 1974.

"To attempt to establish a man's life and character from his works is always a haphazard proceeding. But plays are further the least personal of all compositions. Rarely does a play reach publication intact in its original text." The gist: Robert Greene sold plays to Shakspere. His *Groatsworth of Wit* attack on Shakspere is an attack on someone who abandoned him: "Evidently Greene has been in the habit of selling his work to Shakspere, and evidently Shakspere in this last has cast him off.... Greene tells why Shakspere will have no more of him. The upstart crow imagines that he can bombast out a blank verse himself now as well as anyone; and absolute jack-of-all trades that he is, he seems himself the only showman in the country.... But the adjective 'absolute' qualifies 'factotum' too strongly for 'factotum' to be merely the paraphrase of a literary attribute; further the balancing of 'factotum' with 'Shake-scene' directly speaks of the prompter's profession." Chettle called Shakspere a "vulgar writer," which means that he writes spectacles for common folk. "And for anything more important he hires others." And, "To limit Shakspere's handiwork to the insertion of clownish figures and facetious gags, is not to say that he did not also contribute to the scenario of plays. He knew of course his limitations. That was why he hired these others to write for him." Somebody oversaw and revised what the Marlowes, Greenes, etc. had written. As for courtiers writing, "There existed no reason why courtiers should not have turned to writing. The constant vogue for plays at Court invited any man of talent to exert his wit in their composition." Page 186: "The Poet, gentleman of birth, courtier of the Elizabethan world, poet and philosopher by temperament, drawn for several reasons to play revising, play writing, was the genius of the Shakespearean plays. Will Shakspere, man of the theater, braggart of natural wit, play broker, was the go-between, agent, willing figurehead." The Earl of Southampton is discussed. In his next book, Brooks [1943] will invoke the history of the true author.

Brown, Ivor, and Fearon, George. *This Shakespeare Industry: Amazing Monument.* New York: Harper & Row, **1939**. Reprinted, Westport, CT: Greenwood Press, 1969.

Included is an index plus nine illustrations, including a "Bardolater — Shaw [George Bernard] at Stratford" photo facing title page. There is no bibliography (in text, not full citations). Chapter IX is "Hands Upon the Bard" and covers the authorship dispute. "Where there is so much honor, jealousy and rivalry are likely to accumulate." The authors review the heresies begun by James Corton Cowell and Joseph Hart and covered by Greenwood, Slater, and Walter Thomson. "On the positive side Baconians can justly claim that their hero was over and over again described as a poet." Brown and Fearon admit a riddle but conclude that anti–Stratfordians begin to get snobbish. But what if Shakespeare was discredited? Light metal work, fruit canning and brewing would keep Stratford going, "But the theatre would be closed, the Birthplace would linger on as a curio for sniffing, smiling cynics, the church would no longer be able to charge an entrance fee, and three-quarters of the hotels and lodgings would be shuttered and deserted.... Publishers would have, at some cost, to scrap millions of covers and alter millions of titles."

Ross, William. *The Story of Anne Whateley and William Shaxpere as Revealed by "The Sonnets of Mr. W.H." and Other Elizabethan Poetry.* Glasgow: W. & R. Holmes, **1939**.

This contains shaky contentions and "reading between the lines" while Ross claims to be "reconstructing the story of Anne Whateley and William Shaxpere from the allusions scattered throughout

Elizabethan literature" through deduction. He summarizes claims for Bacon and mentions those of Rutland, Derby and Oxford in passing. The key to understanding the "Sonnets of Mr. W.H." is to realize they were written by a woman. Necessary is a reversion "to their original wording as written, not as published." Of course, publishing as a woman (both Sonnets and the plays) would have hampered her genius. The "black" woman was Anne Hathaway, Mr. W.H. was Shaxpere. Anne Whateley loved him. "Many of the sonnets were sent or given to Shaxpere as explanations, answers, or love-letters as they were written." If true, "The identification of Anne Whateley as the 'concealed poet' in the Shakespearean partnership at once throws light on the genesis of some of the plays." A woman author helps explain mix-up of partners in such as *A Midsummer Night's Dream*. No index.

Barrell, Charles Wisner. "Identifying 'Shakespeare.'" *Scientific American*, January **1940**, pp. 4–8, 43–45.

X-ray exposures reveal portraits of Edward de Vere and the shield of arms of his second wife. Barrell claims that the art of poetry was held in low esteem in Elizabethan times, mentions how many volumes have been devoted to disputing the man from Stratford's claim as bard, but devotes the bulk of his article to an examination of portraits via X-ray and infrared photography. An arresting point: of all the dramatists who sat for portraits, only the Stratford man appeared in noble garb. Featured are the "Ashbourne" portrait of William Shakespeare plus the 1656 Dugdale engraving of the skull symbol on the Stratford monument. Other paintings analyzed include a half-length panel owned by the King of Great Britain and the head-and-bust "Janssen" panel. Barrell claims that in each instance there is clear-cut evidence that the portraits have been changed far in the past by the same person. Lord Oxford's career is summarized.

Freud, Sigmund. *Abriss der Psycho-Analyse,* **1940**. Published in English as *An Outline of Psychoanalysis*. Translated by James Strachey. New York: W.W. Norton, 1963, ©1949.

The "enigma of another dramatic hero, Shakespeare's procrastinator, Hamlet, can be solved by a reference to the Oedipus complex" (page 96, Norton edition). More particularly, footnote 12 on page 96: "The name 'William Shakespere' is most probably a pseudonym behind which there lies concealed a great unknown. Edward de Vere, Earl of Oxford, a man who has been regarded as the author of Shakespeare's works, lost a beloved and admired father while he was still a boy, and completely repudiated his mother, who contracted a new marriage soon after her husband's death." See also Peter Gay's *Freud: A Life for Our Times* (New York: W.W. Norton, 1988), on page 643 of which it is noted that late in life Freud became convinced that the Earl of Oxford wrote the plays, which Gay finds "a farfetched and somewhat embarrassing theory with which he would regale his incredulous visitor and no less incredulous correspondents." The footnote on that page mentions Looney's "Shakespeare" Identified and correspondence on the subject between Freud and Ernest Jones. The latter called it a "harmless mania."

Campbell, Oscar James. "Shakespeare Himself." *Harper's Magazine*, July **1940**, pp. 172–185.

Campbell analyzes Charles Wisner Barrell's X-ray-based contention that the Earl of Oxford is depicted in the "Ashbourne portrait." Conceding that this is indeed a modified portrait of Oxford, he correctly notes that it does not prove Oxford wrote Shakespeare. Any number of paintings have been doctored over the ages to fool prospective buyers. He provides background on the debate, starting with Francis Bacon. On anti–Stratfordians: "Such unrestrained enthusiasts are always the pest and sometimes the gaiety of 'orthodox' librarians and professors." Bacon could not have had the time. The Earl of Rutland is named next, then the Earl of Derby, then Sir Walter Raleigh, but now most often Oxford, "Whose claims are the least grotesque." He says Francis Meres wrote in his *Palladis Tamia* (1598) that not only Oxford but also Shakespeare is listed as "The best for Comedy among us." But why does Shakespeare, not Oxford appear in the "best for Tragedies" list? The Stratford boy/man's life is reviewed in what Campbell sees as a viable biography. According to him, Stratford was not a backwater and its grammar school was one of the best in England. He states that signing with a cross in Elizabethan times was of religious significance. "However, it is not to any one detail in Senator Beveridge's sweeping assertion that exception need be taken [that only a genius could write them, "but genius does not supply learning, facts, experience.]; it is rather to his two major assumptions; first, that the writer of the plays was a man of wide learning; and, second, that literature is a direct reflection of the author's personal experience."

Campbell apparently subscribes to the "new criticism," that the works must be taken out of context. He wonders why Oxford would have concealed his authorship of poems when poets, noble or not, were honored. (They only wrote masques and poems, not plays for the common folk.) "Literary genius still remains inscrutable, but this much we know: it has never been solely in the custody of men of noble birth or of wide learning." In short, "The ways of genius have always been inexplicable."

Pimpernel Smith [film]. British National, **1941**. Screenplay by Anatole de Grunwald, Roland Pertwee, Ian Dalrymple.

Leslie Howard plays Professor Horatio Smith, mild-mannered archaeologist who uses disguise and ruse to foil the Nazis and extract the hunted from the Reich. His nemesis is played by Francis L. Sullivan. They talk Shakespeare at an embassy party and later Smith rushes into the Nazi office and says, "I've been doing a little research work ... on the identity of Shakespeare.... I spent the afternoon in the library, at the embassy. Now this, this proves conclusively that Shakespeare wasn't really Shakespeare at all.... He was the Earl of Oxford. Now you can't pretend that the Earl of Oxford was a German, can you? Now can you? ... Well, there you are.... The Earl of Oxford was a very bright Elizabethan light, but this book will tell he was a good deal more than that." Later, "Perhaps you'd care to read about the Earl of Oxford." At his excavation site, while holding an ancient Teutonic skull, he recites "Alas, poor Yorick" and follows with, "The Earl of Oxford wrote that, you know."

Frye, Albert Myrton, and Levi, Albert William. *Rational Belief: An Introduction to Logic*. New York: Harcourt, Brace, **1941**.

Chapter XVII: Hypothesis is "The Shakespeare Case" and uses Mark Twain's "Is Shakespeare Dead?" and Louis Benezet's *Shakspere, Shakespeare, and De Vere* as background information. "We must start at the beginning, that is, with the plays and other works themselves. What kind of man must the author have been? What must he have known? They consider solutions, identifying the candidates and forming hypotheses such as "Francis Bacon is the author of the plays, sonnets, and other poems made public under the name, William Shakespeare," "William Shakspere of Stratford-on-Avon is the author," and "Edward de Vere, the Seventeenth Earl of Oxford, wrote the plays, sonnets, and other poems made public under the name, William Shakespeare." They conclude, "Such experts as these certainly strongly suggest that their author wrote under a nom de plume and that he wished to immortalize that name. The hypothesis of de Vere's authorship of the plays, sonnets, and other poems is accordingly strengthened. The habit of believing that William Shakspere of Stratford-on-Avon is the author, is however, so strong that perhaps his claim will never be unsettled."

Berg, A. Scott. *Max Perkins: Editor of Genius*. New York: E.P. Dutton, 1978 [**1942**].

This biography of the editor of F. Scott Fitzgerald and Thomas Wolfe contains this passage on page 398: "In 1942 Perkins was reading proofs of a book that did get published only because of his obstinacy. It was Alden Brooks's *Will Shakespeare* [sic] *and the Dyer's Hand*. For some time the book had been a mania with him. At every editorial conference Perkins brought it up and the board unanimously voted it down. 'So, being a man of infinite patience,' one Scribners employee recalled, 'he would reintroduce his suggestion at the next conference, with the same result.' What charmed Perkins about the work was that it credited Sir Edward Dyer, an editor, with Shakespeare's success. Indeed, the book had convinced Perkins that 'the man Shakespeare was not the author of what we consider Shakespeare's works.' Eventually the board gave in, to please Perkins. Max sent copies to many critics, hoping to rouse support. Nearly every one dismissed the work as mere speculation. Still Perkins retained his faith in the book and his respect for it. It made him aware, he told Hemingway, 'how frightfully ignorant I am in literature, where a publishing man ought not to be.'"

Brooks, Alden. *Will Shakspere and the Dyer's Hand*. New York: Charles Scribner's Sons, **1943**.

Part I is "The Man of Stratford"; Part II, "The Man of the Plays." Pages 418–428 assess "The Candidates": Bacon, Oxford, Derby, Rutland, Greene, Peele, Lodge, Kyd, Marlowe, Nashe, Lyly, Daniel, Jonson. "Certainly each of these dramatists did contribute in some part to the Shakespearean plays." But Oxford, for instance, failed to meet the qualifications. "Oxford's outline is without the slightest mark of greatness. He lacked the balance, the wisdom, the all-seeing vision of the Poet." Who was the guiding hand? Edward Dyer, born in October 1543, "conforms to the outline of the Poet." He traveled abroad (Bohemia in 1590) and was a confidant of Leicester. "The Poet was a courtier. Dyer was a courtier." Brooks supports his case with correspondence and poems. What about Shakespeare? "In payment of debt, Will Shakspere claimed manuscripts." Shakspere converted the Blackfriars Gatehouse into a brothel, says Brooks.

Churchill, R.C. "The Baconian Heresy: A Post-Mortem." *Nineteenth Century and After*, November **1946**, pp. 260–268.

Ignoring authors like Twain and James, Churchill takes the tack that only literary critics are qualified to judge literature. He reviews the Baconian theory's history and does correctly observe that many Baconians can't distinguish between plausible and ridiculous arguments. Also, "the plays of Shakespeare can be fitted into every philosophy (including Bacon's, I would add) that has ever been heard of." For him philosophy springs totally from the dramatic context and is not imposed from without. He says the Bacon supporters equate genius with academic attainments "when true intelligence, the intelligence above all of the artist, includes sensibility, the power of imagination." Shakespeare got his knowledge "through miscellaneous reading, conversation and experience."

Allen, Percy. *Talks with Elizabethans*. London: Rider and Company, **1947**.

What at first glance seems tongue-in-cheek is shortly confirmed as serious delving into the authorship problem via mediums and spiritualism, including "automatic script," i.e., messages from the beyond (Bacon, Shakspere, Oxford) taken down by a living psychic, Hester Dowden. Includes index and four illustrations: the Hampton Court and Grafton portraits of Shakespeare, the Ditchley portrait of Queen Elizabeth, and an emblematical portrait of Mary Sidney, Countess of Pembroke.

Johnson, Edward D. *The Shakspere Illusion*. **1947**. 3rd ed., London: Mitre Press, 1965.

If we assume all the plays were published anonymously, "would not the search for the real author be made among contemporary men of letters, whose education, literary ability and experience gained by travel and by extended social intercourse, would qualify them for the undertaking?" Evidence and common sense are needed, for this is not just a matter for literary experts. These remarks are reasonable but Johnson believes Bacon's *Promus* sufficient to prove authorship. He discusses Sidney Lee and the birthplace. There are illustrations in this 194-page work.

Redman, Ben Ray. "New Editions." *Saturday Review of Literature*, June 5, **1948**, p. 46.

Redman's review of G.B. Harrison's *Shakespeare: 23 Plays and the Sonnets* agrees that we know more about Shakespeare than his contemporary poets and proceeds to show how Harrison has "provided a description, running to many pages, of Shakespeare's England," which obviously does not prove that the man from Stratford wrote the plays.

Burgess, Gelett. "Pseudonym, Shakespeare." *Saturday Review of Literature*, October 2, **1948**, p. 22.

Ben Ray Redman's review of G.B. Harrison's *Shakespeare: 23 Plays and the Sonnets* is taken to task. Burgess disputes the fact that we have many facts about Shakespeare, saying we have "perhaps a score of often sordid facts — baptisms, marriage, real estate deals, lawsuits, fines, etc. Not one of these records indicates in the slightest way that the Stratfordian was a writer. Nor do the few recorded items regarding the actor Shakespeare (who may or may not have been the Stratfordian) give any such evidence." He remarks that pseudonyms have been forever common, e.g., Mark Twain, O. Henry, and "it was a common practice in Elizabethan times to use stooges, often ignorant, whose names were put on title pages, even by the clergy. The anonymity of several important Elizabethan works has never been pierced." As for the Earl of Oxford: "he had every possible qualification for authorship, while the dummy of Stratford had not one."

"Letters to the Editor: The Shakespeare Confusion." *Saturday Review of Literature*, November 6, **1948**, pp. 21–22.

Five readers respond to the Gelett Burgess letter supporting de Vere in the October 2 issue. Four are negative, one supports the Oxfordian case and reveals that the publishers' stock of Looney's book was destroyed in a bombing raid on London although most public libraries have a copy. Hoy Cranston's letter includes six points but they are not all valid. (The bust in Holy Trinity Church has a hand resting on a scroll. "So the bust is a memorial to a writer." Originally the hand rested on a grain sack.) "The will also proves that the same Shakespeare produced plays of his own in London theatres. We find in the will the following: 'And to my Fellows ... John Hemmynges, Henry Cundell, Richard Burbage....'" (How does this prove he produced plays?) Clark Kinnaird demonstrates how one might question George Bernard Shaw's literacy from the biographical material at hand.

Galland, Joseph S. *Digesta Anti-Shakespeareana*. Completed by Burton A. Milligan. Evanston, IL: Northwestern University, **1949**.

Never published because of the author's death, this immense and annotated tome (three paperback volumes available from UMI Dissertation Information Service in Ann Arbor, Michigan) is an invaluable resource that covers periodical and book literature in various languages. There are 4,509 entries and a 23-page index.

Halliday, Frank E. *Shakespeare and His Critics*. London: Gerald Duckworth, **1949**.

A detailed family tree of the Shakespeare family fronts Chapter 1, "The Life of Shakespeare," in which Halliday reviews the earliest sketches of the poet, including Thomas Fuller, Thomas Plume, John Ward, John Aubrey, Richard Davies, and Nicholas Rowe. Chapter VII, "Disintegrators and Baconians," discusses those who would question Shakespeare's full title to what is traditionally attributed to him and, in a rather full summary of Edwin Durning-Lawrence's *Bacon Is Shakespeare*, the view that the Stratford man wrote none of the canon. Halliday is no Baconian and believes "The main evidence in favor of Shakespeare's authorship of the plays is their inclusion in the First Folio by Heminge and Condell, Shakespeare's friends and fellow actors, who must have known as well as anybody exactly what he wrote; and in their Prefaces to the Folio they are at pains to make clear how seriously they took their task." So "All argument, therefore, against the authority of the Folio must be based on internal evidence, on the plays themselves." And, "The mere fact of publication with Shakespeare's name, then, is no guarantee of authenticity, but inclusion in the First Folio almost certainly is, just as exclusion almost certainly is a guarantee of spuriousness." Reasonably, Halliday writes that the anti–Stratfordians had grounds for skepticism. "This negative attitude was originally a natural reaction to the hyperbolical claims put forward by the over-enthusiastic Stratfordians of last century, that not only was Shakespeare the world's greatest poet and dramatist but the greatest scholar and philosopher of his time." He considers the weakest part of the Baconian claim the explanation why Bacon concealed his authorship. There are illustrations, a bibliography, an index of critics and a general index.

Evans, Bergen. "Good Friend for Iesvs Sake Forbeare: Was Shakespeare Really Shakespeare?" *Saturday Review of Literature*, May 7, **1949**, pp. 7–8, 39–40.

Northwestern University English professor Evans presents a good case for the Stratfordians after summarizing the controversy and the 4,000+ books and articles about it. "Ironically, this question is founded on the hysterical claims of omniscience for their idol by the bardolaters." Hilariously, "And to support their assumption the various theorists have labored mightily to present The Stratford man as an illiterate oaf and his home town as a benighted spot through whose mired alleys trudged as low a group of cretins as ever gibbered in the suburbs of Dogpatch." One might take issue with Evans' assertion that "All intellectual activity had not yet been sucked into the metropolis," for recall Eric Hoffer's observation that nothing momentous ever came out of a village. Evans believes selecting Shakespeare as a stooge would reflect "little subtlety" by the true author. According to Evans, we know more about Shakespeare than any of the claimants except Bacon. Oxford's candidature is presented. Evans thinks the objection that playwriting was considered a base occupation has been exaggerated. He doesn't buy proof via internal evidence except "Where a metaphor has no particular relation to the character using it or where, as frequently happens, it is out of keeping with the character, it is not unreasonable to assume that it is the author's own." Thus there is a slip in *Othello* which indicates Shakespeare's job as prompter and his familiarity with stagecraft.

"Letters to the Editor: Was Shakspere Shakespeare?" *Saturday Review of Literature*, June 4, 1949, pp. 24–25.

Five respond to Bergen Evans' May 7 *Saturday Review* piece. One is completely humorous (a Martian poet did it), one congratulates Evans, one indicates where there's smoke there's fire, one takes Evans to task for claiming that the plays prove Shakespeare's literacy, and one (Gelett Burgess, see *Saturday Review*, October 2, 1948) presents an "Oxford Primer."

De Chambrun, Clara Longworth. "Was Shakespeare Really Shakespeare?" *Saturday Review of Literature*, June 25, 1949, pp. 27–28.

Written from Paris, De Chambrun takes Bergen Evans' May 7 *Saturday Review* article as a basis for presenting her contention that factual proof of authorship lies in the London Stationers Register, which lists 17 Shakespeare plays. She also believes the Stratford schooling was more than sufficient because Simon Hunt, Bachelor of Oxford, had a license to teach in the Schola Grammaticali in Villa Stratford super Avon, and this same Mr. Hunt later held a high position on the Continent with the Church of Rome.

Campbell, Oscar James. "The Bard's Private Ecstasies & Woes." *Saturday Review of Literature*, September 3, 1949, pp. 10–11.

Reviewed is Ivor Brown's *Shakespeare* (New York: Doubleday, 1949) and although he doesn't like Brown's "biographical interpretation of the poet's work-on the contrary, it is outmoded, being based on a naive conception of the relation of an author's personal experiences to his artistic achievements," or his surmises about the Dark Lady of the sonnets, Campbell appreciates Brown's biography. "His account of the events of the poet's life is spiritual and based on the most reliable scholarship."

Basso, Hamilton. "Books: The Big Who-Done-It." *The New Yorker*, April 8, 1950, pp. 113, 114, 117–119.

Basso reviews a rash of Shakespeare books: Ivor Brown's *Shakespeare*, a new edition of J. Thomas Looney's *"Shakespeare" Identified*, William Bliss' *The Real Shakespeare*, Marchette Chute's *Shakespeare of London*, a new edition of Hesketh Pearson's *A Life of Shakespeare*, and Duff Cooper's *Sergeant Shakespeare*. Most of his compliments go to Looney's work which "has rather cavalierly been neglected."

Humphreys, Philip. "Who Wrote Shakespeare?" *Baconiana*, October 1950, pp. 212–216.

Humphreys takes issue with Folger Library book and manuscript curator Dr. Giles E. Dawson for his piece in the August 10, 1950, *The Listener* titled "Who Wrote Shakespeare?" How come "Shakespeare's works display but little learning" now, wonders Humphreys? He disputes Dawson's view of six signatures. Humphreys says dissidents do not always consider Shakespeare a moron but "neither clerk nor scholar — and, incidentally no genius." The article that follows this is "Can We Educate Dr. Giles E. Dawson?" by Edward D. Johnson; it lists a bevy of notables who did not believe in the Stratford man's claim, including Lord Palmerston, Disraeli, W.E. Gladstone, Dickens, Coleridge, John Greenleaf Whittier, Oliver Wendell Holmes, Whitman, and Emerson.

Ogburn, Dorothy, and Ogburn, Charlton. *This Star of England: "William Shake-speare," Man of the Renaissance*. New York: Coward-McCann, 1952. Reprinted, Westport, CT: Greenwood Press, 1972.

Herein are 1,297 pages examining the life of Edward de Vere, the seventeenth Earl of Oxford, and his claim to the works of Shakespeare. The Ogburns hope to add to Looney's 1920 work and demonstrate how the author's personality is revealed in the plays. There are 16 illustrations, including de Vere, William Cecil, Anne Vavasour, the Ashbourne Portrait, and Henry Wriothesley. It is indexed and contains a six-page bibliography. Like the Stratfordians, the Ogburns resort often to "would seem," "reason to believe," "may allude to," and "must have been." They believe art is not the result of spontaneous generation. "However, even genius must be stocked with experience and knowledge if it is to attain to its full expression." An interesting point is made of Burghley, who as head of the Protestant party would have no interest in "the theatre and vulgar writers." Pages 1220–1248 evaluate what is known of the man from Stratford, to wit: "The facts of Shaksper's life in Stratford, meager as they are, suffice to demonstrate the impossibility of his having had any literary interests or of his capacity to write plays or poems."

Titherley, A.W. *Shakespeare's Identity: William Stanley, 6th Earl of Derby.* Winchester, England: Warren & Son, **1952.**

In his Preface Titherley explains why we should know the identity of the author: "the question fundamentally affects the whole understanding of Shakespeare's Art." He endeavors to "resent conjectures as such and not as misleading statements of fact, the bane of so much Shakespearean biography." He contrasts the early commentators who downplayed Shakespeare's genius with the 19th century generation who appreciated the incredible achievement. He notes that many have questioned authorship for quite some time and calls J.C. Cowell the first Baconian after his 1781 fruitless search for books and papers in the Stratford environs. Greenwood's "sheer iconoclasm" is reviewed and the champions of other candidates are summarized: 'Demblon (Rutland), Looney (de Vere), Lefranc (Derby), Slater (multiple authorship). There are appendices on handwriting, the Northumberland Manuscript, and Canonical Sonnets. There is a Genealogical Tree and an index.

Feldman, A. Bronson. "Shakespeare Worship." *Psychoanalysis*, vol. 2, no. 1 (**1953**): 57–72.

Employing "Freud's dynamic or evolutionary psychology," Dr. Feldman tackles the idolatry surrounding Shakespeare. "It is the remoteness from reason that makes the prevalent attitude to Shakespeare one of piety, of faith." He cites *This Shakespeare Industry*, Mark Twain, Frank Harris' *The Man Shakespeare*, and Henry James' short story "The Birthplace." He shows how the rags to riches story of the lad from Stratford touches a nerve. Also, Shakespeare was "a gentleman of trade, a genius in finance." The Oedipus complex is "the core of his mystery."

Beaton, Cecil, and Tynan, Kenneth. *Persona Grata.* New York: G.P. Putnam's Sons, **1954.**

Famed photographer and stage and screen costume and set designer Beaton and influential critic and writer Tynan profile 100 people they admire: poets and actors, ballerinas and playwrights, prize fighters and painters. Orson Welles completes the cast. He is quoted on Shakespeare: "I think Oxford wrote Shakespeare. If you don't agree, there are some awful funny coincidences to explain away."

Melchior, Ib. "My Solution of the Cipher." *Life*, August 9, **1954**, pp. 88, 90, 92.

Melchior analyzes the four-line inscription on Shakespeare's tombstone, using cryptanalysis to determine if Shakespeare left a secret message providing the whereabouts of a manuscript or some message for posterity. Melchior arbitrarily used Hamlet as his key word and concludes the message could be: "Elsinore laid wedge first Hamlet edition." Preceding this is a photographic essay by William W. Vandivert, "A Hamlet Enigma at Elsinore: Fabled Castle Is Beautiful Setting for Shakespeare Manuscript Search" (pp. 81–87). Is this Ib Melchior the same person who dabbled in film production?

Hoffman, Calvin. *The Murder of the Man Who Was "Shakespeare."* New York: J. Messner, **1955.**

There is no table of contents in this 232-page book. "Parallelisms" constitute pages 203–232. Hoffman reviews his two decades' worth of authorship investigation. He originally did not question the traditional man. He reviews his travels throughout Europe. "I roamed through graveyards, I crawled into dusty tombs, I shivered in the dampness of veritable archives, and in the musty atmosphere of libraries whose book-lined shelves had remained undisturbed for centuries." Doubters like Freud, Twain, and Lord Broughton "have managed to unshackle themselves [from] the handcuffs of a declining tradition" and should not be dismissed as clowns or cranks. In a footnote he disparages W.G. Zeigler's novel about Marlowe, calling it "the purest fiction and fantasy." He cites other Marlowe searchers like Archie Webster, who in a 1923 magazine piece said Marlowe had written the Sonnets. Slater had admitted Marlowe into the group that was headed by Oxford.

Harrison, G.B. "Was Marlowe the Bard?" *Saturday Review of Literature*, July 9, **1955**, p. 16.

　　The author of *Shakespeare's Tragedies* reviews Calvin Hoffman's *The Murder of the Man Who Was "Shakespeare."* Hoffman believes Christopher Marlowe must have been the author, but Harrison presents the facts of Marlowe's life and death in 1593 and vehemently disputes the view that Marlowe went overseas after having had a body substituted for himself.

Amphlett, Hilda. *Who Was Shakespeare? A New Enquiry.* Introduction by Christmas Humphreys. London, **1955**. Reprinted, New York: AMS Press, 1970.

　　This book is accompanied by 15 illustrations, chapter notes, an index, bibliography, and a "Chronology of 'Oxford' Plays 1573–1600." One of Amphlett's best questions is, Why would the first bust of Shakespeare in Holy Trinity Church feature a man with his hands on a sack? She does a workmanlike job explaining the authorship question and presenting the case for de Vere. In her concluding chapter she succinctly and without rancor reviews the claims of other candidates, e.g., "The claims for Raleigh are too slight to merit inclusion here. He was a poet of charm, and a friend of Oxford's if there be truth in Aubrey's account, so that descriptions of cannibals and 'deserts idle' which appear in *Othello* may well have been Oxford's retention of the great travelers' tales." (See Michael Miller, 1990.)

"Empty Theory." *Time*, May 14, **1956**, p. 37.

　　Two paragraphs trace Calvin Hoffman's attempts to secure permission to open Sir Thomas Walsingham's tomb in hopes of finding evidence favoring Marlowe. But he only found sand. "Added the *London News Chronicle*: 'Alas, not even poor Yorick.'"

Evans, A.J. *Shakespeare's Magic Circle.* Westport, CT: Associated Booksellers, **1956**.

　　This 160-page book is ostensibly a group theory book but "Appendix II: Summary of Evidence" comes out on the side of William Stanley, sixth Earl of Derby, as the most likely prime mover — and it's pretty persuasive. Perhaps Derby used knowledge of Oxford's life as background. He was Oxford's son-in-law. Thirty-nine points are made in that summary in Derby's favor. Other candidates examined include Oxford, Bacon, Mary, Lady Pembroke, Sir Philip Sidney's sister, and Roger Manners, fifth Earl of Rutland.

　　Along the way some significant points are made, e.g., "Genius can account for much, but it cannot supply the multitudinous facts of special experience which Shakespeare reveals even in his earliest plays"; there is not connection between Shaksper and Southampton; the orthodox believe is [*sic*] Shaksper composed objectively with no personal turmoils in his life as causes; the point of view is that of a gentleman; dating is crucial to the Stratford claim; Shaksper may have joined the Earl of Leicester's acting troop in 1587 when it passed through; a really keen Stratford businessman should have made provisions for the sale of unpublished manuscripts for his heirs. He examines "Venus" and "Lucrece" and other works, also Bacon and Jonson. He thinks Oxford's surviving works betray none of the humor so often found in Shakespeare. There is a one-page bibliography of two parts: "For the Orthodox Case" with 14 references and "Against the Orthodox Case" with 11 references. Notes are at page bottom. Appendix I is "Shakespeare's Handwriting." There is an index.

Sweet, George Elliott. *Shake-Speare: The Mystery.* Foreword by Erle Stanley Gardner. Stanford, CA: Stanford University Press, **1956**.

　　Gardner doesn't exactly say he believes Sweet's proposition but he likes his logic. ("Sweet's theories fascinated me. I studied his manuscript, I talked with him, and the more I thought about the problem he presented the more fascinated I became.") Sweet tackles the chronology of the plays to support his theory that Queen Elizabeth was the author. "We should label this plan a deliberate, premeditated stratagem rather than a deliberate hoax, for while the author is in part playing a joke on his audience, the secret of authorship was planned for any number of good and sufficient motives." "*Groats-worth of Wit* [*sic*] was published by Henry Chettle in the fall of 1592 and gave to the world the first notice that Shake-speare was a writer or an actor or both." Omission from Henslowe's Diary proves he was "no ordinary dramatist.... To say that Shake-speare moved in a charmed circle is putting it mildly." And, "If Shake-speare was a pen name adopted before 1587, and the manager of the Queen's Men was empowered to hire any potential actor from the provinces with a name similar to Shake-speare, then the nom de plume was no mere whim but an appropriate word-picture highly descriptive of the Bard." As for the Sonnets, "The 'dark lady' sonnets are not personal; Shake-speare is writing drama in a poetic form, he is detailing the volcanic emotional conflict between two individuals, neither to be identified with himself." "Somewhere or somehow there appears to be a misplaced gender about the sonnets." And, "Shake-speare had to appear in the image of a man, not a woman, because sixteenth century England would never forgive a woman, let alone a queen, for writing down-to-earth realism, and that was the way Elizabeth wanted to write." And, "More than any other Elizabethan, the English Queen was the most likely to possess the 15,000 word vocabulary (estimated by one author to be 21,000 words)." Elizabeth was mightily displeased by the secret marriage of Lord Leicester and her cousin, Lettice Knollys, thus "Lettice Knollys is the Dark Lady of the Sonnets." As for the plays' women as men: "The psychic urge that made Elizabeth place Portia, Rosalind, and Viola in men's clothing as a matter of disguise, might partially explain her motivation in disguising her own authorship in masculine raiment.... For every strong and mature Shake-speare heroine we have a weak, vacillating, impetuous hero." Appendices present the "1930 Guess" and the "1955 Guess" concerning chronology and in Appendix C there is discussion of King Henry V regarding dating. There is a bibliography but no index. Not much is said of other contenders.

Wallace, Irving. *The Square Pegs: Some Americans Who Dared to Be Different.* New York: Alfred A. Knopf, **1957.**

Wilbur Glenn Voliva, a flat earth promoter, influenced the ubiquitous Wallace to write this collection that covers Voliva, Baron James A. Harden-Hickey (suicide authority), George Francis Train (millionaire Commune member), Victoria Woodhull (spiritualist and prostitute), Joshua Norton (Emperor of the U.S.), Delia Bacon, John Cleve Symmes (hollow earth), Anne Royall (author), and Timothy Dexter (grammar foe). There are illustrations, an index and references. He presents psychiatric explanations for the eccentric, who have "furthered the cause of science, built great empires, improved the public welfare, and created memorable works of art."

Wallace begins Chapter VI with the background to Delia's theory, covering Herbert Lawrence's *Life and Adventures of Common Sense,* Disraeli's *Venetia,* and Hart's *Romance of Yachting.* As for Delia, "she had initiated a heresy in literature, a controversy in academic circles that would persist generation after generation, that persists even today after more than a century." Her childhood, lectureships, romantic tribulation, and English visit are examined. She believed in "inductive reasoning" (see Karl Popper for deductive). Her relations with Emerson, Hawthorne, and Carlyle are detailed. As for her book, "There followed then, in almost 700 labored pages, the unfolding of a theory that might have been better told in 100 pages." William Henry Smith's simultaneous theory is covered, as are the views of Twain, Slater, Donnelly, Looney, and Alden Brooks.

Benezet, Louis P. *The Six Loves of "Shake-Speare."* New York: Pageant Press, **1958.**

This 126-page book includes footnotes, portraits, and an "Appendix: What the Portraits Reveal," but no index. There is a Preface by the author's son, Roger P. Benezet. The book concentrates on the Sonnets. Background is provided on whoever wrote the canon — how could the Stratford man have read enough to give him a 20,000 word vocabulary, speech of the nobility, and knowledge of Italian and French? Signatures are discussed as are forgeries in the nineteenth century by J. Payne Collier. Benezet mentions that there was a Globe Theatre shareholder William Shakespeare who died in 1615 and says this man is not the same as the Stratford fellow, who died in 1616. The will is analyzed. "The will is dull and lifeless. Not one spark of intellect, to say nothing of genius, is visible anywhere." As for the Sonnets, "Shakespeare's Sonnets and the life story of Edward de Vere, Earl of Oxford, mutually corroborate and illustrate each other." According to Benezet, Anne Vavasour was the "Dark Lady." The Sonnets are experiences of a nobleman who dare not reveal his name to the general public, thus one cannot make sense of them without reference to Oxford's life. Pronouns were changed in gender in the second edition to the Sonnets in order to make them all appear written to young women. Some were to his son, according to Benezet. This is good but a bit idolatrous and containing some factual errors.

Friedman, William F., and Friedman, Elizabeth S. *The Shakespearean Ciphers Examined: An Analysis of Cryptographic Systems Used as Evidence That Some Author Other Than William*

Shakespeare Wrote the Plays Commonly Attributed to Him. New York: Cambridge University Press, **1958**.

The 303-page book has an index but no bibliography although it is chock full of notes and references. "Whoever seeks actively for a cipher usually believes one to be there," write the husband-wife cryptologists, who claim no axe to grind. They cover Gallup, Fiske, Donnelly, and the biliteral cipher and conclude that no one has made a valid case. As for numbers, "Reading messages in them is a fatal pastime; there are so many ways to proving so many things that in the end we see that there is really no way of proving anything at all. As cryptologists we cannot admit that there is safety in numbers." What a genius Bacon would be if he could write a significant work that is meant merely to conceal a secret message! "We suggest that those who wish to dispute the authorship of the Shakespeare plays should not in future resort to cryptographic evidence, unless they show themselves in some way competent to do so."

Churchill, R.C. *Shakespeare and His Betters: A History and a Criticism of the Attempts Which Have Been Made to Prove That Shakespeare's Works Were Written by Others*. Foreword by Ivor Brown. With collaboration in bibliography and research by Maurice Hussey. Bloomington: Indiana University Press, **1958**.

This is worth the bibliography, which is broken down by origins, nineteenth and twentieth century theories, parallel theories, Stratfordian rejoinders, and related questions. As Churchill notes, the authorship question is an international pastime, but few books have surveyed the whole issue, e.g., M. Georges Connes' *Le Mystere Shakespearien*, Gilbert Slater's *Seven Shakespeares*. Churchill's book is divided into two parts, the first tracing the history of the subject from the seventeenth century to 1958, the second a literary and cultural analysis. Churchill believes the inquiry is not for lawyers but for those trained in literary criticism and cultural history. He notes that both sides have been uncivil towards the other, but he calls attention to a personal friendship between Stratfordian J.M. Robertson and iconoclast G. Greenwood. His own view: there is not "a single serious question to be imputed against it [Shakespeare as author]." There is an index.

Pares, Martin. *A Pioneer: In Memory of Delia Bacon*. London: Rydal Press, 1958. 2nd ed., **1959**.

Printed for the Francis Bacon Society, this 70-page tribute contains no index or bibliography. There are some footnotes. Pares supports Bacon as Shakespeare and says the "oppressive power of vested interest" maintains the Stratford man's claim. Regarding Delia's book, he admits that it needed an editor, is "unreadable" yet often throws "light upon some new germ of Shakespearean interpretation." She "surpassed previous commentators in penetrating the hidden motives social and philosophical, underlying the Shakespearean plays." He says authorship has been in dispute since the First Folio. He thinks one had to be learned and a genius to write the plays. He reviews James Spedding's, Francis Bacon's biographer, relationship with Delia, though Spedding "seems to have opposed the Baconian theory of authorship largely on grounds of style." People like Bacon, Sir Thomas More and Campanella "had begun to look ahead to a promised land." He supports Delia in "the belief that there was a purpose, and a more lofty one than that of putting the author in easy circumstances!" Montaigne influenced Delia. "Her plea was unacceptable for the reason that Shakespearean orthodoxy had already become an article of faith." He quotes letters from Carlyle to Delia and Delia to Emerson.

Wadsworth, Frank W. *The Poacher from Stratford: A Partial Account of the Controversy Over the Authorship of Shakespeare's Plays*. Berkeley: University of California Press, **1958**.

In this 174-page work, Wadsworth aims to solve the "romantic dilemma" that is the authorship question. He finds that hatred is a major component of the idolaters. We do know a good deal about the man from Stratford. He and other dramatists were members of a "workaday world — they had little contact with serious affairs of state; and actors, when invited to court, came to provide entertainment, not instruction." (How, then, did Shakespeare acquire intimate knowledge of the court?) Wadsworth claims the anti–Stratfordians believe in class distinctions and deny the "role of vicarious experience in artistic creation." After this Prologue he explores the controversy's history. In his Epilogue he describes the heretics as "romantics of an older, richer, more Keatsian school, enamored of cloud-capped towers and gorgeous palaces, of handsome knights and lovely ladies." There is an index; references are in text. Illustrations include: Constance Pott; facsimile of page from 1623 Folio; Orville Owen's Wheel; Gustavi Seleni's title page; Lichfeld House; Calvin Hoffman; Sir Thomas Walsingham's tomb; Droeschout Portrait of Shakespeare.

Bentley, Richard. "Elizabethan Whodunit: Who Was 'William Shake-Speare'?" *American Bar Association Journal*, February **1959**, pp. 143–146, 204–208.

Bentley, Yale graduate and president of the Chicago Bar Association 1954–1955, claims the authorship question "is not purely a literary question; it is also a question of evidence." He says "we should not reject a new conclusion merely because it may be different from an old one, long accepted." For instance, Richard III was not as bad as he was portrayed. Likewise the Piltdown Man hoax was perpetrated for years. He mentions that Shakespeare is a big business in Stratford. He inspects the candidates William Shaksper, Francis Bacon, Christopher Marlowe, Edward de Vere, and presents the views and evidence put forth by their champions, e.g., scholars, Donnelly, Hoffman, Looney. De Vere seems to have the best claim. Other skeptics are reviewed: Freud, Dickens, James, etc. There is a chart showing the reigns from Edward VI to James I with some significant dates and the birth and death dates of Shaksper, Bacon, Marlowe, and Oxford.

Ogburn, Charlton. "A Mystery Solved: The True Identity of Shakespeare." *American Bar Association Journal*, March **1959**, pp. 237–241.

"The dramatist was obviously a trained lawyer," says Ogburn, citing others who shared this view, like Bismarck, as well as those who didn't, like Sidney Lee. He cites legalese from various plays and sonnets. He says Ben Jonson's comments in the Introduction to the First Folio were "clearly a hoax." He reviews "Shaksper's" biography and de Vere's qualifications.

"Shakespeare Arena." *American Bar Association Journal*, June **1959**, pp. 604–06.

There are responses to Richard Bentley's February article and Charlton Ogburn's March article from 14 men, including Louis Benezet, author of *The Six Loves of "Shake-Speare,"* who would contribute "A Hoax Three Centuries Old" to the May 1960 journal.

Hauser, John N. "The Shakespearean Controversy: A Stratfordian Rejoinder." *American Bar Association Journal*, July **1959**, pp. 704–707, 765–766.

In a more gentlemanly fashion than most, Hauser refutes the Bentley and Ogburn contentions (February and March *American Bar Association Journal*, respectively) that the man from Stratford wasn't the author. He examines (1) some principal anti–Stratfordian points, and (2) Oxford's candidature. Hauser says the Stratford grammar school was free to townspeople of substance, such as John Shakespeare. Ben Jonson's knowledge of classical literature is regarded as superior to Shakespeare and Jonson was not college trained. "There were plenty of opportunities in London for self-education." To back his view, Hauser cites A.L. Rowse's *The England of Elizabeth*, hardly an impartial source. Hauser says 10 of the plays were written after 1604, including *King Lear* and *Macbeth*.

Clary, William W. "The Case for the Defense: De Vere et al. v. Shakespeare." *American Bar Association Journal*, July **1959**, pp. 700–703, 750.

Clary responds to Bentley (February 1959) and, to a lesser degree, Charlton Ogburn (March 1959). He understands the doubt but disputes contentions that there is no direct evidence of authorship. But there is: Shakespeare's will and the First Folio. Clary can in no way believe that actors Heminge and Condell were deceived or became willing parties to the fraud. He proposes that the debate continues because people like to solve problems the hard way. As for Shakespeare's legal and historical knowledge, he got it from Holinshed's *Chronicles*.

Ogburn, Dorothy, and Ogburn, Charlton. "The True Shakespeare: England's Great and Complete Man." *American Bar Association Journal*, September **1959**, pp. 941–943, 990–996.

"His poems and dramas, like the works of all truly creative writers were, in the fullest sense, his life. It had to be so." The Ogburns note that Byron, Tolstoy, Dickens and Goethe used themselves as background. How could the author be an uneducated man for "mediocrity produces mediocrity and greatness greatness." They present 10 facts fundamental to de Vere as the author, such as a cover-up perpetrated by William Cecil. "It is the Cecils' censored version of the Elizabethan era which has come down to us." The Queen would not have allowed a commoner license to write *Henry VI* and *Richard II.* The Ogburns' case is damaged by their contention that de Vere had a son, the "Fair Youth" who was Southampton. His mother: the Queen!

Bentley, Richard. "Elizabethan Whodunit: Supplementary Notes." *American Bar Association Journal*, November **1959**, pp. 1160–63, 1222–30.

    Bentley expands on his February 1959 article questioning the authorship and addresses the Stratfordian replies. He asks us to agree that the records and sources for Shakespeare must come from Edmund Chambers' *William Shakespeare: A Study of Facts and Problems*, "which seem to be acceptable to most Stratfordians." He discusses the signatures, Shakespeare's parents, his education and training (schools "generally required an entrant to be able to read and write Latin and English"), genius, lack of payment for writings ("When Shaksper died, twenty of the Shakespeare plays were unpublished and thus protected, yet the will made no reference to such valuable property"), chronology ("The weakness of the so-called 'Chronology Argument' is that there is no manuscript extant, nor any external evidence whatever to indicate when any of the works was written, except, of course, the fact that each must of necessity have been written at some time prior to the earliest date when it was produced or published…. It should also be remembered that generally dates for each of the works were estimated on the assumption that the Stratford man wrote them"), lack of notice of Shaksper as a literary man, posthumous evidence, the First Folio, bequests to Heminge and Condell, and the financing of the First Folio.

Wright, Louis B. "The Anti-Shakespeare Industry and the Growth of Cults." *The Virginia Quarterly Review*, Spring **1959**, pp. 289–303.

    Wright is guilty of the intolerance he finds in the anti–Stratfordians. "In 1769 Herbert Lawrence published *The Life and Adventures of Common Sense*, in which he suggested that some unidentified person wrote the plays. That was the first and only time the question ever touched common sense." He traces the controversy from the late eighteenth century, noting that "Shakespeare idolatry induced a natural reaction." The reaction he claims is odd and funny books. He claims the "movement is permeated with emotion that sweeps aside the intellectual appraisal of facts, chronology, and the laws of evidence." He complains that anti–Shakespeareans lack a sense of humor. Naively, he thinks a professor would love to be the one who finds a real alternative and that there is no vested interest in keeping Shakespeare and Stratford. "The identity of the individual who wrote the plays is relatively unimportant. The important thing to be remembered is that truth does matter." He compares the antis to trial lawyers, the pros to historical scholars, and identifies four premises upon which the antis built a case. Wright complains that Shakespeare was careless and "demonstrated no profound book learning." After all, he gave a seacoast to Bohemia and garbled history so as to get to the tavern "for a drink with the boys." He writes of good grammar schools in England and says neither Cervantes nor Moliere were well educated. "The 'noble lord' theory of the authorship of Shakespeare's plays is promoted nowadays chiefly by Americans. It represents a kind of snobbery." Plays were not literature at all. Looney is taken to task. The Earl of Derby and Spenser are discussed. "The fact that the later plays are filled with allusions to events after the Queen's death apparently can be dismissed as a matter of no moment." Anti-Stratfordians reside in "Cuckoo-Land."

Hastings, William T. "Shakspere Was Shakespeare." *The American Scholar*, Autumn **1959**, pp. 479–488.

    A member of the advisory board of the *Shakespeare Quarterly*, Hastings has little sympathy for the "lunatics and the unmitigated liars" in this brief rundown of the cases against Shakespeare, for "X," and for Shakespeare. He believes that we know as much about Shakespeare as any other writer of the Elizabethan period. He reviews the positions of most of the anti–Stratfordians and identifies the candidates. "Of them all it may be said categorically that not one theory in support of any one candidate has a single shred of positive evidence behind it. All is pure hypothesis." He contents "the well-established chronology of Shakespeare's works runs from about 1591 to 1613." He stresses the "gentle Shakespeare."

Pares, Martin. "Francis Bacon and the Knights of the Helmet." *American Bar Association Journal*, April **1960**, pp. 401–209.

Pares notes some of Oxford's valid claims but lends his support to Bacon. For instance, Bacon was on the council of the first Virginia Company and two of his colleagues were the earls of Pembroke and Montgomery — to whom the First Folio was dedicated. Bacon would also have known of the wreck of the *Sea Venture* and used the material in *The Tempest*. Pares uses dates that support Bacon, not Oxford. He discusses Ben Jonson's role. Pares does not seem to know that Oxford, like Bacon, was interested in the theater. He examines the Northumberland Manuscript and *The Promus of Formularies and Elegancies*. He uses Shelley and Emerson's views that Bacon was also a poet. He tries to vindicate Bacon's character in regard to the trial of Essex.

Briggs, Arthur E. "Did Shaxper Write Shakespeare?" *American Bar Association Journal*, April **1960**, pp. 410–412.

Briggs supports Francis Bacon, believing that the "Droeschout Print" in the First Folio "was designed to spell the initials of Francis Bacon." He identifies those he believes were Baconians and discusses the Abraham Lincoln argument that an uneducated man could have genius — Lincoln had books. He thinks ideas and purposes are the best evidence and "Bacon, remarkably for this time as well as ours, had a theory of dramatic poetry which elucidates Shakespeare. It provides the basis for criticism, which is otherwise lacking."

Benezet, Louis P. "A Hoax Three Centuries Old." *American Bar Association Journal*, May **1960**, pp. 519–522.

Benezet protests the application of the term "fop" to Oxford, who won two tournaments, studied at Cambridge, and equipped a ship to fight the Spanish Armada. "All of the historical plays of the anti–Armada period were played (or printed) anonymously." As for the list of best comedy writers, "Meres who included in a list of best writers of comedy both Oxford and Shake-speare, may not have known that the two names represent the same man. Or, he may have been aware of it but unwilling to be the one to uncover the pseudonym." John Lyly, writer, confessed how much he'd learned from Edward de Vere. Anthony Munday dedicated *Zelauto, the Fountain of Fame* to Oxford. How come "nothing that we have from his [Oxford's] pen was written after his twenty-sixth year? What was he writing during the rest of his life? Answer: Everything known as that of William Shakespeare." The Sonnets are discussed. Genders of pronouns were changed, Benezet argues. And, "By holding back the publication of the plays until Oxford had been dead eighteen years and paying Ben Jonson, Heminge and Condell a total of some two hundred pounds, slipping a few entries into the Stratford man's will, and erecting a monument in Stratford church with a craftily worded inscription upon it to mystify the populace, the Earls of Derby, Pembroke, Oxford and Montgomery and their wives put over a hoax which has lasted three hundred and fifty years, and is destined to last another fifty if the Folger Library staff can sweep back the rising tide of research and reflection as successfully as they are now doing."

Wham, Benjamin. "'Marlowe's Mighty Line': Was Marlowe Murdered at Twenty-nine?" *American Bar Association Journal*, May **1960**, pp. 509–513.

Christopher Marlowe is profiled and Calvin Hoffman's explorations summarized. In side by side passages, Marlowe and Shakespeare lines are compared. Wham concludes that if Marlowe lived, many questions are answered and the need of an author of tragedy to have experienced tragedy is fulfilled.

Ogburn, Dorothy, and Ogburn, Charlton. "Shakespeare or Shaksper?" *The American Scholar*, Spring **1960**, pp. 271, 290–295.

The husband-wife team complain about William T. Hastings' Autumn 1959 issue attack on their pro–Oxford stance. They disclaim fanaticism and argue that Stratfordians defend "an outworn dogma." "Every man writes what he is," they say, and argue that Shaksper "was a penny-pinching grain-dealer whose parents and daughter could not sign their own names." They dispute Hastings' contention that the solid information about Shakespeare is a lot for the time period. "Although the death of every poet and playwright of the time was marked by memorial verses and other public acclaim, the only notice of Shaksper's was a line in Dr. Hall's diary: 'My father-in-law died yesterday.'" They contend that the plays had all been written by 1603. They explain how Cecilian censorship of Oxford led to the Baconian theory "but Bacon was no poet." They identify seven fundamental facts in favor of Oxford and discuss the First Folio. Following the Ogburns' rebuttal is Hastings' rejoinder. He claims they have offered no proof or evidence. All conclude with a list of recommended readings from both parties.

Holland, Norman N. "Freud on Shakespeare." *PMLA*, June **1960**, pp. 163–173.

Cited are the sources of Freud's comments on Shakespeare. As for genius, it "should not be called upon as an explanation until every other solution has failed" (*Moses and Monotheism*, p. 101). On authorship, he took the Oxfordian view, referring people to Looney and to Gerald H. Rendall's *Shakespeare's Sonnets and Edward De Vere*. Holland does not sympathize: "It is true that Freud's views on authorship were at least eccentric if not downright hostile."

"The Stage: To Man from Mankind's Heart." *Time*, July 4, **1960**, pp. 60–68, 70–72. [www.time.com/time/magazine/article/0,9171,869555,00.htm]

The exemplary state of worldwide Shakespearean performance and interest in the Bard are examined. Deaf-mute students at Gallaudet College mime *Othello*, Southern Rhodesian tribesmen essay *Macbeth* in traditional Zulu costume, John Gielgud's *Ages of Man* recording sells 30,000 copies. The doings at Stratford-upon-Avon ("a shrine and an industry.") are reviewed as are those at Ontario, Canada and Stratford, Connecticut. "If none of the Stratfords is great — too many gimmicky productions betray the fear that the greatest entertainer in the history of the theater is not entertaining enough — they do have the overriding merit of bringing Shakespeare alive for huge audiences." Questions about authorship are labeled "pseudoscholarship" for those theories are based on snobbery. Beyond the historical record, the best refutation "is the plays themselves; the style is the man — the unmistakable code in which life and work meet." Shakspere's family background and presumed schooling are summarized. In London he "was a quick study in success." And "Londoners worshiped him." Reviewed is the esteem or lack thereof in which Shakespeare was held after the Elizabethan era. Extolled are modern purveyors of the Bard's genius: John Gielgud, Laurence Olivier, Maurice Evans, Michael Redgrave. "No single philosophy dominates the plays. The closest thing to it may be Shakespeare's conviction that the social order must be restored." A lengthy endnote on the authorship controversy belittles Delia Bacon and Ignatius Donnelly. J. Thomas Looney "drummed up" the "Oxford boom," his name "a proper foil for the Baconian camp's George M. Battey."

American Bar Association Journal. *Shakespeare Cross-Examination: A Compilation of Articles First Appearing in the American Bar Association Journal*. Chicago: Cuneo Press, **1961**.

This includes the articles appearing in 1959 and 1960 issues of the Journal: "Elizabethan Whodunit: Who Was 'William Shake-Speare'?" by Richard Bentley, "A Mystery Solved: The True Identity of Shakespeare" by Charlton Ogburn, "The Case for the Defense: De Vere et al. v. Shakespeare" by William W. Clary, "The Shakespearean Controversy: A Stratfordian Rejoinder" by John N. Hauser, "The True Shakespeare: England's 'Great and Complete Man'" by Dorothy and Charlton Ogburn, "Elizabethan Whodunit: Supplementary Notes" by Richard Bentley, "Francis Bacon and the Knights of the Helmet" by Martin Pares, "Did Shaxper Write Shakespeare" by Arthur E. Briggs, "'Marlowe's Mighty Line': Was Marlowe Murdered at Twenty-nine?" by Benjamin Wham, and "A Hoax Three Centuries Old" by Louis P. Benezet. Pages 116–125 include excerpts from letters to the editor regarding these articles.

Borges, Jorge Luis. *Labryinths: Selected Stories and Other Writings*. Edited by Donald A. Yates and James E. Irby. New York: New Directions, 2007, ©**1962**.

The selection, "Everything and Nothing," originally appearing in *Version* no. 1, Mendoza, Autumn

1958, appears last in this collection. "Everything and Nothing" is a two-page meditation on the man from Stratford who found on the stage and in writing that he could be someone yet after twenty years "was gripped by the tedium and the terror of being so many kings who die by the sword and so many suffering lovers who converge, diverge and melodiously expire" that he retired to his native home, became another someone who dealt in loans and lawsuits, and "dictated the arid will." Strictly speaking, this is not an essay on authorship doubts but could be cited by either side to support their claims. [See also: Barton, Anne, "The One and Only," *New York Times Review of Books*, May 11, 2006.]

Guthrie, Tyrone. "Threat of Newness to Olde Stratford." *New York Times Magazine*, April 22, **1962**, pp. 12, 60–61.

Guthrie reviews in text and photographs Stratford's penchant for remaining in the past through architecture and discusses the authorship question and ramifications. "But what if it turns out, as it just possibly might, that William Shakespeare of Stratford was not the author of the plays ascribed to him? There is a theory, advanced by reputable scholars, seriously and, in my opinion, plausibly, that Shakespeare merely lent his name as a cover for the literary activities of another person, perhaps the Earl of Oxford. If, by some terrible chance, this theory should be proved, then straightway Stratford's tourist status would dwindle. It would become just one more — and honestly not one in the first ten — of England's picturesque small towns. The Birthplace, Anne Hathaway's Cottage and New Place, where Shakespeare died in 1616, would be discredited; the Theatre would go broke and become the Jam Factory, which it already resembles; hotels, great and small, would be going, going, gone. Once more the beautiful gray church, with its impostor's tomb, would dominate Birmingham's quietest dormitory."

Gibson, H.N. *The Shakespeare Claimants: A Critical Survey of the Four Principal Theories Concerning the Authorship of the Shakespearean Plays*. London: Methuen, **1962**.

Bacon, Oxford, Derby, and Marlowe are considered. Gibson says he began as an agnostic but ended as a Stratfordian. He believes Robertson effectively squashed Greenwood's arguments. There is an index and a three-page bibliography in this 311-page book.

McManaway, James G. *The Authorship of Shakespeare*. Ithaca, NY: Cornell University Press, 1964, ©**1962**.

This is a 50-page Folger Booklet on Tudor and Stuart Civilization. Only Christopher Marlowe and Ben Jonson are better documented, says McManaway. He says actors were held in low esteem in Elizabethan times, that Shakespeare was the first English playwright to have a formal biography written to be published with his works, and that what seems erudition now was common knowledge then. "What is known of Shakespeare's education comes, then, largely from the poems and plays themselves." He names the books in general use in English grammar schools." The testimony of the Reverend Mr. John Ward is unimpeachable [*sic*]." (?) "The truth of the matter is that poetic genius overleaps both space and time." "So it is relatively easy to write the history of English drama from, say, 1585 to 1642 [*sic*]." There are nine plates, e.g., signatures, coats of arms of "Shakespeare the player," a page from an anonymous play, and a receipt signed by George Chapman. "Suggested Reading" constitutes four pages.

McMichael, George, and Glenn, Edgar M. *Shakespeare and His Rivals: A Casebook on the Authorship Controversy*. New York: Odyssey Press, **1962**.

This is an excellent survey of the authorship question. It examines documents such as dedications, wills and Shakespeare's epitaphs. Contemporary references to Shakespeare are provided, from Robert Greene to Ben Jonson. Early biographers are excerpted. All of the major candidates are described. It does not appear that the authors realize that Leslie Stephen's "Did Shakespeare Write Bacon?" was tongue-in-cheek. Appendix B is "Suggested Research Topics and Questions." There is no index, an eight-page bibliography, and 262 pages overall.

Jessup, John K. "Fresh Troops Join the Battle of the Bard." *Life*, September 7, **1962**, p. 4.

Using the appearance of the Ogburns' *Shake-Speare: The Man Behind the Name* and H.N. Gibson's

The Shakespeare Claimants as background, the editor fairly reviews the history of the authorship question and realizes that Oxford's life matches that of a person who could have written the plays. He understands that Elizabethan England had its share of plots and spies and concludes that "there is a Shakespeare problem."

Ogburn, Dorothy, and Ogburn, Charlton, Jr. *Shake-speare: The Man Behind the Name.* New York: William Morrow, 1963, ©1962.

The mother and son say they are taking a fresh, systematic look at the question and conclude that the plays were dynamite commentaries on what was happening in government and that Lord Burghley tried to expunge Oxford from the official record. Included are "Parallel Comparisons Between Shaksper and Oxford" and "The Poems of Edward de Vere." This 282-page book includes seven illustrations, footnotes/bibliography, and an index.

Marder, Louis. *His Exits and His Entrances: The Story of Shakespeare's Reputation.* Philadelphia: J.B. Lippincott, 1963.

There are 386 pages, an index and an eight-page bibliography. In "Chapter V: The Man and the Myth" Marder debunks Baconians and believers in acrostics and ciphers. He covers Bacon, Delia and Francis, Donnelly, mediums, hidden manuscripts, and Calvin Hoffman. "Much more spectacular than any antics of the Baconians were the stories and notoriety that accumulated around the resuscitated notion that Christopher Marlowe was the author of the plays." Marder calls Oxfordians "the most ambitious of the skeptics at the present time." He mentions Looney and the Ogburns. He thinks "the problem of dates" virtually demolishes the claims of Oxford, William Stanley, sixth Earl of Derby and Roger Manners, fifth Earl of Rutland. He cites E.K. Chambers' *William Shakespeare* (1930) which covers group theories. He mentions A.J. Evans' *Shakespeare's Magic Circle* (1956), Sir Anthony Shirley, Raleigh, Essex, William Ross' *The Story of Anne Whateley and William Shaxpere* (1939), and Queen Elizabeth. Page 188: "There is nothing in the plays that was beyond the powers of an alert Elizabethan intimately connected with the stage, a reader of books, a friend to gentlemen and travelers, and, what is not evident in the known works of any other contemporaries except possibly Marlowe, with an insight into humanity and a skill with words and thoughts that has never yet been surpassed."

Montague, W.K. *The Man of Stratford—The Real Shakespeare.* New York: Vantage Press, 1963.

There are seven pages of bibliography and acknowledgments in this 199-page survey with appendices on Shakespeare's legal knowledge, handwriting, and copyright title to plays and manuscripts. He cites the Ogburns, Calvin Hoffman, Durning-Lawrence, and Richard Bentley. A Stratfordian, Montague believes "The grammar school of Stratford had a long and honorable history."

Atkinson, Brooks. "Critic at Large: A Shakespearean Replies to a Baconian and Gets Some Unsolicited Support." *New York Times*, July 12, 1963, p. 22.

Drawing on Louis Marder's views, Atkinson believes there are facts enough about Shakespeare to make a "coherent biography." But "Facts and reasonable assumptions from facts do not influence anti–Shakespeareans. They prefer the fascination of myths." Incredibly, Atkinson uses the "Well, he could because he did" argument for Shakespeare's literacy and authorship. Most of England's great writers were middle class, says Atkinson, citing Chaucer, Milton and Spenser. Isn't it a non sequitur to complain that so many candidates negate the issue? Atkinson advises comparison of Shakespeare's verse with Bacon, Oxford, Elizabeth, and Marlowe. Shakespeare will come out on top, of course, because this presupposes Shakespeare as the author.

Chaplin, Charles. *My Auto-Biography.* New York: Simon and Schuster, 1964.

Page 364: "In the morning Sir Archibald Flower, the mayor of Stratford, called at the hotel and conducted me over Shakespeare's cottage. I can by no means associate the Bard with it; that such a mind ever dwelt or had its beginnings there seems incredible. It is easy to imagine a farmer's boy emigrating to London and becoming a successful actor and theatre owner; but for him to have become the great poet and dramatist, and to have had such knowledge of foreign courts, cardinals and kings, is inconceivable to me. I am not concerned with who wrote the works of Shakespeare, whether Bacon, Southampton or Richmond, but I can hardly think it was the Stratford boy. Whoever wrote them had an aristocratic attitude. His utter disregard for grammar could only have been the attitude of a princely, gifted mind. And after seeing the cottage and hearing the scant bits of local information concerning his desultory boyhood, his indifferent school record, his poaching and his country-bumpkin point of view, I cannot believe he went through such a mental metamorphosis as to become the greatest of all poets. In the work of the greatest of geniuses humble beginnings will reveal themselves somewhere — but one cannot trace the slightest sign of them in Shakespeare."

Brewster, Eleanor. *Oxford, Courtier to the Queen*. New York: Pageant Press, 1964.

Brewster asks the reader to assume from the beginning that Oxford is the author. She wonders why no books were mentioned in Shakespeare's will. Included are some of Oxford's shorter poems and a verse to Oxford by Anne Vavasour. There are illustrations, an index, a three-page bibliography, and 198 pages in all.

Ford, Gertrude C. *A Rose by Any Name*. Introduction by Francis T. Carmody. New York: A.S. Barnes, 1964.

Pro-Oxford, this 302-page book with 11 illustrations contains an explanatory poem by Ford on the left side, extracts from plays and history on the right. Appendix C is an Oxford chronology.

Martin, Milward W. *Was Shakespeare Shakespeare? A Lawyer Reviews the Evidence*. Introduction by Louis Marder. New York: Cooper Square Publishers, 1965.

Bibliographical and subject indexes finish off a 155-page refutation that Martin says "slaughters" the anti–Stratfordian views presented in various issues of the *American Bar Association Journal* in 1959 and 1960. Martin does believe the author counts, not just the works. He says anti–Stratfordians have no evidence but lists their reasons for denying Shakespeare authorship. According to Martin no fraud could have been successful. He speaks of documented evidence increasingly sought through "the millions of papers in the record offices of London and Stratford" (which may actually support the anti–Stratfordians — not much material has surfaced). Robert Greene's *Groatsworth of Wit* (1592) is called upon to support Shakespeare as the "upstart Crow." He notes that "Venus and Adonis" (1593) is by "William Shakespeare" and that Richard Field, publisher, was Shakespeare's neighbor in Stratford. The dedication is to Henry Wriothesley, Earl of Southampton. Other evidence for Shakespeare: the Stratford Monument, and the First Folio. Dismissed is the idea that Shakespeare needed an education. Martin says "every play manuscript ... if published prior to 1700, has totally disappeared." He believes the "dates given by scholars." The "patently absurd" claims of Bacon, Oxford and Marlowe are reviewed and the Sonnets discussed.

Blumenthal, Walter Hart. *Who Knew Shakespeare? What Was His Reputation in His Lifetime?* Iowa City, IA: Prairie Press, 1965.

The author of *The Mermaid Myth; Shakespeare Not Among Those Present* (1959) and *Paging Mr. Shakespeare* (1961) holds the group theory and has two goals: to dispute Shakespeare's alleged literary friendships and his asserted fame during his lifetime. He says Ben Jonson was more esteemed in the seventeenth century than Shakespeare. How come Shakespeare isn't buried in Westminster? Philip Henslowe "knew every playwright. In the Henslowe Diary there are 11 entries of payments to Ben Jonson from 1597 to 1602. But never one mention of Shakespeare?" Why no mention of him in correspondence? — "No other illustrious figure in world literature, since paper and ink were available, has failed to leave written vestiges of correspondence, memorabilia, or documentary evidence, apart from the masterpieces that brought immortal fame." The First Folio is made up of "anonymous printed Quartos, or handwritten promptbooks and transcripts of unknown or uncertain authorship." Blumenthal believes Shakespeare's vocabulary is derivative and has no great regard for the plays: "yet to this day the assumed work of the phantom playwright is regarded with awe by the faithful, while dissenters, like myself, declare the plays to be dated by claptrap devices, puerile disguises, and other outmoded tricks, expounded in stilted dialogue, as fustian as a barrister's old wig." How come there are no tributes, no eulogies by

Shakespeare? "London's population in 1660 was less than one-fiftieth of that of today. The lack of known literary friends of Shakespeare, and his obscurity as an alleged prolific playwright, is therefore all the more incredible. The Mermaid Tavern circle is mute regarding him, and not one of the 'University Wits' alludes to intimacy with him." Blumenthal takes issue with the views of McManaway, Rowse (an "inflated ego") and Marder. "There is no evidence whatsoever that Shakespeare had any personal or patronage contact with any titled personage (including the Earl of Southampton) or with any illustrious literary figure, or that he was personally friendly with anyone outside the theater fraternity." And, "The question of Shakespeare as protagonist of the drama—and bona fide author of the plays attributed to him—is one of belief, not knowledge." Heminge and Condell were collectors, not editors, he says. There were 18 books dedicated to de Vere, none to Shakspere. Joseph Skipsey and Henry James' story "The Birthplace" are covered. On genius: "Because a happening or a human being seems beyond the bounds of comprehension, as manifested in the laws of life, and appears irreconcilable with valid principles and precedents, does not accord any unique status to that event or personage. If an event or a manifestation of genius cannot be explained by such convergence of causation and environment, that obscurity indicates only our deficiency, not an Olympian ordination."

Wraight, Annie D., and Stern, Virginia F. *In Search of Christopher Marlowe: A Pictorial Biography*. New York: Vanguard Press; London: Macdonald & Co., **1965**.

Marlowe is almost as much a mystery man as Shakespeare it seems, although Wraight (Stern is the photographer) says, "the historical documentation of his short and eventful life is more plentiful and precise than that afforded by any other Elizabethan poet." There is little mention of the authorship controversy. Neither Bacon nor Oxford are discussed, and Calvin Hoffman's *The Murder of the Man Who Was Shakespeare* is only mentioned in a footnote. But analysis of the Robert Greene/Henry Chettle *Groatsworth of Wit* (Wraight absolves Chettle, who is probably the actual author) provides comfort to anti–Stratfordians in that Edward Alleyn, not Shakespeare, is posited as the "upstart Crow" and "Shake-scene." Profusely illustrated and 376 pages long, the book contains the presumed portrait of Marlowe found in Corpus Christi College in Cambridge.

Blatty, William Peter. *I, Billy Shakespeare*. Garden City, NY: Doubleday, **1965**.

Before writing *The Exorcist*, Blatty wrote this humorous novel in which Shakspere returns to Earth to condemn the candidates for his literary honor.

Harbage, Alfred. *Conceptions of Shakespeare*. Cambridge, MA: Harvard University Press, **1966**.

Five lectures and three essays celebrate the Shakespeare Quadricentenary. "My theme is the Shakespearean image in after ages—the Shakespearean afterimage—as impinged on the retinas of biographers, critics, actors, theatrical directors, and thinkers, as discriminable although not necessarily mutually exclusive groups." In "A Life of Allegory" Harbage writes, "Surely devotion to Shakespeare as secular saint is preferable to Bacon or Oxford as God." He doesn't think Henry James should have become suspicious about the man Shakespeare just because the relics were spurious. It is, however, "legitimate, or at least inevitable," that questions should be asked about the author's character and personality. After all, the "documented facts admit of no certain interpretation; they are, by and large, neutral." "Shakespeare As Culture Hero" is a 19-page essay on the authorship question. Believing that many recent works (Friedmans, Wadsworth, Churchill, Gibson, Martin) have subjected authorship claims to "sober examination," Harbage seeks to explain the prominent anti–Stratfordians like Wilmot, Delia Bacon, Twain and Freud, not to discredit them, but "In matters of literary history, these four possess no authority that needs discrediting." In short, attacks on authorship must be consigned to the realm of mythmaking. "And mythmaking has its permanent bastion in the twilight zone of the human mind."

Tweedale, Ralph L. *Wasn't Shakespeare Someone Else? New Evidence in the Very Words of the Bard Himself About His True Identity*. Southfield, MI: Verity Press, 1971, **1966**.

Produced under the aegis of The Shakespeare Oxford Society. "Unseen down the centuries, there has lain buried in these masterpieces of literature the most ingenious visual devices, which by the use of a very simple key to their recognition, identify the name of the true author and tie it unequivocally to the pseudonym William Shakespeare." Tweedale does note that the Friedmans found cryptogram decipherment invalid but it's acrostics he believes hold the key. In addition, one must use the original editions. Why the cover-up? Oxford had been Queen Elizabeth's lover and the Earl of Southampton was their child. There are 196 pages, a two-page index, and a one-page "Appendix: Index of Signals by Sonnet Number."

Williams, David Rhys. *Shakespeare Thy Name Is Marlowe*. London: Vision Press Ltd., **1966**.

According to Williams, the case for Shakespeare "rests upon wild speculations and the flimsiest of evidence." Pseudonyms were common, especially for one suspected of heresy like Marlowe. His death was a hoax. Includes appendices, references, acknowledgements and index. 94 pages.

Carlson, Eric Walter, ed. *Introduction to Poe: A Thematic Reader*. Glenview, IL: Scott, Foresman, **1967**.

On pages 522–523 Poe is quoted on Thomas Carlyle's *Hero-Worship*: "Your hero-worshippers, for example — what do they know about Shakespeare? They worship him — rant about him — lecture about him — about him, him, and nothing else — for no other reason than that he is utterly beyond their comprehension. They have arrived at an idea of his greatness from the pertinacity with which men have called him great. As for their own opinion of him — they really have none at all."

Simak, Clifford D. *The Goblin Reservation*. New York: Daw Books, 1982, ©**1968**.

Simak, the pastoralist of science fiction and fantasy and winner of two Hugo Awards, the Nebula Grand Master Award from the Science Fiction Writers of America and the International Fantasy Award, includes references to the Shakespeare-Oxford question throughout his book, as when the main character Professor Peter Maxwell notes a sign: "WILLIAM SHAKESPEARE, ESQ. Of Stratford-on-Avon, England, 'How It Happened I Did Not Write the Plays,' Under the Sponsorship of Time College, Oct. 22, 8 P.M. Time Museum Auditorium." Later Maxwell approaches Time College and after seeing another sign, "He grinned to himself, thinking of it. English Lit would be beside itself. Old Chenery and all the rest of them had never quite forgiven Time for establishing ... that the Earl of Oxford, not Shakespeare, had been the author of the plays. And this personal appearance of the man from Stratford-on-Avon would be rubbing salt into wounds that were far from healed." The historian finally says, "Time found out who really wrote the plays." At one point, "A man suddenly loomed on top of the table and began to sing: Hurrah for Old Shakespeare; He never wrote them plays; He stayed at home, and chasing girls, Sang dirty roundelays."

Honey, William. *The Shakespeare Epitaph Deciphered*. London: Mitre Press, **1969**.

Expanding on Calvin Hoffman's Marlowe hypothesis (*The Murder of the Man Who Was Shakespeare*, 1955), Honey says Hoffman was clumsy, didn't dig deep enough and misinterpreted things. Upon examining Marlowe's life and the epitaph in the Stratford church where Shakespeare rests, he is confident Marlowe was the author. The character and actions of Marlowe fill the vacuum of the Stratford man. Includes the Shakespeare signatures, a bibliography and index.

Freud, Ernst L., ed. *The Letters of Sigmund Freud & Arnold Zweig*. Translated by Elaine and William Robson-Scott. New York: Harcourt Brace Jovanovich, **1970**.

Freud and writer Zweig (*The Case of Sergeant Grischa, Education Before Verdun*) maintained a lively correspondence between 1927 and the former's death in 1939. In this collection the authorship question crops up in six letters, two from Freud, four from Zweig. Zweig borrows Looney's book from Freud but is initially skeptical. Freud warns him against "building fantasies about Sh. on untenable premises." Zweig thinks Oxford is not the author but the "begetter." He writes that there must be some trace of Oxford's death in Shakespeare's work! Freud responds that, "I do not know what still attracts you to the man from Stratford. He seems to have nothing at all to justify his claims, whereas Oxford has almost everything." Zweig tells Freud that Oxford has become an important poetic figure to him but he is not convinced that the aristocrat wrote the canon. He seems to suggest to "Father Freud" that the loss of records during the Civil Wars contributed to our lack of knowledge about Shakespeare.

Schoenbaum, Samuel. *Shakespeare's Lives.* Oxford: Clarendon Press, 1970.

There are an index, notes, illustrations, e.g., Shakespeare Monument in Holy Trinity Church, Dugdale Engraving, Droeschout Portraits, Felton Portrait, Janssen Portrait, Delia Bacon — in what is a biography or at least an examination of past biographers of the Stratford man. "Part Six: Deviations" devotes 100 pages to the heretics. Schoenbaum is no unbeliever himself and although a reasonable critic for the most part, he like many other Stratfordians can be accused of what they label the anti–Stratfordians with: elitism. Example: An 1892 mock trial in Boston featured a jury of "eminent personages" like economist Henry George, Massachusetts governor William E. Russell and actor Henry Irving. They "decided overwhelmingly in favor of Shakespeare. Only one juror, Mr. G. Kruell, found for the plaintiff. Mr. Kruell was a wood engraver." The common man — even Mark Twain — is not qualified to judge or interpret. Can this jibe with Stratfordian opinion that genius sprang from a cottage?

DeMott, Benjamin. "Will the Real Shakespeare Please Stand Up?" *Saturday Review of Literature,* November 7, 1970, pp. 31, 32, 35, 46, 47.

DeMott reviews Samuel Schoenbaum's *Shakespeare's Lives,* Anthony Burgess' *Shakespeare,* Philip Burton's *The Sole Voice: Character Portraits from Shakespeare,* Andrew Gurr's *The Shakespearean Stage, 1574–1642,* Isaac Asimov's *Asimov's Guide to Shakespeare* (Vol. I, The Greek, Roman, and Italian Plays, and Vol. II, The English Plays), and Stanley Edgar Hyman's *Iago: Some Approaches to the Illusion of His Motivation.* Included are six "portraits of Shakespeare" (Chandos, Felton, Flower, Elky Palace, Ashbourne, Hunt). It is obvious that DeMott has no truck with unbelievers: "Or consider the endless succession of snobbery-ridden nonbelievers in Shakespeare — Baconians, Oxfordians, and the like — a crew that isn't limited to chuckle-making names like Looney, Schmucker, and Mrs. Gallup, but includes men as great as Freud."

Eagleton, Terry. "Books: From Postcard-length Data, a Wealth of Images and Legends." *Commonweal,* October 30, 1970, pp. 129–131.

Eagleton reviews Samuel Schoenbaum's *Shakespeare's Lives,* Stanley Edgar Herman's *Iago,* and Anthony Burgess' *Shakespeare.* Schoenbaum's work is "less a re-construction of Shakespeare's shadowy life than a sane and balanced appraisal of other men's re-constructions." Schoenbaum "set out to squeeze every drop of significance from the few known facts and to demolish the constructions of a whole line of editors, myth-makers and legend-spinners who have embroidered our meager knowledge with fictions of their own making." And "There is a particularly hilarious — although properly poker-faced — account of the theories of a certain J. Thomas Looney, a supporter of the claims of Edward de Vere to the authorship of Shakespeare's plays, who doggedly refused his publisher's suggestions of adopting a nom de plume in order to forestall the hilarity of the reviewers."

Ogburn, Charlton, Jr. "Shakespeare's Missing Manuscripts." *Harper's,* June 1972, pp. 94–96, 98, 101.

The importance of Shakespearean manuscripts is stressed, and Oxfordian Ogburn believed that such manuscripts might be hidden behind the monument in Holy Trinity Church, placed there by shrewd contemporaries. "To employ the monument as the repository of the documents that would prove the author someone else and disclose his identity — would this not have been ironical and mischievous in a way that would appeal to the gusto of pre–Puritan Englishmen?" Ogburn was not granted license to disturb the monument. [X-rays revealed nothing — see *Frontline,* 1989.]

Rowse, Alfred Leslie. *Shakespeare the Man.* New York: Harper & Row, 1973.

Admitting that he is at odds with the Shakespearean establishment, Rowse proves why through an obvious self-importance: "I realize all too well, from the uncomprehending way my previous work has been taken by the Shakespeare establishment, that it will take time before this new knowledge [his presumed discovery of the Dark Lady's identity] is absorbed ... for they are the definitive answers." As for Shakespeare, "like any man of genius he was fundamentally self-educated." And, "his unconscious worked for him day and night." Importantly: "After all, a writer writes about his own experience, and willy-nilly betrays himself in his work." "The Sonnets are sonnets of duty from the poet to his patron, from beginning to end, obvious throughout and evident in many of the sonnets individually." "For, make no mistake about this, Shakespeare's interest in the youth [Southampton] is not at all sexual — as Marlowe's or Bacon's might well have been: that was clean contrary to Shakespeare's highly hetero-sexual nature." Obviously it is too bad that there is no existing private Southampton correspondence. Shakespeare is constantly portrayed as neighborly, a responsible family type. Daughter Judith couldn't write because she "evidently took after her mother." There is a good explanation for the willing of the second-best bed to his wife: "the big double-bed would be needed by Susanna and John." Death: "A generation after, the vicar of Stratford recorded the tradition that Shakespeare had a merry meeting with Drayton and Ben Jonson, drank too hard and died of a fever there contracted. Nothing improb-able in that." There's a "Comparative Chronology," illustrations and an index. See also Rowse's *Shake-speare's Southampton: Patron of Virginia* (New York: Harper and Row, 1965).

Barsi-Greene, Margaret (compiled and arranged by). *I, Prince Tudor, Wrote Shakespeare: An Autobiography from His Two Ciphers in Poetry and Prose*. Boston: Branden Press, **1973**.

When the Baconian theory has been subsumed by the Oxfordian, it remains for champions of the former to erect stranger supports for their candidate. Barsi-Greene states that obviously Bacon was the poet. Elizabeth I was his mother. She bases much of her view on Elizabeth Wells Gallup's decipher-ment techniques. There are 319 pages, illustrations, and a bibliography.

May, Robin. *Who Was Shakespeare? The Man — the Times — The Works*. New York: St. Martin's Press, **1974**.

Chapter 5: The Unbelievers is a mocking, condescending, belittling attack on all things anti–Strat-fordian: "a world of vain bibble-babble and sheer madness," "quaint nonsense," "nauseating snobbery," "cypher-crazed experts," "lunacy," "pretentious twaddle." May only accepts the view that Marlowe would make a good candidate. He was a genius, like the Stratford man. No actors believe that anyone other than the Stratford man is responsible for the plays, discounting Leslie Howard at the very least. May briefly recounts the source and progress of the controversy, pointing out the flaws of Delia Bacon, Ignatius Donnelly, etc. Illustrations and index.

Ogburn, Charlton, Jr. "The Man Who Shakespeare Was Not (and Who He Was)." *Harvard Magazine*, November **1974**, pp. 21–28.

The Oxfordian Ogburn begins by citing other authors who used pen names and then surveys heretics like Whitman, Freud, Galsworthy and Henry James. "Is there any creative writer whose works are not a product of his character and experiences, expressions of what he is and has lived through?" He claims Shakespeare's authorship wasn't generally accepted for at least two generations after his death. "'A man's work is autobiographical in spite of every subterfuge,' the poet Wallace Stevens wrote." Ogburn contends that Shakespeare's characters "are almost without exception of the nobility." He says the classics the author had to have read were not yet translated from Greek and Latin. An interesting point: when the Sonnets were published in 1609 the printer's dedication was to the "ever-living," which as Ogburn points out, following J. Thomas Looney, is "a term never applied to a person before his death." Shaksper had seven more years to live. Why was Shaksper the stooge? "Shaksper of Stratford seems to have been picked because of the similarity of names and because, a hanger-on of the theater, he had evidently not been above allowing the credulous to believe he actually was the great but mysterious playwright." Reference is made to Greene's *Groatsworth of Wit*, purported to be the deathbed testament of playwright Robert Greene, who warned his fellows of the "upstart Crow." The final two pages examine Oxford's candidature. Illustrations: John Aubrey, Lumley portrait, Ash-bourne portrait, Marshall engraving, Felton portrait, Droeschout engraving, monument bust, Edward de Vere.

Ward, Bernard Mordaunt, and Miller, Ruth Loyd, eds. *A Hundredth Sundrie Flowres: From the Original Edition of 1573*. 2nd ed. Port Washington, NY: Kennikat Press, **1975**.

Published anonymously in 1573 by Richard Smith, this was believed to have been the work of George Gascoigne. In his 1926 edition Ward proposed the work as that of Lord Oxford. This edition includes Ward's original material plus newer notes, articles and documents from Ward and others. There are indexes and illustrations.

Evans, Gwynne, and Levin, Harry. "Shakespeare as Shakespeare." *Harvard Magazine*, February 1975, pp. 39–43.

Evans, a professor of English, and Levin, Irving Babbitt Professor of Contemporary Literature, both at Harvard, are hard on Charlton Ogburn, Jr.'s November 1974 *Harvard Magazine* presentation favoring Oxford. One must dispute their contention that "The fact that the anti–Stratfordians seldom agree on a rival candidate is itself an argument in favor of the incumbent." They like the inner circle of academia, for "no one professionally versed in historical interpretation has ever challenged the evidence as it stands." They believe Henry James was merely ironic in his criticism. They believe Ogburn is wrong to put Hugh Trevor-Roper in the anti–Stratfordian camp. A good point: if most of Shakespeare's plays were based on pre-existing narratives, they cannot be autobiographical. They counter Ogburn's citation of noble characters in Shakespeare with Shylock and Falstaff. As for Shakespeare's education, "What was he doing from seven to thirteen, at a time when his father was a leading citizen, if not going to school?" They say his source material was available in translation. They find that Oxford led that list of "the best for comedy amongst us" by rules of protocol. Besides labeling anti–Stratfordians social snobs, the authors claim their opponents are unfulfilled men of letters. "For further reading" recommendations are Chambers, Friedman, B. Roland Lewis, McManaway, Schoenbaum, and Wadsworth. Illustrations: bust, Max Beerbohm's caricature of Shakespeare and Bacon, Robert Greene.

Simak, Clifford D. *Shakespeare's Planet*. New York: Berkley, 1976.

The main characters in this science fiction novel open an old book that seems to be *The Complete Works of William Shakespeare* that has no publication date.

Berman, Ronald. "The Shakespeare Industry." *The Sewanee Review*, Fall 1976, pp. 657–668.

Berman reviews a rash of Shakespearean books, devoting the largest chunk to Samuel Schoenbaum's *William Shakespeare: A Documentary Life*. According to Berman, "We now have enough material on him — although of a special kind — to place him thoroughly in his time. Little remains that is intimate; but there is an enormous amount of evidence mustered in this book about the facts of his existence." Berman admits that of the private Shakespeare "it is still difficult to know very much."

Feldman, Abraham Bronson. *Hamlet Himself*. Philadelphia: Lovelore Press, 1977.

Hamlet equals Oxford in this 126-page monograph dedicated to Gelett Burgess and Charles Wisner Barrell, fellow Oxfordians. Feldman investigates the views of Sigmund Freud, correctly finding that "Freud's loss of faith in the official doctrine concerning the author of Hamlet impressed very few of his followers."

The traditional view that Shakespeare of Stratford composed and produced Hamlet between September 9, 1601, and July 26, 1602, is disputed. In short, Shakespeare was too busy with farmland purchases, renting, helping his widowed mother, and performing and rehearsing on the stage. Also, Hamlet was well known in the theater before John Shakspere died in 1601.

Citing G. Harvey's *Marginalia* (Stratford, 1913), Feldman writes, "In 1598 an edition of the poetical works of Geoffrey Chaucer appeared which the erudite Gabriel Harvey bought. In it he scribbled a praise of Shakespeare and his play: 'The younger sort takes much delight in Shakespeare's *Venus and Adonis*: but his *Lucrece* and his tragedy of *Hamlet, Prince of Denmark* have it in them to please the wiser sort.'" Feldman publishes for the first time a translation of the record of an inquiry into the death of a servant while fencing with Oxford.

Huston, Craig. *The Shakespeare Authorship Question: Evidence for Edward de Vere, 17th Earl of Oxford*. Self-published, 1978.

Huston wrote this 35-page case for Oxford to counter McManaway's *The Authorship of Shakespeare* (1962). There are notes and a cover portrait of Oxford.

May, Steven W. "The Poems of Edward De Vere, Seventeenth Earl of Oxford and of Robert Devereaux, Second Earl of Essex," in *Studies in Philology*, Early Winter, **1980**.

Besides the poems themselves, May provides commentary and identifies poems "wrongly" attributed to Oxford and Essex. In his biographical introduction May argues that neither Oxfordians nor Stratfordians have determined what poetry Oxford really did write. He says Looney's *The Poems of Edward de Vere* (1921) is not definitive, for Looney was a novice in both Elizabethan poetry and textual method.

Halle, Louis J. *The Search for an Eternal Norm: As Represented by Three Classics.* Washington, DC: University Press of America, **1981**.

Hamlet, Odysseus and Arthur are examined, and while it is not Halle's aim to analyze the authorship question, nevertheless he does a good job on pages 107–116. "All literature is autobiographical in the sense that it represents the author's experience only: his experience of himself in the first place, his experience of others in the second place. For when he describes the thoughts and feelings of others he is describing what he is able to recognize only because he has know it in himself." He maintains that "an author's works may not be significantly autobiographical in detail, but that taken as a whole they are so." For Halle the problem is that "the identity of the author that comes out so vividly in his works does not match the identity of the man to whom they are attributed." He cites Stratfordian Levin Schucking's admission of the paucity of information on Shakespeare. For Halle, "There is no doubt in my mind that Hamlet is Shakespeare himself." And, "On the internal evidence of the plays and poems as a whole, and of Hamlet in particular, I should then arrive at the conclusion that they had been written by someone who was so high of birth as to be a member of the royal entourage; a man profoundly maladjusted and in rebellion against the requirements of his birth and station." Halle concludes that one member of the court fits the picture: Edward de Vere.

Rooke, Leon. *Shakespeare's Dog.* New York: Alfred A. Knopf, 1983, ©**1981**.

In this nearly unreadable novel — which is not concerned with the authorship question — the dog Hooker discusses canine and human life in backwater Stratford, from which his master Shakespeare longs to leave for London. However, "He'd had ushering at Free School, he's had Hunt and Jenkens and even Cotton that had turned out a Jesuit — all trying to thrash-whip the classics into him.... The strutter knew no Latin and less Greek, but in these areas he smoked like a chimney compared to what he knew of suffering and misery, of the soul and its plumage, of man's most bloated condition. He liked spearing my ear with Cicero or Ovid, loves pronouncing on the four humors, on the stars and on money, on Nature and on Duty, on love for his dark lady (by which he meant one not existing; Hathaway, he'd say, having walled that room up); loved speaking on man's umpteen ages and his 14 sins, on indecision and thwarted ambition, liked speaking his moon doggerel and of unframed oceans; got his syllables rolling as he mocked the flow of the greedy inevitable."

Champlin, Charles. "A Bard by Any Other Name." *Los Angeles Times*, February 12, **1983**.

Critic at Large and *Times* Arts Editor Champlin recalls a dinner party at which some Oxfordians impressed themselves upon him. He summarizes the authorship question, including Bacon and Marlowe, and broaches the question, does it matter? "The issue is more sensitive than might be thought, because Shakespeare is a major industry.... A whole population of scholars would have to rewrite its lectures and revise its footnotes." The dream of finding an authentic manuscript is mentioned. Historian Hugh Trevor-Roper's interest is reviewed.

"Was Shakespeare a Playwright?" *Science Digest*, April **1983**, pp. 10–103.

The "Dr. Crypton: Puzzles, Paradoxes, Pitfalls" section opens with a somewhat witty summary of the controversy and its origins. It is easy for "well-intentioned but self-deluded fanatics to misuse the principles of an entire branch of science, in this case cryptography." Anagrams are explained, and the Elizabethan age labeled "the golden age of anagrams." Even the Queen dabbled in it. The Friedmans' analysis is summarized. Mark Twain is mentioned in passing but not to stress his skepticism but rather to show how "Shakespeare" could be a nom de plume for "Samuel Clemens." The illustration is the

Northumberland Manuscript discovered in 1867 and purporting to show that Shakespeare was the pen name of Bacon.

Churcher, Sharon. "Shakespeare Authorship: A Secret of the Tomb?" *New York*, July 18, **1983**, p. 9.

Calvin Hoffman's application to open Sir Thomas Walsingham's tomb in hopes of finding a chest containing original Shakespeare manuscripts is noted, as well as the claims of Bacon and Oxford. The five-paragraph filler ends quoting Harvard Shakespeare expert Harry Levin: "It's a form of madness to question Shakespeare's authorship."

Johnson, Morse. "Brush Up Your Shakespeare." *New York*, August 15, **1983**, p. 7.

Responding to Churcher's piece on the authorship question in the July 18 issue, Johnson takes issue with Harry Levin's condemnation of doubters by asking if Walt Whitman, Henry James and Leslie Howard were also mad.

Ogburn, Charlton, Jr. *The Mysterious William Shakespeare*. New York: Dodd, Mead, **1984**.

This immense tome (892 pages) by an eminent Oxfordian is somewhat compromised by reliance on such beliefs as that one Arthur Brooke, who wrote *The Tragaicall Historye of Romeus and Juliet* (1562), was a pen name of de Vere, who would have been only 12 years old. Otherwise, the book serves a useful purpose, especially the bibliography and notes. Ogburn believes the disappearance of records illuminating the quest for the true authorship was not accidental. "A conspiracy was not necessary. Autocratic societies are run not by conspiracies but under central direction. And Elizabethan society was autocratic." The book is divided into "The Cause and Question Now in Hand" discussing the authorship question and "Is Not Oxford Here Another Anchor?" presenting Oxford's life and claims. There is a chronology of principle candidates, an appendix concerning the quest for manuscripts, 33 illustrations, and an index.

Hoyt, Richard. *The Siskiyou Two-Step*. New York: William Morrow, **1984**.

In this mystery novel the protagonist-detective is charged with determining, among other things, the authorship of a recently discovered play entitled *Jonathan Cliborne*. Purportedly, a Goan student attending college in Hawaii had found the play in a sea trunk that had belonged to Edward de Vere. The detective had been informed by a respected professor of English that there was a movement to prove that the plays attributed to Shakespeare had been written by Edward de Vere and that there was a movement to obtain general acceptance of his view. J. Thomas Looney is referred to as "the guru who [inspired] such fervor." While consulting the card catalogue looking for information on the identity question, our hero also claims to find references to "Christopher Marlowe — champions, Samuel Johnson — supporters, and all the rest." The results of the quest, at least in regard to the authorship question, were inconclusive.

Lockwood, Allison. "Delia Bacon: The Lady Who Didn't Dig Shakespeare." *American History Illustrated*, October **1984**, pp. 40–46.

Illustrated with portraits of Delia Bacon, Shakespeare, Emerson, Carlyle, Hawthorne and Shakespeare's grave in Holy Trinity Church, English professor and writer Lockwood examines the frequently tragic life of Ms. Bacon, including the affair with the Reverend Alexander MacWhorter. Her professional relationships with Emerson, Carlyle and Hawthorne are explored. There is a vivid description of the September night before the grave in Holy Trinity Church. "After all her years of toil and self-denial, why did Delia Bacon's nerve fail her at the moment of truth? Was it the unseen watcher she suspected? Was it a flash of awareness as to the enormity she contemplated? Was it fear engendered by the legendary verse on Shakespeare's gravestone? 'Good friend for Jesus sake forebeare,/To digg the dust enclosed heare:/Bleste be ye man that spares these stones,/And curst be he that moves my bones.'"

Hamilton, Charles. *In Search of Shakespeare: A Reconnaissance into the Poet's Life and Handwriting*. San Diego: Harcourt Brace Jovanovich, **1985**.

Shakespeare used a "secretary" or "running" hand and "could apparently write this sweet-flowing script with speed." Hamilton provides as examples of bad signatures those of Napoleon, John F. Kennedy and Richard Nixon. According to Hamilton, Shakespeare wrote his own will — his illness is the reason it looks strange. The authorship controversy is briefly reviewed in Chapter IV: "So Long, Francis Bacon." Hamilton presents the possibility that daughter Judith's husband Thomas Quiney murdered Shakespeare with arsenic! This 271-page illustrated and indexed book has a bibliography.

Giroux, Robert. "Happy Birthday, William Shakespeare, and Keep Those Plays and Sonnets Coming." *The New York Times Book Review*, April 28, **1985**, pp. 3, 41.

Upon the celebration of Shakespeare's 421st birthday, the life and obsession of Delia Bacon are presented. Giroux seems sympathetic though he closes with, "As for Ignatius Donnelly, her defender and champion, he gave new life, through his followers and their offshoots, to the anti–Shakespeare madness — which, no doubt we shall always have with us. Happy birthday, 'booby'!"

Taylor, Gary. "Shakespeare's New Poem: A Scholar's Clues and Conclusions." *The New York Times Book Review*, December 15, **1985**, pp. 11–14.

Contending that Shakespeare's poems have been little appreciated, Taylor describes how he found a new one ("the work of a young poet") with the first line, "Shall I die? Shall I fly?" in Rawlinson Poetic Manuscript 160 in the Bodleian Library at Oxford. The entire poem is reproduced and there is a 90-entry list "Verbal Parallels in the Plays and Poems." Taylor does not believe that this can be attributed to Spenser. Is this true: "Although there remain minor disagreements about the relative dating of the canon, in general scholars have little difficulty distinguishing work from Shakespeare's early, middle and late periods: a variety of internal stylistic evidence all tends to suggest that each play and poem belongs in a certain range on a sliding chronological scale." See also: (1) Otto Friedrich, "Shall I Die! Shall I Fly," *Time*, 9 December 1985, p. 76; (2) Anthony Burgess' "Is It Really Shakespeare?" *The New York Times Book Review*, December 22, 1985, p. 3 (Burgess, a Stratfordian, disputes Gary Taylor's contention that in Oxford's Bodleian Library he discovered a new Shakespeare poem dated 1630; "Who's Sorry Now?" is a sidebar counterpoint by Taylor; there is no mention of this controversy); (3) Gina Kolata, *Science*, January 24, 1986, pp. 335–336 (this is virtually the same as Kolata's "So bethumped with words," *Science* 86, May 1986, pp. 65–66). In *Science*, she explains how a statistical method invented by Sir Ronald Fisher to answer a butterfly question was employed by Bradley Efron and Ronald Thisted to determine if "Shall I Die?" was written by Shakespeare; the conclusion: it could very well be); (4) Leonore Fleischer, "Talk of the Trade: Tempest in a Bard's Teacup," *Publishers Weekly*, June 13, 1986, p. 75 (Fleischer reviews *Shakespeare's Lost Play: Edmund Ironside* and contentions based on computer analysis by its editor Eric Sams that *Ironside*, a play known since the nineteenth century, was written by Shakespeare in 1588 — or plagiarized throughout his career; she presents Gary Taylor's contrary opinion, noting that the poem Taylor discovered has been "entered into the Shakespearean canon"; she notes that A.L. Rowse and Anthony Burgess accept Sams' view).

Mitgang, Herbert. "New Answers to Shakespeare Riddle." *New York Times*, March 3, **1987**, p. C13.

A subsidiary Shakespearean debate: Who is "W.H."? Could it be a misprint? How about William Hathaway, Shakespeare's brother-in-law? According to A.L. Rowse, it's Sir William Harvey, Southampton's second stepfather. There are photos of Rowse, Barbara Everett and Donald W. Foster.

Reed, J.D. "Some ado about who was, or was not, Shakespeare." *Smithsonian*, September **1987**, pp. 155–158 & ff.

"Despite the intense research by legions of historians, scholars and biographers over three centuries, what we know — and can prove for certain — about the greatest literary genius in history can pretty well be jotted down on a file card." Reed presents that information before launching into a survey of the controversy, focusing on Charlton Ogburn's then current investigations and book *The Mysterious William Shakespeare*, Lord Oxford's career is examined.

There are deficiencies in Reed's analysis: "The works, after all, are what really matter." He cites those who believe the works are not autobiographical and his contention that the dating leaves something to desire for Oxford's case. He does discuss vested interests in the "Shakespeare industry."

Champlin, Charles. "Shakspere Shaken by Moot Court." *Los Angeles Times*, September 26, **1987**, pp. 2, 3.

The Times Arts Editor contends that the civilized, standing room only mock Supreme Court trial in Metropolitan Methodist Church presided over by justices William J. Brennan, Jr., Harry A. Blackmun and John Paul Stevens means that Edward de Vere's claims can no longer be dismissed. The justices said Oxford's case was not proved but that if another were the author of the plays, he had the best claim. The controversy is summarized from the eighteenth century.

Savage, David G. "Zounds! Much Ado About Poetic Justice." *Los Angeles Times*, September 26, **1987**, part I, p. 2.

Describing the mock trial presided over by Supreme Court justices William J. Brennan, Jr., John Paul Stevens, and Harry A. Blackmun, Savage quotes them and provides a little history of Edward de Vere and Shakespeare. The cases of attorneys James Boyle, representing Shakespeare, and Peter Jaszi, representing Oxford, are summarized. Boyle's contention that de Vere died in 1604 while some of the plays were produced later is not countered by Savage.

"Footnotes." *Chronicle of Higher Education*, October 7, **1987**, p. A6.

Summarized is September's Supreme Court mock debate between Oxford and Shakespeare representatives. It is concluded with mention that Oxford died in 1604, the man from Stratford in 1616, but nothing is made of the fact that Shakespeare's plays are not precisely dated or that a play might be acted or published after someone's death.

Schwartz, Amy E. "Three Justices, a Poetry-Starved Crowd and Shakespeare." *Washington Post*, October 14, **1987**, p. A19.

Schwartz shows how a good-humored debate before three Supreme Court justices on the authorship question attracted 1,800 political and literary types to a church at Ward Circle. She explains how David Lloyd Kreeger, arts patron and friend of Justice Brennan, created the event argued by two American University law professors. Though denied their claim, the anti–Stratfordians made gains, according to Schwartz.

Holden, Constance. "No One Knows If Shakespeare Wrote the Plays." *Washington Post*, October 24, **1987**, p. A19.

Complaining that Amy Schwartz (*Washington Post*, op-ed, October 14, 1987) didn't read Charlton Ogburn's *The Mysterious William Shakespeare*, Holden explains why there has been so much speculation about the authorship — the reason is an absence of concrete information. Accurately, she states that the charge of elitism by Stratfordians "has nothing to do with the argument." She deduces that liberals are more comfortable with the Stratford theory. She finds that "The real issue has to do with whether a man's life has anything to do with what he writes." Read this!

Garber, Marjorie. *Shakespeare's Ghost Writers: Literature As Uncanny Causality*. New York and London: Methuen, **1987**.

Garber begins her heavy duty criticism and Freud-centered analysis by summarizing five arguments typically used against the Stratford man as author. Why is Shakespeare questioned, not Spenser, Raleigh, or Milton? And in a more general sense, why does Shakespeare always emerge unscathed, even "newly canonized," in this age of canonical literature critique? Garber wants to explore the controversy "in order to explore the significance of the debate itself, to consider the ongoing existence of the polemic between pro–Stratford-lifers and pro-choice advocates as an exemplary literary event in its own right." Literature as property is examined in light of Michel Foucault's "author-function." Four investments that motivate the controversy are discussed: institutional, professional, psychological, territorial. Garber aims to determine whether the plays themselves stage the controversy. Includes notes and index.

Sobran, Joseph. "A Fair Shake for Oxford." *National Review*, November 6, **1987**, pp. 54–56.

Sobran discusses the September 25 mock debate and trial before three Supreme Court justices. He believes that although Brennan, Blackmun and Stevens ruled in favor of the Stratford man, "the event lifted the Oxfordian theory out of the crank category." He says both lawyers engaged in character assassination and reviews the bad blood that exists between the champions of each side. He says that Charlton Ogburn, Jr., was disconsolate at the next day's meeting of the Shakespeare Oxford Society. Sobran comments on William Plumer Fowler's *Shakespeare Revealed in Oxford's Letters.*

Young, Arthur M. *The Shakespeare/Bacon Controversy*. San Francisco: Robert Briggs Associates, **1987**.

In this 23-page interview conducted by Faustin Bray at the subject's Institute for the Study of Consciousness in Berkeley, California, Young, who also developed and designed the Bell helicopter and is the author of other New Age publications, expounds on the authorship question. He believes that Elizabeth and Leicester fathered Francis Bacon while ensconced in the Tower. Bacon wrote Spenser, Marlowe, Burton, Shakespeare, Peele, Greene, and of course, himself. The roles of Delia Bacon and Ignatius Donnelly are summarized. Illustrations include the cover of *The Faerie Queen* and Gustavi Seleni's *Cryptomenytices and Cryptographia*, a book on ciphers published in Holland in 1624. There's a bibliography.

Lardner, James. "The Authorship Question." *New Yorker*, April 11, **1988**, pp. 87–94, 96–106.

Despite a first-page comment that the anti–Stratfordians are now after respect if not vindication ("They are aiming for a status comparable to that attained by, say, the partisans of the Loch Ness monster."), this is a generally balanced survey of the controversy spurred by the September 25, 1987 moot court debate. Lardner attended, meeting with Charles Francis Topham de Vere, Charlton Ogburn, Jr., Gordon Cyr, Ruth and Minos Miller, all of them quoted, their backgrounds summarized. Cyr makes the point that "Mozart's genius would count for absolutely nothing if he hadn't had the best musical education that was available to him in eighteenth-century Central Europe, and if he hadn't had one of the best teachers in the world, his father." Famous doubters and important books on the controversy are identified. The moot court session is described in some detail. Lardner recounts meetings and lunch with Stratfordian counsel James Boyle (testified that "arguments in favor of William Shakespeare are overwhelming.") and Peter Jaszi for the Oxfordians ("In some ways, Shakespeare criticism … has anticipated post-structuralist criticism — the kind of criticism that says that the idea of 'author's intent' is an illusion and, thus, that no interpretation is more authentic than another."). The closing comments of Justices Brennan, Blackmun and Stevens are summarized, with findings for the Stratford man but tinged with some degree of uncertainty in Blackmun's and Stevens' case. Stevens urged Oxfordians to develop a coherent theory about how Oxford wrote the plays anonymously. He suggested that Queen Elizabeth and Lord Burghley might have wanted that.

Spark, Muriel. *A Far Cry from Kensington*. New York: New Directions Books, 2000, ©**1988**.

Notable and prolific novelist Spark (*The Prime of Miss Jean Brodie*, *The Girls of Slender Means*) has her main character Mrs. Hawkins apply for an editorial position at the publishing firm of Mackintosh & Tooley. In passing, Sir Alec Tooley informs her, "I hope you don't believe that Shakespeare wrote the plays. The evidence in fact does not stand independent scrutiny. He must be laughing up his sleeve in the next world, if in fact there is one, when he looks down and sees what is in fact going on at Stratford-on-Avon."

Thomas, Sidney. "On the Dating of Shakespeare's Early Plays." *Shakespeare Quarterly*, Summer **1988**, pp. 187–194.

Reviewed are E.K. Chambers' chronology of Shakespeare's plays and the post–World War II lack of consensus. Particular attention is paid to E.A.J. Honigmann's dating. The concluding sentence should be a byword: "The debate should involve vigorous argument and counter-argument, but with a proper respect on each side for the seriousness and intellectual integrity of the opposing side."

Taylor, Gary. "Poem by Shakespeare! Read All About It!" *New York Times Book Review*, June 26, **1988**, pp. 1, 40, 41.

As Peter Levi claimed to have discovered a Shakespeare poem in the Huntington Library in San Marino, California, Taylor, who claimed the same in 1985 for the Bodleian Library, discusses "the peculiar mechanics that govern any encounter between literary scholarship and journalism." Taylor calls Levi unprofessional and says the poem was discussed by John Payne Collier 152 years earlier and that he [Taylor] had rejected it himself.

Trucco, Terry. "Bard on Trial Again, and Again He Wins." *New York Times*, November 28, **1988**.

Trucco reports on "The Shakespeare Moot," the first mock trial on the authorship question to be held in England. Actor and Globe Theater promoter Sam Wanamaker organized the affair which opened with Lord Alexander of Weedon for the Oxfordians and attorney Sydney Kentridge for the Stratfordians. Stanley Wells and Ernst Honigmann testified for the Stratford man. For the other side were L.L. Ware, attorney and founding member of the Mensa Society, and Gordon C. Cyr, former director of the Shakespeare Oxford Society (U.S.). Author Jeffrey Archer had proposed the trial and believed the verdict was correct, i.e., in favor of Shaksper of Stratford. Almost 300 attended.

Austin, Al. "Who Wrote Shakespeare? *WGBH*, April **1989**, pp. 8–9.

From Boston's public television magazine comes an unbiased summary of the controversy that prepares viewers for *The Shakespeare Mystery*, airing on April 18.

Frontline: The Shakespeare Mystery. Public television, WGBH, Boston, **1989**.

Produced and directed by Kevin Sim. Written by Al Austin and Kevin Sim. Hosted by Judy Woodruff. This hour-long documentary explores the authorship question, concentrating on the Stratford man and Edward de Vere. For the Stratfordians, A.L. Rowse and Samuel Schoenbaum. For the heretics, Charlton Ogburn and former British cabinet minister Enoch Powell. Among the scenes: celebrating the bard's birthday in Stratford, the birthplace, Holy Trinity Church, Castle Hedingham, the British Library. The unbelievers receive a very fair hearing, helped by A.L. Rowse's wind-baggish protestations against anyone daring to question the party line.

Hope, Warren. "It Was the Bard of Oxford — Not Avon." *Philadelphia Inquirer*, April 20, **1989**, p. 21-A.

An Oxfordian, Hope reviews the controversy and the lives of an unliterary type, Shakspere, and an educated, literary-type, Oxford, what with the telecast of a debate on the issue on public televisions' *Frontline*. He hopes that the program will facilitate reading and teaching "the plays and poems in the light of a life that illuminates them, rather than continuing to try and force the works to fit a life that is totally alien to them." Hope's op-ed piece engendered letters to the editor for weeks. Most of the respondents railed against him for even suggesting that the Stratford man was a fraud. "This is a position of great snobbery and should not be tolerated by any right-thinking person," wrote Lester I. Conner (*Inquirer*, 17 May 1989, p. 10-A).

Morris, Steve. "Detective Story: Who Wrote Shakespeare?" *Philadelphia Welcomat*, May 10, **1989**, pp. 3, 28–32.

Beginning with the 1964 case of an Englishwoman who left 6,500 pounds in her will to find original Shakespeare manuscripts, Morris reviews objections to the Stratford man's authorship and asks, "Is it possible that the most famous writer in the English language is a fake?" Then he says, "The evidence is substantial that the Shakespeare hoax is unraveling and the mask is about to be removed, revealing the face of a man who, owing to his noble rank, was forbidden in his lifetime to publish anything under his own name: Edward de Vere, 17th Earl of Oxford, scapegrace stepson and son-in-law of William Cecil, Lord Burghley, treasurer and first minister to Queen Elizabeth." He discusses what we know of William Shakespeare, what we know of de Vere. Morris shows how poems and sonnets attributed to

Shakespeare can be traced to Oxford's house. He believes Charles W. Barrell confirmed the "dark lady" as Anne Vavasour, Oxford's mistress. The Earl of Southampton connection is examined as well as the bitter political and religious warfare of the time. Oxford's connection with the state is mentioned. Morris believes Oxford wrote the Sonnets and perhaps *Hamlet*, possibly the comedies and some other of the tragedies. He does think dating damages Oxfordians.

Goldstein, Gary. "Shakespeare Sleuths: Will the Real Bard Please Stand Up?" *Stamford Advocate*, July 21, **1989**.

Goldstein reviews doubts expressed about authorship by such literary lights as Mark Twain, Henry James and Charles Dickens. He complains that "the great majority of professors of English refuse to present the available evidence on the authorship issue either to their students in the classroom or to fellow scholars in the pages of academic journals." He maintains that money is indeed a consideration, what with Stratford attracting over a million tourists each year. If Oxford were the author, "Looking at Shakespeare though [*sic*] Oxford glasses would force scholars to acknowledge that the plays were not designed simply as entertainment for the masses, but as savage social satire about some of the highest officials at the Court of Elizabeth, and as works of political propaganda directed against internal and external enemies of the government, written often at the direction of the monarchy." He mentions John Nassivera's play *All the Queen's Men* performed at the Westport Country Playhouse through July 29, 1989.

Boyd, Bentley. "The Bard: Oxford Earl or 'the Stratford Man'?" *Washington Post*, September 18, **1989**, p. B4.

Boyd profiles Lord Charles Burford, 23-year-old descendant of the Earls of Oxford and Oxford University graduate who enlisted the encouragement and financial aid of William Hunt, retired trader from the Chicago Board of Trade. Burford, who established the De Vere society in 1986, believes credit for the plays must go to the right person, and his grandfather convinced him that the 17th Earl is that worthy. Burford's fear is inertia, "because few want to rewrite literary history." He thinks that "If you get Shakespeare wrong, you get the Elizabethan Age wrong." Burford says Oxford would have been disgraced by revealing his authorship and association with theater types.

Champlin, Charles. "William Shakespeare Is Still News After Four Centuries." *Los Angeles Times*, February 8, **1990**, p. F4.

Times Arts Editor Champlin uses Kenneth Branagh's 1989 film version of *Henry V* to refresh us on the authorship question. He believes "the conspiracy of silence is easier to accept than the miracle." Although the "monumental" evidence for the Earl of Oxford is circumstantial, investigation should be forthcoming because "Orthodox scholarship has chosen almost totally to ignore the possibility that an authorship question exists, retreating behind facades of scorn, contempt, indifference and quick dismissal." Champlin thinks the early Baconians did a disservice through their methods and cipher extolment and that the "authorship question has been left, by default and necessity, to those outside academia." Charlton Ogburn, and the lawyers Judge Minos D. Miller and Ruth Loyd Miller are mentioned.

Oldenburg, Don. "Shakespeare, by Any Other Name?" *Washington Post*, April 17, **1990**, p. D5.

Claremont McKenna College Professor Ward E.Y. Elliott, whose father was an Oxfordian, attempts to determine the authorship of Shakespeare "via computer crunching literary minutiae, from word frequency to punctuation proclivity to use of clauses and compounds." Samuel Schoenbaum, author of *Shakespeare's Lives* (1970), is quoted to the effect that he's sorry he referred to anti–Stratfordians as "lunatic rubbish" and is eliminating that from his revised edition. Elliott's research at the Francis Bacon Library is recounted. Director Elizabeth Wrigley told him there are 58 candidates. Influence of the 1976 statistical tests devised by Ronald Thisted and Brad Efron is noted. Various test results are expressed. Oxford and John Donne came out well. Robert Valenza's test charting strength of relationships between key words find that Sir Walter Raleigh and Queen Elizabeth "matched Shakespeare convincingly." There is skepticism by Carol Sue Lipman, president of the Shakespeare Authorship Roundtable who wants English departments to research the subject.

Miller, Michael. "Computer Test Authenticates Shakespeare." *Washington Post*, April 21, 1990, p. C-3.

   The results of Professor Ward Elliott's computer analysis are in and suggest that the Stratford man was indeed Shakespeare. "Bacon, Oxford and Marlowe come out in Timbuktu" on the modal analysis (Valenza) tests. Guess who rates highest: Queen Elizabeth and Sir Walter Raleigh. The Queen failed five or six of the secondary tests but Raleigh only two. Professor Elliott still believes someone other than Stratford is the author, and rightly so. If Elizabeth and Raleigh achieve such high marks, the Valenza test's validity must be questioned.

"Did Queen Write Shakespeare's Sonnets?" *Science*, May 4, 1990, p. 548.

   Robert Valenza's modal analysis technique and Ward E.Y. Elliott's quest for the true author are reviewed.

"Footnotes." *Chronicle of Higher Education*, May 9, 1990, p. A4.

   Five paragraphs review Professor Ward Elliott's computer analysis of Elizabethan literature in an attempt to prove or disprove that the Stratford man wrote Shakespeare. Using Robert J. Valenza's modal analysis, Elliott finds that "The results appear to take the three major claimants out of contention. While Mr. Elliott is still not persuaded that Shakspere is Shakespeare, he has pretty much given up on his former favorite, the Earl of Oxford." Not mentioned are the high marks given to Queen Elizabeth and Raleigh.

Fleischer, Leonore. "The Bard or Not the Bard?" *Publishers Weekly*, May 11, 1990, p. 228.

   EPM Publications of McLean, Virginia, reprints Charlton Ogburn's *The Mysterious William Shakespeare: The Myth and the Reality* only to find that scholars can't stand the very thought of it. While Fleischer is aware of the controversy, EPM's Peter Exton is not, saying, "We are selling *Mysterious William* enthusiastically, but we've discovered something peculiar about the Shakespearean authorities who should be a part of its audience. They hate the book. We thought serious scholars would value the thoroughness and detail.... The entrenched Shakespearean establishment seems to fear the book. They don't reject it as poorly researched or badly written. They reject it as impossible, unfathomable, although they do not offer evidence that would silence Ogburn's blasphemy. They have been downright nasty, calling him and other Oxfordians 'lunatics.'"

"Computer Study Says Bard Genuine." *Daily Local News* (West Chester, PA), November 2, 1990, p. D3.

   This is but an AP teaser indicating that Ward Elliott and Robert Valenza have via computer analysis and other tests determined that Shakespeare wrote the plays. "Elliott on Wednesday said all of Shakespeare's works are similar, and those of the earl of Oxford look nothing like them." None of the reports on this computer study point out that there are no writings by William Shakspere to analyze."

Oldenburg, Don. "Beating Up on the Bard." *Washington Post*, December 18, 1990, p. B5.

   The Ward Elliott–Robert Valenza computer tests of Elizabethan literature are examined more extensively. Nine convincing Oxfordian objections to Stratfordian authorship are presented. Charlton Ogburn, Morse Johnson, and Peter R. Moore are among those quoted. For once proper objection to the Elliott-Valenza analysis is made when Moore contends that the known Oxford writings would certainly not match Shakespeare's works because "the latter, published between 1593 and 1609, are the mature and developed writings of De Vere and shouldn't be expected to 'match' his earliest attempts to put pen to paper." Such reasonable objections are mitigated by Elizabeth Sears of the Shakespeare Oxford Society. She hopes to prove that Oxford and Queen Elizabeth were lovers and the conspiracy was an attempt to hide their offspring, heir to the throne. But why would Elizabeth hide an heir, illegitimate or not?

"Looking for Shakespeare." *Atlantic Monthly*, October 1991, pp. 43–86.

In "The Case for Oxford" Tom Bethell presents reasonable objections to Shakespeare's candidature and evaluates items favoring Oxford. In "The Case for Shakespeare" Irvin Matus concentrates on Shakespeare as a man of the theater. His best points surface in his reply to Bethell. "The Ghost's Vocabulary: How the Computer Listens for Shakespeare's 'Voiceprint'" examines computer analysis of literature, including the work of Ronald Thisted and Ward Elliott.

"The Nose Job." *Seinfeld*. NBC TV (Columbia Pictures TV/Castle Rock Entertainment. Season 3, Episode 9, November 20, **1991**).

Masquerading as Professor Peter von Nostrand, Kramer (Michael Richards) is queried by a landlord (Roy Brocksmith). Landlord: "Tell me, is it your contention that Shakespeare was an impostor?" Von Nostrand: "My contention?" Landlord: "Yes, your contention." Von Nostrand: "Well yes, that's my contention."

"The Play's the Thing." *Wilson Quarterly* (Winter **1992**): 150.

This comments on Tom Bethell's "The Case for Oxford" and Irvin Matus' "The Case for Shakespeare" in the October, 1991 *Atlantic Monthly*. Bethell is quoted on the implausibility of the Stratford man knowing so much about foreign locales and his lack of sympathy for the "upwardly mobile strivers." The disgust with court life is emblematic of someone who knew it well. Matus argues that the playwright's characters are invariably contemporary Englishmen, thus the Stratford man need not have traveled abroad, and he contends that publicly available material provided enough background for the Stratford man. He notes that Ben Jonson had little formal schooling. Matus wonders how anti–Stratfordian candidates had the inside theatrical knowledge of "William Shakespeare, gentleman of Stratford."

Uncovering Shakespeare: An Update. Stamford, CT: VisNet, September 17, **1992**. [http://www.pbs.org/wgbh/pages/frontline/Shakespeare/debates/gtedebate.html]

This is a transcription of a videoconference hosted and moderated by William F. Buckley, Jr. Guests: Deborah Bacon, Tom Bethell, David Bevington, Charles Boyle, Charles Champlin, Father Francis Edwards, SJ, Rebeca Flynn, Warren Hope, Earle Hyman, Felicia Londre, Ambassador Paul Nitze, Donald Richardson, John Savage, Roger Stritmatter, Gary Taylor, and Charles Vere, Earl of Burford. Despite the length of the program, one feels the participants merely scratched the service. Some are more long-winded than others.

Mantell, S[uzanne]. "Small Colorado House Will Publish 'Lost' Shakespeare Play." *Publishers Weekly*, July 19, **1993**, p. 7.

Reports that *Cardenio, or The Second Maiden's Tragedy* has been discovered by autograph dealer Charles Hamilton. What's more, it has been "authenticated" and will be published by Glenbridge Publishing Ltd. Hamilton says the play "is no *Hamlet*, ... but it compares well" to some lesser Shakespeare items. Perhaps Jennifer Lee Carrell got some inspiration for *Interred with Their Bones* (2008, ©2007) from this discovery.

Stevens, John Paul. "The Shakespeare Canon of Statutory Construction." *Elizabethan Review* (Spring **1993**): 4–20. [Reprinted from *University of Pennsylvania Law Review*, Vol. 140:4, 1992]

U.S. Supreme Court Justice Stevens examines the Oxfordian case based on five canons of statutory construction. First ("Read the statute"), the First Folio identifies the Stratford man as the author, but we have little else. Second ("Read the *entire* statute"), the more Shakespeare we read the more we know about him, and Oxford's noble birth and upbringing would have provided him with background for the plays. Third, read the text in its contemporary context. We know about Oxford's education but have nothing concrete about Shakespeare's. Compare Ben Jonson's "small Latin and less Greek" with his "Drink to me, only, with thine eyes" to identify multiple meanings. Fourth ("consult the legislative history"), where is Shakespeare's library, why did his son-in-law not mention him in his journals, and why the seven-year gap between the Stratford man's death and publication of the First Folio? Fifth, use common sense. Stevens notes that both Stratfordians and Oxfordians label each other's positions absurd on pseudonyms, play dating, and conspiracy. He draws on *Measure for Measure, The Merchant of Venice* and *United States v. James* (1986) to illustrate defense in legal proceedings.

"Letters to the Editor." *Elizabethan Review* (Fall **1993**): 2–6.

Christian H. Gannon, Brooklyn attorney, takes issue with Justice John Paul Stevens' "The Shakespeare Canon of Statutory Construction" (Spring 1993), drawing on Brother Leo's *English Literature, A Survey and Commentary* (1828) to confirm the Stratford man as author. Gannon says, "The authorship argument shifts our focus away from the Canon itself." Psychologist Johanna K. Tabin of Glencoe, IL, addresses two issues she finds unnecessary: the spelling of names in Elizabethan times and the argument that the Stratford lad could not have had the necessary education. She points to Isaac Newton as a self-made prodigy. On the other hand, Tabin contends that Oxford has a case for authorship based on life events reflected in the Canon, recognition during his life of literary ability, his background, and the language and imagery in his early poems. "The total case, thus, is very strong."

Desper, C. Richard, and Vezzoli, Gary C. "A Statistical Approach to the Shakespeare Authorship Question." *Elizabethan Review*, Fall **1993**, 36–42.

Polymer chemist Desper and physicist Vezzoli employ inductive logic to argue that several meanings attend the title *The Winter's Tale*. They identify parallels between its plot and Oxford's life and believe the number of coincidences are telling — and not caused by chance. They find "indirect evidence" compelling, as it sometimes is in law and science. Desper and Vezzoli say they offer not proof but additional evidence favoring Oxfordian authorship.

Wilson, Ian. *Shakespeare: The Evidence: Unlocking the Mysteries of the Man and His Work.* New York: St. Martin's Griffin, 1999, ©**1993**.

Despite the title, this is mostly a biography of a period. Filled with facts about Elizabethan times, it is rife with speculation about Shakespeare, e.g., "arguably indicative," a 1607 portrait of dying man signing his will compared with Shakespeare's death. The main authorship discussion is in "Chapter 2: Was 'Shakespeare' Really Shakespeare?" In Chapter 3, Wilson twice disparages the heretics as "Oxfordians and their ilk," a phrase used throughout (Chapters 5, 8, 12.) According to Wilson, records indicate that Shakspere's father John was not an inconsiderable fellow. Examination of the English theatre before Shakespeare and the traveling companies suggests that "we might be forgiven for envisaging the five-year-old William sitting on his father's knee while watching these performances." For Wilson, drawing on the works of such Shakespearean scholars as Edmund Chambers, Leslie Hotson and A.L. Rowse, Shakespeare didn't *have* to earn a living, he was an actor; he probably got his books at the stalls in St. Paul's Churchyard, or Ferdinando Stanley, Lord Strange, could have been Shakespeare's patron and supplied books and insight into court life. Perhaps the most compelling revelation in Wilson's book is that Richard Stonley of Aldersgate, a teller of the Exchequer, entered in his diary on June 12, 1593 purchase of *Venus and Adonis* along with the *Survey of France*. In 1972 the Folger Shakespeare Library obtained a copy of the diary and curator Laetitia Yeandle discovered the notation, "12th of June, 1593. For the Survey of France, with the Venus and Adhonay pr Shakspere, xii.d." Wilson says this is the first known original record of any purchase of a Shakespeare publication — and the earliest known notice of him as a published author. Writer's cramp is suggested as the reason for the poor signatures of his later days. Perhaps some chronic ailment caused his retirement. Although Wilson reviews other wills in which books were identified and passed on, he hazards no guess as to why Shakespeare didn't do this. If Shakespeare had Catholic sympathies, it explains "both his compassion towards all vagaries of the human condition, and also his guardedness — discreetly balancing everything, avoiding disclosing his own political and religious affiliations, above all, unlike Jonson, setting his plays in anything but the here and now of his England." Includes map of Shakespeare's London, 54 illustrations [question marks follow many], Notes and References, Family Trees, Chronology, Miscellaneous Documents, Bibliography, and Index.

Baker, Elliott. "The Philosophy of the Plays of Shakespeare Unfolded — and Abridged." *Elizabethan Review* (Spring **1994**): 6–14.

Novelist (*A Fine Madness*) Baker adapted this from the foreword to his abridgement of Delia Bacon's *The Philosophy of the Plays of Shakespeare Unfolded*. "In the few critical notices granted her book, none mentioned what it was about." For Delia, authorship was incidental to the consistent philosophy of the plays. She wanted to "perceive its intent and establish its origins." Baker does not deny the book is overwritten. "It's as if Delia didn't believe the elements of her theory could be absorbed from a single exposure." Thus repetition enters. "She overestimated her readers' familiarity with the plays and Bacon's philosophic writings and also granted them a classical knowledge equal to her own." Such miscalculations doomed acceptance for Raleigh as organizer of the group, Francis Bacon as "philosophic mentor." Montaigne's influence is explained and the new enlightenment summarized. Baker says Delia Bacon did not use circumstantial evidence. He notes that even before Delia Bacon's January, 1856 *Putnams Monthly* article, many had questioned Stratford authorship, e.g., Pope, Coleridge, Emerson. Delia "was the first to offer an alternative." Includes notes.

Chandler, David. "Death Put Off by Cunning and Forc'd Cause." *Elizabethan Review* (Spring **1994**): 15–20.

Doctoral candidate in English at Corpus Christi College, Oxford University, Chandler takes the opportunity of the 400th anniversary of Christopher Marlowe's death in 1593 to review the literature naming Marlowe as Shakespeare. He discusses the tradition that permitted Marlowe to survive, perhaps — according to some biographers — to substitute for himself his victim, Francis Frazer or, Shakespeare, said to closely resemble Marlowe. William Taylor of Norwich is credited with initiating "new interest in Marlowe's life, more speculation, and more fiction." James Broughton, John Payne Collier and Alexander Dyce stepped in with their biographies. Wilbur Gleason Zeigler weighed in with his 1895 novel, *It Was Marlowe*. "Did Marlowe Write Shakespeare?" by Thomas Corwin Mendanhall followed. A physics professor, Mendenhall developed "fingerprinting" based on word length and found a correlation between Shakespeare's and Marlowe's style. This caused a sensation. Leslie Hotson penned *Death of Christopher Marlowe* (1925). Then came Gilbert Slater's *Seven Shakespeare* (1931) in which the Shakespeare canon was attributed to Bacon, Marlowe, William Stanley, Roger Manners, Edward de Vere, Walter Ralegh, and the Countess of Pembroke. Calvin Hoffman's *The Man Who Was Shakespeare* (1955) came next in importance. Denigrating reviews didn't stop anyone. William Honey accepted Hoffman's premise and wrote *The Shakespeare Epitaph Deciphered* (1969). Honey followed with the privately published, *The Life, Loves and Achievements of Christopher Marlowe Alias Shakespeare* (1982).

Edwards, Francis. "William Shakespeare: Why Was His True Identity Concealed?" *Elizabethan Review* (Autumn **1994**): 23–48.

Edwards explains that the Elizabethan stage was not what theater is today, i.e., it was an occupation for rowdier elements of society. Masques were favored by Elizabeth and James I. Money was made in running the theaters, not playwriting. Edwards quotes various contemporary sources denigrating plays. Oxford's dramatic inclinations needed to be discreet because the Cecils, to whom Oxford was beholden to financially as well as for favor with the Queen, had no truck with the theater. Oxford had relations with "lewd friends," according to a 1587 William Cecil letter to Francis Walsingham. And why would the Cecils, newly arrived as gentlemen, countenance any actions by their ward that would stain nobility? On concluding pages Edwards discusses the probability that Oxford and the man from Stratford were well acquainted with the latter being one of those "lewd friends."

Matus, Irvin Leigh. *Shakespeare, In Fact*. New York: Continuum, **1994**.

An independent scholar on the Stratfordian side outdoing normal scholars in research and often wearying detail, Matus believes the central question is how Shakespeare stood in relation to his contemporaries. He counters all anti–Stratfordian claims, whether it be that Shakespeare was unique in not having a literary paper trail, that playwrights controlled publication ("playwrights did not keep copies of their plays"), or that the thousand pounds Elizabeth granted Oxford was not to provide plays but merely to maintain an earl's solvency. Indifference to manuscripts, the ravages of the English Civil War, using pages underneath cooked pies — no wonder not much survives. Matus notes that Ben Jonson's education was just about as sketchy as Shakespeare's. But Stratford's grammar school was good. Although Matus claims friendship with some Oxfordians and refuses to label all as cranks or "kooks," he gets in a dig at J. Thomas Looney's name and spends much time drubbing and pillorying Charlton Ogburn (*The Mysterious William Shakespeare*, 1984) on, among many things, lack of references to Shakespeare as actor and provides documents contradicting him. Matus decries Ruth Loyd Miller's ability for "conjuring a story" yet offsets a plethora of facts with speculation, e.g., "likely," "it is probable," "likelihood," "may be conjectured," "suggests," "within the realm of probability." In discussing play length, Matus quotes Algernon Charles Swinburne to the effect that Shakespeare wrote for the "studious reader," not just for the stage. [Contrast with Diana Price's opinion in *Shakespeare's Unorthodox Biography*, 2001.]

Dating is no real problem, and Matus is definite that *The Winter's Tale* could not have been written before 1610, six years after Oxford's death. Matus quotes 17th century sources labeling plays harmful to the state but doesn't make the argument that this leaves the Stratford man less than a proclaimed genius and provides a reason for Oxford to officially camouflage authorship. Matus seems to accept Lord Henry Howard's attacks on Oxford without scrutiny. Commoner John Chamberlain sent letters that indicate he had connections in court circles and kept company with folks around St. Paul's to catch gossip. This proves that a commoner could understand court life, says Matus. As for falconry, anyone could have picked up enough information to make it sound as if he were a courtier. There are plenty of analogies and facts, some only tangentially bearing on Shakespeare himself. Although the jacket says this is for primarily for general readers, those readers are likely to bog down. Fully illustrated. Includes notes by chapter, a lengthy bibliography, and index.

Phillips, Graham, and Keatman, Martin. *The Shakespeare Conspiracy*. London: Century (Random House), **1994**.

The authors aim "to remove the cloak of secrecy" surrounding the mystery that is Shakespeare. They examine myth and reality, historical evidence, the man from Stratford, Francis Bacon, Lords Derby and Oxford, Marlowe, and the "superspies." Amongst other reasons, Bacon can be eliminated on the grounds that he attacks contemporary drama in *De Augmentis Scientarium*. They believe Oxford's case is much stronger than Derby's but that as Oxford was senior — and older than — Southampton, he could not have written and dedicated *Venus and Adonis* or *The Rape of Lucrece* to that earl. The final chapter speculates that Shakespeare might have been one William Hall, whose actions were instrumental in sending Sir Walter Ralegh to prison for 13 years. Ralegh was released on 19 March 1616, six days before Shakespeare made his will. Shakespeare died on 23 April. Poisoning? The authors also wonder why no verifiable portrait exists. Had he been disfigured? After all, Ben Jonson had suggested Shakespeare's portrait was not true to life. Includes two dozen illustrations, chronology, bibliography and index.

Whalen, Richard F. *Shakespeare—Who Was He? The Oxford Challenge to the Bard of Avon*. Westport, CT: Praeger, **1994**.

Aiming at a general audience unfamiliar with the debate or befuddled by its complexity, Whalen focuses on the writings of eminent Shakespeare biographers and scholars. "No [theater] records give him any role in any play, not even in the plays he is supposed to have written." Whalen admits that the dearth of manuscripts is not unusual because they were owned by acting companies and printers. "But no one has been able to find anything written by the hand of Will Shakspere, supposedly the well-known and successful poet and playwright of Stratford and London." In "The Missing Apprenticeship," Whalen makes compelling objections to the Stratford man as author: young, new to London and presumably active in the busy theater yet having the time to learn French and Italian, familiarize himself with aristocratic lifestyles, study English history — all this while running his Stratford real estate and grain businesses. Would this not have required "superhuman genius" if not "divine inspiration"? Whelan also contends that the Stratford man's Warwickshire dialect and accent would have been barely intelligible in London and would have to be shed, and fast. A valuable chapter analyzes the spelling of the name and whether Shakspere was Shakespeare, which for Whalen is manifestly not so. As for *genius*, "Unlike music or mathematics, great and sustained writing is the result of genius working on life experience and acquired knowledge, neither of which can be part of the innate gift of genius. Even if endowed retrospectively with a genius that is almost superhuman, Will Shakspere still, according to the records, had precious little time to gain the life experience demonstrated so dramatically in the early plays."

Fully explored are objections to Oxford's candidature. Oxford's life is matched with elements in *All's Well That Ends Well*, *Romeo and Juliet*, *The Merchant of Venice*, and *Hamlet*. A "conspiracy" to hide Oxford's role is examined. Play dating is discussed. A superb case is made for scholarship opportunities if, first, academic resources are used to explore alternate candidates and, second, if Oxford were determined to be the true author. "The plays and poems would take on new meaning, new depth, and heightened emotional significance." This is one of the most entertaining and reasonable analyses of the authorship question. Appendix A: Records of Will Shakspere's Theater Activities, Appendix B: "Shake-scene," *Groatsworth*, and Chettle, Appendix C: Ben Jonson's Notebook, *Timber*, Appendix D: The Benezet Test [comparing Shakespeare lines with Oxford's early poetry]. Includes informational notes, selected annotated bibliography, and index. Illustrations: the signatures, the Dugdale and more recent Trinity Church monument, and the Droeshout portrait.

Michell, John F. *Who Wrote Shakespeare?* New York: Thames & Hudson, 1999, ©1996.

Claiming agnosticism — and not belittling any side — Michell provides an informative and hugely entertaining analysis of the debate accompanied by over a hundred exceptional illustrations. He maintains that there is indeed an authorship problem. ("No comparable figure in history has ever been so anonymous.") In his estimation, Stratfordians are sincere but not as secure as they think. "Whenever one party in a debate resorts to abusing its opponents, it is a sure sign that it is uncertain of its ground." In the final analysis, everything has been said and we approach a dead end. The central question is how could a man from out-of-the-way Stratford accomplish this art? Along the way, Michell notes Tolstoy's opinion that Shakespeare did not identify with the common people; the importance of the enigmatical Ben Jonson, who satirizes then pans the author; and the lack of acknowledgment of Shakspere's death — or burial in Westminster Abbey — in contrast to Jonson, Francis Beaumont, Michael Drayton, Edmund Spenser. As for those claiming manuscripts have been lost for others as well as Shakespeare, Michell says there are plays in manuscript by Marlowe, Jonson, Green, etc. He addresses Shakspere's literacy, the Stratford school's quality, why an attorney like Bacon wouldn't see to a better edited First Folio, the Sonnets (in middling depth), and the non-mention of Shakespeare at the Essex trial.

A plus for the Stratfordians is the unequivocal inscription beneath the bust in Holy Trinity. Contenders receive individual chapters. "Baconians are often very reasonable, well-informed people, but below the surface of their movement is its underworld, a region of darkness and fantastical illusions." As for Ignatius Donnelly, "He saw through the racket of Shakespeare." The ciphering that damaged the Baconian case must be viewed in terms of its times, a time of spiritualism, mysticism and channeling. In Chapter 6: The Oxford Movement, Michell begins with Freud. Michell finds Oxfordian claims cumbersome. William Stanley, Sixth Earl of Derby, is considered in light of Professor Abel Lefranc's studies. How could Shakspere have been received at the Court of Navarre and there gleaned background for *Love's Labours Lost*? Derby traveled abroad and most probably witnessed the Court of Navarre. Eventually "Lefranc and his French colleagues lost patience with the Stratfordian theory. It made a mockery of their historical and literary scholarship." As for Roger Manners, Fifth Earl of Rutland, he actually visited Denmark. Yet "Everyone's life, not just Rutland's, is reflected in Shakespeare's plays." According to Michell, Marlowe has been acknowledged by Stratfordians as author of some of the canon. Thomas Mendenhall's analysis of word lengths matched Marlowe with Shakespeare. Now we have "stylometrists" who analyze sentence-length, numbers of words in sentences, common or uncommon words, but it's become chaotic. No one has used computers to duplicate Mendenhall's 1901 work.

In a summary chapter, Michell explores Group Theory, which he finds acceptable in part but problematic when it comes to identifying the members. In any event, William Shakspere had to have been involved in some way. Investigating the Stratford man's life for clues has been a failure, however. Michell notes that Leslie Hotson's unearthing of the 29 November 1596 writ for Shakspere's arrest would have dismayed Victorian biographers for it proves Shakspere was involved in the "rackets" of "gangsters." "Shakspere did well in theatre business, but he had no great reputation among colleagues. If he had written and sold plays or been prominent on the stage, he would have been mentioned often in Henslowe's diary, Alleyne's records or the notes and letters that people wrote about the theatre. He was never mentioned and left no record or memory of any part he acted." Shakspere was discreet as well as an opportunist.

Michell addresses the work of George Connes, saying one cannot honestly join Connes in his "waveringly" support for the Orthodox. "The fact that it has been impossible to establish any alternative theory of Authorship does not vindicate the Orthodox position, merely preserves its respectability." There are equal and opposite experts for everything. "If it were not for the taboos and inhibitions that prevent young scholars from approaching it, this would be a popular and rewarding subject." Includes bibliography by candidate and index.

Sobran, Joseph. *Alias Shakespeare: Solving the Greatest Literary Mystery of All Time.* New York: Free Press, 1997.

Dismissing as irrelevant anti–Stratfordian cranks, Sobran finds the established account of the author's life "also fails to offer any literary insights." And "'Genius' is not an explanation." In fact, "Inverted snobbery" can be cast at the feet of the Bardolaters. "The most dispiriting trait of the professional scholars is not their consensus about Shakespeare's identity, but *their refusal to admit that there can be any room for doubt.*" Regarding the death of the Stratford man, Sobran wonders why no one saluted him? Sobran traces the development of the biography, pointing out various frauds and forgeries. He confirms the author's knowledge of Italy. Fulsome attention accrues to the Sonnets and the trouble they give traditionalists. "A poet of Mr. Shakspere's age and rank, writing in praise of his noble patron, would hardly bring himself and his mortal prospects into the foreground so insistently; he would merely praise his patron, and leave himself and his own passions out of it. He wouldn't have to beg his employer to forget him and not mourn for him too much…. The Sonnets were all too likely to compromise the man they sought to glorify. We can safely rule out any notion that Southampton paid Mr. Shakspere for writing poems that might have led the public to infer, rightly or wrongly, that they were homosexual lovers." Sobran emphasizes the authorship clue given by Oxford's 1573 letter to Thomas Bedingfield, translator of *Cardanus Comfort.* The cases for Bacon and Marlowe are summarized. Vocabularies are discussed. Despite his faults, de Vere is called loyal, generous, and never underhanded. Quoted are contemporary sources on the common suppression by nobles of their writings. Sobran wonders why when Elizabeth I railed against a planned performance of *Richard II* for its subversive qualities only actor Augustine Phillips was taken to task, not the author "Shakespeare"? (Sobran finds support for the view that *Richard II* is older than the convention date of 1595.) Stressed is the importance of William Barkstead's 1607 poem *Mirrha the Mother of Adonis,* e.g., why is "Shakspeare" spoken of in the past tense? As for retiring, "Writing is not an activity you retire from, especially at forty-five." Sobran examines Walt Whitman's view that the author is feudal. Also analyzed in depth are the poems *Venus and Adonis* and *The Rape of Lucrece.* According to Sobran, Shakespeare researchers have unearthed next to nothing confirming Mr. Shakspere as author or to put the lie to Oxford's claim. "The Oxfordian view, trimmed of its crankish excesses, opens a door to a completely new understanding of the great plays and poems, promising rewards, now hardly imaginable, for those readers and scholars who can bear to let go of the old view." Appendices: 1: Mr. Shakspere's Will, 2: Oxford's Poems, 3: Oxford's Letters, 4: The Preface to *Cardanus Comfort,* 5: The Funeral Elegy [Sobran finds inconsistencies that later would cause its proponent Donald Foster to dismiss his claim that Shakespeare wrote it. At the time Sobran thought it could have been early Oxford.] Includes notes, bibliography and index. Illustrations: Droeschout portrait, Elizabeth I, Edmund Spenser, Ben Jonson, Phillip Sidney, Henry Wriothesley, Henry Howard, William Cecil, William Herbert, Philip Herbert, Oxford (2).

Bate, Jonathan. "Bard Beyond Belief." *The Wall Street Journal,* May 1, 1997, p. A16.

This is a "Bookshelf" review of Joseph Sobran's *Alias Shakespeare* by the Stratfordian professor of English literature at the University of Liverpool. Bate's first paragraph could provide the heretics with ammunition as it says the Stratford man's life was very mundane and the "only raw materials he needed … were a grammar school education and a lifetime in the theater as actor, scriptwriter and shareholder of the King's Men, the most successful playing company of the age. He became the most admired dramatist of his generation, but nobody expressed any surprise when in about 1612 he handed over the role of in-house scriptwriter … to John Fletcher and retired to his hometown of Stratford-upon-Avon, where he died four years later." Bate then summarizes Shakespeare's reputation, fluctuating over the next century but during the 19th century's Romantic movement synonymous with genius. As for Sobran's tome, Bate finds it "much shorter and much better written than most works in the genre," but minus new evidence. "The belief that there ought to be connections between an artist's work and his life is a classic Romantic fallacy." Thus making the Sonnets autobiographical is false. Sonnets "were elaborate games, … not necessarily confessions from the heart." On dating, Bate finds cause to believe certain works were written after Oxford's death and wonders why "Mr. Sobran fails to provide any explanation for the historical specificity of Shakespeare's Jacobean works." He says Sobran doesn't investigate the genius of creating fully-drawn characters from all walks of life. Bate finds it refreshing that Sobran does delve into Oxford's warts. "It is good to have a book that paints Oxford in his true cruel colors." Shakespeare, by contrast, was "a respectable family man."

Bethell, Tom. "Outing Shakespeare." *The American Spectator* (May **1997**): 22–23.

Anti-Stratfordian and admitted friend of Joseph Sobran, Bethell reviews Sobran's *Alias Shakespeare*. "I have no hesitation in saying that this is the best book ever written on the subject." He notes that the "academy" has framed the debate as one between the correct view and conspiratorialists. To Bethell, knowing the true author makes a real difference. "The easy recourse to 'genius' as an explanatory device, our blithe faith in the Common Man, our understanding of English literature and of Western culture itself could be shaken by the radical revision offered here. Much is at stake." He traces the history of the controversy, admitting the proliferation of cranks in the Age of the Amateur (when Twain and Whitman lived) and points out that Ignatius Donnelly's *The Great Cryptogram* severely tarnished the heretics' case. Bethell touches on the dating debate. "Some plays are conventionally dated after that year [1603] but it is all guesswork, not dictated by any fact." Oxford's biography is provided. Summarized is the 1987 moot court debate at American University in which the pro–Stratford lawyer made much of Oxford's character flaws, at which Justice Stevens replied, "Sounds like a playwright to me." The debate is compared to a jigsaw puzzle with a plethora of missing pieces. Bethell says that new information about Oxford remains in virgin archives. "If Sobran is correct, remember, much of the historical research has been done in the wrong place."

"A Shakespeare by Any Other Name...." *The Wall Street Journal*, May 15, **1997**, p. A23.

Letters to the Editor respond to Jonathan Bate's review of Joseph Sobran's *Alias Shakespeare*. In support of Oxford are Nancy Ann Holtz, Patrick R. Sullivan, and Sobran. Holtz (San Antonio) finds the argument that Oxford chose Shakspere as a beard compelling. "Mr. Bate seems to believe that ideas can take root in a cultural desert." She wonders if Shakspere was any more respectable than Oxford. Sullivan (Tukwalla, WA) argues that there is no evidence that the man from Stratford could write and that the letter about a Bermuda shipwreck that would seem to nullify Oxford's candidature was published in 1625, nine years after the Stratford man's death. Sobran (Burke, VA) says Bate's review of his book was "kind (though critical)" and focuses on the Sonnets, maintaining that they are indeed autobiographical. He concludes by stressing that "the poet confidently expects his poetry to be 'immortal,' yet he predicts that he himself will be 'forgotten.' All this is an eerily accurate description of Oxford, the fate of his works, and his centuries of oblivion."

"From Nowhere, a Genius for All Time." *The Wall Street Journal*, June 10, **1997**, p. A19.

In Letters to the Editor, Anna L. Irwin and R.C. Hughes respond to Joseph Sobran and two other readers supporting Oxford. Irwin finds Jonathan Bate's "Bard Beyond Belief" admirable and argues that Ben Jonson wouldn't have provided a "laudable" "prefatory poem" to the First Folio if he knew William Shakespeare were a counterfeit. "He knew Shakespeare. Shakespeare was a friend of his." Irwin quotes conversation between Louis B. Wright and Virginia La Mar at the Folger Shakespeare to demonstrate that the authorship controversy is bunk. Hughes is "always fascinated and appalled by the perennial pushiness of those who favor that second-rate Earl of Oxford (or Francis Bacon or the professor down the street) as the real Shakespeare." Hughes draws attention to Charles Hamilton's *In Search of Shakespeare* and argues that Hamilton was a "premiere autograph expert" and found 29 extant signatures of Shakespeare and revealed that Shakespeare corrected several Bacon essays. Hughes identifies geniuses who, like Shakespeare, came from nothing: Einstein, Beethoven, Rembrandt, Leonardo, Michelangelo, Lincoln, Edison.

Dickson, Peter W. "Unmasking the Bard." *Book World* [*Washington Post*], August 17, **1997**, p. 11.

Reviewed are John Michell's *Who Wrote Shakespeare?*, Richard F. Whalen's *Shakespeare: Who Was He?* and Joseph *Sobran's Alias Shakespeare*. Dickson suggests newcomers to the issue could benefit very much by beginning with Michell's overview. However, Dickson feels Michell isn't terribly comfortable questioning conventional wisdom and "grudgingly concedes that Oxford (de Vere), who did visit Italy, is now the primary rival claimant." Whalen's bias in favor of Oxford is obvious, says Dickson, but he compliments Whalen's lucidity and splendid bibliography. Dickson says Whalen scores a major point by proving that Bermuda shipwrecks were publicized prior to 1610. Therefore Oxford's death in 1604 cannot be used to dispute his authorship of *The Tempest*. As for Sobran, Dickson thinks his "dense analysis of the key issues" is valuable in concert with Michell and Whalen. Dickson identifies two significant pieces of evidence in Sobran: (1) a passage in William Barkstead's *Mirrha Mother of Adonis* (1607) referring to Shakespeare as deceased, and (2) Oxford's references to lameness. Dickson is impressed with Sobran's point that hard chronological data rather than textual analysis can validate or invalidate a claimant. As for the reason for secrecy, Dickson relates a deception by Columbus' bastard son Ferdinand that lasted for 500 years, namely a cover-up of Columbus' adultery and his aristocratic Portuguese wife's family's involvement in the Braganza conspiracy to murder the Portuguese king. Neither Columbus' family nor the Portuguese rulers when they came to power wanted this revealed. Included are a portrait of Oxford and the Janssen monument of William Shakespeare.

Brennan, Patricia. "On Shakespeare and 'Cadfael.'" *Washington Post TV section*, August 23, 1997, p. 6.

Respected actor Derek Jacobi is profiled when he was guest of honor at the Folger Shakespeare Library's 65th anniversary gala in April and appearing as *Brother Cadfael* on TV. He says, "What I'm 95 percent convinced of is that the man who lived in Stratford didn't write the plays." He thinks that man probably did act but his name was likely a front for Edward Devere. He confronts the position that "Even if Shakespeare becomes Edward Devere, so what? The plays are still there." And, "I think if it was one man, it wasn't that man who lived in Stratford.... But you'll never get scholars to acknowledge that. Economically, Stratford-on-Avon would die. But something in my bones tells me it wasn't that man. Even [Sir John] Gielgud, Einstein, Freud—all expressed doubts."

Allen, Ron. *Who Were Shake-Speare? The Ultimate Who-Dun-It!* San Diego, CA: Silverado, 1998.

"People of substance and discernment, not crazies, have grappled with the thorny question, 'Who really wrote the plays and poems of Shake-speare?'" Amusingly yet seriously, Allen makes the case that Oxford ("neither angel nor devil") was the "patron-teacher of his brash young collaborator, Shaksper." The former was expert on the upper class and possessor of a fine library, the latter on the lower rungs of society. Books were rare and out-of-print editions were obviously used for background, therefore they were Oxford's. Allen stresses the importance of collaboration, e.g., Henry Chettle and Ben Jonson, Anthony Munday and Michael Drayton, Francis Beaumont and John Fletcher. Allen maintains 16th century stage writing was held to be a "low craft," thus providing one reason Oxford used a pseudonym. The feudal state of "unmerry Olde England" is described. Shaksper is proposed as the "artistic director" of the Chamberlain's Men. Oxford didn't have many governmental functions so he had time to write—and rewrite. Shaksper was born too late to come to London and all by himself write the canon even with his obvious talent. Allen disputes Oxfordians who claim Shaksper was a "straw man," for how would that have been allowed by a theater company? The frequent ad-libbing by actors in that period is compared to improvisation of Mozart cadenzas. To Allen it is obvious that after Oxford and Shaksper were gone many people had a hand in modifying the plays and that Cecil tarnished Oxford's reputation. Illustrations and lists include questioners, play sources, Shake-Speare's knowledge based on available books, Elizabethan actors and writers, editions of Shake-Speare's works, Elizabethan Theater Companies, London area theaters. The six Shake-Speare signatures are reproduced. Appendixes: A: Ten Myths Revisited, B: Shaksper Biography, C: Research Aplenty, D: On Shake-Speare Claimants. Includes Selected Bibliography and Index.

Altschuler, Eric Lewin. "Searching for Shakespeare in the Stars." *Physicsworld.com*, October 23, **1998**. [http://arxiv.org/abs/physics/9810042v1]

Altschuler identifies contenders for Shakespeare's throne. He finds the question of authorship to have "intrinsic interest, and, as well, the vast amount of informal and professional study of Shakespeare might be enhanced by knowledge of his identity." He discusses references in Shakespeare to astronom-ical and geophysical discoveries in 1572 and 1600, "but not to similarly important events of 1604, 1609 and 1610." To Altschuler it is singular that Shakespeare omits mention of Galileo's various discoveries publicized in his 1610 book, *Sidereus nuncios*. "There are many possible explanations why Shakespeare did not write about any of these topics, however, the most parsimonious is that the Bard was not alive to know of these new developments in astronomy. This would be consistent with Oxford (1550–1604), but not Shakspere (1564–1616) as Shakespeare." Includes references, from Joseph Sobran's *Alias Shake-speare* to Tycho Brahe's *De nova stella* and C. Clark's *Shakespeare and Science*.

Bate, Jonathan. *The Genius of Shakespeare*. New York and Oxford: University Press, **1998**.

Well-traveled lecturer and King Alfred Professor of English Literature at the University of Liver-pool, Bate explores the origins and the effects of Shakespeare, defining genius and explaining its mean-ing in various eras. Chapter 3 is "The Authorship Controversy." For Bate, the only mystery about Shakespeare is that some people question authorship for which there is hard evidence. Although he'd considered the question when "a brilliant but eccentric Greek master" tried to convince him, Bate became "skeptical when I discovered that the original proponent of de Vere's claim was an Edwardian schoolmaster who rejoiced in the name of J. Thomas Looney." For Bate, De Vere's death in 1604 con-founds his claim because Bate is adamant that *Macbeth* could not have come before the Gunpowder Plot of 1605, *The Winter's Tale* was licensed no earlier than 1610, *The Tempest*'s shipwreck was inspired by a 1609 sinking, and *Henry VIII* was cited a "new play" in 1613. Treating Oxfordians as if all are of one mind, he says they virtually ignore dating and "admire every word of the works indiscriminately." For Bate, the author was a man of the theater who knew staging and technical details. Bate ignores the likes of Leslie Howard when he writes that "no major actor has ever been attracted to Anti-Stratfor-dianism." Disputing those who say no one wrote about Shakespeare as a writer, he counters with tes-timony by Ben Jonson, verses by Francis Beaumont, and the marginal notation "W.S." in John Davies' *Microcosmos*. Bate considers Shakespeare "letters" the prefatory material at the beginning of *Venus and Adonis* and *The Rape of Lucrece*. Changes in the idea of Shakespeare and authorship in the 18th century inspired the questioning, the "Romantic idea of authorial genius" impelled the mystery. Bate identifies and traces the course of two authorship controversies: (1) between 1700 and 1740 when Alexander Pope and Lewis Theobald dueled over pristine texts and forgeries, and (2) the William Henry Ireland for-geries of the late 18th century that turned Shakespeare into a commodity but spurred historical inves-tigation. Nationalism and class began to play a role in the debate. Bate agrees with Harold Bloom that "Freud submitted to the Looney hypothesis as a way of taking revenge on William of Stratford for being the one person in the history of the world with a more powerful map of the human passions than his own." Contains Notes, Index and 20 illustrations, including the Droeschout engraving; *Henry Wrio-thesley*, third Earl of Southampton; *John Florio*, Max Beerbohm's *William Shakespeare, His Method of Work*; Laurence Olivier as Hamlet; and *John Keats* by Joseph Severn with Chandos portrait on wall.

"Funky Winkerbean." Cartoon. *Philadelphia Inquirer*, October 27, **1998**.

In frame two of three, student Matt says, "So they think that this Edward de Vere is *really* the guy who wrote Shakespeare's plays?" The teacher responds, "Some people do!" In frame three Matt says, "And here you were gonna get on my case for taking credit for someone else's work on my Shakespeare term paper!"

Woods, Michael. "Bard's Genius Is Not Universally Accepted." *Philadelphia Daily News*, November 20, **1998**. [Reprint *from Toledo Blade*.]

Woods cites Eric Altschuler's study, "Searching for Shakespeare in the Stars," which posits Oxford as the true playwright based on play references to celestial phenomena and astronomical discoveries prior to Oxford's death. Heavenly events post–1604 are not mentioned in the plays. "Altschuler identified a common thread in these and other references to physics and astronomy in Shakespeare's plays: None involved events that occurred after 1604. De Vere died in 1604 at age 54." Woods notes that Ward Elliott of Claremont McKenna College considers Altschuler's study "could-be evidence" and that Elliott's word usage patterns nixes Oxford as author.

Chua-Eoan, Howard. "The Bard's Beard?" *Time*, February 15, 1999, pp. 74–75.

Chua-Eoan reviews the "circumstantial but rather sexy evidence" for Oxford as Shakespeare what with newfound interest in the Bard. He notes that the film *Shakespeare in Love* (1998) bears resemblance to a 1941 novel *No Bed for Bacon* by Caryl Brahms and S.J. Simon. Summarized is the splash made by the discovery of Oxford's annotated Bible in the Folger Shakespeare Library. Quoted are Stratfordians like Jonathan Bate, who believes the Stratford man would have received a strong education at the Stratford Free School. University of California professor Alan H. Nelson is quoted that "The Earl of Oxford was perhaps the most egotistical and self-serving person of his day in England.... Many Elizabethan noblemen wrote and published." Yet Chua-Eoan concludes, "Of the man from Stratford we have only a sheaf of facts slimmer than a Gospel redacted by atheists. He is a man about whom it is impossible to write the literary biography as we know it today." Included is a chart comparing eight plays and the Sonnets to the lives of Oxford and the Stratford man.

"Contenders in the Shakespeare Shake-Out," *Time*, March 8, 1999, p. 16.

Readers of the February 15 issue (Howard Chua-Eoan's "The Bard's Beard?") pose Marlowe (Russell Mason, NYC) and Bacon as likely authors while Richard E. Kramer (NYC) brings up the mock trials that find for the Stratford man and concludes that "De Vere's claim just doesn't hold up under scrutiny."

Ignatius, David. "Honor the True Bard," *Washington Post*, March 21, 1999, p. B7. OP/ED Section.

As he awaits awards on Oscar night for the film *Shakespeare in Love*, Ignatius, formerly "part of the docile throng who dismissed the issue of who wrote Shakespeare's plays as useless pedantry," is convinced that Lord Oxford was the playwright. The *Harper's* special April issue devoted to the controversy turned him toward the nobleman. "This Stratfordian version celebrated the universality of genius — but it divorced the plays from any historical context." And, "This holy fool version of Shakespeare is a comfortable myth, but ultimately an unsatisfying one." Ignatius summarizes his friend Tom Bethell's sleuthing style of historical investigation, i.e., putting together "thousand-piece jigsaw puzzles. In the case of the Kennedy assassination, he says, investigators are overwhelmed by millions of pieces — most of them junk. But with Shakespeare, there are 50-odd pieces to arrange and rearrange."

"The Ghost of Shakespeare." *Harper's* (April 1999): 35–62.

One of the most significant periodical articles on the authorship question include, for Oxford, Tom Bethell, Daniel Wright, Mark K. Anderson, Joseph Sobran, Richard F. Whalen. On Shakespeare's side are Gail Kern Paster, Marjorie Garber, Irvin Matus, Harold Bloom, and Jonathan Bate. For Bethell, "The great problem with the conventional biography is that it conflates what we know about the man from Stratford (1564–1616) and the author of the works." Pointedly, "He must have been the only great writer to 'retire' so young and in the midst of such triumph." As for genius, "Genius does not convey knowledge. Yet the author was surely one of the best-educated men in England." Oxford's history is recounted. Wright traces authorship doubts to Reverend Dr. James Wilmot in the early 1780s. "For playwrights, the need to dissemble was especially urgent, particularly as the public theater — already much mistrusted and often suppressed by authorities for its alleged traffic in corrupt material — was exiled in Shakespeare's day to the darker districts of London (such as Southwark), where the theater's supposed viciousness could be restricted to people who commonly were regarded as derelicts and scoundrels." Anderson maintains that Oxford has become the leading candidate and posits his Geneva Bible as more proof, citing Roger Stritmatter's investigations. "One favorite rejoinder to the Oxfordian argument is that the author's identity doesn't really matter; only the works do. 'The play's the thing' has become the shibboleth of indifference-claiming doubters." And, "Nowadays, assertions that one can recover the author's perspective from his own dramatic self-portraits are often ridiculed as naïve or simplistic. Yet the converse — that Shake-speare somehow evaded the realities and particulars of his own life in creating his most enduring, profound, and nuanced characters — is absurd on its face." As for Oxford, "*everything* seems to have found its way into Shake-speare." With this in mind, Hamlet, Helena, Falstaff and Prospero are connected to Oxford's life. Sobran discusses the Sonnets, maintaining that they've baffled academe because they "clearly refer to real people and situations in the poet's life." And,

"As many scholars now acknowledge, the Sonnets to the youth are homosexual. No common poet would have dared make amorous advances to an earl, but another earl might." Sobran points out that only the pun on the name "Will" "supports the traditional identification of the poet as William." "But the context doesn't tell us whether this is his real name, a pen name, a nickname, an inside joke, or an alias his mistress knew him by." Whalen examines the silence at the time of the Stratford man's death, the Dugdale portrait and monument. He says Samuel Schoenbaum recognized the problem but concluded that Dugdale or the engraver got it wrong. As for the will, it is "totally devoid of anything literary; it is the will of a businessman." He notes that Oxford lived his last years on a country estate just outside the London suburb of Stratford. There's no mystery in the dedication of the First Folio to the earls of Pembroke and Montgomery because they financed publication. Montgomery was the husband of Susan Vere, Oxford's daughter. Pembroke, his brother, was Lord Chamberlain, responsible for play perform-ance and publication. How does one explain the cessation of "first editions" of Shakspere plays after Oxford died in 1604? Whalen notes that even some scholars aren't sure about play chronology and addresses whether the shipwreck in *The Tempest* refers to a 1609 Bermuda wreck or Sir Walter Raleigh's description of one in 1591. Whalen disputes Stratfordian claims that a "vast, implausible conspiracy" would have been necessary to cloak Oxford's role by arguing that "Shakespeare's true identity was prob-ably an open secret; there would have been little reason to 'reveal' Oxford as the author after his death." He says many questions need yet to be answered and that archives will certainly contain more infor-mation about Oxford, "but it is unlikely that much more will be found about the Stratford man."

In the Stratfordian camp, Gail Kern Paster says the author's life "remains strongly off-limits to most scholars." Yet for her, the authorship question "does have the merit of returning the scholarly mind, with sudden and surprising violence, to the real salience of biographical interpretation." But anti–Stratfordians are guilty of "a ferociously snobbish and ultimately anachronistic celebration of birthright privilege." And, "The anti–Stratfordian position is a summary judgment about the curse of provincial origins and barbarian rusticity, one that radically underestimates the classical rigors of Tudor public education and overestimates the scope of aristocratic learning. It is pernicious doctrine." Strat-fordians merely need prove "that such a man from Stratford could have written the plays, not that he did so." Paster believes the Stratford man "remained a provincial man of Stratford ... whose main pur-pose in undertaking the business of writing plays was personal and familial advancement in Stratford-upon-Avon." Marjorie Garber uses the film *Shakespeare in Love* as a stepping stone to discussion of what people want: the true author but also "How does great writing happen? Where does it come from? And why?" She investigates the institutional, psychological, and territorial "investments" of each side. As an "effect" and a "myth," Shakespeare's identity, for Garber, seems not especially important. "Were he more completely known, he would not be the Shakespeare we know." Irvin Matus calls the works "miracu-lous creations" and argues that we must not view Shakespeare's age "through the glass of one's own." Most Oxfordian arguments are countered. He says the first students of Shakespeare in the early eigh-teenth-century interpreted the plays as literature, not theater, yet "The primacy of the page over the stage is agreeable to the Oxfordians." [On this subject, see Diana Price, *Shakespeare's Unorthodox Biog-raphy*, 2001.] Matus identifies the crux, the "mystery" Oxfordians aim to solve: why did Shakespeare's contemporaries fail to extol his paramountcy? He contends that dating the plays is the most difficult problem for Oxfordians. He says there are "relatively few allusions that suggest the author of the plays was particularly well-read in the ancients." As for Oxford, he was "singularly self-obsessed" which mil-itates against the humanity in the plays. Harold Bloom labels Oxfordians "the sub-literary equivalent of the sub-religious Scientologists." He concentrates on the Sonnets. "These are 'his [Shakespeare] sug-ared sonnets among his private friends,' doubtless a socially varied group extending all the way from lowlife actors (and Lucy Negro!) to the petulant Southampton, patron and (perhaps) sometime lover." And, "The poetic achievement of the Sonnets has just enough of the playwright's uncanny power to show that we confront the same writer, but the awesome cognitive originality and psychological per-suasiveness of the major dramas are subdued in all but a few of the sequences." Jonathan Bate finds in the Stratford man's will "evidence of another life" than that of the small town burgher, e.g., a house in the London theater district of Blackfriars, money for memorial rings of fellow-actors John Hemynges, Richard Burbage and Henry Condell. Bate argues that the earliest monument in the Stratford church did show a man with pen and paper, not the woolsack. He traces the daunting task of publishing the First Folio. He argues that the sometimes use of a hyphen in the name Shake-Speare is "quite arbi-trary — a printer's vagary." He considers Elizabethan grammar schools "very good." The relationship between Shakespeare and Jonson is analyzed. Bate maintains that Leonard Digges's poem "To the Memorie of the deceased Authour Maister W. Shakespeare" and his own upbringing in the vicinity support the Stratford man as author. "In establishing the author's identity, what you need to look for are the quirky things." Bate concludes that "my money and my reputation will always be staked firmly on the friend of Jonson and Digges, 'our Will,' the Stratford lad. There is too little room for doubt."

Sidebars quote doubters Walt Whitman, Ralph Waldo Emerson, Henry James, Mark Twain, Charlie Chaplin, and Sigmund Freud. Appearing in the prestigious *Harper's*, this has been known to convince even academics that there is an authorship issue worth investigating.

"Merchants of Venom" [editorial]. *Philadelphia Inquirer*, July 24, **1999**, p. A10.

Taking the April 1999 *Harper's* forum and plethora of big-screen Shakespeare adaptations as cue, this lengthy editorial labels "bunk" the possibility that the Stratford man did not write Shakespeare. Incongruously, the editorial's author is himself venomous, describing the authorship question as "one of the nuttiest chestnuts in Western culture," "hoary," and its proponents "hermetically sealed" and "astigmatists." He contends that we know plenty about the Stratford man ("not a particularly mysterious figure as non-royal Renaissance men go."). The editorial will strike some as laughable in its so-called arguments, e.g., "And the man could write.... Will was Will. And only Will."

"Who Wrote the Works Attributed to Shakespeare?" *Philadelphia Inquirer*, July 31, **1999**, p. A16.

Readers of the July 24 "Merchants of Venom" respond. Warren Hope (Havertown, PA) wonders about the name-calling. "Apparently a visceral fear that those who doubt the traditional myth of William Shakspere (not Shakespeare) rising from illiteracy to eloquent genius with little schooling and less thought are fast establishing intellectual respectability." As for the statement that "Will was Will. And only Will. Be thankful for the miracle of his words," Hope says this "reflects the mind of someone who hates, literally cannot stand, rational, cool-headed, public examination of an intellectual issue." Michael Nolan (Malvern, PA) labels the quest for the true identity a "noble cause. We can gain a deeper understanding of these magnificent works, which have contributed so much to our culture, by knowing the man." Emanuel E. Garcia (Philadelphia) had his mind changed by Charlton Ogburn's *The Mysterious William Shakespeare*. "There the mountains of misinformation, guesswork, hyperbole and plain-old fiction about the lad from Stratford were meticulously exposed." Starr Whitney (Haverford, PA) indicates that her Haverford High School students in the Shakespeare elective class are introduced to the controversy via Warren Hope's book, *The Shakespeare Controversy*. "They digest the possibilities, discuss them, and eventually ask me what I think." She responds by calling attention to the emergence of genius, using William Faulkner and Emily Dickinson as examples. The class then read and acted Shakespeare's genius rather than "dwelling in possibility." When the class cut the cake on April 23, 1999, to celebrate Shakespeare's birthday, a student said, "This is really swallowing the party line." Whitney would rather "see it as celebrating the triumph of genius."

Oldenburg, Don. "Shakespeare in Trouble." *Washington Post*, January 24, **1999**, pp. F1, F4.

Oldenburg describes ex–CIA analyst Peter Dickson's research, especially his investigation of Henry Peacham's *The Compleat Gentleman*, in four editions from 1622 to 1661, none of which place Shakespeare amongst the greatest Elizabethan poets. Those who are mentioned in Peacham are Oxford, Lord Buckhurst, Lord Paget, Philip Sidney, Edward Dyer, Edmund Spenser, and Samuel Daniel. As for the controversy, "both sides run circles around the available facts, which are astonishingly few." The connection of Mary Sidney, Lady Pembroke with the house of Oxford is explored. Objections to Oxford's candidacy by Irvin Matus are presented. Summarized is a 1998 Shakespeare Mock Trial sponsored by the Lawyer's Committee for the Shakespeare Theatre of Washington in which Supreme Court Justice John Paul Stevens broke a tie vote to find for Oxford.

Reno, Jamie. "Shakespeare in Doubt." *Newsweek.com*, April 21, **1999**.

Summarized is Eric Lewin Altschuler's forthcoming paper suggesting that Oxford was the author based on frequent mention of astronomical events in Shakespeare and their omission after Oxford's death in 1604, e.g., Galileo's telescope. On Oxford as author, Altschuler says, "It's beyond a reasonable doubt."

"Letters: A Tale Told by Idiots." *Harper's,* July **1999**, 6–11.

Weighing in on "The Ghost of Shakespeare" in *Harper's,* July 1999 are folks from Quebec, Ridgewood, NJ, New York City, Norwalk, CT, Ontario, Mount Vernon, NY, Oak Park, IL, Santa Fe, NM, Johnson City, NY, Norwich, VT, Poolesville, MD, South Yorkshire, U.K., Kennett Square, PA, Utica, MA, Louisville, KY, Brooklyn, Ithaca, NY, and Vicksburg, MS. There is plenty of castigation and nastiness by the Stratfordian coterie. Chad Poove of Vicksburg considered "The Ghost of Shakespeare" of "parasitic material," and "Those of us who love his works love the bard unconditionally. That is, we don't give a damn who he was." Teymoor Nabili of New York City couldn't believe the "scion of the hermetically sealed world of sixteenth-century aristocratic England could absorb the voices and behavior of the working class, and then expertly render them into blank verse." Alexander Scala of Ontario wonders if Twain, Whitman, Emerson, and Dickens were concerned about the "contradiction between the grandeur of Shakespeare's plays and the mercenary preoccupations of the man." As they too were of middle class origin, perhaps their skepticism "derived precisely from uneasiness about their own status: were they artists, or were they merely entrepreneurs?" On the skeptical side, Mark Woodward of Norwich, VT, writes, "What forever cools me to the notion of a Stratford Shakespeare is his quiet early retirement. This squares with nothing we know about great artists.... Writers write until they die." Leonard Sax of Poolesville, MD, is "struck by the shrillness of the Stratfordians" and credits Oxfordians for presenting facts rather than insults.

Heller, Scott. "A Fresh Look at a Cryptic Drawing Puts 'Titus Andronicus' in a New Light." *Chronicle of Higher Education,* June 4, **1999**, pp. A19, A22.

Heller reviews the conclusions of June Schlueter, Lafayette College English professor and provost. Schlueter studied the 1595 Henricus (Henry) Peacham drawing of a scene taken till now to be one from *Titus Andronicus* and the only existent picture of an Elizabethan play and concludes that it is a depiction of a German play, *A Very Lamentable Tragedy of Titus Andronicus and the Haughty Empress,* performed by English actors on the Continent. The evidence satisfies George Washington University English professor Gail Kern Paster but not Jonathan Bate, English literature professor at the University of Liverpool, who argues too much significance has been attached to the Peacham drawing. The drawing is included in the article.

Heller, Scott. "In a Centuries-Old Debate, Shakespeare Doubters Point to New Evidence." *Chronicle of Higher Education,* June 4, **1999**, p. A22.

Heller describes the annual banquet of the Shakespeare Oxford Society in the basement of the Harvard Faculty Club. The mood is "festive" on the heels of the *Harper's* cover story that gave the Oxfordians' side a fair hearing. Aaron F. Tatum, society president, insurance executive and amateur scholar, believes the message might not reach professors but that the electronic media can help it reach students. Briefly profiled are Roger Stritmatter and Daniel L. Wright, the latter of whom organized the first Edward de Vere Studies Conference three years previously. Included is a portrait of de Vere and photos of Wright and Stritmatter. Although the orthodox label Oxfordians elitists, heretics like Wright consider the orthodox anti-democratic. "The Stratford myth tells us to be passive and acquiescent before the claims of tradition.... It tells students who themselves would be writers, 'You'll never be a great writer like Shakespeare. Shakespeare only accomplished what he did because he was a genius. And absent such genius, you have no hope for the future.' What blasphemy such rot is! And in any other discipline of the academy, could there be perpetuated such an anti-intellectual, anti-education myth as this that would not be derisively dismissed as an offense against the very raison d'etre of the educational enterprise?" Roger Stritmatter's investigation into De Vere's Geneva Bible and his plans to defend his dissertation the following year are reported. The history of authorship doubt is summarized. It is noted that Naseeb Shaheen, professor of English at the University of Memphis and author of *Biblical References in Shakespeare's Plays* (University of Delaware Press, 1999) will not support Stritmatter. Alan Nelson, professor of English at the University of California at Berkeley, formerly an agnostic on the question, upon researching de Vere for a biography, says, "the more I get to know him, the more impossible that this dreadful creature could have written the generous, self-effacing works of Shakespeare." Anti-Stratfordians are irked by literary studies that ignore an author's biography.

Heller, Scott. "The Illustrator of 'Titus Andronicus' Also Figures in Authorship Controversy." *Chronicle of Higher Education*, June 4, 1999, p. A19.

This is a short insert in Heller's "A Fresh Look..." article in the same issue. Heller calls attention to Henry Peacham's 1622 *The Compleat Gentleman* literary survey wherein Edward de Vere is placed at the head of the list of outstanding poets—and Shakespeare not at all. Heller cites Charlton Ogburn on the argument that as the tutor of the sons of a cousin of the Earl of Oxford, Peacham knew Oxford authored the plays and Sonnets.

Howe, Norma. *Blue Avenger Cracks the Code*. New York: HarperCollins Children's Books, 2000.

Blue Avenger, formerly David Schumacher, is a bright 16-year-old at San Pablo High in Oakland, CA. In Dr. Wood's junior English class, Blue hears about the distinct possibility that Edward de Vere is the true author of Shakespeare's plays and Sonnets. Dr. Wood offers Charlton Ogburn's *The Mysterious William Shakespeare* and *Alias Shakspeare* (Joseph Sobran) as guides to the issue. As "secret champion of the underdog, modest seeker of truth, fearless innovator of the unknown," Blue decides that his latest mission will be confirming this theory and giving Lord Oxford his due. This is merely the central thread in a skillful and smart young adult novel with numerous subplots and intriguing characters, even Monty Python's Michael Palin, appearing (briefly) incognito in Venice. In that city, Blue hopes to find manuscripts with Oxford's signature, perhaps notes for *Romeo and Juliet*. This novel suggests or even confirms that secondary school teachers are more open to the authorship issue than those in collegiate academe. In "Author's Final Note," Howe reveals that she was drawn to the subject after watching a 1996 rerun of "The Shakespeare Mystery" on the public TV series *Frontline*.

Kositsky, Lynne. *A Question of Will* (Out of This World Series). Montreal, Quebec, Canada: Roussan, 2000.

During a semester abroad, spunky Canadian adolescent Perin Willoughby is rather abruptly transported back into Elizabethan London, there to meet both Will Shakspere and Edward de Vere. Lodging with Shakspere, Perin finds him and his abode a mess. Sent to De Vere's residence, she returns with a parcel for Shakspere. Thought a boy, Perin gets to play Juliet and Rosalind at the Theatre (and performs a salsa dance after one performance). Interesting details abound, e.g., scribing and cutting up a manuscript for the various players. Ben Jonson, Queen Elizabeth, Richard Burbage and many others appear. Kositsky, a poet and former teacher of English and drama, does a fine job imagining Elizabethan stagecraft and Elizabeth's less than sanitary court, and cleverly inserts her heroine into amusing situations. In an Afterword, Kositsky succinctly explains the authorship question. Her sympathies lie with De Vere.

Satchell, Michael. "Hunting for Good Will: Will the Real Shakespeare Please Stand Up?" *U.S. News & World Report*, July 24/31, 2000, pp. 71–72.

Part of the magazine's "Mysteries of History" issue, Satchell summarizes the authorship question and addresses the circumstantial evidence for someone other than the man from Stratford, most notably Edward de Vere. De Vere's modern descendant, Charles Francis Topham de Vere Beauclerk, Earl of Burford, is quoted. Famous skeptics and other possible authors are identified. Satchell claims that "Despite more than two centuries of research beginning with [James] Wilmot, there isn't a scrap of documentation that Shakspere, the Warwickshire merchant, ever wrote anything in his life." He says the Stratfordians "cherish their orthodoxy but have scant evidence to bolster their case." Gail Kern Paster is quoted to the effect that it's only necessary that "Shakspeare could have written the plays and sonnets, not that he did." De Vere's background is traced. Satchell says "William Shake-speare" is likely a pseudonym. "The pen name was almost certainly for protection. Many of the plays deal with court intrigue and political corruption and contain thinly veiled satires and parodies of politicians and courtiers." Satchell lays significant weight on de Vere's Geneva Bible for the many highlighted passages that appear in Shakespeare. Professor Daniel Wright, director of the annual Edward de Vere Studies Conference at Concordia University in Oregon says, "These works are the mature achievements of a worldly and urbane litterateur who could not tell the world his name." Includes portrait of De Vere and smaller one of "Shakespeare."

Price, Diana. *Shakespeare's Unorthodox Biography: New Evidence of an Authorship Problem.*
Westport, CT: Greenwood Press, **2001**.

"It is highly unusual, if not unique, to find only posthumous literary evidence remaining for an individual who supposedly lived by his pen." There were many Shaksperes, so why pick the Stratford man? Shakspere was frequently absent from London so how important was he to the theater company? Examined is frequent use of the hyphenated name. "No other Elizabethan or Jacobean author appeared in hyphenated form with comparable frequency." Ben Jonson didn't write anything about Shakespeare or Shakspere during the latter's lifetime, "a surprising omission for an author who wrote explicitly about most of his literary colleagues." Price shows how Stratfordian biographers spin facts and allusions to make the author "good" and "gentle Will." With liquid assets and business acumen, Shakspere is touted as seminally important in behind-the-scenes activities. Why, then, is there no real, literary, paper trail? Many Elizabethan writers are buried in Westminster Abbey. Shakspere isn't one of them. Price argues that Shakspere's signatures are "*not* evidence of a literary career." For her, the plays were intended to be read as literature. [Contrast with Irvin Matus' view in "The Ghost of Shakespeare," *Harper's*, April 1999.] There is detailed analysis of Jonson's contradictory allusions in dedications and plays. "Jonson's two conceptions of Shakspere/Shakespeare are inherently incompatible, but his conflated testimony makes sense if he recognized Shakspere and Shakespeare as two different people. Jonson knew better than to comment explicitly in print on the professionally performed plays of an aristocrat." As for Michael Drayton, poet and Warwickshire man treated by the Stratford man's doctor son-in-law, "he concluded the poem [*Elegies upon Sundry Occasions*] by talking about aristocratic poets who had written for the stage, but whose names he would not reveal." If the Sonnets of 1609 are dedicated to "OVR.EVER-LIVING.POET.," he'd most certainly be dead. Price investigates the lack of Shakspere's literary bequests and absence of books in his home. She argues that statistically the lack of any literary personal records for Shakspere is "a virtual impossibility." No conspiracy was necessary. Think about the mores of the time. Aristocrats would not write for profit, nor would men of humble origin incriminate one who did write for the theater. Facts are needed despite genius, so where did Shakspere get those? Why were his daughters "functionally illiterate"? The author knew Italy and falconry and royal tennis and used his knowledge to create metaphor. The dating of *The Tempest* is examined. "Shakespeare" was an "entrepreneur and financier," not a dramatist. There are thirty-one illustrations, including applications for John Shakspere's coat of arms, letters with signatures of Elizabethan authors, Shakspere's signatures, the Holy Trinity Church monument, the Dugdale sketch, portrait engravings of various writers. Appendix: Chart of Literary Paper Trails, bibliography, index.

Rubinstein, William D. "Who Was Shakespeare?" *History Today* (August **2001**): 28–35.

This is an extensive analysis of the controversy by a Professor of Modern History at the University of Wales, Aberystwyth. "If Shakespeare was a perambulating actor during the 'lost years' he cannot also have readily been a law clerk, or acquired a working knowledge of court life or European politics." Rubinstein finds the story that Shakespeare accidentally held the horse of a gentlemen at a theatre door upon arriving in London more credible than most because it's from distant kinsman J.M. Smith in 1818. However, it contradicts the most popular current versions of Shakespeare's introduction to the capital. Rubinstein notes the author's coining of words and phrases and his massive vocabulary. As for his vast knowledge, "It is this incredible incongruity which has led so many to question whether the Stratford man wrote the plays attributed to him — not, as is often alleged by orthodox scholars, snobbery on the part of proponents of other writers, who allegedly insist that only a nobleman could have been England's national poet." How did a man from a community based on conformity develop an "unprecedented ability to empathize with his characters, among them foreigners, Catholics, Jews, Moors and women, bringing them to life"? The heresy is traced to Reverend James Wilmot. Discussed are Oxfordian claims via John Thomas Looney. Rubinstein believes the most convincing part of the Oxfordian claim lies in the Sonnets. Tenuous, even nonexistent, links between Shakespeare and the Earl of Southampton are mentioned. The issue of dating of the plays is considered. Rubinstein notes that balanced articles on the subject have been appearing in mainstream American magazines. He concludes that Oxford's candidacy is not the only legitimate one and shows how even now there are "possible links between Bacon and Shakespeare," including a wall-painting in a St. Albans inn of a hunt scene in Shakespeare's *Venus and Adonis*. Briefly considered are William Stanley, Roger Manners, Christopher Marlowe, and group candidacies. [See James, Brenda, and Rubinstein, William D., *The Truth Will*

Out, 2007, for a view of Sir John Neville as Shakespeare.] For Rubinstein, it is crucial that contemporaries took for granted that Shakespeare was the author. "Yet the thesis that someone else was the author, and the Stratford man a front or agent of some kind, is not at all absurd." Rubinstein suggests the authorship question may never be resolved and might even become more heated in future. There are many illustrations, including the Stratford monument, the First Folio title page, portraits of Lord Oxford and the Earl of Southampton, the painting *Queen Elizabeth Dancing with Robert Dudley*, Earl of Leicester, the mural in St. Albans' White Hart inn. Recommended for further reading are Schoenbaum, Honan, Michell, Price, and Sobran.

Sanford, John. "Panel Featuring Shakespeare Scholars Discusses Whether the Bard Was a Beard." *Stanford Report*, January 9, **2002**, 3 pp. Online at www.stanford.edu/dept/news/news/2002/january9/shakespearesidebar-19.html)

Briefly summarized are the origin and rise of the Oxfordian movement, traced to J. Thomas Looney. Parallels between Oxford's life and elements in the plays are cited. Described is the Pigott Theater panel discussion held by Stanford Continuing Studies in connection with the American Conservatory Theater (ACT) production of Amy Freed's *The Beard of Avon*. Panelists identified: Freed; Larry Friedlander, English professor; Marco Barricelli, artistic associate at ACT who plays Oxford in the play; Deborah Sussel, core-faculty member of ACT's Master of Fine Arts program; and Ron Bebholz, Professor Emeritus of English who considers doubters snobs. "Most people who take [the authorship question] seriously look down upon somebody who had nothing more than a grammar-school education in a small town in Warwickshire." Curiously, he thinks "it distracts from the study of the texts." Stratfordians are said to contend that Shakespeare's classical knowledge wasn't special.

Niederkorn, William S. "Theater; A Historic Whodunit: If Shakespeare Didn't, Who Did?" *New York Times*, February 10, **2002**.

Much ground is covered pursuant to a Smithsonian Institution "Who Wrote Shakespeare?" seminar. Niederkorn says the argument has gathered steam and identifies scholars and writers on all sides. He reviews the 1987 moot-court debate and reveals that Supreme Court Justices Stevens, Blackmun and Brennan, originally siding with the Stratfordians, changed or modified their views. Play dating is discussed. Parallels in Oxford's life with authorship are presented. "For many actors and playgoers, biographical references that connect Oxford to the Shakespeare canon open up a new dimension that is otherwise missing when the plays are thought of as the work of the inscrutable genius of Stratford." Actors Derek Jacobi and Michael York are identified as Oxfordians. Niederkorn notes that most of the establishment remains on the Stratford side and has champions in Irvin Leigh Matus, Alan H. Nelson, David Kathman, and Terry Ross. Most research funds still go to Stratfordians. Examined is Roger A. Stritmatter's dissertation on Oxford's Geneva Bible. Presumed — or forged or unknown — portraits of Shakespeare are reviewed. Australian filmmaker Michael Rubbo has produced *Much Ado About Something*, a film investigating Christopher Marlowe's candidature. Niederkorn reveals that Mark Rylance, the Globe Theater's artistic director, has gone from not caring to caring about the issue and favors Oxford.

"Shakespeare; A Megaconspiracy." *New York Times*, February 24, **2002**.

Colin Norman of Kingston, Ontario responds to William Niederkorn's February 10 article by maintaining that a conspiracy to hide the real author is unbelievable in "an intimate world in which players, playwrights and theater managers rubbed shoulders with one another constantly." He believes the First Folio seals the deal because Heminges and Condell took great pains to publish it "In order to keep the memory of so worthy a friend and fellow alive." Norman notes that Shakespeare's name appears on the title page beside his portrait and that there was a tribute by Ben Jonson, "who knew Shakespeare well."

"Shakespeare; American Grain." *New York Times*, February 24, **2002**.

Roger Stritmatter of Northampton, MA, commends William Niederkorn's February 10 article. "I especially enjoyed the description of Dr. Gail Kern Paster's lecture in Washington, in which she concluded her defense of the orthodox view with a rousing patriotic appeal to her audience." Stritmatter finds it ironic that skeptical opinion by the likes of Nathaniel Hawthorne, Herman Melville and Walt Whitman can be "appropriated for the purpose of wrapping bad history up in the American flag." He says Whitman was prescient in his authorship comment that "one of the wolfish earls" might be the true author.

"Shakespeare; Any Actor Knows." *New York Times*, February 24, **2002**.

Playwright Kevin O'Morrison of Edmonds, Washington replies to William Niederkorn's February 10 article with dismay. He is astounded that theater people would entertain the idea that someone else wrote Shakespeare. He says actors know who the author is as soon as they join a company producing one of the plays. He cites the First Folio dedication by Ben Jonson and says all alternate candidates are known to have written inferior work.

"Shakespeare; Avoiding Disgrace." *New York Times*, February 24, **2002**.

Christopher Adams of Langport, England responds to William Niederkorn's February 10 article "A Historic Whodunit: If Shakespeare Didn't, Who Did?" He argues that the surviving families related to De Vere were not prepared to identify him with actors and playwrights as they were still considered not much more than vagabonds, and the Sonnets could not be pinned on Oxford due to "overtones of homosexuality (a capital offense)." And, "If the world was happy to accept William Shakespeare as the author, why stir up a hornet's nest? And some of the world are still happy in their illusion, but not all, as the article made clear."

"Shakespeare; By Committee." *New York Times*, February 24, **2002**.

Stephen M.D. Day of Washington responds to William Niederkorn's February 10 article by promoting the group theory. He thinks Oxford was important but not sole author. He notes the first English dictionary was published in 1604 with 2,500 words whereas Shakespeare's plays and Sonnets contain 15,000 to 17,000 words. "Fascinating that a man with no documented education could achieve this."

"Shakespeare; Lack of Evidence." *New York Times*, February 24, **2002**.

Diana Price of Cleveland, OH (*Shakespeare's Unorthodox Biography*), responds to William Niederkorn's February 10 article. She agrees that the case for Oxford is circumstantial but that one must question the Stratford man because there is not a lick of "documentary evidence to support his alleged career as a professional writer. In the genre of Elizabethan literary biography, that deficiency is unique."

"Shakespeare; No Standards." *New York Times*, February 24, **2002**.

Responding to William Niederkorn's February 10 article, David Kathman of Chicago and Terry Ross of Baltimore decry "space devoted to the fringe belief" that the Earl of Oxford wrote the plays. "Rejecting the ample evidence for Shakespeare's authorship requires a wholesale abandonment of the most basic standards of historical evidence, which is why Oxfordians are not taken seriously by real scholars."

"Shakespeare; Read the Poetry." *New York Times*, February 24, **2002**.

Richard H. Low of Manhattan responds to William Niederkorn's February 10 article: "There is at least one fatal flaw in the old chestnut that Shakespeare was Edward de Vere. It can be found by reading de Vere's poetry."

"Shakespeare; Sins of Omission." *New York Times*, February 24, **2002**.

Replying to William Niederkorn's February 10 article, English teacher Lori Barnett of Upper Montclair, NJ, says she mostly agrees with the Stratfordian "the play's the thing" but identifies a problem with the orthodox view: in less than a classroom period students can learn all that exists about the man from Stratford. She considers it a disservice not to let students consider this "fascinating debate." Barnett says she was surprised by fellow academics who "wish to believe that genius is responsible for the conundrum, and not the fop, the rogue, the outcast of court accounts of Edward de Vere. I, too, want to believe that an uneducated man wrote the plays, Virginia. But what if the real author's story still cries out to be heard?"

"Shakespeare; The Door's Open." *New York Times*, February 24, **2002**.

In a response to William Niederkorn's February 10 article, Wayne Shore of San Antonio, TX, contends that authorship is an open question, that "no side has been able to close the sale" on authorship. He commends to interested parties Diana Price's *Shakespeare's Unorthodox Biography*.

"Shakespeare; With Enough Time." *New York Times*, February 24, **2002**.

Peter Farley of Freeport, NY, responds to William Niederkorn's February 10 article by suggesting that with time and energy he could posit Wilkie Collins as the author of Charles Dickens' novels.

Bottum, J. "A Ford, Not a Shakespeare." *The Weekly Standard*, July 15, **2002**, pp. 38–39.

Bottum reviews Donald Foster's recanting of his 1995 contention that the 1612 poem "A Funerall Elegye" was by the Stratford man, basing his conclusion on scholarship and computer analysis of the language using the Renaissance "Shaxicon" database. G.D. Monsarrat of the University of Burgundy and Brian Vickers, author of *Counterfeiting Shakespeare*, concluded that John Ford was the author. Bottum complains that Foster's discovery was unwisely heralded in public and despite owning up to the error, Foster made a name for himself. "Bardolators" are touched upon.

Goldman, David. "The Bard or Not the Bard: Who Wrote Shakespeare's Plays?" *Biography Magazine* (August **2002**): 23.

Goldman says that more and more authors and scholars doubt traditional authorship and summarizes key points in the debate. The standard alternate candidates are identified. Oxfordians are reported to bemoan a lack of funding for research that would upset the academic apple cart. A somewhat flippant conclusion: "So the debate rages on. To the doubters, there's a method to their madness, while the Stratfordians insist the whole thing is just a tale told by an idiot. But whatever the truth may be, in the end, the play's the thing." Included are the standard Shakespeare portrait plus Joseph Fiennes as Shakespeare and Rupert Everett as Marlowe in the 1998 film *Shakespeare in Love* and a traditional portrait of the Stratford man.

Nolen, Stephanie. *Shakespeare's Face: Unraveling the Legend and History of Shakespeare's Mysterious Portrait.* New York and London: Free Press, 2004, ©**2002**.

While a reporter for Toronto's *Globe and Mail*, Nolen heard about her mother's neighbor in Ottawa who purportedly possessed a portrait of William Shakespeare handed down through the generations of his family. Nolen inquired of museum curators and scholars about this "Sanders" portrait. John Sanders had been born in 1576 and in 1603 "prepared a sturdy oak panel and some bright oil paint and recorded the face of his colleague, William Shakespeare." Shakespearean scholars weigh in via chapters they write: "The God of Our Idolatry" (Stanley Wells), "Picturing Shakespeare in 1603" (Andrew Gurr), "Scenes from the Birth of a Myth and the Death of a Dramatist" (Jonathan Bate), "Looking the Part" (Marjorie Garber), "An Actor's Face?" (Robert Tittler), "A Painting with a Past" (Tarnya Cooper), "The Conundrum of the Label" (Alexandra F. Johnston, Arleane Ralph, Abigail Anne Young), and "The Man Who Will Not Meet Your Eyes" (Alexander Leggatt). Nolen admits there is a strong case against this portrait as Shakespeare because there is no documentation showing ownership before the mid–1800s. Nevertheless, dendrochronology confirms a date circa 1603. In what she admits is a "fanciful scenario," Nolen imagines Shakespeare sitting for the portrait. The center section of black and white and color plates features full and detailed views of the Sanders portrait, as well as portraits of Ben Jonson, Richard Burbage, John Fletcher and Southampton. Includes notes, "Useful Sources," and an index.

Anable, Stephen. "Loving Shakespeare." *Publishers Weekly*, May 19, **2003**, p. 51.

This is an interview with Sarah Smith, author of the novel *Chasing Shakespeares*. Smith studied Shakespeare with Robert Lowell. Anable and Smith discuss whether the novel is a true mystery. Smith equates it with Josephine Tey's *Daughter of Time*. She says she thinks she found a "good, Shakespearean-sounding poem probably written by the Earl of Oxford." She claims the book "has major factual revelations about the authorship controversy."

Nelson, Alan H. *Monstrous Adversary: The Life of Edward de Vere, 17th Earl of Oxford*. Liverpool, England: Liverpool University Press, **2003**.

The "warts and all" style of biography is carried to extremes in this disparaging analysis of the subject. A clue to Nelson's bias lies deep in the book when Lord Burghley, Oxford's father-in-law — and thorn in his side — is branded as "The greatest Englishman of his age." Nelson begins with a detailed review of the 17th Earl's forebears. He notes that Oxford was not the only young squire railing against the wardship of Lord Burghley but adds, "I myself assume that an individual born into power and privilege must sooner or later be held accountable for his own actions." Conjectures are many, e.g., one paragraph on page 59 contains "to be imagined," "perhaps," "probably," "We are free to imagine," and "may be." Nelson maintains that misspellings in Oxford's letters demonstrate that Oxford was not a Latin scholar or "even a fully competent practitioner of his native English." Yet later, "Orazio [Coquo, an Italian page in Oxford's home] testifies further that Oxford was a fluent speaker of both Italian and Latin." To Nelson, Oxford was a spendthrift, worse, a "thug" with bad friends. His troubled relationship with wife Anne Cecil is probed. (Oxford's treatment of his wife reminds one of Roman aristocrats who divorced and remarried in accordance with their political interests). Nelson buys wholesale anti-Oxfordian claims by such enemies as Henry Howard and Charles Arundel. There is detailed analysis of Oxford's known poetry where an "egocentric, cry-baby attitude" prevails. Some praise is forthcoming: Oxford's verse has received "unjustified praise and unwarranted denigration" but his poems are "astonishingly uneven." Nelson openly ignores the work of the Ogburns, *This Star of England* and *The Mysterious William Shakespeare*. He is kinder to J. Thomas Looney and Bernard M. Ward for they at least shed light on the earl and his milieu. Nelson does a service in having ferreted out and printed original documents, and his book is used by both Stratfordians and heretics for those elements. Contains notes, 14 figures (illustrations), four maps, an appendix citing Oxford's letters, memoranda and the libel documents involving Oxford, Henry Howard and Charles Arundel, bibliography, and index.

Rubbo, Michael. *Much Ado About Something*. Boston: WGBH Educational Foundation and the Helpful Eye, **2003**.

Film from Australian Broadcasting Corporation broadcast as part of the PBS *Frontline* series. Producer Rubbo explores the authorship question with a concentration on the case for Marlowe.

Stritmatter, Roger A. *The Marginalia of Edward de Vere's Geneva Bible: Providential Discovery, Literary Reasoning, and Historical Consequence: A Dissertation*. Northampton, MA: Oxenford Press, June **2003**. (Originally a dissertation submitted to University of Massachusetts Amherst, 2001.)

Analyzed is Edward de Vere's "Geneva Bible," now in possession of the Folger Shakespeare Library. Its provenance is traced. Stritmatter says the Bible is not a "smoking gun" but provides a revealing look into the annotator's creative life. The marginalia reveals more Biblical verses in Shakespeare than previously identified. De Vere was a true student of the Bible. "The annotations in the de Vere Bible are striking for their inclusion of relatively obscure Biblical books, for their attention to theological and editorial detail, and for their systematic approach to key points of doctrine such as sin, economics, and redemption." In one of the many appendices Stritmatter addresses criticisms, including supposed "randomness," by the likes of Bruce Smith, Alan Nelson, David Kathman, and Gerald Downs. Included is a biography of de Vere, the history of the authorship question, "figures" (120 illustrations), appendices and bibliography. To quibble with editing, contents page numbers don't correspond with the actual locations of appendices and figures.

Niederkorn, William S. "Seeing the Fingerprints of Other Hands in Shakespeare." *New York Times*, September 2, **2003**.

Niederkorn reviews the debate between scholars using ingenious methods to dissect a text for co-authorship clues and the "conservators," those "who ridicule those efforts and want no deviation from the idea that the entire canon was written by a solitary genius." He examines Brian Vickers' *Shakespeare, Co-Author*, which identifies work by other playwrights in *Titus Andronicus* (George Peele), *Timon of Athens* (Thomas Middleton), *Pericles* (George Wilkins), *Henry VIII* and *The Two Noble Kinsmen* (John Fletcher). Vickers complains that he's attacked by Stratfordians-conservators and praised by anti–Stratfordians "trying to use me as grist for their mill." Diana (*Shakespeare's Unorthodox Biography*) Price expresses disappointment that Vickers didn't explore the nature of the co-authorship arrangements. Reviewed is Vickers' *"Counterfeiting" Shakespeare* in which he demonstrated that the poem "Funeral Elegy" was not by Shakespeare and caused Donald W. Foster and Richard Abrams to retract that contention. It is reported that Gary Taylor, co-editor of the *Oxford Shakespeare*, plans to re-examine "Shall I Die" based on Vickers' research. Controversy surrounding authorship of *Sir Thomas More* is summarized.

Niederkorn, William S. "Theater; Where There's a Will, or Two, or Maybe Quite a Few." *New York Times*, November 16, **2003**.

Niederkorn traces Manhattanite Amy Freed's inspiration to create the satirical play, *The Beard of Avon*. She says neither Stratfordians nor anti–Stratfordians have denigrated the production. She started writing it as if De Vere was patently the author but "then the innocent rustic guy really started fighting back." Niederkorn wonders what coincidence put four playwrights in principal roles? In the end, Freed believes the authorship issue should be tackled. "I also think that it does matter about Shakespeare. It certainly matters to writers and artists and practitioners of language in any way. It's the high-water mark achievement of our language. Why would it not matter that we know how it came to be?"

"'The Beard of Avon,' No Evidence." *New York Times*, November 23, **2003**.

Earl L. Dachslager of The Woodlands, TX, responds to William Niederkorn's November 16 article, "Where There's a Will, or Two, or Maybe Quite a Few." Dachslager calls Amy Freed's play *The Beard of Avon* bad history, arguing that there is no evidence to support anyone but the Stratford man as author. He equates anti–Stratfordians with creationists and "intelligent design" advocates who disparage opponents' views but have no real proof of their own.

Bolt, Rodney. *History Play: The Lives and Afterlife of Christopher Marlowe*. New York: Bloomsbury Publishing, 2005, ©**2004**.

South African-born graduate of Cambridge and travel writer, Bolt explores Marlowe's life and the probability that he wrote the canon in this hybrid of biography and historical fiction. In endnotes, Bolt identifies his numerous "embellishments" and inventions, e.g., "I treat Devlin's theory as fact, and have turned the idea on a notch. I have used the evidence that he assembles — the people involved, the planted letter, the chain of events that leads to things going wrong — but have added another layer to Cecil's motive: that he would use his 'exposure' of the plot to further his political standing. Marlowe's role in the affair is conjecture." In the Afterword, Bolt explains further: "This book is, of course, an exercise of purest (or most impure) conjecture. But then so is the work of countless other writers of lives of Shakespeare and Marlowe.... The book may very well have been called *The Impossibility of Biography*." Beyond examining Marlowe's life, this is an exploration of the time, its theater, its literature, the "ongoing, collaborative effort" that was playwriting, the upheaval caused by the Copernican revolution — and spying, spying, spying. Bolt has Marlowe escape Thomas Walsingham's web by letting his companions murder a "ruffler," a vagabond dressed in his clothes. For Bolt, Marlowe's grief over the murder can be found in *Richard III* and *Measure for Measure*. Marlowe continued writing in Mantua and sending his work back for Shakespere ("flaming with aspiration") to use. Sometimes "Kit" Marlowe was irked. "Kit felt impotent, anonymous and ill understood. Later he would accuse Will of 'dulling my lines, doing me disgrace.'" (Sonnet 103). An "Interlude" explains how Shakespere entered playacting, i.e., when the Queen's Men visited Stratford in 1587 there were two empty spots. Shakespere joined up to make money and as an act of rebellion. Similarly, Marlowe's move into play writing "was a step of dissent, tinged by social ambition and spurred by financial need. So, too, with Will."

Includes notes, bibliography, index and Appendices (I: Passport issued to players led by Will Ireland written by the Lord Chamberlain, 14 June 1581 [Translated from the French]; II: Computer face-ageing technology applied to the Corpus Christi portrait of Christopher Marlowe; III: Transcription of letter from William Larkin to Dr. Norgate (Master of Bene's College 1573–97), circulated among the Fellows of Corpus Christi College by Dr Mara Kalnins and Dr Linne Mooney on 1 April 1996, after being found behind a skirting board during renovations in Old Court; IV: Cecil's Plot to Create a Fake Conspiracy Incriminating Lord Strange, 1593 [flow chart]; V: Lament of Arianna [musical notations with libretto]; VI: A full and perfit Catalogue of W–H his books both got in England and acquired and bought in forraine parts.

Dawkins, Peter. *The Shakespeare Enigma*. Dublin, Ireland: Polair, **2004**.

Founder of the Zoence Academy (to synthesize wisdom traditions) and The Francis Bacon Research Trust, Dawkins is also an architect, adviser to actors and directors, and creator of Wisdom of Shakespeare seminars and workshops. *The Shakespeare Enigma* is an extension of Dawkins' articles in the *New Ireland Review*. Ciphers are investigated. The Rosicrucian impact on the upper class is discussed. Dawkins is cautiously optimistic that the truth is in the wings. "There can be no doubt of the ultimate result of the present controversy.... Recent events seem to point to a speedier victory than could be hoped for a few years ago. Distinguished scholars ... have forced the matter to the front, so that it is now a world-wide discussion, and it seems to be one which the world in the long run will make up its mind to know the truth about." Includes introduction by Mark Rylance, notes, illustrations, bibliography, and index.

Niederkorn, William S. "To Be or Not to Be ... Shakespeare." *New York Times*, August 21, **2004**.

The Globe in London is promoting discussion of the authorship issue. Quoted is artistic director Mark Rylance, in process of investigating the major candidates and planning a research library of 600 books currently the collection of the Shakespearean Authorship Trust, successor to the Shakespearean Authorship Society and before that the Shakespeare Fellowship. Trustee John Silberrad is quoted on the open-mindedness of the trust. "We merely say that in the present state of knowledge, we certainly don't think that the Stratfordians have made out their case ... but we equally don't believe that the Oxfordians have either." Brian Vickers, author of *Shakespeare, Co-Author*, who though making a case for contributions to some Shakespeare plays by others, complains that Mark Rylance and actor Derek Jacobi aren't scholars. "No serious scholar I know of bothers with the doubters." Niederkorn notes that Jacobi and Rylance, John Gielgud and Orson Welles and other actors "approach Shakespeare from the inside, committing the plays to memory, getting under the skins of the characters, finding ways to make their parts work onstage — and perhaps discovering in that intimacy more things than are dreamt of in scholars' philosophy." Rylance views the scholars as "repressive of different ideas," and "Even if we all agreed that the man from Stratford wrote the plays, we'd all have very, very different images of who that man is."

Paul, Christopher. "A Monument Without a Tomb: The Mystery of Oxford's Death." *The Oxfordian* (October **2004**): 7–68.

Did Edward de Vere actually die on 24 June 1604 or did he pass away a few years later? Paul examines the evidence: letters, petitions, grants and manuscripts. And where exactly was Oxford buried? Why no elegies or epitaphs, no record of a funeral, no will? Paul is not attempting to show Oxford writing plays post–1604, rather to demonstrate how primary sources present their own set of problems and are to be taken literally at one's peril. Includes map, Oxford's signature, a page from a parish register at the Church of St. Augustine-at-Hackney, notes and bibliography.

Smith, Sarah. *Chasing Shakespeares*. Washington Square Press, **2004**.

While examining an Elizabethan manuscript collection at Northeastern, grad student Joe Roper unearths a letter supposedly from the Stratford man that if true reveals that he did not write the plays. Skeptical, Roper nevertheless lets bumptious scioness Posy Gould corral him into flying to London to determine the letter's provenance. In this excellent novel, Smith demonstrates a firm grasp of the authorship controversy. Roper stands in for the Stratfordians, Gould for those questioning authorship. Their actions and words will rile up both sides. Roper comes to believe that the man from Stratford lived in Oxford's London house known as Fisher's Folly and there obtained his literary background, reading and listening to the lord and his chums. "Books? Fisher's Folly must have had books. Court info? Legal training? Sports, tournaments, falcons, hunting? Poetry? Drama? Oxford had two companies of players, for shit's sake." And at Fisher's Folly, Shakespeare would have had a first-hand view of Bedlam Hospital: "Fools and Lears, melancholic Hamlets, guilty Lady Macbeths, suicidal Ophelias, right across the street." [Compare to Jennifer Lee Carrell, *Interred with Their Bones*, 2008.]

"Symposium: Who Wrote Shakespeare? An Evidentiary Puzzle." *Tennessee Law Review* (Fall 2004): 1–453.

Contents: "Mark Twain's Evidence: The Never-Ending Riverboat Debate" by Daniel J. Kornstein, "Connecting the Dots: The Catholic Question and the Shakespeare Authorship" by Peter W. Dickson, "Jumping O'er Times: The Importance of Lawyers and Judges in the Controversy over the Identity of Shakespeare, as Reflected in the Pages of the *New York Times*," by William S. Niederkorn, "Burden of Proof and Presumptions in the Shakespeare Authorship Debate" by William F. Causey, "Evidence for a Literary Biography" by Diana Price, "Stratford Si! Essex No! (An Open-and-Shut Case)" by Alan H. Nelson, "A Law Case in Verse: *Venus and Adonis* and the Authorship Question" by Roger Stritmatter, "The Seventeenth Earl of Oxford as Poet and Playwright" by Steven W. May, "Who Wrote Shakespeare? The Preponderance of Evidence" by Richard F. Whalen, "A Response to 'Burden of Proof and Presumptions in the Shakespeare Authorship Debate'" by Richard F. Whalen, "A Response to 'Oxford by the Numbers'" by Richard F. Whalen, "Reading the 1592 *Groatsworth* Attack on Shakespeare" by D. Allen Carroll, "The Shakespeare Authorship Debate and the Proper Standard of Proof," by Marion Buckley, "Using Circumstantial Evidence to Discover Shakespeare: The Importance of Good Legal Analysis" by Amy L. Gibson, and "Oxford by the Numbers: What Are the Odds that the Earl of Oxford Could Have Written Shakespeare's Poems and Plays" by Ward E.Y. Elliott and Robert J. Valenza. Except for the Whalen responses and Buckley's article, these were presented June 4–5, 2004, at the University of Tennessee College of Law. Kornstein's opening article commends the College for teaching the interrelated nature of law and literature. He delves into the nature of Shakespeare's legal expertise, using Twain's 1909 essay "Is Shakespeare Dead" and also his 1894 novel *Pudd'nhead Wilson*. Dickson explores the debate within Stratfordian ranks over Shakespeare's religious affiliation. Niederkorn surveys the authorship debate between legal experts covered *in The New York Times*, 1866 to 2002. Causey urges creation of a formal mechanism to further debate. Price argues that if Shakespeare was the author of the plays he was by definition a professional writer, so why no literary paper trail? Nelson says there is enough historical evidence to support the Stratford man as author while conspiracy theorists attack and destroy evidence. Stritmatter analyzes *Venus and Adonis* which if read in a political and cultural context provides justification for concealing the author's true identity. May finds a gulf between the styles of Shakespeare and Oxford. Whalen's "Who Wrote Shakespeare?" surveys evidence for Oxford and against the Stratford man. Carroll argues that to accept a vast conspiracy "puzzles the intellect and numbs the imagination." Buckley believes the authorship question provides ground for critical thinking and proposes a debate in which the Stratfordians not rest on the status quo and the heretics not be bound to prove a negative. Gibson, a student, introduces newcomers to the controversy's basics. Supporting their case with 10 appendices of baseline data, Elliott and Valenza discuss their internal-evidence stylometric tests they say fail to connect Oxford to the canon.

Anderson, Mark Kendall. *"Shake-Speare" by Another Name: The Life of Edward de Vere, Earl of Oxford, the Man Who Was Shakespeare*. Foreword by Sir Derek Jacobi. New York: Gotham (Penguin), **2005**.

A modern biography of Oxford extrapolates and points to de Vere's interest in Plato, Ovid and Castiglione. "Between the ideals de Vere set forth in the Latin translation of *Castiglione* (1572) and the English translation of *Cardano* (1573), the earl had laid out his recipe for literary mischief.... Treat the court as if it were a theater and the theater as if it were a court." Anderson details so far as possible Oxford's sojourns in Venice, Greece, Sicily and Italy but much is conjecture with plenty of "would have," "may have," "must have found," "tempting theory," "probably." Regarding the plays and masques performed for Queen Elizabeth, de Vere wrote or rewrote some of these for the public stage in the 1590s and early 1600s. "A year in Italy had transformed de Vere, twenty-six-year old chronic pain in the ass, into a chronic pain in the ass with an astonishing capacity for court comedy." (Later in life a "Contradictory amalgam of misanthrope and humanist.") There are well-founded arguments that plays were propagandistic. In 1586 Elizabeth gave Oxford one thousand pounds in annual salary. Why? "The quid pro quos — whether stated or not — lurking behind de Vere's annuity remain one of the more vexing unsolved problems of his biography. Was Her Majesty intentionally buying him the time needed to develop what would become the Shake-speare history plays? Or was she subsidizing other related activities, such as his supervising a workshop of playwrights (e.g., Munday and Lyly) who were themselves generating the Queen's Men's playscripts? Or was the queen just being exceptionally, inexplicably, generous?" (An Anderson note mentions a letter to Robert Cecil from Oxford's second wife Elizabeth Trentham saying Oxford used his money to maintain his estates.) Anderson ties many a Shakespearean heroine (Ophelia, Hero, Hermione, Desdemona) to Oxford's long-suffering wife, Anne Cecil. *Love's Labor's Lost* is a doorway into Oxford's public and literary life. "There is no documentary record of de Vere and Shakspere ever meeting." There is analysis of the Sonnets, of *Venus and Adonis*. Use Occam's Razor, i.e., simplicity is the best answer. To Anderson, examination of *Willobie His Avisa* proves the London literati knew de Vere's identify as "W.S." There are speculations on the Southampton relationship, Shakspere's role, and Jonson's poet-ape. For Anderson, the isle in *The Tempest* is not Bermuda or some other esoteric venue, rather England itself. The play is "a fantastical and even dangerous satire." After de Vere's death in 1604 and until 1623 there were no new Shakespeare plays. "The Shakespeare canon contains no unambiguous references to literary sources or events after 1604." Nor were new scientific discoveries referred to after 1604. Elizabethan nostalgia reared its head quickly. In 1615 the "prolific scribbler" Richard Brathwait blew Shakespeare's cover in a short piece Anderson says tells us some material from the Elizabethan theater was written "Prettily shadow'd in a borrowed name." The Stratford church epitaph is a red herring, writes Anderson. Susan de Vere found books for Anthony Munday. The First Folio's publishers tread lightly, using "Shakespeare" so as not to offend King James who was negotiating a marriage alliance with Spain.

In summary, if de Vere is Shakespeare, (1) the plays and poems become more integrated, (2) boundaries between comedy, history and tragedy overlap, (3) Shake-speare becomes a "venturesome cosmopolitan and a true citizen of western Renaissance Europe," (4) the artistic arc goes from "preening young champion to a betrayed and jealous middle-aged skeptic to a resigned and bitter old man," and (5) his "development as a writer traced his development as a human being." De Vere's writing had become a cathartic exercise. Anderson provides a comprehensive, in-print biography — and antidote to Alan Nelson's *Monstrous Adversary* (2003). Includes maps of England, London and Europe, Timeline, Dramatis Personae, notes, "Frequently Cited Sources," index. Appendices: Edward De Vere's Geneva Bible and Shake-speare, The Shake-speare Apocrypha, "The 1604 Question," The Ashbourne Portrait of Shake-speare.

Broach, Elise. *Shakespeare's Secret*. New York: Square Fish/Henry Holt Books for Young Readers, **2005**.

In this engaging young adult novel, 12-year-old Hero and her 14-year-old sister Beatrice, named by their Shakespearean scholar father for the characters in *Much Ado About Nothing*, find themselves in a new home in Maryland. Their dad has accepted a position at the Maxwell (read D.C.'s Folger Shakespeare Library). The neighbor lady produces for Hero a necklace she believes belonged to Anne Boleyn. The woman who used to live in Hero's house was a Vere, a descendant of Elizabethan England's Edward de Vere. Hero's father summarizes the case for De Vere. Author and historian Broach is sympathetic to De Vere's case but in an "Author's Note" says she's not yet ready to topple the Stratford man from his pedestal.

Cavanaugh, Rebecca. "West Chester Library Examines Collections: Shakespeare's Works to be Appraised." *Daily Local News* [West Chester, PA], July 5, **2005**, pp. A1, A5.

"'There's a notion that the author sends a manuscript to the publisher and it comes out exactly as is,' Richard Swain said. 'But forget it with 17th-centry printers. They did it any way they wanted. Anything you could think of could happen and lots of things you couldn't think of.'"

Niederkorn, William S. "The Shakespeare Code, and Other Fanciful Ideas from the Traditional Camp." *New York Times*, August 30, **2005**.

Playwright, composer and an editor in the *New York Times* culture department, Niederkorn remarks on new biographies, including James Shapiro's *1599: A Year in the Life of William Shakespeare*, Stephen Greenblatt's *Will in the World*, and Claire Asquith's *Shadowplay: The Hidden Beliefs and Coded Politics of William Shakespeare*. "All these books are provocative and have generally been well received. But in the end their reliance on coded writing or shaky circumstantial evidence raises doubts." Niederkorn says academics consider the possibility that anyone other than the Stratford man was responsible for the plays mere "baloney" (Dominic Dromgoole, Globe Theatre's new artistic director) and vent fire-and-brimstone-like against heretics (Brian Vickers). Niederkorn wonders why the Stratford man let his plays languish and return nothing for his heirs. And why did descendants leave no word of their fore-bear's literary excellence. Reviewed is Mark Anderson's *Shakespeare by Another Name: The Life of Edward de Vere, Earl of Oxford, the Man Who Was Shakespeare*. It seems that even the dicey connections between Oxford and Shakespeare are no dicier than Greenblatt's between Shakespeare and the Warwickshire Catholic teacher Shakeshafte. Niederkorn points out that Anderson takes at face value attribution of *Sir Thomas More* to Oxford. He wonders what would happen if authorship studies became part of the Shakespeare curriculum?

Rosenbaum, Ron. "The Shakespeare Code: Is Times Guy Kind of Bard Creationist?" *New York Observer*, September 18, **2005**.

Rosenbaum takes rather strident issue with *New York Times* culture critic William Niederkorn's series of articles on the authorship question. He says Niederkorn "has drawn criticism from an array of Shakespeare scholars," bemoans a lessening of emphasis on Shakespeare in the classroom, and maintains that including authorship would further erode the curriculum. Why not spend time on controversies not being investigated, e.g., *King Lear* variations, *Hamlet*'s three texts? Summarized is a "skirmish" between Niederkorn and Stephen Greenblatt over the *Funeral Elegy*. For Rosenbaum it's more important to read and reread the plays.

Talcott, Christina. "Will the Real 'Beard of Avon' Please Stand Up?" *Washington Post*, October 21, **2005**, p. WE26.

Summarized is Amy Freed's 2001 play, *The Beard of Avon*, a comedy in which the bumpkin but engagingly human fellow from Stratford helps De Vere put humanity into his plays. The Rorschach Theatre's co-artistic director Randy Baker believes stage achievements then and now are "inspired collaborations" between writer(s), actors, and designers.

Marks, Peter. "Rorschach's 'Beard' Playfully Tweaks the Bard." *Washington Post*, October 25, **2005**, p. C01.

Marks reviews Amy Freed's *The Beard of Avon*, ranking it "charming, cheeky" but a bit long-winded. Will Shakspere was a front man for the nobles. Queen Elizabeth authored *The Taming of the Shrew*. Marks says the play "is chockablock with wacky fractures of conventional Elizabethan wisdom — its anachronistic sensibility owes a thing or two to the Oscar-winning film comedy *Shakespeare in Love*," combining academic satire with slapstick. "You'd need a Shakespearean search engine at the ready to catch all the references to the canon, not to mention the cockeyed digs that Freed slips in at the expense of Dickens and Rodgers and Hammerstein." The play is about the love of the stage with Will Shakspere "the purest expression of that love. Unlearned and consigned to a rube's anonymity, he is smitten after Anne takes him to an awful local production in Stratford." The twist: actor Eric Singdahlson's De Vere is a master of plot with simple Will, a quasi-savant, providing the play's common touch.

Fields, Bertram. *Players: The Shakespeare Mystery*. New York: Harper Perennial/Regan Books, **2005**.

A famous entertainment industry attorney, Fields assumes nothing. After summarizing the Elizabethan era, he discusses "Shaksper's Life" and "The Playwright's Life." Coming under scrutiny are the Sonnets, the will, the monument, the First Folio, sexual orientation, religious outlook, portraits. In Part III Fields devotes chapters to Oxford, Marlowe, Bacon, William Stanley, Roger Manners, Queen Elizabeth and group theories. He finds John Michell's analysis of the controversy good but disputes

Michell's and Celestin Demblon's assertion that Rosencrantz and Guildenstern are mentioned in Padua University records, which would give some credence to Rutland's candidacy. Curiously, while Fields mentions Stephen Greenblatt, Samuel Schoenbaum, Charlton Ogburn, Joseph Sobran, John Michell and others and has an index, he doesn't provide the titles of their works or include a bibliography. Regarding the genius of Shakespeare, Fields writes, "The cry of 'genius' seems an unpersuasive response, as does the claim that all of this is the product of a fine grammar school education, plus diligent research." All in all, this is an excellent introduction to the question that will have those new to it shaking their heads. However, the summing up chapter strains credulity. In it Fields uses the standard — and understandable caveats — "Perhaps" and "someone, somehow" to create a scenario in which Oxford wrote most of the plays, paid homage to Marlowe and others by quoting from their works, and employed the Stratford man as his front. This may be true or entirely false.

McCrea, Scott. *The Case for Shakespeare: The End of the Authorship Question.* Westport, CT and London: Praeger/Greenwood Publishing Group, **2005.**

For McCrea, anti–Stratfordians are subjective, anti-historical, and their case a con game, but they are neither cranks nor fools and their research has some value. (Sonnet 138 is the best anti–Stratfordian argument in its mention of age but a reference to lameness is only metaphorical.) McCrea's aim is to "bring them to their senses," while simultaneously vindicating some of their doubts. McCrea himself speculates mightily and can be contradictory, e.g., "we can be certain William and his brothers learned to read and write at the attached petty school." On the next page, "If Shakespeare did attend the petty school and then the grammar school." And later, "As huge as such an assumption is." Regarding Shakespeare's problems with the authorities over malt speculation, "Whoever was looking after his household in Stratford was the real malt speculator." John Shakspere was more literate than we think and son William felt superior and privileged, soon "associating with citizens of substance." Disregarding Georges Connes admonition not to build on the quicksand that is Ben Jonson, McCrea seems to swallow Jonson whole. To McCrea the only oddities in Shakespeare's life are the six signatures (and knowledge of French). "Either he didn't sign his name very often and thus his autograph never developed a consistent pattern, or he was a man so creative he never let it become static, or both." And, "Their oddness might just as easily reveal their maker's teeming imagination." As for Italian, Shakespeare might have read it in the original or in old plays based on Italian sources. He might have seen manuscripts in translation. Maybe he heard about them from someone who'd read them. McCrea disputes Joseph Sobran and others who contend canals connected Verona and Milan. While McCrea believes Shakespeare's familiarity with the law was genuine, he contradicts Mark Twain's view that Shakespeare never made mistakes in his legalese. Other writers used more legal terms than Shakespeare. Lest we forget, Shakespeare's father engaged in litigation. McCrea is adamant that we can't extract personal biography from the plays. He cites those who say Shakespeare didn't know much about aristocratic life, such as Muriel S. Clare Bryne. As for falconry, a man of property like John Shakespeare is likely to have engaged in it. As for Burghley equaling Polonius, no court inside knowledge was necessary to skewer Burghley. "Possibly, the Author learned things about Burghley from someone who was indeed a courtier." The Author relied on Holinshed for his history. The Author was not a courtier, lawyer, scholar, or soldier. "He could have been William Shakespeare. And because he could have been, and because the external evidence — the Folio epistles, the Stratford monument, the posthumous references — all tell us he *was*, we are obligated, as historians, to conclude this was the case." Stratford citizens' names appear in some plays. The Chandos portrait is "almost certainly an authentic likeness." So, "at least we know what he looked like."

Part II examines alternate claims, beginning with a brief rundown on Rutland, followed by longer investigation of Bacon, Lord Stanley ("a wonder Derby is not the favorite Authorship claimant."), Marlowe (staged murder superfluous because no extradition; style not Shakespeare's), and Group Theories (would that work like a quilting bee?). Beginning with Chapter 10: The Accused, Oxford's biography and candidacy are investigated. McCrea disputes Oxford's learning, i.e., the Author used "Bishops" Bible in early plays as often as the Geneva Bible; Oxford was not a good historian. The only event in Oxford's life with a legitimate if indirect connection to the plays is the 1573 incident when his former employees told Lord Burghley they feared for their lives after an ambush by three of Oxford's other men. A similar scene is in *Henry IV Part One.* Some plays can only be dated post–1604 [*King Lear*] due to astronomical occurrences. [Contrast with Eric L. Altschuler's "Searching for Shakespeare in the Stars,"

Physicsworld.com, October 23, 1998.] Although there had been Bermuda shipwrecks for years, "Without a doubt, the Author read Strachey. So, without a doubt, de Vere cannot be the Author." (The Bermuda shipwreck in question was found in Strachey's *True Reportory of the Wrack and Redemption of Sir Thomas Gates, Knight* [written 1610, published 1625; in manuscript shared by members of the Virginia Company].) Applying Ockham's Razor, McCrea says the Oxford theory is "riddled with wild, improbable assumptions." McCrea believes the Authorship Question is rooted in the question of education and also the nature of greatness. Yet Shakespeare wasn't superhuman, he was an "upper-middle-class actor-playwright who never learned to empathize completely with the servant classes beneath him." In conclusion, "Anti-Stratfordianism ... exposes how little we really know about the Elizabethan period,... Oxfordians know even less." Sigmund Freud, Orson Welles and John Gielgud can doubt Shakespeare's authorship because they lack knowledge, not intelligence. McCrea is disturbed that some Supreme Court Justices favor Oxford and equates this with conspiracy theories. "The idea that one must be born an earl to empathize with earls is a misunderstanding of the power of human imagination. It's a child's view of reality, in which one can gain knowledge only through experience. Oxfordians look through the wrong end of the telescope and should stop inviting others to do the same." Includes notes, bibliography, and index.

Jordan, Mary. "Shakespeare's Likeliest Likeness, Forsooth." *Washington Post Foreign Service*, March 4, **2006**, p. C01.

Jordan describes the Chandos portrait in the "Searching for Shakespeare" exhibit at London's National Portrait Gallery, which will travel to the Yale Center for British Art in New Haven, CT and open June 23, 2006. Tarnya Cooper, the gallery's 16th-century curator, says people connect with the writer who offered "such an enormous range of human emotions." Summarized are the x-rays, ultraviolet exams and other methods used on various likenesses thought to be Shakespeare. Although it might not be Shakespeare, the Chandos portrait was, according to Cooper, "certainly painted during Shakespeare's era and there is much evidence to support that it is, in fact, a rendering of Shakespeare." Visitors' opinions are provided. Cooper thinks the man in the portrait looks "slightly bohemian" and "someone you could have an interesting conversation with." Chairman of the Shakespeare Birthplace Trust Stanley Wells opines that Shakespeare was much interested in what people looked like. ("The exhibit points out that other portraits of men with earrings around the same period included maritime adventurers, courtiers and 'men of creative ambition.'")

Barton, Anne. "The One and Only." *New York Times Review of Books*, May 11, **2006**.

Barton reviews five recent Shakespeare books to sensibly examine the never-ending supply that "seem alarmingly on the increase." The books are James Shapiro's *A Year in the Life of William Shakespeare: 1599*, Richard Wilson's *Secret Shakespeare: Studies in Theatre, Religion and Resistance*, Clare Asquith's *Shadowplay: The Hidden Beliefs and Coded Politics of William Shakespeare*, Peter Ackroyd's *Shakespeare: The Biography*, and David Ellis' *That Man Shakespeare: Icon of Modern Culture*. Barton draws on various literary lights in her investigation, including Matthew Arnold, who suggested that biographers "might as well interrogate Mont Blanc about its personal history and opinions" as seek the essence of Shakespeare's life. She notes that anti–Stratfordians also engage in "unremitting efforts" to identify an aristocrat as the "craftily hidden author." While noting that biographers say more is known about Shakespeare than other contemporary literary figures save Ben Jonson, Barton points out how very much we know about Jonson and delves into the reactions to the deaths of both Jonson's and Shakespeare's first-born sons. Shakespeare biographers "scrabble about desperately among the plays for passages that might somehow reflect his presumable paternal grief—a task made more difficult by uncertainties about their chronology." Not the second-best bed but the possibility that Shakespeare was Catholic is, according to Barton, the main subject of contemporary biographical dispute. Barton quotes Shapiro on the fluidity, the "layered nature of what Elizabethans, from the queen on down, actually believed." Wilson and Asquith use "misty allegorical readings." Barton says Asquith's allegories will not sway most readers and that her book contains inaccuracies and misunderstandings. She finds that Ackroyd's biography "also trespasses upon the terrain of fiction." And, "He is also given to totally unfounded pronouncements about Shakespeare's creative processes." Barton reserves most of her praise for Shapiro, finding him a tonic, his book containing much to illuminate the plays and their author. As for Ellis, he is "shrewd and perceptive" in his analysis of methods biographers use sans new information.

Barton calls for a moratorium on Shakespeare biographies but that there might be a book on why they sell — and "a proper investigation of the psychology uniting all those continued attempts to demonstrate that he [Shakespeare] was only the front man for the true author, whether Marlowe, Edward de Vere, Bacon, Sir Henry Neville, or Mary Sidney." Barton concludes with reference to Borges' short story "Everything and Nothing," in which Shakespeare is haunted by never possessing any character or personality. [See Borges, Jorge Luis. *Labyrinths: Selected Stories and Other Writings*. Edited by Donald A. Yates and James E. Irby. New York: New Directions, 2007, ©1962.] Endnotes cite Brenda James and William D. Rubinstein's *The Truth Will Out: Unmasking the Real Shakespeare*, Robin P. Williams' *Sweet Swan of Avon: Did a Woman Write Shakespeare?*, William F. and Elizabeth S. Friedman's *The Shakespearean Ciphers Examined*, the Peter France and William St. Clair-edited *Mapping Lives: The Uses of Biography*, and Jorge Luis Borges' *Collected Fictions*. Barton also references Samuel Schoenbaum's *Shakespeare's Lives*, "that witty and exhaustive account of all the biographical attempts from the very beginning."

Cooper, Tarnya. *Searching for Shakespeare*. With essays by Marcia Pointon, James Shapiro, and Stanley Wells. New Haven, CT: Yale University Press, **2006**.

This beautifully illustrated tome might be construed as a coffee table book. Among the plates are the Chandos portrait and Janssen effigy, Shakespeare's will, a draft of John Shakespeare's grant of arms, and portraits of Edward de Vere ("Despite continued interest in this theory, few established scholars now consider him as a likely candidate."), Mary Sidney, and Francis Bacon ("but most modern Shakespeare scholarship dismisses this view" [as the true Bard]). Select Bibliography and Index.

Farina, William. *De Vere as Shakespeare: An Oxfordian Reading of the Canon*. Foreword by Felicia Hardison Londre. Jefferson, NC, and London: McFarland and Company, **2006**.

Amateur Shakespearean enthusiast Farina tackles the authorship question by examining the comedies and romances, histories, tragedies and poems attributed to Shakespeare and tying them to events in Oxford's life. For Farina, literary biography is hardly irrelevant. Imagine studying modern playwrights such as Tennessee Williams or Eugene O'Neill without considering those writers' backgrounds. Farina points out that "conspiracies," even literary ones, have continued. For instance, blacklisted Hollywood writer Dalton Trumbo penned scripts under other names. Although he doesn't buy the interpretation, Farina notes his reliance on Alan Nelson's fact-filled life of Oxford, *Monstrous Adversary* (2003). He is more impressed with Bernard Ward's 1928 biography, *The Seventeenth Earl of Oxford (1550–1604)*. In his Conclusion, Farina touches on "genius," the probable necessity for a pseudonym or beard due to the propagandistic nature of the plays, and group theories. Although open to whatever research unearths, Farina is optimistic that skepticism about Stratfordian authorship and research will increase despite "orthodox academics and other traditionalists who fiercely need a Bard that is a sympathetic voice of the common man and an uplifting role model for aspiring mediocrity everywhere." Includes notes, bibliography, and index.

James, Brenda, and Rubinstein, William D. *The Truth Will Out: Unmasking the Real Shakespeare*. Foreword by Mark Rylance. New York and London: Harper Perennial, 2007, ©**2006**. First published in Great Britain in 2005.

James is an English literature lecturer, Rubinstein professor of modern history at the University College of Wales, Aberystwyth. Sir Henry Neville is their candidate. Mark Rylance, actor and Artistic Director Shakespeare's Globe 1996–2005 and Chairman of the Shakespearean Authorship Trust, provides a foreword in which he hails the book as "pioneering." The authors admit to using suppositions, including "shrewd guesses." They insist that "Shakespeare" had a huge library, was a "deeply learned and well-educated linguist." They dispute publisher (and Stratford native) Richard Field's role as purveyor of weighty tomes into the Stratford man's hands. They make the convincing case against the Stratford man in that there are no letters by or to him. Taking on Shakespearean biographers, they wonder how the latter can dismiss literary biography but use the death of Shakespeare's son Hamnett to comment on the Bard's evolution? Diana Price (*Shakespeare's Unorthodox Biography*) is frequently cited. James and Rubinstein contend that there are so far three pieces of documentary evidence in favor of Neville as the Bard: (1) the Tower Notebook of 1602 with notes and annotations made during Neville's sojourn (near

Southampton) in the Tower, (2), Halle's *Chronicles* with marginal notations, and (3) the Northumberland manuscript, originally tied to Francis Bacon. (These are more fully explored in Chapter 11: Documentary Evidence: Analyses and Shakespearean Parallels.) Neville's biography includes travel on the Continent between 1578 and 1582 with Merton College tutor, Henry Savile. He gleaned Continental learning, in particular that of Hungarian humanist Andreas Dudith and especially astronomy. James and Rubinstein attempt to answer four questions about Neville "becoming" Shakespeare: (1) why write? (2) when did writing begin? (3) why use a pseudonym? and (4) why Shakespeare? The traditional chronology of the plays is accepted — possibly because that fits Neville nicely (1562–1615). Neville was distantly related to the Stratford man, thus the latter was an "ideal factotum." Oxford's candidacy is rejected on such grounds as he died too young (1604) and the supposedly 1609 Bermuda shipwreck reference in *The Tempest*. The authors cite Alan Nelson's hardly unbiased *Monstrous Adversary* for some Oxford commentary. The authors are premature: "He [Neville] died without knowing, or suspecting, that he would eventually be regarded as the greatest Englishman of the past thousand years." They dismiss other candidates yet say, "In complete contrast, with Sir Henry Neville there is apparently direct evidence and a biography which matches the chronology and evolution of Shakespeare's works at every point." This Harper Perennial Edition (2007) includes an Afterword in which Brenda James summarizes reaction to the book's first appearance in 2005 ("lack of *informed* academic response"). She says that many readers were surprised and delighted to find Neville "the first credible candidate that they had ever heard of." She proceeds to examine Shakespeare as a fantasy and "tabula rasa on which every individual can project an image that best pleases him or her." There are intriguing comments about Shakespeare of Stratford becoming written in stone post–World War II and criticism of vested interests, especially academics who don't leave their ivory towers to armchairs to conduct real research. Anti-Stratfordians are lauded for bringing light to Shakespeare's times. Because Neville was distantly related to Shakespeare and more closely to Francis Bacon, he seems most appropriate to reconcile factions. James discusses meetings and debates with Stratfordians Stanley Wells and Jonathan Bate. In a prescient moment, she writes, "My continuing research has discovered a hint that the 'secret' of Sir Henry's authorship may have traveled with some of the earlier settlers in America." Shades of Jennifer Lee Carrell's novel *Interred with Their Bones* (2008, ©2007)! Includes illustrations, Neville family trees, notes, index. Appendices: (1) Commendatory Verses and the Three Suns, (2) Sir Henry Neville and the Essex Rebellion, (3) Sir Henry Neville's Voyage to France, and Its Double, (4) A Review of *Shakespeare and the Founders of Liberty in America*, (5) Genealogical Notes, (6) The Chronology of Shakespeare's Works.

Williams, Robin P. *Sweet Swan of Avon: Did a Woman Write Shakespeare?* Berkeley, CA: Peachpit Press, **2006**.

Described as an independent scholar, Williams marshals a plethora of evidence in favor of Mary Sidney, Countess Pembroke, as the author. As with Oxford, evidence is circumstantial but weighty, e.g., Sidney fostered an important literary salon and traveled in Europe (but apparently not Italy). Williams implies that the canon turned dark when Sidney's life took a downturn. Women characters in the canon elicit such comments as, "The playwright consistently ennobles and strengthens the female characters and makes them more virtuous than their original counterparts." And "This playwright, unlike any other dramatist of the time, displays a reverence for the wit, intelligence, maternity, capacity, and strength of women." Williams says the history plays — and Sidney knew court life well — were among the earliest plays written, so how could Shakespeare of Stratford be the author? The rules of court life explain why Mary didn't publish under her own name. Williams calls De Vere the "ever-arrogant Earl of Oxford" with a "well-documented misogyny" incapable of creating the great women of the plays. A chapter summarizes the cases for other candidates. Williams' initially compelling case is somewhat compromised by "Chapter 18: Mary Sidney, Alias Shakespeare" in which Williams inserts in italics many possibilities, e.g., "Mary's son William is outraged by her affair with the lower-class doctor and for *writing plays for the public theater that threaten his career in the royal court. In 1609, he steals her sonnet collection and has it printed in Shakespeare's name.* The sonnets are dedicated from the publisher to Mr. W.H." The "W.H." could signify Mary's son William Herbert. Nevertheless, Williams proves that Sidney's candidacy deserves scrutiny. Appendices: A: Old School (Mary Sidney's importance to); B: The Other Candidates. Bacon, Oxford, Marlowe, Henry Neville, William Shakespeare, Mary Sidney Herbert; C: Jonson's Eulogy (in which Williams paraphrases each line on the opposite page); D: The Narrative Poems. ("Documentation exists verifying that William Shakespeare composed and published these two overwrought and melodramatic poems."); E: Literary Allusions. (all literary references to William Shakespeare in his lifetime); F: The History Plays (real characters and their relation to Mary Sidney); G: English Peerage; and H: Real Money. Filled with illustrations, sidebars, charts, timelines, genealogy, footnotes, bibliography, and index. A fold-out compares Sidney's documented life, the plays and poems attributed to Shakespeare, and Shakespeare's documented life.

Stewart, Doug. "To Be or Not to Be Shakespeare." *Smithsonian* (September, **2006**): 62–66, 68–71.

"At heart, the Shakespeare debate is about more than missing records. It's driven by an unquenchable need to slip past Shakespeare's verses and locate the real-life artist behind them, whoever he or she might be." Stewart describes the "Searching for Shakespeare" exhibit at the Yale Center for British Art in New Haven, CT — six paintings (reviewed in some detail) plus other artifacts and documents. A dearth of documents is noted. Quoted are supporters and doubters, including Mark Anderson *("Shakespeare" by Another Name)*, Richard Whalen *(Shakespeare — Who Was He?)*, University of Warwick Stratfordian Jonathan Bate ("He didn't insert his own opinions, and he steered away from the topical controversies of the day. That's why it's so easy for directors and filmmakers today to make his plays contemporary."), and Marjorie Garber *(Shakespeare After All, 2004)*. Garber maintains that manuscripts weren't that important back then and were not saved once set in type. Summarized is the Oxfordian case, but "One by one, mainstream scholars knock down the Oxfordians' debating points." Stewart notes Garber's "Many people prefer to keep the idea of a transcendent, universal Shakespeare." Illustrations: portraits (Flower, Grafton, Sanders, Soest, Chandos, Janssen; De Vere, Bacon, Marlowe (unauthenticated), Elizabeth I, Raleigh; Ben Jonson and the ©1620 memorial effigy; doubters (with quotes): Twain, Welles, Whitman, Freud. There are photographs of Jonathan Bate and Richard Whalen. "Folio, Where Art Thou?" by Paul Collins is a lengthy sidebar reviewing the attempt by Anthony James West *(First Folio: The History of the Book)*, senior fellow at the University of London, to identify and dissect all of the First Folios, some of which are still being unearthed.

Carrell, Jennifer Lee. *Interred with Their Bones*. New York: Plume, 2008, ©**2007**.

In a thriller moving at breakneck speed between Europe and North America, American stage director Kate Stanley prepares a production of *Hamlet* at London's Globe theater only to have a former mentor appear, invite her to a mysterious rendezvous and end up dead. Kate opens the package her friend had given her, discovering clues to ... what, exactly? With a criminal on her trail, Kate returns to Harvard and in the Widener library searches the First Folio and *Don Quixote* to make sense of her late friend's enigmatic notes about a Shakespearean manuscript surviving until today. Occasionally interspersed with episodes from Elizabethan times, this is a solid if occasionally confusing historical mystery novel that bears comparison with Sarah Smith's *Chasing Shakespeares* (2004). The authorship issue raises its head in references to Delia Bacon, the Earl of Oxford, Marlowe, Derby and the character who says, "Because I rate what's in the plays higher than what's on their title pages.... The man who wrote the plays had a broad and deep classical education, and he had easy access to fine books. He had an aristocratic outlook.... He distrusted women, adored music, and despised grasping after money. He knew intricacies of English law and of navigation and sailing; he knew Italy and spoke French and Latin. Above all, he lived and breathed poetry. So far as can be proven — not assumed from the plays, but proven from the records of his life — William Shakespeare of Stratford exhibited none of these characteristics. Ergo, he did not write the plays." In a 10-page concluding "Author's Note," Carrell traces the history of the authorship controversy and identifies what is real and what is fictionalized in her saga.

Geoghegan, Tom. "Shakespeare: The Dossier." *BBC News Magazine* (news.bbc.co.uk/2/ hi/uk_news/magazine/6988670.stm) September 11, **2007**.

Geoghegan uses the Jacobi/Rylance "declaration of reasonable doubt" and the initiation of Shakespeare authorship studies at Brunel University to run a side-by-side comparison of "For Stratford" and "Against." Topics: Historical Documents, No University Education, It Was Edward De Vere, 17th Earl of Oxford, There Was More Than One Writer, Other Arguments. Ten comments from readers are presented. Most are comfortable with the Stratford man, and several wonder why we need to know?

Alberge, Dalya. "Double, Double, Shakespeare Oil in Trouble." TimesOnline, October 25, 2007, 2 pages. (http://entertainment.timesonline.co.uk/tol/arts_and_entertainment/visual_ arts/article27336)

Examined is Hildegard Hammerschmidt-Hummel's contention that a copy of the "Flower" portrait in the collection of the Royal Shakespeare Company in Stratford-on-Avon since 1892 has been replaced by a 19th-century fake. The University of Mainz professor claims the current portrait is not the one she examined between 1995 and 2005. The Royal Shakespeare Company counters that "perceived differences are caused by lighting conditions and different equipment." According to Stanley Wells, Shakespearean scholar, the German professor "knows her way round the archives, but she barks continually up the wrong tree. At least she's not saying Shakespeare didn't write Shakespeare." This concludes with a list summarizing various Shakespearean forgeries.

Bryson, Bill. *Shakespeare: The World as Stage.* New York: Atlas Books (HarperCollins), **2007**.

Bryson, a well regarded, popular writer (*A Walk in the Woods*, *A Short History of Nearly Everything*) provides this 199-page entry for the publisher's Eminent Lives Series. To Bryson it's definitely not passing strange that no play manuscripts or promptbooks were found among Shakespeare's personal effects when he died. Such things belonged to the performing company, says he. For Bryson, Shakespeare "had some command of French, it would seem, and evidently quite a lot of Italian (or someone who could help him with quite a lot of Italian), for *Othello and The Merchant of Venice* closely followed Italian works that did not exist in English translation at the time he wrote." Bad geography in the plays suggests that Shakespeare "was not conspicuously worldly." In the end, "Shakespeare's genius had to do not really with facts, but with ambition, intrigue, love, suffering — things that aren't taught in school. He had a kind of assimilative intelligence, which allowed him to pull together lots of disparate fragments of knowledge, but there is almost nothing that speaks of hard intellectual application in his plays — unlike, say, those of Ben Jonson, where learning hangs like bunting on every word." Bryson admits that what little we know of Shakespeare's life only adds to the mystery. The reader wonders if "everything in his private life seemed to indicate a pronounced longing to be in Stratford." Stratfordian Stanley Wells is frequently cited. As usual, such caveats as "probably," "Inexplicable" and "it would seem" are used. The final of nine chapters is "Claimants." Shakespeare was a country boy who "lurks in all the texts." Curiously, Bryson belittles unbelievers, taking a cue from Samuel Schoenbaum and using the distinctly un-academic argument that some anti–Stratfordians had "mirthful" names. Most amazing is this closed-mindedness: "So it needs to be said that nearly all of the anti–Shakespeare sentiment — actually all of it, every bit — involves manipulative scholarship or sweeping misstatements of fact." A bibliography is included. Also available as an unabridged, 6-hour, 5-CD set from HarperAudio (2007).

McClinton, Brian. *The Shakespeare Conspiracies: Untangling a 400-Year Web of Myth and Deceit.* Aubane, Ireland: Aubane Historical Society, **2007**.

Editor of *Humani*, the journal of the Humanist Association of Northern Ireland, McClinton traces his doubts to 1964 when he was studying *The Tempest*. He failed to grasp that "this colossus of literature ... had supposedly no intellectual life outside such masterpieces." He decided that Ben Jonson's First Folio reference to Shakespeare acting as Mercury to "charm" the age indicated someone else was the true author. Two conspiracies are identified and explored: (1) "a secret plot to convey the truth of the human condition and expand our understanding of it through a myth," and (2) a collective effort by priests-scholars to maintain the myth rather than search for the truth. Chapter 1 sets the stage with an examination of the mysteries — of missing Shakespeare books and commendations, of silence about him by others, of confusion about play attribution, of nonexistent records from theatre owners acknowledging receipt of his plays, of a "caricature" portrait. The prime alternate candidates are featured in Chapter 5: The Good Pens and the Master-Workman: Marlowe (fails to fit all the criteria), Derby (wrote nothing during the last two decades of his life), Oxford (character flaws), Rutland (coincidences), and Anthony Bacon (died in 1601). The "master-workman" is revealed as Francis Bacon. The "good pens" supplied basic materials while the master mind (Bacon) molded them "into something rich and strange that would endure." "Shakespeare," for McClinton, was "the very acme of Renaissance humanism." So was Bacon. Ten objections to Bacon's candidacy are identified and discussed as are 10 reasons to consider him the Bard. Features six appendices: Bacon's Verse Translation of Psalm 104, Shakespeare's Humanism, Just William: Greenblatt's *Will in the World*, The Bard Stripped Bare: Ackroyd's Biography, *Much Ado About Nothing*: Germaine Greer on *Mrs. Shakespeare*, and Timeline: Shakespeare and Bacon. Includes two dozen illustrations, bibliography and index.

Stritmatter, Roger. "Is This the Bard We See Before Us? Or Someone Else?" *Washington Post*, March 18, 2007, p. B1, B5.

Stritmatter, vice chairman of the Shakespeare Fellowship and English professor at Coppin State University in Baltimore, calls the controversy "the elephant in the living room of modern Shakespearean criticism." He calls attention to the fact-challenged "seemingly endless procession of books that roll off the presses every year." Yet the Stratfordians "have a monument without a man." There remains "populist resistance" to the Stratford man. Stritmatter identifies such candidates as Bacon, Marlowe, Elizabeth, and Oxford "but we all believe that the real author was forced to conceal his identity and allow his works to be published under another man's name." He argues that anti–Stratfordians are not "unrepentant conspiracy theorists." Rather, unbelievers are astounded that biographers speculate on a man "who contradicted the literary thumbprint of his creation in every way." Summarized are objections to Stratfordian authorship by notable authors such as Mark Twain and Henry James. The traditionalists believe in a man "Born to a comfortable middle-class existence, [who] evades the stark class realities of Elizabethan society and conquers the literary world through Will-power, re-creating the lives of kings, queens and courtiers simply by deploying his superabundant imagination." To Stritmatter, "A papier-mâché author who accomplishes everything through sheer genius fortifies the American myth that anything is possible if you just click your heels three times and wish hard enough." He contends that concealed authorship has not been uncommon and was practiced in 15th-to 17th-century Europe. Because art is never merely art, the stage was indispensable for political dissent. Summarizing Oxford's life, Stritmatter portrays him as a man with the means, opportunity and motive to write *Hamlet*.

Wells, Stanley. "There's No Doubt It's Will." *Washington Post*, March 18, 2007, pp. B1, B5.

The Chairman of the Shakespeare Birthplace Trust identifies the Warwickshire clergyman [Reverend James Wilmot] as the man who started the "nonsense" about the Stratford man not being the author. According to Wells, the authorship issue has become "an immense monument to human folly." He says no one till 1785 doubted authorship and notes that in 1598 a poet named Richard Barnfield praised Shakespeare and that same year clergyman Francis Meres did likewise. According to Wells, Shakespeare became the "first literary pinup." He draws attention to "indiscreet remarks" made by Ben Jonson in 1618, e.g., Shakespeare "wanted art." Wells points to the name *Shakespeare* on books and poems. He is incredulous that doubters say that Shakespeare "was the pen name of writers who were so modest that they not only concealed the fact that they had written the greatest plays ever, but also were so generous as to allow an obscure actor to take all the credit." Reverend Wilmot's doubts are reviewed, and it is noted that he wanted his research burned but that a friend publicized his theory. Summarized is Joseph Hart's *Romance of Yachting* (1848) and his idea that Shakespeare "had added all the dirty bits to plays by unknown authors." The latest candidates are mentioned, including Sir Henry Neville and Lady Mary Sidney. Wells intimates that anti–Stratfordians prefer an educated, traveled and preferably aristocratic man as author. He argues that the Stratford man could have learned of far away places from books or conversation. Stratford's grammar school is extolled.

Niederkorn, William S. "Shakespeare Reaffirmed." *New York Times*, April 22, 2007.

In an *Education Life* survey of 265 American professors of Shakespeare, 82 percent found no valid reason to doubt authorship by the man from Stratford. Six percent found good reason, 11 percent possibly good reason. Sixty-one percent said there was no convincing evidence to deny the Stratford man. Thirty-two percent found it a waste of time, 3 percent saw it as an "exciting opportunity for scholarship," 2 percent declared "it has profound implications for the field." Seventy-two percent of the professors said they bring up the issue in class. The professors were well versed in Oxfordian claims. Anti-Stratfordian literary supporters Looney, Ogburn and Mark Anderson had been read by 29, 26, and 17 percent, respectively. Stratfordians Scott McCrea and Irvin Matus had been read by 11 and 10 percent, respectively. A common view was expressed by one professor: "I would be thrilled if people would get half as excited about the plays as they did about wondering who wrote them."

Billington, Michael. "I Am Shakespeare." *The Guardian*, September 3, **2007**.

Billington reviews the play, *I Am Shakespeare*, conceived by and acted in by Mark Rylance. Billington finds "a few passages of inspired madness" but the ending "eagerly awaited." "The show is at its best when it pins down the destructive nature of single-issue obsession." Billington isn't moved. "As so often, they [anti–Stratfordian arguments] boil down to a snobbish incredulity that a middle-class Warwickshireman could be a great dramatist, and to a romantic association of aristocracy and genius." He says the show never sets on one candidate. Billington references Stratfordian Jonathan Bate (*The Genius of Shakespeare*).

Doran, D'Arcy. "Coalition Aims to Expose Shakespeare." *Associated Press*, September 8, **2007**.

Summarized is the decision by actor Derek Jacobi and Mark Rylance, former artistic director of the Globe Theater, to sign the Shakespeare Authorship Coalition's "Declaration of Reasonable Doubt" about whether the man from Stratford wrote the plays. Jacobi believes in the group theory and suspects De Vere was the "leading light." Almost 300 people have signed online. The document was presented by Jacobi and Rylance to William Leahy, head of English at Brunel University in west London. Leahy heads up the first graduate program in Shakespeare Authorship Studies. Leahy says the point is that they won't answer everything, rather "It is, of course, to question."

Thorpe, Vanessa. "Who Was Shakespeare? That is (still) the Question." *The Observer*, September 9, **2007**. [http://arts.guardina.com.uk/theatre/news/story/0,,2165581,00.html]

Thorpe reviews the "Declaration of Reasonable Doubt" devised by actors Derek Jacobi and Mark Rylance as a prod to investigate the authorship question. Jacobi leans toward De Vere and believes an author writes about his own experiences. After the last matinee performance of the authorship-questioning play *I Am Shakespeare* at Chichester's Minerva Theatre, the *Declaration* was given to Dr. William Leahy, head of English at Brunel University in London where Leahy is to convene the first MA in Shakespeare authorship studies. Leahy is quoted on the legitimacy of the question.

Van Gelder, Lawrence, comp. "Arts, Briefly: Alas, Poor Shakespeare." *New York Times*, September 10, **2007**. [http://www.nytimes.com/2007/09/10/arts/10arts.html?_r=1&oref=slogin]

The Associated Press announces that following the final matinee of the play *I Am Shakespeare*, Derek Jacobi and Mark Rylance promulgated a "Declaration of Reasonable Doubt" about the Stratford man's authorship. The declaration was presented to William Leahy, head of English at Brunel University where the first graduate program in Shakespeare Authorship Studies will be convened. According to Leahy, the point is "to question."

Aaronovitch, David. "What Links Shakespeare and the McCanns?" *TimesOnline*, September 11, **2007**.

This is an odd equating of authorship doubters ("a harmless waste of time") such as "that lovely man Derek Jacobi" and Mark Rylance who signed the "declaration of reasonable doubt," with those who question recent terrorist bombings in England and wonder about the missing Madeleine McCann. As for Shakespeare, "an elaborate hoax or fraud would have to have been perpetrated over two decades by someone seeking to disguise authorship of plays that were popular but not seditious." Aaronovitch views anti–Stratfordianism as a way, "possibly unconscious — to pull the supreme poet down from his tower." He argues that Freud and Twain came from humble stock, therefore the Stratford man's literary credentials remain viable.

"Much Ado about Shakespeare." *TimesOnline*, September 12, **2007**.

Three letters to the editor respond to David Aaronovitch's September 11 article. Derek Wakeham of Eastham, Wirral wonders how de Vere can be a viable candidate since he died in 1604. Jeremy Crick of Wolstanton, Staffs. questions why the Stratford man left 17 of his plays unpublished at his death.

He says De Vere "had no need to publish his works—his career as a dramatist was bent primarily on satisfying Queen Elizabeth's passion for dramatic interludes and masques." He adds that orthodox scholars must explain why many early quarto editions of the plays were published anonymously. As for conspiracy theorists, "It doesn't take a conspiracy for an author to write under a pen-name. It was common practice then as it is now." Terry Deary, Burnhope, Co Durham writes, "Sir, The truth is that these middle class uber-snobs don't want to accept that their working-class 'inferiors' are capable of producing great art. Shakespeare's plays were written by a tradesman's son, without a university education, called William Shakespeare. End of drama."

Farouky, Jumana. "The Mystery of Shakespeare's Identity." *Time.com*, September 13, **2007**. [www.time.com/time/arts/article/0,8599,1661619,00.html]

Farouky reviews the unveiling by Derek Jacobi and Mark Rylance of the "Declaration of Reasonable Doubt" created by the California-based Shakespeare Authorship Coalition. Other signatories are identified, including Charles Champlin, former Los Angeles Times arts editor, Michael Delahoyde, English professor at Washington State University, and Robin Fox, social theory professor at Rutgers University. Farouky notes the perplexing item that someone so prolific left behind so very little evidence of his life, identifies the prime candidates for authorship, and reports that Stratfordians dismiss doubters as snobs. Quoted is Stratfordian Jonathan Bate, arguing that it was not necessary for the Stratford man to write autobiographically. "That's the modern image of the writer as someone who puts his own experiences into his plays, a very romantic idea of writing. But it's just not how plays were written back then." It is suggested that a whole new interpretation of the plays would occur, as history professor at the University of Wales, Aberystwyth, Bill Rubinstein, says, "if we knew who wrote them. If he was heavily involved in politics, for example, every line in every play would have a different motivation." Included is a Hulton Archive/Getty artist's depiction of Shakespeare reading *Hamlet* to his family.

Whalen, Richard F., ed. *Macbeth*. Truro, MA: Llumina Press (Horatio Editions), **2007**.

This is part of The Oxfordian Shakespeare Series, Shakespeare plays annotated from an Oxfordian perspective. Play text on the right-hand page is complemented by left-hand page definitions, explanation of terms and passages, and how Oxford's life and, in this case, knowledge of Scotland, is reflected in the play. The book concludes with "Acting MacBeth," a 17-page essay by actor Derek Jacobi. Other similarly edited plays in the series include *Othello* (Ren Draya), *Antony and Cleopatra* (Michael Delahoyde), *Hamlet* (Jack Shuttleworth), *The Tempest* (Roger Stritmatter), *Henry the Fifth* (Kathy R. Binns-Dray), *King John* (Daniel L. Wright), *Love Labours Lost* (Felicia Londre), and *Much Ado About Nothing* (Anne Pluto).

Blumenfield, Samuel L. *The Marlowe-Shakespeare Connection: A New Study of the Authorship Question*. Jefferson, NC and London: McFarland and Company, **2008**.

Overlooking the authorship question "is to close one's mind to history," writes Blumenfield. Dedicating this to Calvin Hoffman, Blumenfield traces his interest in the authorship question to Hoffman's *The Murder of the Man Who Was "Shakespeare"* (1955), a book he reprinted as editor of the Universal Library at Grosset & Dunlap. "As history has shown, it is easier to believe a credible falsehood than an incredible truth." Blumenfield believes an author's biography can be as important as his works. He contends the Sonnets match Marlowe's autobiography. The first 17 Sonnets were "probably commissioned by Lord Burghley who knew Marlowe well as a very skilled poet." Chapter 39 traces the chronology of the authorship question, identifying key exponents of alternate authors. According to Blumenfield, there was no collaboration: "Only one mind could have written them ... it was Marlowe's forced isolation that precluded any collaborative effort. And that is why the plays in the First Folio stand out as the miraculous work of an extraordinary genius working alone." A rather speculative "Postscript" conjectures connections between Anthony Bacon and Monsieur Le Doux, who might have been Marlowe. For Blumenfield, a list of books Le Doux purchased match Marlowe's reading habits and Le Doux's letters are thus Marlowe's. Marlowe continued his spying activities on the Continent for the Burghleys. Includes bibliography and index.

Waugaman, Richard M. "The Pseudonymous Author of Shakespeare's Works." *Princeton Alumni Weekly*, March 19, **2008**.

Initially skeptical about non–Stratford claimants to authorship and "chagrined" that Freud named Oxford the true Bard, psychoanalyst Waugaman (Georgetown University School of Medicine) traces his conversion to a 1999 *New York Times* article. He took up the topic and became a "reader" at the Folger Shakespeare Library where he found de Vere's Geneva Bible a veritable "smoking gun." He cites a friendship with Roger Stritmatter, who wrote his dissertation on de Vere as Shakespeare based on annotations in that Bible. Waugaman expresses fascination with the range of reactions to the issue. He says we should generally trust experts, "But literary studies lack a reliable methodology to evaluate such authorship claims." He posits an analogy between Wegener's once-derided proposal on continental drift and the plethora of evidence that marks de Vere as Shakespeare. Waugaman concludes de Vere used a pseudonym because "Elizabethan nobility did not publish poetry under their own names during their lifetimes." Nor was the theater held in high repute. It is possible the history plays, which complimented the Tudor line, were propaganda possibly "enhanced by attributing them to a commoner." Waugaman draws on his own studies of the psychology of pseudonymity to contend that many writers are more creative when concealing authorship. As for those who wonder why bother, Waugaman knows these same folks would seek connections between the life and the psychology of any other great writer. "What we know about the man from Stratford is so limited that we can imagine almost anything we want about him." De Vere was complicated, thus evidencing the complexity to be expected in the author of the canon.

Akbar, Arifa. "Rylance Reveals Why He Had to Quit the Globe Over Iraq." *The Independent* (U.K.), May 5, **2008**.

Mark Rylance explains why he resigned his position of artistic director at Shakespeare's Globe in 2005: vocal opposition to the Iraq war and curiosity about who might really have written Shakespeare. "I became more and more convinced that Francis Bacon was the doorway into it.... Undoubtedly the Stratford actor [Shakespeare] is involved in the creation of the plays because he is a shareholder in the Globe but I have not seen a convincing argument that he was capable of writing the plays." (Current Globe artistic director labels this heresy as "baloney.") Rylance says he never injected authorship views into any Shakespeare play. His lauded acting roles at the Globe are identified.

Appendices

Associations and Websites

Francis Bacon Foundation (founded 1938)
655 N. Dartmouth Avenue
Claremont, CA 91711
  714–624–6305
  http://www.sirfrancisbacon.org/index.htm
  contains the Francis Bacon Foundation Library;
    publishes Annual Report

Francis Bacon Society (founded 1886)
Canonbury Tower
Islington
London N1 2NQ
England
  http://www.sirbacon.org
  questions authorship; publishes Baconian Jottings,
    Baconiana, Terminologia e Fortuna nel SVII
    Secola

International Shakespeare Association (founded
  1973)
The Shakespeare Centre
Henley Street
Stratford-on-Avon, Warwickshire CV37 6QW
England
  Or: World Shakespeare 2006, c2007 The Univer-
    sity of Queensland, Brisbane, Australia ABN
    63 942 912 684; http://www.shake-
    speare2006.net
  publishes Congress Proceedings after World
    Shakespeare Congresses

Irvin Leigh Matus' Shakespeare Site (Stratfordian)
  www.willyshakes.com

The Marlowe Society
c/o Valerie Colin-Russ, Secretary, General En-
  quiries
27, Melbourne Court
Randolph Avenue
London W9 1BJ
  www.marlowe-society.org

Marlowe Society of America (founded 1976)
c/o Professor Sarah Scott

Dept. of English
Mount St. Mary's University
16300 Old Emmitsburg Road
Emmitsburg, MD 21727
  http://aps.carleton.edu/hosted/msa/membership
  publishes Marlowe Bookreview, Marlowe
    Newsletter

Mary Sidney Society
  www.marysidneysociety.org
  Marysidney.com (Robin P. Williams)
  www.marysidney.com

The Master of Shakespeare (Fulke Greville,
  Lord Brooke, 1554–1628)
  www.masterofshakespeare.com

Shakespeare Association of America (founded
  1972)
Georgetown University
37th and O Streets, NW
Washington, DC 20057–1131
  http://www.shakespeareassociation.org/main.asp
  publishes a Bulletin and Directory of Members

Shakespeare Authorship Coalition
  http://www.doubtaboutwill.org
  contains the "Declaration of Reasonable Doubt
    About the Identity of William Shakespeare"

Shakespeare Authorship Roundtable
P.O. Box 1887
Santa Monica, CA 90406
  http://www.shakespeareauthorship.org
  questions authorship

The Shakespeare Authorship Research Centre
Concordia University
2811 NE Holman
Portland, OR 97211–6099
  http://www.authorshipstudies.org/contact/index.c
    fm

Shakespeare Authorship Sourcebook
  http://www.sourcetext.com/sourcebook/library/ba
    rrell/index.htm
  contains "The Writings of Charles Wisner Barrell"

Shakespearean Authorship Trust (superseding
    Shakespeare Fellowship, 1922, and Shake-
    spearean Authorship Society, 1959)
P.O. Box 53619
London SE24 OYS
England
    http://www.shakespeareanauthorshiptrust.org.uk
    questions authorship; publishes pamphlets; main-
    tains library

Shakespeare Birthplace Trust (founded 1847)
The Shakespeare Centre
Henley Street
Stratford upon Avon
Warwickshire CV37 6QW
England
    http://houses.shakespeare.org.uk
    publishes *The Shakespeare Newsletter*

The Shakespeare Fellowship
P.O. Box 421
Hudson, MA 01740

http://www.shakespearefellowship.org
    publishes *Shakespeare Matters*

Shakespeare Oxford Society (founded 1957)
P.O. Box 808
Yorktown Heights, NY 10598–0808
    http://www.shakespeare-oxford.com
    questions authorship; publishes *The Shake-
        speare–Oxford Society Newsletter*

The Shakespeare Society
500 Eighth Avenue, 5th Floor
New York, NY 10018
    212–967–6802
    http://www.shakespearesociety.org

Shakespeare Society of America (founded 1967)
432 Airport Road
Watsonville, CA 95076
    http://www.shakespearesocietyofamerica.org
    publishes *Hamlet's Proclamation* and *Shakespeare's
        Proclamation*; has library

Libraries

Most university and large public libraries have Shakespearean collections in which are included books on the authorship question. In general, the older the library the more likely is one to find such items as Ignatius Donnelly's *The Great Cryptogram*. The libraries below are those with large Shakespearean holdings.

American Players Theatre, Inc. (APT) Library
P.O. Box 819
Spring Green, WI 53588
    www.playinthewoods.org
    email: aptmaster@americanplayers.org

Beloit College Library
Beloit College
731 College Street
Beloit, WI 53511
    email: libref@www.beloit.edu

Birmingham Shakespeare Library
Birmingham Central Library
Chamberlain Square
Birmingham B3 3HQ
United Kingdom
    email: arts.library@birmingham.gov.uk

Bodleian Library
University of Oxford
Broad Street
Oxford OX1 3BG
United Kingdom
    www.bodley.ox.ac.uk
    email: bodleys.librarian@bodley.ox.ac.uk
    includes Robert Burton's books

Brighton Reference Library
Brighton Public Library
Church Street
Vantage Point
Brighton BN1 2GW
United Kingdom
    includes James Orchard Halliwell Phillipps Col-
        lection

British Library
96 Euston Road
London NW1 2DB
United Kingdom
    www.bl.uk

British Museum
Great Russell Street
London WC1B 3DG
United Kingdom
    www.britishmuseum.org

Brown University (John Hay Library)
20 Prospect Street/Box A
Providence, RI 02912
    http://dl.lib.brown.edu/libweb/about/hay/index.
        php
    email: hay@brown.edu

Carnegie-Mellon University Libraries (Hunt Library)
4909 Frew Street
Pittsburgh, PA 15213
www.cmu.edu

Cleveland Public Library (Literature Department)
Main Library
Main Building, 2nd Floor
325 Superior Avenue
Cleveland, OH 44114
www.cpl.org
email: Literature@cpl.org

Dartmouth College (Sanborn House Library)
Dartmouth College Library
Hanover, NH 03755
http://library.dartmouth.edu/cdp/read.php?cdp_id=24

Folger Shakespeare Library
201 E. Capitol Street, SE
Washington, D.C. 20003
www.folger.edu
includes authorship material

Francis Bacon Foundation Library
655 North Dartmouth Avenue
Claremont, CA 91711
www.sirfrancisbacon.org/index.htm
includes authorship material

Free Library of Philadelphia Rare Book Department
1901 Vine Street
Philadelphia, PA 19103
www.library.phila.gov

Globe Theatre *see:* Shakespeare's Globe Theatre

Guildhall Library
Department of Printed Books, Literature Collection
Aldermanbury
London EC2V 7HH
United Kingdom
email: printedbooks.guildhall@cityoflondon.gov.uk

Harvard University Library *see* Widener Library

The Huntington Library
1151 Oxford Road
San Marino, CA 91108
www.huntington.org/LibraryDiv/LibraryHome.html

Indiana University *see* The Lilly Library

John Harvard Library (Southwark Local Studies Library)
211 Borough High Street

Southwark
London SE1 1JA
United Kingdom
www.southwark.gov.uk
email: southwark.libraries@southwark.gov.uk
Globe Theatre material only

John Rylands University Library
The University of Manchester
Oxford Road
Manchester M13 9PP
United Kingdom
www.library.manchester.ac.uk

Library of Congress
Rare Book and Special Collections
101 Independence Avenue, SE
Room LJ239, Thomas Jefferson Building
Washington, D.C. 20540
www.loc.gov/rr/rarebook
includes authorship material

The Lilly Library
1200 East Seventh Street
Bloomington, IN 47405
www.indiana.edu/~liblilly/index.php

Milwaukee Public Library
814 West Wisconsin Avenue
Milwaukee, WI 53233
www.mpl.org

The Newberry Library
60 W. Walton Street
Chicago, IL 60610
www.newberry.org

New York Public Library

Humanities and Social Sciences Library
Fifth Avenue at 42nd Street
New York, NY 10023
www.nypl.org/research/chss

The New York Library for the Performing Arts
40 Lincoln Center Plaza
New York, NY 10023
www.nypl.org/research/lpa/collections

The Rare Books Division
Fifth Avenue and 42nd Street
New York, NY 10018
www.nypl.org/research/chss/spe/rbk/rbooks.html

Penfield Library
7060 State Route 104
Oswego State University of New York
Oswego, NY 13126
www.oswego.edu/library/index.html

Princeton University Library
Firestone Library
One Washington Road
Princeton, NJ 08544
    http://firestone.princeton.edu.ghrd

Queen Mary University of London
Main Library, QMUL
328 Mile End Road
London E1 4NS
United Kingdom
    www.library.qmul.ac.uk/contact_us/index.htm
    includes Sidney Lee's collection

Queen's University of Belfast
Bishop (Thomas) Percy Library
University Road
Belfast BT7 1NN
Northern Ireland
    www.qub.ac.uk/directorates/InformationServices/
        TheLibrary
    includes authorship material

University of St. Andrews Library
North Street
St. Andrews
Fife KY16 9TR
Scotland
    www.st-andrews.ac.uk/library

St. Mary's School (Sarah Graham Kenan Library)
900 Hillsborough Street
Raleigh, NC 27603
    www.saint-marys.edu/pages/sitepage.efm?page=
        72610

San Diego Public Library
Literature and Language Section
820 East Street
San Diego, CA 92101
    www.sandigeo.gov/public-library
    includes authorship material

The Shakespeare Centre Library and Archive
The Shakespeare Birthplace Trust
Henley Street
Stratford-on-Avon CV37 6QW
United Kingdom
    www.shakespeare.org/uk/content/view/19/19
    email: library@shakespeare.org.uk

Shakespeare's Globe Theatre
21 New Globe Walk
Bankside
London SE1 9DT
United Kingdom
    www.shakespeares-globe.org

Shakespeare Society of America
432 Airport Road

Watsonville, CA 95076
    www.shakespearesocietyofamerica.org

Stratford Upon Avon Library & Information
    Centre
Henley Street
Stratford-on-Avon CV37 6PZ
United Kingdom
    email: stratfordlibrary@warwickshire.gov.uk

Trinity College
The Wren Library
Cambridge CB2 1TQ
United Kingdom
    www.trin.com.ac.uk/index.php?pageid=44&stop=
        10

University of Illinois at Urbana-Champaign
University Library
1408 West Gregory Drive
Urbana, IL 61801
    www.library.uiuc.edu

Senate House Library
University of London
Malet Street
Bloomsbury
London WC1E 7HU
United Kingdom
    www.ull.ac.uk
    includes (1) Sir Edwin Durning-Lawrence Library, and (2) (Katherine) Eggar Collection
    (www.ull.ac.uk/specialcollections/dll.shtml)

University of Michigan
University Library
Department of Rare Books and Special Collections
Ann Arbor, MI 48109
    www.lib.umich/edu

The Louis Round Wilson Library
University of North Carolina at Chapel Hill
Tannenbaum Shakespeare Collection
CB#3930
Chapel Hill, NC 27514
    www.lib.unc.edu/wilson

University of Nottingham Library
Department of Manuscripts & Special Collections
University Park
Nottingham NG7 2RD
England
    http://mss.library.nottingham.ac.uk

University of Pennsylvania (Horace Howard
    Furness Memorial Library)
Van Pelt Library
3420 Walnut Street

Philadelphia, PA 19104
  www.library.ukpenn.edu/collections/rbm/furness.
  html

University of Texas Libraries
P.O. Box P
Austin, TX 78713
  www.lib.utexas.edu

Thomas Fisher Rare Book Library
120 St. George Street
St. George Campus
University of Toronto
Toronto, Ontario M5S 1A5
Canada
  www.library.utoronto.ca/fisher

University of Virginia Library
P.O. Box 400113
Charlottesville, VA 22904
  www.lib.virginia.edu

University of Wisconsin
University of Wisconsin-Milwaukee
2311 East Hartford Avenue
Milwaukee, WI 53211
  www.uwm.edu/Libraries

Widener Library
Harry Elkins Widener Memorial Collection
Harvard Yard
Harvard University
Cambridge, MA 02138
  http://hcl.harvard.edu/libraries/#widener

Yale University (Beinecke Rare Book and Manuscript Library)
121 Wall Street
New Haven, CT 06511
  www.library.yale.edu/beinecke

Index